EDUCATION IN COLONIAL INDIA

Education in Colonial India

Historical Insights

Edited by

DEEPAK KUMAR
JOSEPH BARA
NANDITA KHADRIA
CH. RADHA GAYATHRI

MANOHAR
2025

First published 2013
POD reprint 2025

ISBN 978-81-7304-987-3

Published by
Ajay Kumar Jain *for*
Manohar Publishers & Distributors
4753/23 Ansari Road, Daryaganj,
New Delhi 110 002

Printed at
Replika Press Pvt. Ltd.

For
Professor Aparna Basu

Contents

Acknowledgements

This volume was originally conceived as a panel titled 'Emergence of Knowledge Societies and Educational History' of the XXth Congress of the International Association of Historians of Asia (IAHA), which was organized by the Zakir Husain Center for Educational Studies and Educational Records Research Unit, Jawaharlal Nehru University (14-17 November 2008).

The panel on education was an integral part of the XXth IAHA conference and we benefited from the generosity of Maulana Abul Kalam Azad Institute of Asian Studies, Asia Project, India International Centre, and Project on International Migration and Diaspora Studies, JNU. We thank the Indian Council of Cultural Relations, Indian Council for Social Science Research, Ministry of Environment and Forest, B.P. Koirala Foundation and Indo-Sri Lanka Foundation for their support.

We are grateful to all those who participated and later agreed to revise and submit their papers for publication. Four papers, i.e. of S. Irfan Habib, Dilip Chavan, Ch. Radha Gayathri and Savitri Das Sinha were solicited later. We are grateful to Sage Publications for granting us permission to reproduce S. Irfan Habib's article originally published in *Contributions to Indian Sociology*, vol. 34, no. 1, copyright Institute of Economic Growth, Delhi. All rights reserved and reproduced with the permission of the copyright holders and the publisher, Sage Publications India Private Limited, New Delhi.

Dr. Kapila Vatsyayan was the guiding spirit and chair of the panel. Thanks to her patronage, this panel could be held at the India International Centre. Professor Sabyasachi Bhattacharya, former Director ERRU, was with us, as ever and delivered the keynote address of the panel. His affection and support will always remain a source of encouragement for us. Our sincere thanks to Shri Ramesh Jain, our publisher, for all his care and help.

EDITORS

Introduction

> 'Well, Mr. Puntoji', said the President of a School Committee in a provincial town, some few years ago, to a Native who had just arrived from Bombay having been sent to establish an English School in the town, under the auspices of the said Committee, 'Well, Mr. Puntoji, and what do you mean to teach these young gentlemen?
>
> 'Oh!' replied the new arrival, 'reading, writing, arithmetic, grammar'.
>
> 'Grammar! uuh!' said the President.
>
> 'And', continued the newcomer, 'geography, and . . .'
> 'Geography!!' interrupted the worthy President,
> 'My grandmother! What do black fellows want to know about geography?'
>
> *The Bombay Quarterly Magazine,*
> vol. I, no. II, January 1851, p. 109

Questions like what to teach, how to teach and whom to teach have been central to debates on education in India. Big changes in both knowledge production and generation came riding the wave of colonization. Here it is important to note that under the East India Company, perhaps for the first time in Indian history, the State had emerged as the producer of knowledge and the sole arbiter of what was to be delivered and to whom. The recipients had limited options and limited access. Moreover, they had their own prejudices and requirements which were not always congruent with those of the rulers. Rather they differed greatly. It is in the realm of education that cultural encounters take place and unfold the complications of civilizational interactions. Knowledge is essentially a contested term, as much as education itself is a contested terrain.[1]

These days it has become fashionable to talk in terms of knowledge society and knowledge economy. Why this obsession? Is it because of the success of information technology in our country and in our times? What kind of knowledge is this? What did our forefathers think about knowledge? Quest for knowledge has never been alien to Indian society. And there were institutions in pre-colonial times too. What new changes came in the nineteenth century? Can these be explained in terms of metropolis – periphery relationship or impact/response studies? How to 'straddle the spatial and epistemological divide' between metropolis and colony? Was this a one-way transfer? One can add, was this knowledge merely or largely derivative? Could it produce autodidacts or intellectual-migrants who could hold on their own?

Clear-cut answers are difficult to attempt, for colonialism was no monolith and it left several facts and questions open which can be interpreted either way. The same is probably true for post-colonial India! The organs of colonialism did differ in their views and implementation programmes. But these differences were not of a very basic nature. They differed in matters of detail and execution. That is why the implementation part appears ad hoc and half-hearted, but when one looks at the policy pronouncement, particularly at the higher levels, one is struck by its generosity and utilitarianism. Full trust or emphasis on them, however, could be misleading, for they tend to hide the 'real' requirements and intentions of a colonial power.

Education is an important constituent and dimension of knowledge society as it empowers people with requisite skills and knowledge to access productive employment. The British colonizers were not entirely oblivious of it, though Macaulay's project to educate the 'natives' through English medium was also equally aimed at limiting the expenditure on education. At the same time, on a larger socio-cultural scale, it aimed at emphasizing existing differences as well as at creating new ones within the colonial society.[2] The transition from the pre-colonial, local systems to a colonial education system was, however, a multi-dimensional process with many actors playing active roles in it. The pace of knowledge diffusion has increased, particularly over the last century, but the education system in India even today is basically a legacy of the two centuries of colonial rule, with still limited and uneven access to knowledge. The entry of market and consumerism, which is actively engaged in the process of transforming education into a marketable commodity, has further added to this unevenness.

To examine the debate on knowledge and its transmission through institutions of education in modern India from a historical perspective, a panel was organized on 'Knowledge Societies and History of Education' at the XXth Conference of the International Association of Historians of Asia, held in New Delhi at the Jawaharlal Nehru University in November 2008. The roots of the present volume may be traced to this exercise. Some of the papers included here were presented at the conference and revised subsequently. However, many were solicited later to make the volume a comprehensive and meaningful one. The papers have been thematically sub-divided and arranged under three sections titled 'Making of a Knowledge Society', 'Institutional Sites' and 'Women and Education'. Situated in different periods and locales, these essays deal with development of ideas and institutions of knowledge, delineating the educational systems as evolved during the colonial rule in India and carried over as legacy to the contemporary period. As in other areas of research, most of these works are parts of the respective contributor's larger projects under investigation and, as such, introductory at best. The editors thank them all for their efforts and patient cooperation.

II

The evolution of modern knowledge and education system of India needs to be situated in the larger context of the encounter between two civilizations in colonial India – European and Indian – in the background of an overarching cultural hegemony of the colonizers over the colonized societies and cultures of Asia.[3] Studies on the impact of colonialism on culture and society have been predominant in the past two decades with specific focus on colonialism and the economy, society, religion, law, medicine, and so on, as also their sub-categories. They have contributed to the understanding of the transformative interfaces between India and Europe from 1800 onwards.[4] However, what one needs to ensure in such a project is the knowledge of the pre-colonial realities that colonialism encountered. In other words, in order to determine how colonialism changed South Asia we need to know what was being changed in the first place.[5] With respect to scientific knowledge and scholarship, especially for the early modern period, in-depth research is virtually non-existent as it requires a sound knowledge of the classical languages. This is despite the fact that the Mughal era, from the latter half of the sixteenth century onwards, had ushered in a new and dynamic period of intellectual inquiry in many parts of the subcontinent. The rich material, however, for the most part, has remained untapped[6] – perhaps due to language constraints as one of the most disturbing but little remarked legacies of colonialism and modernization. Despite the wealth of culturally and historically significant materials most regional language materials remain untapped. Perhaps the central ideology of British imperialism and its civilizing-modernizing mission, which devalued the late pre-colonial period as an object of study, is also responsible for this stunted development of the intellectual and cultural histories of South Asia.[7]

The recent historiographical trend of delineating history in the vernaculars may be taken as a corrective step towards enhancement of historical knowledge in the context of the Indian subcontinent.[8] There has also been a renewed interest amongst some British scholars to review the imperial records 'more dispassionately', in order to counter the historiography condemning the British as 'cultural and economic imperialists who needlessly exploited the colonies for their own aggrandisement',[9] and to put forward the argument that without a detailed investigation into the socio-educational and attitudinal aspects of the imperialists or the colonial executives on the ground it was not possible to understand what imperialism was.[10] In this fresh zeal to revisit the past, focus is being shifted to the educators and people responsible for spreading Western education in India and the other British colonies from the erstwhile centrality given to the other types of colonial officers in the administration of the empire.

The universalistic agenda of early liberalism had appealed to the Indian elites as the early 'civilizing' mission of the colonizers was inclusive and the idea of Western and racial discrimination was covert in it. As observed by Metcalf, the liberal enterprise had the effect of disseminating the notions of Indian difference more widely than before, and in fact this ideology of difference continued as a legacy even in independent India. The indigenous elites were attracted by the possibility of bringing cohesive changes to society which the colonial encounter had produced by means of popular schooling, school book societies, etc. Though by the mid-nineteenth century powerful currents of disillusion had set in, liberal ideals continued to shape British perception of their imperial mission in India till the uprisings of 1857.[11] In course of the nineteenth century, however, the Company's education policies in India had become more interventionist following its consolidation of political power and a changed perspective towards the colonial civilizing mission. The downward filtration policy, which was opted as the course to transform Indian society, started neglecting the vernacular schools, and it was the flow of Christian missionaries from the second decade of the nineteenth century onwards, together with the activities of native educational societies that promoted popular education through new contents and methods of education.[12]

The civilizational discourse which was started by James Mill with his critical evaluation of the Indian civilization at the beginning of nineteenth century was joined by Bankim Chandra Chatterjee and R.G. Bhandarkar in the late nineteenth and early twentieth centuries and still later entered a new phase with Gandhi's publication of the *Hind Swaraj* (1910).[13] Gandhi did not blame the European people but the civilization which he considered to be the enemy of Indian civilization, and to counter the claim of civilizational superiority of the West he glorified the 'Indian' civilization which was syncretic in nature and not a 'Hindu' civilization.[14] This legacy of Gandhi was carried forward by many nationalist leaders and it continued to influence several generations in India. Gandhi believed that colonial policies had uprooted the culturally meaningful and socially integrative indigenous education from its base.[15] Rabindranath Tagore too emphasized the portrayal of India as a symbol of unity amidst diversity, although he had difference of ideas on many other issues with Gandhi. In fact, from Gandhi and Tagore onwards India's assimilative civilization received a central place in nationalist thinking.[16]

The national education movement also resulted in the generation of a large and influential literature by personalities like Aurobindo Ghosh, B.G. Tilak, Annie Besant, Lajpat Rai and others who emphasized the centrality of Indian culture and civilization in the education process.[17] The middle-class Indians expressed their new hopes and vision through periodicals, pamphlets and other contemporary publications. Their larger vision included growth of technical and medical education, scientific research and agricultural experiments, and institutional dissemination of knowledge. This 'new vision' was unitary in a broad 'national' sense, but ridden with discourses, and controversies and differences of opinion clouded over the 'national' goals in education. Despite this, however, all educated members of the civil society influenced the civilizational discourse or interface and carried the education in Indian schools and higher institutions beyond classrooms. In the process of nation building, appeal to civilizational unity and continuity was found to be both necessary and effective for combating the notions of Indian differences.

III

The quest for a techno-scientific knowledge in the last two decades of the nineteenth century had brought in people belonging to different walks of life – people who realized that the limitations of being colonized also meant that no scientific curriculum was introduced in schools and colleges with practical applications in mind. As contended by Deepak Kumar in his essay, the science interlocutors therefore questioned the purpose of scientific knowledge as disseminated through a mechanized educational system which failed to adopt a 'holistic' view of education. They blamed the failure on the 'distorted' influence of colonial system and its bureaucracy and some of them boycotted the Westernization of education, which they equated with commercialization – while others were ready to accept modernization, but not commercialization of education. Visionaries like J.C. Bose and P.C. Ray were realistic enough to accept English as the language of the scientific world although they were in favour of vernaculars for early education. Both looked at education as the 'most effective vehicle' for assimilation and gradual diffusion of scientific ideas for harnessing the economic resources of the country. Like an accomplished sociologist, Ray situated science in the social context and believed more in alleviation of poverty and literacy among the disprivileged than creating institutions for scientific training of the few. Gandhi, on the other hand, was concerned about dissemination of knowledge through curriculum, to the extent he believed that the use of science could be for the benefit of the masses, and as such, humanitarian. Thus he too linked scientific knowledge to social accountability. But his followers did not share his vision of a 'new India' – particularly its modalities based on decentralization and rural framework were not acceptable to them.[18]

In the decade before Independence, the pace of institutionalization increased but the proliferation of institutions did not mean enhancement of quality in research or coordination between academic scientific research and industrial needs. The era following Independence was one of mixed economy and politics in spite of Nehru's initial leanings towards planned development on the Soviet pattern. In this period, despite attempts by scientists like S.S. Bhatnagar and Homi Bhaba, a composite structure combining pure and applied sciences did not emerge, rather the appeal for pure sciences continued unabated. However, despite this colonial legacy, the notion of a definite link between science and technology assigned a greater responsibility and authority to the State for coordinating the two, thereby putting greater emphasis on institutions than on individual ideas.[19]

Western imperialism had generated a reaction against certain sciences, which were seen as 'un-Islamic' by the orthodox in the Muslim community.[20] Situating the article in the context of the resurgence of political Islam in recent times, which is marked by a call for 'the Islamization of sciences', Irfan Habib deals with the aspect of reconciliation of modern science with Islam in the nineteenth century through an in-depth analysis of the ideas and experiments of Syed Ahmad Khan and Jamaluddin Afghani, two very prominent ninteenth-century intellectuals and reformers. Whereas both believed that science had been central to early Islam from the eighth to the thirteenth or fourteenth centuries, they had serious differences on the way in which science was to be reconciled with Islam. Syed Ahmad was a revitalist and a reconstructionist who tried to freshly interpret the Quran to assimilate modern scientific knowledge. On the other hand, Afghani, in the Indian context, was known to be a pragmatist and an anti-imperialist to the extent that despite his faith in modern science he did not approve of imitating the West blindly.

Habib argues that the issue of reconciliation of science with Islam in nineteenth-century India is not separable from the broader issue of locating the place of modern science within colonial societies, particularly when the recipient countries like India had centuries' old civilizational and knowledge base. Here, there was a similarity between the early nineteenth-century critical assimilation of modern science by Western-educated Hindu middle-class intelligentsia and the late nineteenth-century attempts of Muslim intellectuals in reconciling science with Islam, in that both the religious streams engaged with modern scientific knowledge 'from the vantage point of their own political and cultural contexts, not always in isolation from each other'.[21] In this late awakening of the Muslim intellectuals Syed Ahmad became a reformist and protagonist of Western education and science from being a religious scholar. The compelling force behind his transformation was the political repercussions of the uprisings of 1857 on the Muslim community, which turned him into the most radical modernizer of Islam in the nineteenth century. So much so that he broke away from tradition to propose a reinterpretation of the Quran to remove the apparent contradictions, although he never tried to interpret the Quran as a book of science. To his over-enthusiastic modernist zeal the distinction between imperialism and progress was very marginal.

In contrast, Jamaluddin Afghani was a pragmatist and a cautious advocate of modernity, though at the same time critical of the orthodoxy of the *ulema* for not adopting modern science and technology. In the Indian context he advocated anti-imperialism over pan-Islamism, which gets reflected in his writings while in India where he emphasized nationalistic ideas and his attempts at reconciling science with Islam in India. He was convinced that of all religions Islam was closest to science and knowledge and as such there was no need for its reinterpretation. However, despite a difference of approach both the intellectuals were promoters of modern science and knowledge, and as attempted in the article by Habib, the points of convergence and divergence of their ideas lay in their respective political and social contexts.

Education had been an important tool in the hands of the colonizers for demonstrating racial supremacy. Since native character was taken to be 'deficient' in colonial constructions, character formation was projected as the main purpose, with the contents taking a secondary place in education. The result was the growth of a system imparting literary rather than scientific and technical knowledge. A need for the latter was felt only with the construction projects of buildings, roads, bridges and railways. It was thus the need for local overseers, mechanics, surveyors and assistant engineers that led to the introduction of modern scientific and technical education in India. From the administrators' point of view a basic technical education was necessary, but not at the cost of disturbing the social *status quo*. Hence preference was given to the teaching of and training in crafts and agrarian skills over academic education of science and technology. But the newly emergent elite demanded academic education based on higher levels of scientific and technical knowledge. This conflict of interest is brought out in the essay by Suvobrata Sarkar.[22]

The Bengali intelligentsia was the first group in modern India to interact with the British system of law and governance, and most of all Western education. To start with, Western education was perceived as a vehicle for professional mobility by the middle-class Hindus. But the initial expectations of the class were followed by disillusions when the Bengali middle class realized that professional opportunities were too restricted for them. Still they believed in a cultural synthesis of the Western and the Indian, which gave them the best of both worlds. Nigel Crook has made relevant observations about British political power being accompanied by the control, transmission and reproduction of knowledge; the system of education that developed therefore was also geared towards preservation and reproduction of colonial authority among the indigenous people in the colonies.[23]

Engineering education was introduced with the specific objective of meeting the needs and requirements of the government, and it went hand in hand with the expansion of activities of the Public Works Department, particularly civil engineering. The other branches, like mechanical, electrical and mining engineering got importance only in the 1930s. Interestingly, institutionalization of engineering education started and crystallized in India before it did in England and its academic structure helped provide models for replication in England – a reverse flow from the periphery to the centre which is barely noticed in the diffusionist historiography of education.[24] Indian education responded to economic and political pressures from both the colonized and the colonizer, which were often contradictory. But despite Indian aspirations engineering education remained confined to lower levels of training, in a similar fashion as the literary education with its focus on training clerks and pleaders. Therefore, education – particularly technical education – became a political issue in the second half of the nineteenth century in the wake of Indian nationalism, as many Indian leaders believed that India must have a strong base in scientific-technical education for the required industrial development. The issue of diffusion of scientific and technical education in colonial India was entrenched in the discourse of colonial power and domination, which created powerful hierarchies as the sustainability of the empire itself depended on the strength of such a hierarchical structure. The Bengali intelligentsia on its part welcomed such moves and became advocates of technical education. Their approach of a cultural synthesis of Western and Indian knowledge systems and emphasis on technical education saw a notable expansion of medical, engineering and scientific education in Bengal.

However, the intelligentsia was resentful of the preferential treatment meted out to the Europeans on the issue of employment and this in turn resulted in a close connection between scientific research and nationalism, manifest in the institutions set-up by intellectuals like Mahendralal Sircar or by the efforts of Dinanath Sen. The partition of Bengal in 1905 also added political stimulus to the zeal. The National Council of Education, started in 1905, was intended to be a 'national' university free of European control with equal emphasis on literary, scientific and technical education. This was followed by the setting up of the Bengal Technical Institute in 1906 by P.N. Bose and others – which aimed at providing industrial education to Indians that was ignored by the Calcutta University and the Director of Public Instructions. In this phase of institutionalization of technical education by the nationalists, Japan and Germany were taken as role models and their main objective was development of science-based industries without the evils of Western industrialization. Scientists like M.L. Sircar, P.N. Bose, J.C. Bose and P.C. Ray played a catalytic role in this movement from the last quarter of the nineteenth century. Sarkar's paper delineates this process with the help of contemporary publications, especially Bengali journals.

Developments in the field of scientific knowledge, emergence of market economy and day-to-day requirement of the colonial government had affected the traditional position of Sanskrit learning in Mithila. This is brought out in the paper by I.K. Chaudhary, which deals with the state of Sanskritic learning in Mithila under the British rule, with special reference to the episode of its freak revival in the face of Anglicization of Indian education. Chaudhary explains the structure and the stream of learning in Mithila and the patronage for learning by the Darbhanga raj. Chaudhary says that the stoppage of aid to the *tols*, where Sanskrit was taught and which did not teach vernacular led to the imposition of vernacular and the decline of Sanskrit. The colonial government not only withdrew support but also encouraged the policy of discouraging the grant of rent-free lands to endowments which were crucial for the sustaining of the teachers of the *tols*. This kind of policy affected the working of Sanskrit *pathshalas* and *madrasas* together. The zamindars and rich cultivators were no more in position to discharge a part of their social obligation.

The Christian missionaries were ideal missionaries in the field of religion in modern history. Towards the fulfilment of missionary interest, they made prominent use of education. By education the Christian knowledge and principles were presented to the audience of prospective converts in an arranged capsule of instruction. The essay by Joseph Bara examines how the missionary idea and object was pursued and nuanced in the nineteenth- and early twentieth-century colonial India. It takes the case of missionary college education, which dealt with advanced instruction and more sophisticated presentation of Christianity to a select audience of higher mental level. Such education was supposed to foster deeper spiritual formation in the recipients and the converts so obtained would be pillars of the upcoming church.

With that in view, the Christian colleges addressed the upper classes of the Indian society. It was hoped that the latter, being the social leaders, would lead the large masses to Christianity. This projection was, however, mired in complications. Firstly, the attitude of the upper-class Indians was not always constant. Sometimes criticism of Indian religion and culture that the missionaries practised to prepare way for the spread of Christianity was accepted or tolerated. At times criticism ignited reaction against missionary operations. The missionaries also did not find the colonialists a reliable ally. In the nineteenth century, they were largely seen as disturbers of peace by playing with the fire of sensitive subjects like local religion and culture. And later, the colonial state even suspected many Christian colleges as centres of 'sedition'. Taking into account such uneven cultural terrain, the essay describes how the missionary idea and the object of Christian college was buoyed in colonial India between 1818, when the first institution, the Serampore College, was started and 1910, when the Christian colleges encountered Indian nationalism and responded to nationalistic quizzing for the first time. The essay takes different models to describe the trend of the missionary idea.

The first phase, *c.* 1818-30, describes how the Serampore College was launched by the British Baptists, the Serampore 'Trio' (William Carey, Joshua Marshman and William Ward) with an aggressive note of severe criticism of Hinduism and making use of the Orientalist knowledge system and vernacular languages. The thrust of the college was to raise local missionary as a helping hand for a large missionary enterprise to demolish local faith structures and pave way for the spread of Christianity. The subject of the second phase, from 1830 to 1850, was the effort of the Scottish missionary Alexander Duff, who established the General Assembly's Institution at Calcutta (1830) to impart Christian teachings through English education. A diehard Anglicist, he had complete faith in the efficacy of the English education in stirring spiritual change in the recipients. Unlike the Serampore missionaries, who opened their college to all classes and sections, Duff admitted only upper-caste Hindus. Both Serampore College and General Assembly's Institution stood for the conversion and creation of a local Christian leadership.

From the mid-nineteenth century, English mania and degree culture in higher Indian education and Indian social reform movements thwarted the above missionary objects. This heralded a third phase of the missionary idea of Christian college. Prominence of English literature and philosophy and of Western scientific knowledge continued. But through those the thrust now lay on evangelization, i.e. diffusion of Christian knowledge and principles. The thinking that guided the rise of St. Stephen's College in Delhi depicted this well in north India. Conversion of individuals or training of Christian leadership was a secondary object. Two notable efforts – science education by Eugene Lafont at St. Xavier's, Calcutta and English literary education by William Miller at Madras Christian College – are described as specimen under this phase.

The last phase of the essay begins from the late nineteenth century, when nationalistic developments challenged the Christian colleges as the arrowhead of Western culture and imperialism. The monopoly of missionary colleges on quality Western education was eroded by many local efforts. Further, the Indian nationalism imposed upon the missionaries to orient the missionary church as national church and turn attention to the lower-class Christians. By the opening years of the twentieth century, the chain of these and related other events instilled in the missionary mind a sense of 'Christian community' and forced the missionaries to review the existing evangelization agenda of the Christian colleges. Many missionary leaders were unhappy with the amorphous composition of the Christian community and neglect of the chances of individual conversion and of training Christian leadership in the Christian colleges. Christian community interests thus dominated the missionary thinking on the idea of the Christian college.

Narrowing the canvas down to the actual sites of learning, the paper by Dilip Chavan studies the development of two famous educational institutions in western India, the Sanskrit *pathshala* in Pune and Elphinstone Institute in Bombay, which were established in the early decades of the nineteenth century with the professed aims of cultivating Sanskrit and dissemination of English education, respectively. By comparing these two institutes this article aims to study the differentiation in language policy of the colonial government and the shifts in its patronage. Arguing on the lines of Gauri Viswanathan and Kumkum Sangari, Chavan says that the establishment of the Sanskrit college was not merely an Orientalist design for improving and encouraging Hindu learning but also for power consolidation. Realizing the volatile base of the British empire and the deeply institutionalized structure of patronage to Sanskrit learning in Pune during the Peshwa regime, Mountstuart Elphinstone followed a policy of conciliation by establishing the Sanskrit college. It was not long before there was demand for English language in the Sanskrit college both from the utilitarians who sought functional education through any medium and also from some sections of Brahmins who were aware of the fact that their arrival in the portal of colonial employment was possible only through English education. Subsequently the Sanskrit college turned into a modern institute having Sanskrit, English-vernacular and vernacular departments. Thus the earlier social elite emerged as an informed and linguistically modernized class of intelligentsia which mediated between the colonial state and the colonized subjects and thereby consolidated its hegemonic position in the caste society.

Unlike Pune where English was introduced by the state, in Bombay the demand came from society itself leading to the establishment of the Elphinstone College. There was a growing demand for English in Bombay as people hoped that proficiency in English would help them either in their business pursuits or qualify them for government jobs. From the study of these two institutes Chavan infers that given the socio-cultural conditions the language policy was predetermined to be selective which lead to a differentiated language policy, resulting in the uneven distribution of English education. In fact, this differentiated language policy exhibits the brilliance with which the colonial rulers dealt with early predicaments like the dominant castes' urge to continue their hegemonic position. The thread of commonality underlying the seemingly contradictory policy and the variety of ideological trends which surface above the commonality were the different expressions of the ideology of the empire, benefiting both the empire and its indigenous allies.

Expansion of Indian universities truly gathered momentum in the wake of Indian Independence, and co-incided with as well as was inspired from expansion of universities in the developed world including the United States of America. From the time the first modern universities came into existence in the mid-nineteenth century, till the early part of the twentieth century, the universities in India were like 'islands in a country the vast majority of whose population went without the benefit of elementary education and even literacy'.[25] The articulation of demand for a university in the Assam Valley since the late nineteenth century and consequently, the establishment of the Gauhati University in 1948 were seen as much as a fulfilment of economic and cultural, and therefore, regional need, as educational by the people of Assam. Situated in the larger context of linguistic and ethno-cultural identity, the essay by Nandita Khadria traces the roots of the demand for higher education in Assam through an analysis of the articulations of the educated middle class in the first half of the twentieth century. Here the issue of demand for educational institutions was entangled with many others, overshadowing the multi-ethnic, multi-lingual society of Assam. When neighbouring Bengal was critically re-viewing the quality of general as well as scientific and technical education its inhabitants received, the entire north-east region lacked a single institution for higher education – being dependent over three quarters of a century on the Calcutta University for higher education. The first two colleges in the region were set-up in 1891 (M.C. College, Sylhet) and 1901 (Cotton College, Gauhati) with classes up to the First Arts standard of the university. Despite representations from individuals and associations, the higher educational institutions in Assam continued to be controlled from Bengal. By 1921 the two colleges were ranked among the best in the university, with Cotton College being the only college outside Calcutta offering instructions beyond honours degree; but Assam still did not have any representation in the governing body of the university, and the Government of India Act of 1935 further passed the control of secondary and university education of Assam to the Bengal legislature.[26]

Interestingly, it was the long association and impact of Bengal renaissance and development in modern education that contributed substantially to the growth of Assamese aspirations for regeneration of its own language, literature and culture, and development of institutions of higher learning facilitating this. Representations of demand for higher education in Assam go back to 1860s, which had resulted in the opening of four secondary schools. By the end of the nineteenth century there was an increase in private English schools which led to a strong demand for colleges. The government managed to stall this demand by offering fellowships to students of the region at the Calcutta University, but when the fellowships started getting channellized to medical and engineering education exclusively, the Assamese intelligentsia like M.C. Barua and others freshly articulated the demand for a local college. This was supported by Sir Henry Cotton, the Chief Commissioner of Assam, and was followed by the establishment of Cotton College in 1901.

The issue of higher education was also embroiled in the larger political issue of partition of Bengal and of joining Assam with the region of East Bengal for administrative purposes, which further marginalized the educational institutions in Assam both from the perspectives of comparability and language. Associations as well as Assamese students' forums in Calcutta expressed their anxieties over the developments, following the tradition of using the public platform of *Raijmels* of Assam. Student activists and later on renowned personalities like K.K. Handiqui, Lakshminath Bezbarua and Padmanath Gohain Barua stressed on the need for improving the quality of education along with its expansion. The national movement in its *swadeshi* form also influenced the Assam Students Association. Members of the Assam Association, though more modern than the Assamese *Chhatra Sanmilan*, debated upon the issues. But it was the students' efforts that soon created a strong public opinion for the establishment of a separate university in Assam. The Assamese students at Calcutta in the early twentieth century were a progressive lot and much influenced by L.N. Bezbarua – the editor of the journal *Banhi*. They had the platforms of associations and newspapers and journals to voice their demands and aspirations under the able leadership of educated Assamese like Chandra Prasad Agarwala, Madhab Bezbarua and Jyoti Prasad Agarwala, all of whom articulated their demand for a university in Assam.

Language and culture were such significant issues in this context that they occupied the primary attention of the Assamese intelligentsia in this period. Their aspirations were articulated in terms of an immediate desire to escape from the control of the Calcutta University by having a university of their own at Gauhati – essentially to promote the study and stimulation of Assamese literature and culture, but also to be more selective and practical than the Calcutta University by combining the unitary and affiliating systems. The courses were to meet not only the requirements of the services and professions, but also the cultural and economic needs and aspirations of the people of the valley. The intelligentsia was also aware that on the academic front the university must face and deal with the question of educated unemployment, be relieved of the organizational and coordinating role of an intermediary, and set a high standard for itself and maintain it. These were unanimous voices across divergent groups, and when it came to their perception of the regional educational and economic needs their voices matched with one another.

Who are the marginalized groups or communities whose education needs special care and commitment? The poor, the low-income groups, the socially backward communities and women are some of the categories whose historical experiences, travails and need for education are discussed in the second part of this volume. One such less privileged group was the children of traditional artisanal families. The essay by Bidisha Dhar examines the problems of this neglected group for whose training industrial schools were specifically designed.[27] Dhar's study of the Lucknow Industrial School is relevant since here the traditional weaver castes were hard hit by the Industrial Revolution in Europe and the subsequent competition from machine-made textile products, and were forced to abandon their traditional livelihood. More than the concern for rehabilitation of the uprooted artisans, the colonial imperative was to construct railways and improve roads, dockyards, etc., to connect the cotton-producing district with the metropolis for supply of raw cotton. It was as a result of the dual need for skilled workers and pacifying nationalist opinions that the technical schools were promoted by the colonial state in the late nineteenth and early twentieth centuries. Far from being passive followers of the imperial schemes, however, the trainees from artisanal families had their own aspirations of upward mobility in the profession. While they were imparted manual training through the curriculum, most of them wanted to learn drawing and English at an advanced level so as to be able to understand drawings as well as written orders and instructions of English-speaking supervisors at railway workshops and other such workplaces. The clash of interest between the provider and the recipient of education is visible in this context of technical education in this period and is the main focus of Dhar's article. The artisan was willing to give up his traditional occupation only so long as the industrial school provided a springboard for him to achieve upward social mobility, and at the same time enabled him to retain his independent identity as a draughtsman. The artisans had to accept their fate in most cases, but individual attempts had continued for changing it.

There were 45 industrial schools with less than 1,500 students in 1886, which were run mainly by missionaries and, the PWD division of the railways as reformatory institutions and some of them were affiliated to technical schools or engineering colleges. Because of its locational importance the North-West Province Oudh saw a growth of engineering and technical training institutions under the Allahabad University as well as a rearranged system of examination at the matriculation level. Through this more students could seek admission in the mechanical engineering course or workshop instructions at Roorkee. It was also planned that the Roorkee College of Engineering would offer preparatory training courses in various technical skills in addition to the existing civil engineering and irrigation courses, and a separate industrial school set-up under the Roorkee College of Engineering for the purpose.

The Lucknow Industrial School was associated to the Technical School, Lahore, which was also a training institution for apprenticeship in railways and other large workshops. Though reserved for the artisans mainly, some seats were open for other industrial communities in the city. A very strong contender in the post-1870s phase of promotion of technical education was the group of low-skilled European workers, who competed with Eurasians and Indians for lower-paid subordinate posts in the railways and related industries through the schemes of free training for them in technical institutions. Dhar links this to the issue of racial discrimination as the imperial policy clearly favoured training these 'denigrade' European/English young men technically so as to enable them to maintain their racial supremacy over their Indian counterparts. The general colonial perception regarding the comprehensive and analytical skills of the local Europeans, Eurasians and artisanal clan of Indians was also low enough to keep the curriculum to its basics. This in turn restricted the aspiration of upward mobility of Indian artisanal groups and led to their alleged 'aversion' to manual education. It also reflected in the falling attendance and withdrawal of students from the courses. The situation improved only at the turn of the century when technical schools affiliated to the Roorkee College were offered additional grants to facilitate better instructions as well as fellowships so as to prepare them for entry into mechanical apprentice classes offered at the institution. It was only after the railways offered employment to the pass-outs of the Lucknow Industrial School that the enrolment and stability increased in the institution and it became ready for promotion to a mechanical engineering college in 1918.

The Lucknow Industrial School has undergone many travails to survive and it became a success by the turn of the century when it got affiliated to Roorkee College of Engineering. However, not all professional education experiments were successes. The next essay by Savitri Das Sinha looks into one such short-lived experiment of Vernacular Medical Education (VME) during the nineteenth century, where Western medicine was taught through Indian languages. Her article primarily looks at VME through the eyes of the *Indian Medical Gazette* (*IMG*) which has been in regular publication since its inception in 1866 to date. Though it was a medical journal edited by the Indian Medical Service personnel, it had many non-medical contributors and was a reflector of social and medical conditions.

Besides the idea of propagating knowledge of Western medicine, the need to address the medical needs of the people of the villages and *moffusils*, and to supplant practitioners of indigenous systems of medicine like *hakeems* and *kobirajs* led to the establishment of VME institutions. As in the case of the Lucknow Industrial School, through these institutions the colonial state tried to utilize the hereditary physician castes of the country for their colonial purpose. Medical schools were very popular initially, so much so that it was suggested that medical schools be opened in every district. *IMG* articles show that the VME suffered from financial constraints and were mostly dependent on philanthropy and local government assistance. Though VME professionals constituted the major bulk of the medical practitioners, they were always treated as 'hospital assistants' and never as doctors. The deficiencies in selection, curriculum, lack of vernacular texts, and difference in social status all led to the natural death of VME in early twentieth century. In her conclusion Savitri Das Sinha tries to bring in similar developments in China and the USA. She shows through her study of IMG that the desire for social mobility through English education was operative in the nineteenth century and was responsible for the decline of VME.

The next essay in the section, by Susheel Prasad, brings out the discourses around institutionalization of education in this period of transition through the prism of the Central Advisory Board of Education (CABE).[28] The Government of India Act of 1919 had transferred education from the centre to the provincial governments and CABE was formed as the body to coordinate among various provincial education departments with the objective of getting better results. Though its functioning was suspended between the years 1923 and 1935 due to 'financial constraints', in the subsequent years till 1947 it was active in its attempts at reconstructing Indian education. It was the first education minister of independent India Maulana Azad who strongly supported CABE and felt that in a free, democratic India it should be able to exert real power in the field of education and take Indian education forward.

The need for providing assistance by a central advisory body to the local bodies in matters of education and acting as an impartial arbiter in cases of dispute, was first emphasized by the Calcutta University Commission. The formation of CABE was, however, looked at critically by Indian leaders – particularly its composition and the omission of important Indians from its membership, although in the initial phase of three years the CABE had created a niche for itself, as an advisory body, by attempting to understand the complex interplay between nationalism, imperialism and Indian education. Prasad's article poses the important question as to why the Indian members of the board neglected to use the platform to popularize aspects of the national education movement in which they were active participants, and link it up with the larger question as to whether education itself had lost significance during the peak of the national movement.

From the revival of CABE in 1935 to the Sargent Plan of 1944, a great deal of discussions took place between the government and non-government stake-holders. Of particular importance was the issue of unemployment, which the board felt must be tackled with radical reforms in the education system. The Wood-Abbott Committee in its report recommended the duration, scope and content of most of the courses that ought to be followed by the Indian technical institutions. The B.K. Kher Committee analysed Gandhi's Wardha Scheme together with the Wood-Abbott Committee Report and taking essence from both recommended vocalization of Indian education by the introduction of basic education in rural areas to begin with. Hindustani, using Hindi and Urdu scripts, was recommended as the common Indian language of instruction. Emphasis was also put by the committee on teacher training and women teachers' recruitment in order to promote women's education. The CABE approved of all the recommendations of the Kher Committee and continued working in the general direction of its recommendation with focus on adult education and social service, among others. A more important contribution of the CABE in this period of transition was the preparation of a comprehensive national policy on education. The Sargent Plan of 1944, despite its limitations was insightful in many ways, though it attracted severe criticism over issues, particularly on the cost involved in the process of recruitment of trained teachers at the primary level.

The CABE was put to more challenging tasks in the period after Independence with Nehru's emphasis on improvement of India's education. This was also reiterated by Azad and the board's area of jurisdiction widened in the post-Independence period, but the plans for educational reconstruction were not implemented immediately. The CABE nevertheless was successful in defining the future of Indian education. As shown in the essay by Prasad, provincialization of education was more of a rhetoric, at least in the initial phase of its inception, as the union government found ways to intervene in its function through loopholes and ignored issues that were considered sensitive and likely to cause embarrassment to the government. But the uniqueness of CABE lay in the fact that, unlike in some other areas of governance, policies on education were guided by Indian educationists, teachers and civil servants. As such the transfer of power did not affect the basic commitment of the board towards its primary objectives and it could make a dent in the education scenario of the country.

Aspects of women's education, ranging in scope from training of teachers, women's education in the princely state of Mysore, education of Muslim women as part of the greater Aligarh movement, to women's access to medical education – extending from early nineteenth century to the Indian Independence – are the focus of the articles dealing with women's education in this volume. Contemporary historians have increasingly concerned themselves with the processes involved in the making of institutions and the discourses around them. Recent research studies have also focused on the wider conceptual issues related to the notion of gender and creation of an ideal Indian woman. While Bengal had set the precedence of reform movement as a tool to respond to challenges posed by colonial rule, the movement soon spread to other parts of the country and in northern India it was led by the Arya Samaj.[29] Studies have also highlighted the debates on women's education in the late nineteenth and early twentieth centuries – on what sort of education women should receive and the attitudes of social reformers towards women's education.[30] There were some reformers who emphasized on the enlightening aspect of education whereas others viewed education as a continuation – as reproducing rather than fundamentally challenging social inequality. Though the social reformers in the nineteenth and early twentieth centuries stressed on the need for education as the first step towards women's enlightenment and empowerment, their patronage was also defined by an attempt towards identifying certain common standards of social behaviour and cultural norms.

From 1854 onwards, concern for 'female education' became one of the anxieties of the colonial administration as a result of the recognition given by the Wood's Despatch which linked it to the 'educational and moral tone' of the people. Particularly for women its significance lay in the gap between a premature imposition of Western professionalism and the existing tradition of female education of indigenous origin. Tim Allender's essay points out how, though uneven, there existed some indigenous girls' schools of mixed clientele, attended by low-caste girls along with the elites who usually preferred to educate their women more exclusively.[31] By virtue of there being strong collaborations between Europeans and Orientalists in Bombay and the NWP the native societies started schools for education of girls by engrafting Western knowledge on Indian language by 1820s. In this tradition many more girls even attended boys' schools and crossed the barrier for women's education more easily. This was further strengthened by educating girls in the village circle Halkabandi Schools earmarked for boys by enthusiastic administrators like Henry Reid, the DPI. This in turn was catalytic in opening more girls' schools in the area. The Victorian moral norms of family, character and respectability, introduced through the Western educational models in Bengal in the 1820s, led to the growth of women's education in India both for elites and the backward. In its turn this created a demand for more female teachers and was instrumental in the introduction of the Lancaster model of education by the intervention of Mary Carpenter, a follower of the Unitarian ideology.

Carpenter's ideas echoed that of the new colonial mentalities of the Raj, and in this scheme training of female teachers, even for the indigenous schools, was to be modeled on European experience. As another imperative of the Raj to promote education and employment of the Eurasian children it was also decided, by late 1850s, to channelize Eurasian girls towards training as teachers of good moral character. Thus Carpenter's ideas were supported by the state for the rest of the century, though it soon appeared to be a much more expensive system than employing female indigenous teachers in place of the European superintendents and headmistresses, and most of Carpenter's teacher training schools were closed down on economic as well as ethical grounds. The issue of training Eurasian women was much more complex due to its definitional as well as social complexities, but it did engage colonial preoccupation, and combined with other similar preoccupations it diverted the state attention from the more urgent need of focusing on the lower order of schooling first. Funding for Indian girls' schooling was scarcer and most funding for female schooling went to Eurasian children over Indian, which was not the case with the Philipinos under the American or the Koreans under Japanese control.

Outside the state sphere, however, were women like Eleanor McDougall, in-charge of the Women's College in Madras from 1914 for almost a quarter of a century, who not only developed a degree and a diploma course each for teacher training in 1923 but also infused in the trainees an ethic of service to the poor and needy girls of south India. Allender's essay also touches upon the development of a new Hindu female ethic with strong cultural traditions of responsible motherhood in the household and combining it with public action or social service to combat illiteracy, child marriage and other evils of society. Some women activists also developed their own sense of sisterhood for the same issues across caste and religion and independent of the nationalist forums, which they saw as male domains. Still others encouraged female professional education and used their higher education for furthering social reform.

In the inter-war period the All India Women's Conference stressed on the importance of physical and moral education in the Indian context, and the radical Hindu feminists, while remaining within the religious fold, were driven by male rigidity to pursue a separate social agenda. There were attempts at reform by individual women converts and leading activists with Western professionalism, however, these were rejected by the broader women's reform movement of the early twentieth century in the radical *swadeshi* atmosphere. Girls' education had become a social issue in their campaigns. Between 1921 and 1931 educational institutions for women and the enrolments in them had increased substantially – helped by some generous funding from private sources. Simultaneously, the racial boundaries regarding enrolment in European, Eurasian schools *vis-à-vis* schools for Indians too blurred, and this ushered in greater Indian schoolgirl participation in education. Despite the dominance of Western stereotypical thinking, the Indian national movement developed a different role for Indian women and this was reflected in the post-Independent Nehruvian policy of assuming a direct responsibility in providing equal opportunity for women in professional education by offering them far greater access to it and with a professional ethic far more suited to the needs of the country.

The essay by Parimala V. Rao shows how a popular aspiration coupled with state support could achieve within a short time what meticulous planning and interpersonal rivalries of various factions of the Mysorean elite had failed to do over a long period of time. The princely state of Mysore, taken over by the British in 1832, was put under the administration of Mark Cubbon with primary focus on maintenance of law and order and very little priority to the development of educational institutions. This state of affairs was found suitable by the privileged traditional elite and continued for about a quarter of a century at the cost of progress of general and particularly female education. In Mysore, therefore, it was primarily through the missionary initiatives that schools developed for girls of mixed social backgrounds. The local demand for education also became evident when the administration changed hands in 1862 and passed on to Chief Commissioner Bowing. The petitions urging the state to start schools for boys and girls came from the highest to the lowest in the Hindu society as well as from the Muslim community there. Rao attributes the change in people's perspectives to the two statesmen's contrary perspectives primarily, and the response the colonial government received from individuals collectively for funding schools.[32]

Though highly factionalized, the Mysore elites in government services were also critical of colonial rule and it was the efforts of personalities like Dewan Sheshadri Iyer that saw the expansion of women's education in the state following the restoration of the Maharaja in 1881. By the turn of the century, women's education had received full support from most people and the only areas where there were reservations were on issues of teaching English and sciences in school. However, these oppositions were worn down by firm stands taken by visionaries like Rangacharlu and Iyer who countered all opposition to women's education stemming out of caste, gender and religious dynamics of the Mysore society in the representative assembly. This was possible because of the holistic approach adopted by them towards the gender issue and the social abuses surrounding it. As a result the pattern that emerged in the state in the field of women's education was more egalitarian than the general trend, though oppositions continued towards higher education on various pretexts. It was the firm hand of administrators like Visvesvaraya, particularly his efforts at implementing compulsory education for girls, that helped overcome opposition to progress in the mission. Like in other parts of India the 1920s saw greater attention being given to political reform, and in the state of Mysore this shifted focus from the agenda of women's education. The dynamics of the multi-ethnic elite conflict in Mysore during the colonial period put challenges to the issue of educating women, which impeded as well as pushed the issue towards a more positive outcome than in many other parts of the country as evident from the article by Rao.

Education of Indian Muslim women in the wider context of women's education in a highly differentiated social structure of India holds an important place and is probed at length by Gulfishan Khan. Her essay elucidates how the English-educated Muslim elite in their confrontation with ideological and institutional challenges of colonialism and nationalism redefined their cultural identity and reconstructed the social position of Muslim women. Following the course of Shaikh Abdullah's life and activities, it chalks out the complex process of intellectual influence on social change. Khan focuses on Abdullah's ideas which broadly echoed the themes articulated by nineteenth-century social reformers and the intellectuals associated with the Aligarh movement. But Abdullah's uniqueness lay in his focus on education – in particular women's education – as the route to social advancement of the country and a prelude to emancipation of women.[33]

In a comparative analysis the article brings in the contributions of Syed Ahmad Khan towards Muslim women's education in a harmonious patriarchal set-up, with family stability as the first priority. Sir Syed believed that the deteriorating position of Muslim women was a direct result of the colonial ascendency and the declining social and economic status of Muslim women at home in traditional ways. Shaikh Abdullah on the other hand, showed a better understanding of the development and progress of feminist issues through his Western education and exposure to the English print media, though in his endeavour to bring the liberal notions of equality and emancipation of women he sought to provide an Islamic model. He translated the intellectual debates of the Aligarh movement relating to women's education into a social reality. Empowering women with literacy and education and their integration into public life remains a unique contribution of Abdullah to the Islamic feminist thought, and in his contribution to the modern Islamic feminist ideology he was as influenced by the reformist movements of other Islamic countries as by the pluralistic discursive context of India. As pointed out in the essay by Khan, perhaps this was a legacy of his being born in a Brahmin family and having later embraced the faith of Islam due to its appeal of the philosophy of egalitarianism. It was therefore his pledge to appeal to the conscience of the Muslims to grant women the status granted by Islam but denied by social practice. Abdullah founded the Women's College at Aligarh Muslim University, and the main focus of his reformist agenda was progress in higher education for Muslim women, which he expressed through essays, articles, pamphlets and biographical reminiscences. Shaikh Abdullah firmly believed that there was no inherent difference in the intellectual capacity of men and women and argued in favour of teaching them the same subjects. He also argued that knowledge was universal in nature and did not follow regional distinctions like Eastern, Orientalist and Anglicist.

Despite acknowledging the need for enhancing women's health care facilities the colonial government's emphasis and research fund allocation was more on areas like tropical medicine. In comparison, the maternity and health welfare infrastructure was poor and the institutes particularly set up for training professionals in these had to struggle for survival at every stage of their development. Women's access to medical education and research on women-specific diseases and obstetric care are two important issues in medical education in India dealt in the essay by Ch. Radha Gayathri.[34] Maternal and child welfare care had drawn attention only as late as the post-Second World War period, when the approach changed from a moral to a social issue basis with particular emphasis put on antenatal care, and schools were opened for training women as health visitors and midwives. It was a movement that spread all over India and support from provincial governments sustained the training schools. The demand for trained medical professionals and hospitals, however, far outnumbered its supply, and it were the welfare centres that provided viable alternatives for such needs. On the curative field, training of medical professionals also had a male bias. Despite this, institutions providing medical education to women grew by 1920 as a result of demand for women doctors. Women's access to medical education further eased after this, but the demand continued to exceed the supply substantially.

Medical research on maternal and infant mortality was at best intermittent and sporadic as brought out by Gayathri. No special department for research into maternal and child health care came up in this period in any university or research organization till the establishment of the All India Institute of Hygiene and Public Health in the early 1930s, and this single institute continued to offer a postgraduate diploma in maternity and child welfare for a very long time, though it had to suffer from inadequate and irregular grants. Despite great demands for the diploma course it was not opened to medical licentiates on grounds of it being of too high a standard till 1938, when a resolution was passed in its favour. The first institute imparting quality training to health visitors was Lady Reading Health School in Delhi, started in 1918, but its diploma was not recognized officially in many provinces of India for about a decade due to certain technicalities involved in the process. It was only in 1935 that more such training schools came up.

IV

The collection of essays in this volume aims at examining the debates and developments towards the making of an inclusive knowledge society in colonial India, and the transmission of knowledge through agents and institutions of education in modern India, from a historical perspective. The relevance of such an exercise lies in the fact that the education system in India even today remains a legacy of the two centuries of colonial rule, with still limited and uneven access to knowledge, and the added entry of more clearly defined market and consumerist ideologies, which are now actively engaged in the process of transforming education into a marketable commodity. The neo-liberal policies of the 1990s facilitated the growth of a middle-class enamoured with the prospects of a new knowledge-economy and a new knowledge-society. Today's quest for knowledge is shorn of certain moral or social values. Students emerging from our distinguished engineering institutions seldom opt for manufacturing units or research laboratories; finance or sales attract them more.[35] Our forefathers knew how to grow sugar cane, so when sugar was considered a high-end product in the international market, they were uprooted from their villages and sent to far-off Fiji, Trinidad or Mauritius to grow sugar cane.

They were called *coolies*. Now software is the high-value product and the new *techno-coolies* equipped with degrees from prestigious institutions are all grabbing the opportunities. And they do not have to be uprooted! They practise this new skill taking advantage of the time-zone for a dime which would have cost a dollar in the other hemisphere. As for the companies, the watchword is profit and profit alone. The public resources (even air-waves) are ripped at a pace which could easily shame the buccaneers of the East India Company. Governments are willing partners in this game. Hope lies in the strengthening of the civil society and making knowledge and its institutions quality and equity-oriented.

The volume traces the growth of knowledge in India in modern times and its conflict with the existing societal and religious expectations, as also the conflict between individual and institutional ideas. The societal expectations of market-oriented modern education stunted the growth of indigenous classical and vernacular-language educational institutions. It also addresses the question of missionary involvement in the spread of education, bringing out its interplay with nationalism and the resultant change in the perspective of educational and larger religious objectives of the missionaries, rather than accepting it as a monolithic development as is made out to be in many scholarly writings. In tracing the growth of institutions and patrons of education, the volume has attempted to address the issue of social exclusion – be it sectional, regional or gender oriented. Despite the apparent diversity and exclusivity, the themes presented here are interwoven and reflect an overarching interest in broader issues, with the primary focus being on the growth of a new system of education in modern India with its obvious as well as subtle implications for the larger society. Notwithstanding the sincere efforts to make it a comprehensive one, some major gaps remain in the volume. It will therefore rest on a future volume to address the issues left unaddressed by this one.

NOTES

1. The debate pertaining to the term 'knowledge society' can be traced back to the writings of J.S. Mill in the 1830s and Adam Smith in the 1860s in Britain. However, the popularization of the concept in the post-industrial society is attributed to Daniel Bell through his book, *The Coming of the Post-Industrial Society*, published in 1973.

For a treatment of the concept in both historical and present-day contexts see, Nico Stehr, *Knowledge Societies*, London: Sage, 1994. For a discourse on Indian education and its historical contexts, see, S. Bhattacharya (ed.), *The Contested Terrain: Perspectives on Education in India*, New Delhi: Orient Longman, 1998. This volume was based on a conference held earlier at JNU with the perspective of education as a terrain of contestation.

2. T.R. Metcalf, *Ideologies of the Raj*: *The New Cambridge History of India III*, 4 (paperback edn.), Cambridge: Cambridge University Press, 1998.
3. This cultual hegemony was built upon the attribution of cognitive authority to metropolitan Western culture, centralization of knowledge production in the metropolis, and marginalization (de-legitimization) of knowledge systems and educational institutions indigenous to the natives of the colony. S. Bhattacharya (ed.), *Education and the Disprivileged: Nineteenth and Twentieth Century India*, New Delhi: Orient Longman, 2002; and *Educating the Nation: Documents on the Discourse of National Education in India, 1880-1920*, New Delhi: Kanishka, 2003.
4. D.A. Washbrook, 'Orients and Occidents: Colonial Discourse Theory and the Historiography of the British Empire', in *The Oxford History of the British Empire*, vol. 5, *Historiography*, ed. Robin W. Winks, Oxford: Oxford University Press, 1999. Cf. Sheldon Pollock, 'Forms of Knowledge in Early Modern South Asia: Introduction', *Comparative Studies of South Asia, Africa and Middle East*, 24: 2, 2004, p. 19.
5. Pollock, 2004.
6. There are materials from which one could make some serious sense of culture and power in early modern India (1500-1800)—after which the British colonial power consolidated itself in the subcontinent and changed the definitions of knowledge in the Indian context. South Asia has an impressive literary record in terms of number of texts and centuries of unbroken multilingual literacy, as compared to that of Greek and Latin and medieval European culture combined. S. Pollock, (ed.), *Literary Cultures in History: Reconstructions from South Asia*, Berkeley: University of California Press, 2003. Cf., Pollock, ibid.
7. Ibid., p. 20.
8. For an informed discussion on this, see 'Introduction', in Raziuddin Aquil and Partha Chatterjee (eds.), *History in the Vernacular*, New Delhi: Permanent Black, 2010.
9. On this recent historiographical trend see Clive Whitehead, *Colonial Educators: The British Indian and Colonial Education Service 1858-1983*, London: Tauris, 2003.
10. See Foreword, by Kirk-Greene, in ibid.
11. Metcalf, 1998.

12. Krishna Kumar and Joachim Oesterheld (eds.), *Education and Social Change in South Asia*, Hyderabad: Orient Longman, 2007.
13. S. Bhattacharya: 'Contested Pasts: The Concept of Civilization in the Nationalist Discourse of Education', paper presented at the Conference on Learning in the Past, Research Agendas for the Future: Connecting Histories of Education, 1700-2000, IDS, Kolkata, February 2010.
14. Ibid., p. 8.
15. Bhattacharya, 1998.
16. V.R. Taneja and S. Taneja, *Educational Thinkers*, New Delhi: Atlantic, 2004, p. 123.
17. Bhattacharya, 2010, p. 8.
18. Deepak Kumar, '"New" Knowledge and "New" India: Lessons from the Colonial Past', *Infra*, Section I.
19. Ibid.
20. S. Irfan Habib, 'Reconciling Science with Islam in 19th Century India', *Infra*, p. 63.
21. Ibid., pp. 64-5.
22. Suvobrata Sarkar, 'Bhadralok Aspirations and the Quest for Technical Knowledge (1830-1900)', *Infra*, Section I.
23. Nigel Crook (ed.), *The Transmission of Knowledge in South Asia*, New Delhi: Oxford University Press, 1996; Bhattacharya (ed.), 1998, op. cit.
24. Bhattacharya, 2010, op. cit.
25. Andre Beteille, *Universities at the Crossroads*, New Delhi: Oxford University Press, 2010, p. 13.
26. Nandita Khadria, 'Popular Demand for Higher Educaiton: The Genesis of University Education in Assam', *Infra*, Section I.
27. Bidisha Dhar, 'Educating the Artisan?', *Infra*, Section II.
28. Susheel Prasad, 'Advising Indian Education: Evolution of the Central Board of Secondary Education', *Infra*, Section I.
29. The most apt example would be of a recent study by Meena Bhargava and Kalyani Dutta, *Women, Education and Politics: The Women's Movement and Delhi's Indraprastha College* (2006); Shanti Kamath and Narain Prasad, *The Saga of Indraprastha College for Women*, Delhi: Indraprastha Education Trust, 2000. Sabyasachi Bhattacharya et al. (eds.), *Development of Women's Education in India: 1850-1920*. The last is a collection of primary documents, published and unpublished, highlighting the negotiations between the indigenous intelligentsia and the British-Indian government and the forms of institutional and education system that ensued as a result.
30. Partha Chatterjee, 'Nationalist Resolution of Women's Question', in Sangari and Vaid (eds.), *Recasting Women,* New Brunswick: Rutgers University Press, 1989; Malavika Karlekar, 'Kadambini and the Bhadralok: Early Debates over Women's Education in Bengal',

Economic and Political Weekly, vol. 21, no. 17 (26 April 1986); Sumit Sarkar and Tanika Sarkar, *Women and Social Reform in Modern India: A Reader*, Bloomington: Indiana University Press, 2008.

31. Tim Allender, 'Colonial Anxieties: The State Embodiment of the Female Teacher "trainer", 1808-1939', *Infra*, Section II.
32. Parimala Rao, 'The Impact of Elite Conflict on Women's Education in Princely Mysore, 1860-1920', *Infra*, Section II.
33. Gulfishan Khan, 'Shaikh Muhammad Abdullah (1874-1965) and Muslim Female Education Movement', *Infra*, Section II.
34. Radha Gayathri, 'Training of the Maternal and Child Welfare Professionals: The Demands and Constraints', *Infra*, Section II.
35. In the realm of fundamental research or cutting-edge knowledge, colonial India produced more brilliant and original scholars and scientists than post-colonial India.

PART I

MAKING OF A KNOWLEDGE SOCIETY

CHAPTER 1

'New' Knowledge and 'New' India

Lessons from the Colonial Past

DEEPAK KUMAR

The onset of the twenty-first century was treated with a great deal of media hype and forecasts as a century of knowledge and incredible developments. As we move to the close of the first decade of the new century, the hype refuses to die down. Talks and claims about knowledge-society and knowledge-economy (even in the midst of apparent economic meltdown) continue to pour in as if the earlier societies or economies were not shaped or influenced by knowledge. Perhaps every age is an age of knowledge and change. Turn of a century can be a good time for historical reflections. How did the Indians feel when they entered the twentieth century? How did they look at the then existing techno-scientific knowledge? How different was it going to be from the past? What was their vision of 'new' India? How was 'new' knowledge perceived? What new strategies were thought of? The beginnings saw the apogee of the Empire but things were to change soon. Even the colonial government had to shift gear and talk about development. The new middle class that had emerged out of the colonial experience appropriated the right to speak on behalf of all people and pondered over the ways and means to improve their lot. On the new agenda figured technical education, scientific research, medical intervention, agricultural experiments, institutional dissemination of knowledge, and so on. Could the newly emerging middle class succeed in making a clear blueprint? Differences of opinion and controversies dogged the discourse all the time. The present paper discusses not only the contours of the 'development discourse' but also the views that still lay on the margins.

The turn of the twentieth century saw intense debates on what the Indians had received at the end of a century-and-half of British rule. A cursory look at the periodicals, pamphlets and publications of the time would show the high level of discontent with the contemporary situation.[1] Even the then Governor-General agreed that a huge stratum of the society retained 'the primordial elements far away from the reach of progress'.[2] In the first decade of the twentieth century amelioration was sought through the slogans of *swadeshi* (self-reliance) and *swaraj* (self-rule). These were more than political slogans, rather they symbolized an intense yearning for change.[3] The 'new vision' of India that came to be debated so intensely in the years to follow had its beginnings in the last two decades of the nineteenth century. The quest for 'techno-scientific knowledge' preceded and facilitated the emergence of this 'vision'.

The Scientific Pioneers

A large number of Indian interlocutors, belonging to different disciplines and walks of life, contributed to the new quest for techno-scientific knowledge. Among those who were the first to take scientific research and teaching as their career were Pramatha Nath Bose (1855-1934), Ramendra Sundar Trivedi (1864-1919), Jagadish Chandra Bose (1858-1937), and Prafulla Chandra Ray (1861-1944). P.N. Bose specialized in geology at the University of London and later joined the Geological Survey of India. In 1886 he wrote a pamphlet 'Technical and Scientific Education in Bengal' and a decade later published three volumes titled *A History of Hindu Civilization*. Fierce nationalism had transformed a geologist into a historian. From physical mapping he shifted to cultural contours. He held the Brahmanical system responsible for neglecting physical science 'to a most serious extent'. 'The Hindu civilisation carried the germs of its decay within it', he argued. But he would never agree to his (geological) chief's perception of Indians as 'utterly incapable to any original work in natural science'.[4] He could see no reason why 'with an improved system of scientific education, and with just and sympathetic treatment of the young men trained in India, they will not be able to take a place in the modern scientific world'. The Japanese 'instead of being thwarted, discouraged and set down as incapable, have been aided, encouraged and stimulated by their government to pursue science'.[5]

Bose only forgot to mention that Japan was not a colony! But he did realize (at his own cost) that a just and sympathetic treatment was not always possible in a colony. Every concession had to be literally wrung out. It was a struggle in slow motion but on a high pitch. In 1886 P.N. Bose asked for a science course at the F.A. (intermediate) level to facilitate early specialization. It was not until 1906 that an intermediate science course was introduced. Bose also pointed out the defects in the B.Sc. course which in itself was divided into literary and scientific curriculum. The Presidency College had no chairs in botany, zoology and geology and officers of the Geological Survey of India were asked to teach geology on a purely temporary basis. One could imagine what progress would come from such intermittent lectures. So was the case in Bengal Engineering College at Shibpur where chemistry, physics, geology and metallurgy would be taught by one and the same teacher.[6] Bose wanted science subjects to be taught with an eye to their application to industry. But at the same time he warned against the dark sides of industrialism in Europe which was feeding the growing spirit of militarism and imperialism in the West.[7] He would have preferred the cultivation of science and technology within the 'limits of intellectual culture'. Later, the experience of the First World War made him revert to the propagation of ancient culture (as represented by India) which 'would rescue the humanity from the morass of militarism, malevolence, destitution, disease etc.'.[8] Thus P.N. Bose wanted change and progress but on his cultural terms and without losing Indian values.

A sharper articulation of the cultural dimensions of techno-scientific education came from Ramendra Sundar Trivedi, a science teacher at Ripon College (later its principal) in Calcutta. He wrote a number of thematically-rich yet seemingly popular science articles in Bengali which were published in books titled *Prakriti* (1896) and *Jigyasa* (1904). Thanks to the English education one may have learnt a great deal. But 'have we acquired the ability to learn on our own?' Trivedi asked:

> Have we assimilated scientific into our system? The very word science throws us into raptures but what we ultimately imbibe is basically pseudo-science. Having heard that human hair is a non-conductor of electricity we immediately begin growing pigtails: and as soon as we learn that changes in lunar position cause tides we take our horoscopes to the astrologer. Can one think of a more piteous situation?[9]

This comes from a person with a supposedly Brahmanical and revivalist bias. But such poignant questions would have occurred only to those who had a deep understanding of their own time and locale. Trivedi even tried to expand the realm and definition of science: 'Science! Science! We all aspire for scientific research. As if science is confined only to physics, chemistry and physiology. As if anthropology is beyond the scope of science – as if historical analysis is outside science's concern.'[10]

Such a holistic view may not be appreciated by the scientists now but a century ago it was not so. In fact, scientists like P.N. Bose and P.C. Ray turned into sound historians. Like them Trivedi could see the distorting influence of the colonial system and its bureaucracy. How 'mechanized' the educational system had become, the universities nothing or little more than degree-granting machines. Even private efforts had come to a naught with M.L. Sircar's Association for Cultivation of Science lying in a virtually moribund state. Trivedi criticized the content and quality of education in the *tols* and *chatuspatis*, but thought that these had at least some genuine respect for knowledge. Modern educational institutions, because they followed a mechanized routine, failed to inculcate this genuine respect. They became what P.C. Ray later called *golam-khanas* (slave-factories) churning out munsifs, clerks, assistant surgeons and overseers as per the requirements of the colonial job market. Trivedi realized that this 'mechanization' could not altogether be avoided. It was part of the global change. That is why unlike Gandhi he did not attack the West with anything he could lay his hands on! Trivedi kept grappling with the two different texts. He would accept modernity but not Westernization; modern university system of education but not its commercialization. Several Indian thinkers and reformers of his age like Vivekananda and Aurobindo held similar views. But Trivedi was a little different in the sense that he was deeply aware of the philosophical issues concerning science, and even then he would deny modern science any epistemic superiority (unlike P.C. Ray). He would rather describe Western scientists in Hindu terms, for example, Copernicus as one with *dibyachakkhu* (spiritual vision), Newton as a *rishi* (sage) and Helmholtz as an *abatar* (incarnation).[11]

In contrast the two most creative scientists that the late nineteenth-century India produced, J.C. Bose and P.C. Ray, would fully accept the epistemic superiority of modern science and treated education as the most effective vehicle for assimilation and gradual diffusion of the new ideas. Both were well-steeped in Indian history and culture and could differentiate between what was to be taken and what not. J.C. Bose was a bio-physicist who worked on electrical impulse and response in the living and the non-living. Borrowing from the technical language of his discipline he thus described the role of education in the East-West encounter:

> An impulse from the outside reacts on impressionable bodies in two different ways depending on whether the recipient is inert or fully alive. The inert is fashioned after the pattern of the infinite repetition of one mechanical stamp. But when an organism is fully alive the answering reaction is often of an altogether different character to the impinging stimulus. The outside shocks stir up the organism to answer feebly or to the utmost in ways as multitudinous and varied as life itself. So the first impetus of Western education impressed itself on some in a dead monotony of imitation of things Western; while in others it awakened all that was greatest in the national memory.[12]

Unlike P.N. Bose and P.C. Ray, J.C. Bose did not undertake any investigation into the 'national memory' (i.e. history). But he did try to identify his works with what he considered to be the greatest in his cultural inheritance. His propositions that life emerges out of non-life and that there exists an underlying unity between the living and the non-living were taken as scientific manifestations of the Samkhya philosophy. J.C. Bose used to quote from the Vedas and had a poetical flavour in his writings: he even gave Sanskrit names to his instruments and did not see any conflict between science and religion. The contemporary opinion did not consider it mystical or 'oriental'; rather he was hailed as a syncretic mind.[13] His works were the first authentic rebuttal of the colonial view that Indians were incapable of original scientific investigations. But his was not an ivory tower projection of education and research. He was convinced of the utilitarian value of science and wanted its widespread diffusion through proper science education. It had to be not only for the sake of scientific knowledge but also to harness the economic resources of the country and to show how to discriminate between industries which can and which cannot be profitably carried on under the climatic and other conditions prevailing in India.[14] To achieve this were needed a satisfactory science course, good laboratories and scholarships. Bose was particularly perturbed over the science curriculum in Indian universities. At the graduate level in Calcutta University for example, the vast area of acoustics, heat, light, electricity and magnetism formed only half a paper! To add to the woes of the students too many textbooks were prescribed. The result was they looked for help books. Second-hand knowledge thus took the place of 'living science'. Even this could not be put to any use because in the absence of any post-degree scholarship or employment the students would shift to a career in law or administration. Like his compatriots, Bose excelled in diagnosis but his solutions were limited and heavily dependent on the government. All through he remained a devoted researcher, not an activist.

P.C. Ray, on the other hand, showed a higher degree of social commitment. He was an educationist, a scientist, an entrepreneur, a Gandhian activist – all rolled into one. He spoke and wrote extensively on educational matters with rare passion, sincerity and clarity. Himself a working scientist and deeply conscious of its industrial applications he was one of the earliest to see science in its social context and to talk of its social relevance and accountability. He did some original research on India's scientific heritage and attempted a social explanation of what went wrong, when and how. Unlike Trivedi and others, he held the Indian social (caste) structure responsible for the cleavage between mental and manual work and the resultant stagnation.[15] He wanted modern education to bridge this gulf. In his view education had to be quality oriented, not for degree but for generation of employment and wealth. The average graduate was found to be 'a licensed ignoramus' and the degree itself served as a cloak to hide the degree-holders' ignorance. Higher education should be restricted to only those who feel an instinctive call in that direction.[16] The other great defect in his opinion was the undue stress on a literacy curriculum. A Calcutta University student for M.A. degree in 1930 had to attend 230 classes in English and only 65 in mathematics. He was equally unhappy about the intellectual narrowness of the specialist in science. He visualized a broad 'mental culture' in which science, literature, history and philosophy were given almost equal attention. Legal studies which thrived on the colonial requirement had no place in this scheme. Gandhi had severely criticized the legal profession. Similarly Ray would exclaim, 'if I am made the dictator of the university for one day, I would shut down the Law Department for at least three years!' Apart from the defective curriculum what hurt Ray most was the medium of instruction. He was convinced that learning through a foreign medium killed originality:

> Imagine for a moment what would happen if the English lad were compelled first of all to learn Persian or Chinese or say German or Russian and then had to read through the medium of such a tongue . . . in India we have adopted the most unnatural system and have to pay a heavy penalty for it.[17]

Ray realized that his own forefathers had gone 'mad' over English education but he appreciated their dilemma. In the first half of the nineteenth century English education was necessary to acquire new knowledge. Rammohun and Vidyasagar who asked for it had also written extensively in Bengali. Later the whole process degenerated into a 'service-seeking mania'. This Ray resented. He was not against English. He only asked for its late introduction after the mother tongue had laid the base. J.C. Bose held similar views and recalled with pride how his father had sent him to a 'vernacular' school. This did help him relate to his surroundings. But higher education and publication of research had to be in English – the language of the scientific world.[18] They had no doubt about it. Then the existing institutions of science education and research had to be strengthened through fellowships, laboratories and private donations. When J.N. Tata (a leading Bombay merchant) floated the idea of an Indian Institute of Research, Ray was reticent. He would have preferred private munificence to encourage the existing institutions in different parts of the country rather than create one single island of excellence. He argued, 'India is not a compact homogenous country like Japan; a central Research Institute with an "Imperial University" like that of Tokyo does not seem to commend itself'.[19] Later in 1931 when the eminent engineer M. Visweswaraya pleaded for a technological university, Ray called it a delusion and argued, 'in every country industrial progress has preceded progress in science and technology'.[20] In this industrial progress he envisaged a greater role for businessmen and workers than graduates in science and arts. The key to prosperity lay in the spirit of entrepreneurship and not in mere technical expertise.

Ray did not advocate higher education for everyone but primary education was a different matter. As late as 1934 the Bengal government was spending only Rs. 27 lakh on primary education while it raised Rs. 32 crore as revenue from the province. It was a mere 0.9 per cent of its earning while Japan and Denmark spent about 20 per cent of their gross revenue on primary education. Ray cited from the Famine Commission of 1880 and the Agricultural Conference of 1888, etc., on how beneficial primary education could be for the peasants. Millions perished in epidemics and the ignorant masses steeped in superstition looked to Goddess Sitala. It was useless to 'din Pasteur's researches into their ear', Ray would argue, 'an ignorant people and a costly machinery of scientific experts go ill together'. He shared the belief that 'it is education and nothing but education that can remove social evils, sanitary troubles and economic distress from the country and can awaken political consciousness and create social solidarity in the people. Self-government without literacy would be nothing but a farce and might possibly be a tragedy'.[21]

Gandhi: An Alternative

Amidst the growing demands for self-rule, democracy, industrialization and development, Gandhi emerged as an extraordinary dissenter. Gandhi condemned the West precisely for the same virtues it had prided itself, i.e. modernization and industrialization. He seldom used the terms science or technology. His concern was civilization and mechanization and on these he talked and wrote profusely. He considered machinery 'the chief symbol of modern civilzation'; 'it represents a great sin', he wrote, though many times Gandhi would say he was not opposed to machinery. In his words:

> How can I be when I know that even this body is a most delicate piece of machinery? The spinning wheel itself is a machine. What I object to is the craze for machinery . . . today machinery helps a few to ride on the backs of millions. The impetus behind it all is not philanthropy to save labours but greed. It is against this constitution of things that I am fighting with all my might.[22]

So machinery as an ally of capitalism was Gandhi's anathema. How about machinery under state control as in the communist system? Here, he could foresee the state emerging as a super-capitalist and becoming equally oppressive. Means and ends both had to be 'pure'. He would not mind villagers plying their implements with the help of electricity. But the village communities or the state must own the power houses, just as they have their grazing pastures.[23] Later, in 1946, he even agreed that 'some key industries are necessary'. He would not enumerate these but would prefer them to be under state ownership provided the state professed non-violence.[24] Gandhi was worried less about production and more about distribution. He would have supported the Soviet experiment in production and distribution had it not been based on force. He was not for mass production, but for production by the masses, using the tools that the masses could afford to possess and repair.[25] A simple cottage machine like *charkha* (the spinning wheel) solved the problem of distribution. There would be no concentration of wealth and power.[26] Gandhi talked of developing round the *charkha* programmes of anti-malaria campaign, improved sanitation, conservation, cattle-breeding, etc. His critique was thus no mere denunciation of the West, rather it involved the development of a whole network of what Gandhi called 'ameliorative activity'.[27]

Two of the few occasions on which Gandhi touched the issue of science directly was when he talked to students at Trivandrum in 1925 and when he visited the Indian Institute of Science at Bangalore in 1927. He declared that he was not an opponent of science. But he wanted to put certain limitations 'upon scientific research and upon the uses of science'. These limitations were those of non-violence, humanity and morality. To these, he added:

> How will you infect the people of the villages with your scientific knowledge? Are you then learning science in terms of the villages and will you be so handy and so practical that the knowledge that you derive in a college so magnificently put and I believe equally magnificently equipped – you will be able to use for the benefit of the villagers?[28]

There were no easy answers. The system prepared them for an urban or industrial India, or for a slot abroad. An Indian student specializing in wood-chemistry in America once asked Gandhi, 'Would you approve of my going into industrial enterprise, say pulp or paper manufacturing? Do you stand for the progress of science? I mean such progress which brings blessings to mankind, e.g. the work of Pasteur of France or that of Dr. Benting of Toronto?' Gandhi had no objection to an industrial enterprise so long as it remained humanitarian. After all, it added to the productive capacity of the country. Similarly, with his admiration for the 'scientific spirit of the West' came a plea for limitations upon 'the present methods of pursuing knowledge'. One may not agree with Gandhi's great emphasis on non-violence and anti-vivisection, but he definitely provided a notion of social accountability with which it is almost impossible to differ. Similarly, his search for an 'alternative' cannot be overlooked.

Westward Ho!

The sharpest criticism of Gandhian views came from Meghnad Saha (1893-1955), a pioneer astrophysicist and an illustrious student of P.C. Ray, who wanted India to choose 'the cold logic of technology' and not the vague utopia of Gandhian economics. In the very first issue of his celebrated journal, *Science and Culture*, while appreciating Gandhi's genuine sympathy with the 'victims of an aggressive and selfish industrialism', Saha firmly refuted the claim that better and happier conditions of life could be created by 'discarding modern scientific technique and reverting back to the spinning wheel, the loin cloth and bullock cart'.[29]

Saha was a staunch advocate of industrial progress through careful and deliberate planning backed by scientific research. His thought had two significant strands. First, he treated science and technology as distinct yet connected knowledge systems without hierarchical relations, and second, he wished to introduce changes through a mixed economy in which both state and private enterprise had significant roles.[30] Saha was suspicious of Indian capitalists and would therefore assign the state a greater role.[31] Many Indian scientists and technologists sought solutions for the country's problems but their methods differed. P.C. Ray saw the remedy in *swadeshi* and *charkha*. Visvesvaraya, an eminent engineer (1860-1962), demanded rapid industrialization through the use of Indian capital and enterprise.[32]

By the mid-1930s, the long-drawn-out freedom struggle had begun to yield significant results. Provincial autonomy was introduced in 1935 and debates on planning for national prosperity began. Visvesvaraya's *Reconstructing India* was perhaps the first attempt to make Indians plan-conscious.[33] In 1934, he wrote *Planned Economy for India*. The same year G.D. Birla, a major industrialist and follower of Gandhi, pleaded for planning.[34] But it was Saha who convinced the national political leadership of its necessity. In 1937, he persuaded the Congress President, Subhas Chandra Bose, to constitute a National Planning Committee (NPC). This materialized at the end of 1938 under the chairmanship of Jawaharlal Nehru. As many as twenty-nine expert sub-committees were constituted to deal with different areas of national reconstruction, including agriculture, industries, population, labour, irrigation, energy, communication, forestation, health, housing and education.[35] Nehru was amazed at both the utility and vastness of the planning process. He wrote: 'One thing led to another and it was impossible to isolate anything or to progress in one direction without corresponding progress in another. The more we thought of this planning business, the vaster it grew in its sweep and range till it seemed to embrace almost every activity.'[36]

With nationalist feelings bursting at seams, the NPC provided an opportunity to recast the old arguments in terms of national regeneration, self-sufficiency and all-round progress.[37] But it also laid bare inherent tensions and contradictions. Gandhians like J.C. Kumarappa and S.N. Agarwal preferred traditional technology and village industries, and attacked the NPC.[38] Even within the Congress, younger leaders leaned towards modern science, technology and heavy industrialization. Some wanted to follow the socialist path, others favoured capitalist models such as envisaged in the Bombay Plan of 1944. The indigenous business class was no less divided. Gandhi's politics was convenient but not his economics. Although socialism remained an ideal for many (including Nehru and Saha), a version of democratic socialism with a mixed economy was accepted by the NPC as the basis for future development.[39] Saha resented this dilution, and even called the Congress leaders 'puppets in the hands of big industrialists'. He and Nehru gradually drifted apart. Later Nehru leaned more towards S.S. Bhatnagar (1894-1955) and Homi Bhabha (1909-66) which led to the growth of government-controlled industrial and defence research. By 1945 the political leadership took a conscious decision to modernize, and the dualism of the previous decades came to an end.

Reflections

For India, the twentieth century began on an interesting note; it saw the apogee of the Empire and, at the same time, the seeds of decolonization sprouted. Like the eighteenth century, it was an era of transition. The direction of change, however, remained unclear. Many critiques appeared and many options were debated. A renowned art critic, Ananda Coomaraswamy criticized his contemporary *swadeshi* protagonists for having ignored the skilled artisans and village craftsmen.[40] Officials like Chatterton (Director of Industries, Madras) differed and asked for industrial development under government patronage.[41] Towards this end, the Holland Commission attempted some sort of national planning in a bureaucratic guise. But nothing could impress the British government, which conveniently and regularly took refuge in the situation created by war and depression.

The last decade of the Raj saw some flickers of 'constructive imperialism', but these came too late. By then, nationalism had gathered strength and thanks to its demand for total indigenization, the British government could conveniently leave the core sectors of agriculture, health and education in Indian hands. Both Indian leaders and the government now vied with each other to raise development issues. Dissenters were gradually marginalized. To the government, Gandhi was important politically, but not otherwise. His vision of a new India was not fully shared even by his own followers!

The period 1937-47 deserves more attention. Many committees were formed and their reports published. Apart from the NPC, the Bombay Plan and Hill's Report, other significant reports emerged. Health and industrial research were explored under the chairmanship of Joseph Bhore and Shanmukham Chetty, respectively.[42] All these committees had at least one thing in common. They all asked for greater institutionalization. The importance of coordination everyone recognized, but even for this they asked for a coordinating institution![43] The proliferation of institutions did not necessarily bring quality research, nor could it bring academic science and industrial needs together. In Britain the work of the Board of Education, the University Grants Commission and the Department of Scientific and Industrial Research reflected widely varying pressures.[44] Indians were entering a similar situation. The race was on to make India a modern nation state. The new watchwords in the development discourse were planning, industrialization, institutionalization, and coordination. All major political leaders, and even the colonial government, joined the chorus.[45]

At first sight, there seemed to be a unity of purpose, but in reality this was not so. The thin veneer of the development discourse evaporated when put under pressure by class interests. The discourse was run by 'experts', middle-class professionals who stood for the state and through the state for the nation. Politicians and bureaucrats added their own flavours. And all this was done in the name of the 'masses', who 'entered the picture only as the somewhat abstract ultimate beneficiary'.[46] In the name of the 'masses', the authors and defenders of the Bombay Plan asked for a shift from an 'over-agriculturalized' economy to an industrial economy.[47] At its core was the notion that industrial production was more capitalistic than agricultural production. Even those who argued for industrialization felt the heat:

> The real bottleneck is the attitude of capitalists, and civil servants in league with them, who oppose all industrial production in excess of the proved absorptive capacity of the market and threaten that such production is unprofitable. They forget that planned development ultimately aims at giving plenty to all and not profits to few.[48]

A more viable proposition was planned development on the socialist (Soviet) pattern. Nehru's heart lay in this but the pragmatist in him led to compromises at every step. Lest right-wing leaders feel alienated, Nehru spoke of independence and a democratic structure first, to be followed by socialism and planning.[49] After Independence, he perfected the art of mixed economy and mixed politics.[50] He tried to combine Gandhi and Visvesvaraya, but finally could do justice to neither.

Another casualty in the era of mixed policies was the traditional distinction between pure and applied science. S.S. Bhatnagar, Homi Bhabha and many others looked for a composite structure that combined the two. But to 'purists' like Meghnad Saha, pure science was the seed of applied science, and 'to neglect pure science would be like spending a large amount on manuring and ploughing the land and then omit the sowing of any kind'.[51] Satyen Bose and C.V. Raman had similar views. Academic science still held a greater appeal for the Indian mind. However, the notion that science and technology were two sides of the same coin had two interesting results for an undeveloped country. First, it meant assigning a far greater authority and responsibility to the state.[52] Secondly, in the name of coordinating the two, the tendency in practice was to centralize.

From the pluralistic and a deeper cultural exploration of the late nineteenth century, the science-society discourse among Indians gradually moved towards the paradigms laid by the dominant Western concepts and practices. Far greater emphasis was put on institutions than on men and ideas. Freedom and democracy should have led to decentralization and upward mobility. But the results were exactly the opposite. The post-colonial state in India emerged no less centralized, bureaucratized and top-heavy than the colonial state. Now that knowledge has become a fiercely competitive industry, the ideas of the preceding generations need to be looked at again.

NOTES

1. 'The Danger of the New Century', *The Pioneer*, 28 January 1901; 'Good bye 1800-1900', *The Statesman*, 4 January 1900; K. Zulaskar, 'India Entering upon a New Era of Enlightenment', *Modern Review*, 21, V, 1913, pp. 535-8.
2. 'Lord Curzon on Higher Education', *The Dawn*, 25 December 1900.
3. Manu Goswami, 'From Swadeshi to Swaraj: Nation, Economy, Territory in Colonial South Asia, 1870-1907', *Comparative Studies in Society and History*, 40, 4, 1998, pp. 609-37.
4. Note by H.B. Medlicott, Director, GSI; Revenue-Agriculture, Surveys, Proc. No. 25, September 1880, National Archive of India.
5. P.N. Bose, *A History of Hindu Civilization*, vol. III, Calcutta: n.p., 1896, pp. II-V, 98.
6. P.N. Bose, *Essays and Lectures on the Industrial Development of India*, Calcutta: Newman and Co., 1906, pp. 65-85.
7. Prophetically he wrote, 'the great wars of the future will be fought not for interests in Europe, but for interests outside Europe', ibid., pp. 241-58.
8. P.N. Bose, *Swaraj, Cultural and Political*, Calcutta: n.p., 1929, pp. 275-6.
9. R.N. Trivedi, quoted in Santanu Chacraverti, 'Ramendra Sundar Trivedi and Bengal's Response to Modern Science', unpublished Ph.D. thesis, Jadavpur University, 1996, pp. 42, 80.
10. Ibid., p. 85.
11. Ibid., p. 183.
12. *Modern Review*, February 1917, reprinted in D. Sen and A.K. Chakraborty (eds.), *J.C. Bose Speaks*, Calcutta: Puthipatra, 1986, pp. 31-2.
13. *The Dacca Review*, vol. VI, December 1916, in J.C. Bose Trust Press File No. 2, p. 247.
14. *The Englishman*, 22 May 1897, in J.C. Bose Trust Press File No. 1, p. 58.

15. P.C. Ray, *History of Hindu Chemistry*, vol. II, Williams and Norgate, Calcutta, 1909, p. 195.
16. P.C. Ray, *Life and Experiences of a Bengali Chemist*, Calcutta: Chuckrevertty, Chatterjee and Company, 1932, pp. 261, 299.
17. Ibid., p. 289.
18. Those who were not too happy with J.C. Bose (probably Sir Asutosh Mukherjee) would make fun of his professed love for the mother-tongue: 'Why does not Sir Jagadish publish his original articles in Bengali? Who knows, there may flock in Bengal, thousands of devotees from the remotest corner of the earth to learn the Bengali language only to read the valuable researches published in that language?', *The Century Review*, January 1918, in J.C. Bose Trust Press File No. F/94.
19. P.C. Ray, 'The Problem of Scientific Education in India', *Calcutta Review*, vol. CVIII, 1899, pp. 347-95.
20. Ray, *Life and Experiences*, p. 321.
21. Ibid., vol. II, Calcutta, 1935, pp. 82-100.
22. *Young India*, 13 November 1924, pp. 377-8.
23. *Harijan*, 22 June 1935, p. 146.
24. Ibid., 1 September 1946, title page.
25. Ibid., 2 November 1934, pp. 301-2.
26. As Gandhi once beautifully explained:

    'No amount of human ingenuity can manage to distribute water over the whole land as a shower of rain can. No irrigation department, no rules of precedent, no inspection and no water-cess. Everything is done with an ease and gentleness that by their very perfection evade notice. The spinning wheel, too, has got the same power of distributing work and wealth in millions of houses in the simplest way imaginable.' *Young India*, 27 December 1923, p. 430.
27. Gandhians find in it a concept of 'technology-practice'. Sunil Sahasrabudhey, 'Gandhi and the Challenge of Modern Science', *Gandhi Marg*, V, September 1983, pp. 330 7.
28. The *Hindu*, 19 March 1925, quoted in Raghvan Iyer (ed.), *The Moral and Political Writings of Mahatma Gandhi*, vol. I, Oxford: Clarendon Press, 1986, pp. 310-15.
29. *Science and Culture*, vol. I, 1935, pp. 3-4.
30. Dinesh Abrol, 'Colonised Minds or Progressive Nationalist Scientists: The Science and Culture Group', in R. MacLeod and D. Kumar (eds.), *Technology and the Raj*, New Delhi: Sage, 1995, pp. 265-88.
31. *Science and Culture*, vol. IV, 1938, p. 367.
32. M. Visvesvaraya, *Planned Economy for India*, Bangalore: Bangalore Press, 1934.
33. M. Visvesvaraya, *Reconstructing India,* London: King and Sons, 1920.
34. G.D. Birla, *Indian Prosperity: A Plea for Planning*, Annual Speech

delivered on 1 April 1934 at FICCI, New Delhi, later published in Allahabad: Leader Press, 1950.

35. The Second World War disrupted the work of the NPC which could be resumed at the end of the war. Before dissolving itself in 1949, the NPC published 27 volumes of reports outlining a ten-year plan to be implemented by a government of free India. K.T. Shah, *Report: National Planning Committee*, Bombay: Vora & Co., 1949.
36. J.L. Nehru, *The Discovery of India*, Calcutta: Signet Press, 1946, p. 396.
37. J.N. Sinha, 'Technology for National Reconstruction: The National Planning Committee, 1938-49', in R. MacLeod and D. Kumar (eds.), *Technology and the Raj*, pp. 250-64.
38. J.C. Kumarappa, *Why the Village Movement?*, Wardha: All India Village Industries Association Publications, 1936; S.N. Agarwal, *The Gandhian Plan for Economic Development for India*, Bombay: Padma Publications, 1944.
39. This was done to accommodate the views of the Indian industrialists as outlined in Purshotamadas Thakurdas, *Plan of Economic Development for India*, Bombay: Penguin Books, 1944 (popularly known as the Bombay Plan).
40. Ananda Coomaraswamy, *Art and Swadeshi*, Madras: Ganesh Press, 1910.
41. For details see, Nasir Tyabji, *Colonialism and Chemical Technology*, New Delhi: Oxford University Press, 1995.
42. *Report of the Health Survey and Development Committee,* 4 vols., Delhi: Manager of Publications, 1946; *Report of the Industrial Research Planning Committee*, New Delhi: CSIR Publication, 1945.
43. The Chetty Committee recommended a National Research Council (consisting of the representatives of science, industry and administration) to coordinate all research activities and to function as a National Trust for Patents. Ibid.
44. R. MacLeod and E.K. Andrews, 'The Origins of DSIR: Reflections on Ideas and Men, 1915-1916', *Public Administration*, Spring 1970, pp. 23-48.
45. Bidyut Chakraborty, 'Jawaharlal Nehru and Planning, 1938-41: India at Crossroads', *Modern Asian Studies*, 16, 2, 1992, pp. 275-87; I. Talbot, 'Planning for Pakistan: The Planning Committee of the All India Muslim League 1943-46', ibid., 28, 4, 1994, pp. 877-86; Vinod Vyasulu, 'Nehru and the Visvesvaraya Legacy, *Economic* and *Political Weekly*, 29 July 1989, pp. 1700-4.
46. Benjamin Zachariah, 'The Development of Professor Mahalanobis', *Economy and Society*, 26, 3, 1997, pp. 434-44.
47. An interesting debate for and against the Bombay Plan can be seen in: P.C. Malhotra and A.N. Agarwala, 'Agriculture in the Industrialists' Plan', *Indian Journal of Economics*, XXV, 99, 1945, pp. 502-10.

48. J.C. Ghosh, 'Industrial Planning for India', *Science and Culture*, XII, 1947, pp. 345-7.
49. S. Gopal (ed.), *Selected Works of Jawaharlal Nehru*, vol. IX, New Delhi: Orient Longman, 1976, pp. 377-99.
50. In a chance meeting in Beijing in 1954, Nehru confided to J.D. Bernal: 'Most of my Ministers are reactionary and scoundrels but as long as they are my Ministers I can keep some check on them. If I were to resign they would be the Government and they would unloose the forces that I have tried ever since I came to power to hold in check. I have to work with the people who are actually influential with the country. They may not be the kind of people I like but it is the best I can do.'

    To this Bernal added, 'He treated the rule of a country of hundreds of millions as if it were the management of a college in Cambridge'. *Bernal Papers*, MSS Add. 8287, Box 48, B.3.349, Cambridge University Library.
51. *Science and Culture*, IX, 1943, p. 571.
52. This was not something new. The colonial requirements had initiated the concept of state scientist. The post-colonial state strengthened it further.

CHAPTER 2

Reconciling Science with Islam in Nineteenth-Century India

S. IRFAN HABIB

> The Qur'an does not prove that the earth is stationary, nor does it prove that the earth is in motion. Similarly, it cannot be proved from the Qur'an that the sun is stationary. The Holy Qur'an was not concerned with these problems of astronomy; because the progress in human knowledge was to decide such matters itself . . . the real purpose of a religion is to improve morality . . .
>
> SYED AHMAD KHAN,[1] cited in Bary, 1958: 74

> The strangest thing of all is that our ulema these days have divided science into two parts. One they call Muslim science and one European science. Because of this they forbid others to teach some of the useful sciences. How very strange it is that the Muslims study those sciences that are ascribed to Aristotle with the greatest delight, as if Aristotle were one of the pillars of the Muslims. However, if the discussion relates to Galileo, Newton, and Kepler, they consider them infidels.
>
> SAYYID JAMALUDDIN AFGHANI[2]

The resurgence of political Islam today is marked by a call for the Islamization of sciences. Western imperialism has generated a reaction against certain sciences which are seen as un-Islamic.[3] In this context, it would be useful to go back to a ninteenth-century debate on reconciling science with Islam. Through the works of two important figures, Syed Ahmad Khan and Jamaluddin Afghani, we observe a concern with the multicultural nature of modern science and the crucial contribution of Islam in its progress.

The reconciliation of science with Islam in nineteenth-century India is enmeshed with the broader issue of locating the place of modern science within many colonial societies. It is not an easy task, and becomes all the more problematic if the introduction of science is visualized not merely as a passive process of diffusion, but as a struggle for subversion and cultural redefinition of scientific knowledge.[4] The recipient cultures, particularly those like India with centuries old civilizational history, confronted modern science armed with their own stock of knowledge. Besides, India being a multi-religious society, the process of cultural encounter was all the more colourful and complex. The two major religious streams, Hinduism and Islam, engaged with modern scientific knowledge from the vantage points of their own political and cultural contexts, not always in isolation from each other. Within Hinduism, Western-educated middle-class intelligentsia took the lead in advocating the critical assimilation of modern science, as well as in making it a morally legitimate activity.[5] A similar attempt was made within Islam by certain reformers and intellectuals. However, the two responses were qualitatively different. The former was led, as just stated, by a Western-educated modern elite, which was socialized through colonial education in 'British colonial values', but which later ended up subverting those values. Within Indian Islam, there was no equivalent of a modern elite: rather, most of the interlocutors were grounded in an Orientalist intellectual context, where exposure to Western education and culture was minimal. The relatively early exposure of Bengal to British influence could produce a Rammohun Roy, followed by a host of others who could press for reform within Hinduism and for the legitimation of modern science. Nothing similar occurred within the Muslim community, though sporadic attempts were made during the early nineteenth century.

Mirza Abu Talib Londoni was a thinker, traveller and historian who visited Europe between 1799 and 1803 and recorded his impressions in a travelogue. He pleaded for the acquisition of modern scientific knowledge and emphasized 'the significance of economic factors both in the rise and fall of states'.[6] Another example is Maulvi Karamat Ali, who was born in Jaunpur but spent most of his active life in Calcutta. His outlook on Islam and its relation with the world at large forms a radical departure from that of the majority of the *ulema* of his time. Karamat Ali welcomed the establishment of Western institutions in India and, according to Garcin de Tassy, even competed for the Sir Charles Trevelyan Prize for the best Indian essay on 'The influence of the Greeks and Arabs on the Renaissance in Europe'. For lack of an English translation, however, his essay was not accepted.[7] Hinting at the cross-cultural character of modern science, Karamat Ali held that:

> Muslims had developed Greek sciences into modern sciences and transmitted them to Europe through their centres of education in Spain. This process of cultural and intellectual diffusion, he noted, had resulted in the 19th century scientific discoveries of Europe from which the Muslims of India could justly benefit without any sense of inferiority. (Ali 1867: 15-22)

Abdur Rahim Dahri (known as *Dahri*, i.e. non-believer or sceptic, because of his unorthodox views) also emphasized the need for Muslims to take to the new learning from the West. He wrote a booklet titled *Arzdasht dar Bab-i-Zarurat Tarvis-i-Zaban-i-Angrezi-o-Ulum Firant* (An Appeal for the Study and Dissemination of the English Language and Western Learning).[8] Abdul Latif in Bengal founded the Mohammedan Literary Society in the 1860s. He delivered lectures on the accessibility of European science and technology, and denied that Islam opposed the study of such subjects. In his estimation, the glorious periods of Islamic history had been characterized by the flowering of rationalism and science, whereas Muslim decline had stemmed from ignorance of this intellectual heritage.[9] After the uprising of 1857, he felt, like Ahmad Khan, the need to bring his co-religionists more into harmony with English institutions of learning.

The overall Muslim reaction, however, was very different. While the professional middle-class Hindu perceived the shift from Mughal to English rule as one more departure in its history, the Muslim viewed it as a calamity. The British were usurpers, and anything associated with them, including modern science, was to be looked upon with apprehension. 'European science' was seen as the enemy's ruse for subverting Islamic religion and culture. A combination of hurt, pride, defiance and conservatism led the Muslims to reject modern learning.[10] What the Battle of Plassey in 1757[11] did to the Muslims of Bengal and the east, the 1857 uprising[12] did to the Muslims of the north. It was only in the latter half of the nineteenth century that realization of the need for modern learning dawned, and attempts were made to bridge the gap.

Towards the end of the nineteenth century, the Islamic response to modern science was broadly along the same lines as David Kopf describes for the early nineteenth-century Bengali *bhadralok:* revivalist, revitalist, and complete Westernization.[13] Within Indian Islam as well as in the Arab world, the reactions varied. The Wahhabi response to modern science was to reject anything Western, including Western ideas, seeing a return to early puritanical Islam as the only remedy for their stagnant society.[14] Others attempted to adapt Islam to the modern techniques as well as sciences of the West. Still others advocated complete Westernization as the only means of achieving progress.

Syed Ahmad Khan was a reformist India modernizer who founded the Aligarh Muslim University, while Jamaluddin Afghani was peripatetic pan-Islamist and anti-imperialist[15] who spent a few years in India during the 1880s. Both tried to adapt Islam to the modern techniques as well as sciences of the West, and thus they fit into the second category of responses. However, they pursued different strategies to realize this objective. Syed Ahmad inaugurated a school of revitalists, or reconstructionists as Pervez Hoodbhoy puts it in his recent work, who were convinced that some adjustment was needed to equip Islam to face the challenges of modern civilization, particularly modern science. He was ably supported in this task of reconstruction by Munshi Zakaullah[16] and Syed Amir Ali.[17] Jamaluddin Afghani, on the other hand, was a pragmatist who advocated the use of pan-Islamism as an ideological bulwark against imperialism. This commitment to anti-imperialism forced him to ignore pan-Islamism in India, and to emphasize the unity of Muslims and Hindus to strengthen the emerging nationalism. Yet he could not overlook the imperative of cultivating modern science and technology and criticized the orthodoxy within Indian Islam for being retrograde in its outlook. Within this framework, Afghani preferred to ignore theological interventions and believed that Islam as a faith was well equipped to deal with the demands of modern science. This was his position while dealing with the *umma*, the community of believers. Afghani's pragmatism took him to the other extreme when confronted with the academic and philosophical world, for example in his exchanges with the famous French Orientalist and Islamist, Ernest Renan. This will be taken up in detail at the end of the article.

The Reconstructionist Approach

What really compelled Syed Ahmad Khan to enter the dangerous and sensitive domain of reinterpreting the Quran and Shariat under the gaze of modern science and civilization? The year 1857 seems to have been decisive in this regard. Prior to 1857, Syed Ahmad, like most other Muslim scholars of the period, spent his entire intellectual energy 'in seeking to escape reality by having recourse to dreams of the golden age when Islamic civilization flourished in India'.[18] His two most important works, characteristic of this stage in his career, are the *Asar-us-Sanadid* (1847), an inventory and description of the old monuments of Delhi and its surroundings including an account of the famous people who once resided in Delhi,[19] and a recension of the *Ain-i-Akbari* (1856), Abul Fazl's administrative and statistical return of Emperor Akbar's government in the sixteenth and seventeenth centuries.[20] The tumultuous days of the 1857 uprising were catastrophic enough to bring about a decisive change in Syed Ahmad Khan's attitude towards life. He realized the potential of modern scientific knowledge and institutions, which he felt accounted for the victory of the British over the decaying medieval institutions represented by the Mughal emperor. He was quick to initiate a policy of reconciliation between the rulers and the ruled (particularly Muslims who were considered the enemies of the British), between Islam and Christianity, and finally between East and West. It is against this social and political background that we need to locate Syed Ahmad Khan's policy of reconciliation between Islam and modern science.[21]

Syed Ahmad Khan was one of the most radical modernizers of Islam during the nineteenth century, and still remains a controversial figure almost a century later. His revitalist position – in sharp contrast to the virulent anti-science and anti-modernist stance of the orthodoxy – was essentially to reinterpret the faith in order to reconcile the demands of modern civilization with the teachings and traditions of Islam. For him, early Islam until the time of the *Khalifa-i-Rashida* (the four early Caliphs) was progressive, revolutionary, liberal and rational. One must look to that early Islam to seek inspiration and guidance to emerge from the present rut. As a matter of fact, this return to early Islam is common to both the revivalists as well as the revitalists or reconstructionists. For the Wahhabis, Islam in all its ramifications was frozen in the seventh and eighth centuries, oblivious of any future social, economic, intellectual or political advancement. They were committed to removing from Islam such accretions as borrowings from Hinduism, while the reconstructionists like Syed Ahmad and Amir Ali projected an ideal Islam in which all that was conformable to the spirit of the modern age was qualified as 'genuine', and all that contradicted it was styled as 'foreign' and put aside. They used early Islam as a rhetorical ploy to convince the nineteenth-century Indian Muslim that he/she needed to think Islam afresh to reconcile the faith with modernity, particularly science. The Wahhabis were interested chiefly in the revival of orthodox religion, while Syed Ahmed strove, first of all, for a social, economic and cultural revival of his co-religionists with the motto: 'the more worldly progress we make, the more glory Islam gains'. To underline the significance of science in this progress, the reconstructionists went back to the sayings of the Prophet emphasizing the supreme value of learning and science in Islam. For instance, the Prophet said: 'the ink of the scholar is more holy than the blood of the martyr', and, 'to listen to the words of the learned and to instill unto others the lessons of science is better than religious exercises'. The Prophet repeatedly impressed on his disciples the need to seek knowledge 'even unto China'.[22]

Syed Ahmad Khan knew that the task at hand was a difficult one. It needed a radical reinterpretation of Muslim theology to extract 'pure' Islam from irrelevant and fossilized dogma: 'My inquiring mind never left me. . . . This made me arrive at the truth which we believe to be *thet* Islam [pure Islam] although conventional Muslims may hold it to be *thet* kufr [pure unbelief].' Writing on the intellectual history of the Muslims in the Indian subcontinent, Pervez Hoodbhoy points out that after the end of Akbar's reign, there was an uninterrupted period of anti-science and anti-rationalist conservatism.[23] Some 200 years before Syed Ahmad Khan, Sheikh Ahmad Sarhindi and many other influential *ulema* had issued *fatwas* against mathematics and the secular sciences, demanding that the education of Muslims be conducted exclusively along religious lines. Even Aurangzeb had protested to his teacher about the futility of the subjects taught him. In harsh tones, he expostulated:

> What did you teach me? You told me that the land of Franks is a small island where the greatest king had previously been the ruler of Portugal, then the king of Holland and now the king of England. You told me about the kings, of knowledge of geography and history you displayed! Was it not your duty to instruct me in the characteristics of the nations of the world—the products of these countries, their military power, their methods of warfare, their customs, ways of government and political policies?
>
> You never considered what academic training is requisite for a prince. All you thought necessary for me was that I become an expert in grammar and learn subjects suitable for a judge or a jurist.[24]

Indian nobles like Danishmand Khan were drawn to the study of modern science and the arts, but their individual efforts could not crystallize into a movement for the popularization of modern science and technology.[25] Had the anxiety of the Indian mind to keep abreast of Western learning in various spheres of science and art, evinced in the attitude and behaviour of Danishmand Khan, not vanished as quickly as it did, the transition from the medieval to the modern would have taken place much earlier in India.[26] Syed Ahmad rebelled against the established orthodoxy, writing:

> Now with great humbleness I ask: of the different religious books, which exists today and are used for teaching, which of them discusses Western philosophy or modern scientific matters using principles of religion? From where should I seek confirmation or rejection of the motion of the earth, or about its nearness to the sun? Thus it is a thousand times better not to read these books than to read them. Yes, if the Musalman be a true warrior and thinks his religion right then let him come fearlessly to the battleground and do unto Western knowledge and modern research what his forefathers did to Greek philosophy. Then only shall the religious books be of any use. Mere parroting will not do.[27]

For Syed Ahmad, who was primarily a religious scholar, the task of scientific exegesis was of paramount importance. In a startling break with tradition, he proposed that the Quran be reinterpreted so as to remove all apparent contradictions with physical reality. Since the Quran was the word of God, he argued, and since scientific truths were manifestly correct, any contradiction could only be apparent and not real.[28] For him, Islam as a natural religion contained no dichotomy between the 'word' and the 'work' of God.[29] He therefore suggested interpreting the Quran using the following methodology:

1. A close enquiry be made into the use, meaning and etymology of Quranic language so as to yield the true meaning of the word and passage in question.
2. The criterion employed to decide whether a given passage needed metaphorical interpretation, and which of the several interpretations ought to be selected, is the truth established by science. Such truth is arrived at by *aqli dalil* (rational proof) and demands firm belief.
3. If the apparent meaning of the Scripture conflicts with demonstrable conclusion, it must be interpreted metaphorically. In this, Sir Syed follows Ibn Rushd in his problem of reconciling *maaqul* (demonstrative truth) with *manqul* (Scripture truth). Yet he makes clear that such metaphorical and allegorical interpretation is precisely what the Author of the Scripture intended.[30]

However, Syed Ahmad Khan never attempted to interpret any religious book, including the Quran, as a book of science. This is an effective antidote against the current belief that modern scientific discoveries can all be located in the Quran, and that there is nothing outstanding in the claims of present-day scientists. Maurice Bucaille (1990), a French surgeon-turned-spiritualist, began this trend with the publication of his exegesis, *The Bible, The Qur'an, and Science*. He concludes that the Bible is often wrong in its interpretation of natural phenomena, while the Quran is invariably correct in anticipating many of the scientific discoveries of modern science. Syed Ahmad's views were almost diametrically opposed to Bucaille's fundamentalist interpretation of the Quran and science. He held all attempts to derive scientific truths from the Book as entirely misplaced.[31]

Syed Ahmad was not alone in adopting this approach. Several intellectuals in other parts of the Islamic world tried to grapple with the problem along similar lines. Ibrahim Hakki, the noted Turkish scholar of the late eighteenth century, whenever in need of clarification concerning the relationship of religion and science, always quoted the following *hadith* of the Prophet: 'you are more knowledgeable on worldly matters', and expressed the view that 'explanations of material facts' in non-religious matters should not be judged according to religious precepts.[32] For Al-Biruni, described by C.A. Nallino as 'the greatest Muslim scientist', the task of the Quran was not that of imparting secret knowledge, but of giving practical and ethical laws that had nothing to do with science.[33] This was very clearly stated in an apparently unimportant and not often quoted passage in his Chronology where, arguing with those who wanted to derive from the Quran a more or less precise definition of the concepts of 'day' and 'night', he wrote; 'Now if people say that God in this verse (Qur. II, 183) wanted to teach mankind the beginning of the day and night, which is simply absurd (*muhal*). . . . And how could we believe a thing the contrary of which is evident to our senses?'.[34] This approach to the interpretation of the holy scriptures finds resonance in the famous line by Galileo Galilei in his letter to B. Castelli (21 December 1613) discussing the interpretation to give the passage of the Bible (Joshua X, 12-13) in which Joshua arrests the course of the sun. 'I think it prudent not to bind the passages of the Holy Scriptures forcing them, as it were, to affirm as true certain theories of natural sciences, the contrary of which could eventually be proved by our senses and necessary demonstrative reasons'.[35]

Syed Ahmad has often been called an apologist in his interpretation of the Quran, particularly his work *Tafsir al Quran*. According to Baljon, one can trace a direct relation between his educational work and his apologetic efforts. As a consequence of the introduction of modern knowledge in Muslim India, he was charged with the task of evolving a new interpretation of Islam which would make it possible for Muslim youth to remain faithful to their religious convictions. Therefore, Quranic conceptions and teachings were formulated anew in terms of the rationalist-thinking Western world.[36] However, this cannot be the only angle in evaluating Syed Ahmad's apologetics. Perhaps he was not very concerned in the 1860s and 1870s about Muslim youth losing their faith under the spell of modernity. Rather, his sole mission was to redefine Islam, to reconcile it with modern science and encourage Muslim youth to cultivate it. For him, the acquisition of modern knowledge was primary, although he never lost sight of faith.

Inspirations

We need to digress a little here to understand some key influences in the formulation of Syed Ahmad's views on religion and the need to reconcile it with science. His trip to England in the 1860s certainly inspired him in many different ways, even though he was unable to read or write English. After his return from Europe, Syed Ahmad graduated to the Newtonian view of nature. It helped him adopt a rational approach towards fundamental Islamic convictions including the role of the Prophet, revelation and the 'proofs' of prophecy – the miracles.[37] This intellectual transformation earned him the sobriquet of *Niechari,* the naturist. Though there are not many references in his works to European writers of the period, the progressive and industrialized West was a permanent reference point in all his formulations. If we go by his own acknowledgement, Mutazilism and Shah Waliullah seem to have been his two main inspirations.

Mutazila (dissenters) was a radical school of rationalist philosophers of the eighth and ninth centuries. It was declared a State doctrine by the Abbasid Caliphs al-Mamun and al-Mutassim and, more than ten centuries after its birth, Mutazilism played a key role in shaping the ideas of Muslim reformers of the European colonial era. It even inspired Hindu social reformers and modernizers like Rammohun Roy, whose *Tuhfat-ul-Muvahidin* is replete with Mutazila influences. Reacting against the Jabria orthodoxy of that period, the Mutazila sought a reconciliation of faith with reason.[38] This synthesis of Muslim theology with Greek logic gave birth to a theological science known as *ilm-ul-Kalam*, which was to form the basis of Muslim scholasticism and dominate Islamic thinking for centuries to come.[39] Syed Ahmad found Muslim religious thought confronted with the same complex situation which the Musalmans of the early Middle Ages had faced in their encounter with Greek philosophy:

> Today we are in need of a modern *ilm-i-kalam*, by which we should refute the doctrines of modern science and undermine their foundation, or show that they are in conformity with the articles of Islamic faith. When I am endeavouring to introduce these sciences among the Muslims then it is my duty to defend the religion of Islam and to reveal its original bright face.[40]

This famous quote has invited the ire of many scholars. Syed Ahmed has been accused of prioritizing science over Islam. Ismail

R. Al Faruqi even said in one of his papers that Syed Ahmed belonged to the school that:

> . . . has little notion of what Islam is about, aside from the observance of ritual and some customs, and the overt expression of one's Muslimness through self-declaration . . . it's so-called harmony with science and the principles of nature, therefore, cannot but be superficial, for it is not a harmony with the inner principles and values of Islam, but merely with formal adherence to Islam.[41]

If one is oblivious of the historical context and the exigencies of politics, this criticism may seem convincing. Even outside the Indian subcontinent, the Muslim world was encountering the challenge posed by the triumph of Western power which was equally the triumph of science at the turn of the century. Syed Ahmad was trying to do what his contemporaries were doing in Turkey, Egypt and other countries. The differences in their approaches were governed by their respective political and social contexts.

Apart from Mutazila – which had always been an irritant to the orthodox – Syed Ahmad was deeply influenced by an Indian mystic and scholar, Shah Waliullah (1703-61).[42] Epitomizing the 'modern full-dressed rationalistic revolt against the stupor of orthodoxy and the immobility of legal thought in Islam, Shah Waliullah can be easily recognized as the pioneer and chief source of inspiration'.[43] For Iqbal, he was the first Muslim, 'who felt the urge of a new spirit in him'.[44] What Syed Ahmad found most attractive in Waliullah's programme was his call for a fresh interpretation of religion according to the needs of time and place in order to justify it as a universal creed. Shah Waliullah opened the door of *ijtihad*[45] which had been closed and sealed off many centuries earlier.[46] Syed Ahmad also did exactly that. His commitment to *ijtihad* is reflected in a letter written to his friend and close associate Nawab Mohsin-ul-Mulk:

> Listen, dear brother! This is not the time that I should conceal my conscience from you. I tell you frankly that if people will not give up blind adherence (*taqlid*) and will not search out that particular light which can be had from Qur'an and the reliable tradition of the Prophet and will not compare [reconcile] religion with modern sciences the religion of Islam will disappear from India. This anxiety for the well-being of Islam has forced me to carry on all these researches and I do not care for the traditional rut. Otherwise you know well that in my view, to remain a Muslim and to be

entitled for Paradise it is enough to follow Maulvi Habbu, not to speak of the great jurists of Islam.[47]

Syed Ahmad opposed the acceptance of religion as a traditional reality. Religion should have value in terms of current human experience and should help human society in its onward march.[48]

Underlying Multiculturalism

In the nineteenth century, when the distinction between imperialism and progress was almost blurred for modernists like Syed Ahmad, any reference to the contribution of non-European civilizations to the advancement of knowledge should be viewed as admirable. Syed Ahmad raised questions at a very rudimentary level, trying to convey the idea that modern civilization, represented by the Euro-American world, was the outcome of joint human effort, cutting across cultural or religious boundaries. It may be anachronistic to locate the current understanding of multiculturalism or Needhamian ecumenism in his writings, yet he did have a vision of knowledge as premised on the cross-cultural exchange of ideas through the ages.

The Europe that Syed Ahmad visited in the 1860s was the Europe of the Industrial Revolution, of Victorian England and the Second Empire in France, and age of optimism and belief in progress. His trip came soon after the publication of Darwin's *Descent of Man*, and he was impressed by the view that isolated forms of life are relatively backward and that intercourse between species makes for progress. He adopted this idea and applied it to cultural development, stating that the march of civilization was essentially the result of intercultural contact.[49] This became the cornerstone of his theory of progress, and made it logically possible for him to persuade people to adopt such Western traits as would further their own national development. All his efforts to convince people of the legitimacy of modern science were based on cross-culture perspective. For instance, he said:

> The blind prejudice of Muslims is preventing them from emulating [Western] education, sciences and technology; Muslim society erroneously admires the blindness of those who are stubborn and haughty and considers all nations except their own inferior.[50] There is not a single nation in the world which acquired excellence, material progress, and spiritual happiness entirely by virtue of its own efforts.[51]

Zakaullah, his enthusiastic supporter, adopted a similar framework. He too lamented the fact that most Hindus and Muslims in India viewed the achievements of science and their contribution to development as nothing but a hoax: 'How could you call it knowledge? Most of it is based on the professional skills of blacksmiths, carpenters and cobblers, and whatever little knowledge it could boast has been borrowed from us.'[52] Zakaullah further stated:

> [I]t is ignorance to dub the ancient sciences or the Eastern sciences irrelevant. And the ignorance is compounded if we do not give preference to the modern or Western sciences over the ancient or Eastern sciences . . . once we are able to restore this balance in our approach, we will be able to see the splendors of nature and the miracles of human ingenuity.[53]

For him, knowledge or science was the outcome of cumulative human effort over the centuries, and each century added a new chapter to the progress of science. The nineteenth century, in particular, had been an auspicious century in the history of science, as it had brought about revolutionary changes in knowledge never even conceived of by earlier generations.[54]

Despite Syed Ahmad's overenthusiastic interpretations and arguments, which often clashed with the rising nationalism and the emerging identity consciousness of late nineteenth-century India, he certainly has a message for present-day proponents of Islamic science or Hindu science, viz., that fanaticism and *taassub*, i.e. prejudice, can never lead to the promotion of knowledge. He believed that:

> Nations always benefit from each other; only bigots deny themselves the fruits of their fellowmen's labour. They are like wild animals, happy in [the narrow life of] their own flock, and are deaf to the sweet melody of the nightingale and the chirping of little sparrows, and know not how the garden [i.e., the world] was laid out and what makes the flowers bloom. Prejudice and progress will never mix.[55]

Syed Ahmad was voicing a nineteenth-century faith in and fascination for science and its achievements. Such uncritical acceptance of science's magic is impossible to conceive of today, after Kuhn and Feyerabend. Yet, despite all these criticisms, Syed Ahmad's cross-cultural perspective is still valid and, following the fall of Eurocentrism, is on the ascendant in the form of a well articulated and theorized multiculturalism. Under the pretext of challenging Eurocentrism, some proponents of Islamic science have put forward an Islam-centric alternative, at least for believers, if not for all. The most articulate among these is Syed Hossein Nasr, who has attempted the re-sacralization of science through his gnosis-oriented approach. Hossein Nasr's own view is seen as anti-democratic, since it involves a denial of the equality of forms of human experiences, while privileging the particular Islamic one he supports.[56] Syed Ahmad at least did not believe in the exclusivism of present-day interpreters who envisage an uncontaminated, pure, Islamic science with a distinct epistemology. On the contrary, he proudly referred to that stage of Islamic intellectual efflorescence when the Greek arts, philosophy and sciences were introduced to Muslims.[57] After this early synthesis, an Asharite reaction threw the baby out with the bath water and banned Greek learning, calling it *ulum-ul-awail* (foreign sciences).[58] A similar sanitization and purification is now sought by some in the name of Islamic science (Jameelah, 1977; Nasr, 1968, 1978; Sardar, 1989).[59] Unfortunately, such attempts tend to be merged with current critiques of modern science that emphasize the destructive nature of some of its products and claim that its application has led to the dehumanization and robotization of society. All these are valid criticisms, but they do not necessarily derive from insights emanating from a particular faith.[60]

Syed Ahmad's liberal approach to Islam transcended religious parochialism and involved a larger concept of religious pluralism. This is particularly interesting when viewed against current fundamentalist formulations, not just in science but generally. Referring to Muslims, he asserted: 'God sent his prophets for their moral improvement. It is absurd to believe that the prophets appeared only in Arabia and Palestine to reform a handful of Arabs and Jews, and that God condemned the peoples of Africa, America and Asia to ignorance.'[61] He went further and said that whoever followed God's prophets achieved salvation and it was immaterial whether the prophet was from China, America, Mongolia, Africa, India or Iran, or if he preached God's message to savages or civilized men.[62] In this way, Syed Ahmad tried to broaden the world-view of the nineteenth-century Indian Muslim, and in the process conveyed an important message in eclecticism to the future. His reconciliation of science with Islam should be viewed against this cultural, civilizational and religious pluralism.

The Pragmatist Approach

The pragmatists were not really concerned with Quranic reinterpretations like the reconstructionists. They found this a somewhat redundant and arcane exercise. Preferring to treat requirements of religion and faith as essentially unrelated to the direct concerns of political and economic life, or to science and secular knowledge, the pragmatist is satisfied with the vague belief that Islam and modernity are not in conflict.[63] Yet there is an essential agreement with the reconstructionist on opposition to fundamentalist thinking.

Syed Jamaluddin Afghani is the most fascinating example of the early pro-modernity and pro-science pragmatist. His ideas deeply influenced the Muslim world, particularly his view of Islam as a unifying force against Western imperialism. A pioneer of Islamic resurgence, he has been referred to as the *Sage of the East*.[64] Afghani, with his Persian upbringing, was deeply under the spell of Ibn-Sina's rationalist thinking, and remained a constant source of worry and discomfort for the orthodox. He was expelled at their behest from Istanbul for pressing for the establishment of a *Darul-Funun*, a new university to impart instruction exclusively in modern science.[65] We will not deal here in detail with his political life, though it was enmeshed with his work as a modernizer. It is particularly interesting to explore Afghani's views on science and modernity because, in contrast to reconstructionists such as Syed Ahmad Khan, Afghani did not make a serious attempt to reinterpret Muslim theology. His central concern was the mobilization of people against Western colonialism, and Islam seemed the most potent rallying force for this purpose. His advocacy of modernity was also marked by caution. He never emphasized the Western origins of the elements he borrowed, for fear that it might encourage a trend of admiration for the West and feelings of Islamic inferiority and helplessness.[66]

We shall refer mostly to the three years that he spent in India (1880-2). As a matter of fact, 'he acquired in India his first knowledge of the sciences and mathematics of Europe'.[67] He spent these years delivering lectures and writing a few insightful articles. The most controversial of these was *Al-Radd ala al-Dahriyyin,* the 'Refutation of Materialists' or, in its original Persian title, 'The Truth About the Neicheri Sect and an Explanation of the

Neicheries'. The Refutation can, however, be understood properly only in the context of his other writings. Six of these were written for the first issues of a Hyderabad journal, *Mu'allim-i-Shafiq*, while five more lectures were published along with these original six in the first edition of the collected articles of Afghani titled *Maqalat-i-Jamaliyyeh* from Calcutta in 1884.[68] According to Keddie, the three striking features of Jamaluddin Afghani's writings in India, which make them distinct from his writings elsewhere in the Islamic world, are: (a) advocacy of nationalism of linguistic or territorial variety, meaning unity of Indian Hindus and Muslims, with little said about the unity of Indian Muslims with Muslims abroad. Pan-Islamism is shelved and local nationalistic ideas emphasized instead, which might seem at variance with pan-Islam; (b) stress on the benefits of philosophy and modern science; (c) attack on Syed Ahmad Khan as a lackey of the imperialist government. All these three features appear, in one way or another, in Afghani's attempts at reconciling science with Islam in India. When he talks of nationalism of a linguistic variety, he emphasizes the cultivation and teaching of modern science in the local language of the people. He goes to the extent of preferring linguistic ties as being more durable than religious ties. In his own words:

> A single people with one language in the course of a thousand years changes its religion two or three times without its nationality, which consists of unity of language, being destroyed. One may say that the ties and the unity that arises from the unity of language have more influence than religious ties in most affairs of the world. (*Maqalat-i-Jamaliyyeh*, 75-87)[69]

Ironically, even his *bete noire* in India, Syed Ahmad Khan, began as an enthusiastic campaigner for Urdu as a medium of instruction for science. He turned into an Anglophile after his trip to England, and also due to an unfortunate Hindi-Urdu controversy in the 1880s.

For someone better known for his pan-Islamism, Jamaluddin Afghani's emphasis on a non-religious nationalism is an apt reflection of his pragmatic approach. His address at Calcutta in 1882 was directed primarily at a Muslim audience, yet it had affinities with extreme Hindu nationalist sentiments. This cultural nationalism was not based on a sifting of symbols and ideas on religious lines.[70] He said:

> Certainly I must be happy to see such offspring of India, since they are the offshoots of that India that was the cradle of humanity. Human values spread out from India to the whole world. These youth are from the very land where the meridian circle was first determined. They are from the same realm that first understood the zodiac. . . . Thus we can say that the Indians were the inventors of arithmetic and geometry . . . the Code Romain, the mother of all western codes, was taken from the four Vedas and the Shastras. Greeks were the pupils of the Indians in literary ideas, limpid poetry, and lofty thoughts.
>
> [The Indians] reached the highest level in philosophic thought. The soil of India is the same soil; the air of India is the same air; and these youths who are present here are fruits of the same earth and climate. (*On Teaching and Learning* 101-2)[71]

Afghani exhorted Indian Muslims to take pride in the Hindu past. He did the same in Egypt, where he appealed to the Egyptian Muslims to seek inspiration from pre-Islamic Egyptian greatness. Jamaluddin Afghani glorified Vedic civilization in a conscious attempt to forge Hindu-Muslim unity through the message of composite nationalism. However, some scholars have placed him in the classical Islamic scholarly tradition of Al-Biruni and Al-Jahiz, and deem it anachronistic to find any allusions to nationalism in his work.[72] His reconciliation of science with Islam was premised on the belief that science was not something alien to non-European cultures, or an exclusive domain of the white man. His underlying nationalist agenda constantly sought indigenous sources of intellectual and cultural inspiration. Afghani was not very different from Syed Ahmad Khan in stressing the benefits of philosophy and science. In his Calcutta lecture titled 'On Teaching and Learning', he emphasized the importance of modern science and philosophy. He was passionate in his desire to convince nineteenth-century conservatives to embrace modern science and philosophy. Although he desired intensely to modernize, he strongly emphasized the need to avoid identification with the West. Syed Ahmad, on the contrary, had resolved this contradiction. He had no hesitation in openly conceding the superiority of modern Western civilization and the need to borrow and learn from its advancements in knowledge. Despite his opposition to the West, Afghani went on to say that all great empires had been supported by science, up to and including the European conquerors of his time. Ignorance is always subjugated by science, which is the basis of advanced technology in all fields.[73]

According to him, it was not the French or the English who had colonized the non-European world, but rather the greatness and power of science. In his lecture at Calcutta, Afghani discussed the medieval philosophers' concept of philosophy as the organizing soul of the sciences: 'the science that has the position of a comprehensive soul and the rank of a preserving force is the science of *falsafa* or philosophy, because its subject is universal. . . . It applies each of the science in its proper place.'[74] He was critical of the Indian *ulema* who, he said, were still busy reading and teaching *sadra* and *shams-i Bazegha*, a seventeenth-century Indian text by Mulla Mahmud Jaunpuri. They 'vaingloriously call themselves sages, and despite this they cannot distinguish their left hand from their right hand, and they do not ask: Who are we and what is right and proper for us? They never ask the causes of electricity, the steam boat and railroads.'[75]

In today's context, his most serious criticism of the *ulema* is quoted at the beginning of this article. Afghani was surprised that the *ulema* had divided science into Muslim science and European science, and thus forbidden the teaching of some of the useful sciences. He said that all 'those who forbid science and knowledge in the belief that they are safeguarding the Islamic religion are really the enemies of that religion'. The terms 'rational' and 'revealed' sciences were also used by the *ulema*, emphasizing a methodological distinction between the so-called Muslim and non-Muslim sciences. While the *awail* sciences, or the present-day European sciences, were products of the human mind, the Islamic sciences were based on revealed truth, i.e. they had sprung from Muslim religion or were closely connected with it. Conservative clerics also made a distinction between 'native' and 'foreign' learning[76] and between the 'praiseworthy sciences' (Islamic) and 'blameworthy sciences' (*awail*).[77]

Afghani, however, was convinced that Islam was the closest of all religions to science and knowledge, and that there was no incompatibility between them. Hence, he did not feel the need, like Syed Ahmad, to reinterpret Islam to make it compatible with the requirements of modern science. For him, the culprits were the leaders of Islam, the *maulvis*, who needed to radically change their attitude towards not only science but the world in general, which had made rapid strides in the past few hundred years. The minds of the Muslim logicians in India, according to Afghani, were filled with superstition and vanity, and there existed no difference between their ideas and those of the masses of the bazaar. He described the *ulema* as a very narrow wick topped by a very small flame that neither lights its surroundings nor gives light to others (*on teaching and learning*).[78]

Despite his anti-imperialist stance, Afghani warned the Indian *ulema* against the rejection of foreign sciences and innovation, saying that while:

> The desire to protect fatherland and nationality (*watan wa jins*) and the wish to defend religion and co-religionists, that is patriotic zeal, national zeal and religious zeal are essential and lot can be accomplished through them, but the Muslims in India have applied the desire to defend religion, or religious zeal in a very bad way. For they have carried zeal, through misuse, to a point where it has become a cause of hatred for knowledge and the sciences, and a reason for aversion toward industries and innovation. They believe they must out of religious zeal, hate and abominate what was connected with the opponent's faith, even though these things were sciences and arts. (*Maqalat-i-Jammaliyyeh*)[79]

According to Afghani, for the Indian *ulema*, anything not mentioned in Ibn Sina's *Shifa* or in the illuminist philosophy of Shihab ad-Din Suhrawardy was to be ignored and condemned. This led them to abandon the investigation of innovations like the phonograph,[80] the camera, the telescope and the microscope. Given Afghani's evolutionist perception of Islam, which will be taken up in some detail in the following section, the Indian *ulema's* understanding appeared to him not only un-Islamic but ahistorical as well.

Afghani's Encounter with Ernest Renan

Jamaluddin Afghani's pragmatism is best reflected in his exchanges with the French Islamist and Orientalist Ernest Renan in Paris. Afghani was one of those few Asiatics who travelled to Europe and had first-hand experience of the European perception of other people and religions, particularly Islam.[81] He was in Paris in 1883, just a few days before Renan delivered his lecture, 'Islam and Science' at the Sorbonne, published subsequently in the *Journal des Debats* in its 29 March 1883 issue. The same journal carried Afghani's 'Answer to Renan' on 18 May 1883.

Renan's lecture was an articulation of the ninteenth-century racist and Orientalist construction of Islam and the Arab world. It can be better understood by looking at his other speeches, e.g.:

> The Semitic race appears to us to be an incomplete race, by virtue of its simplicity. This race – if I dare to use the analogy – is to the Indo-European family what a pencil sketch is to a painting; it lacks that variety, that amplitude, that abundance of life which is the condition of perfectibility . . . the Semitic nations . . . have never been able to achieve true maturity.[82]

Thus, for him, Islam as a Semitic religion and the Arabs as a Semitic race were too simple and trivial to make any meaningful contribution to the growth of science and philosophy. He was convinced that the Semitic-Oriental sensibility never reached the heights attained by the Indo-Germanic races. What is generally called Arab science and philosophy is really Greek and Persian. Renan's argument buttressed the Orientalist theory of origins, viz., that the Indo-European race is the source of science and philosophy. His first meeting with Afghani produced on him a 'vivid impression'. He wrote:

> Sheikh Jemmal-Eddin is an Afghan [read: not an Arab] entirely divorced from the prejudices of Islam; he belongs to those energetic races of Iran, near India, where the Aryan spirit lives so energetically under the superficial layer of official Islam. . . . Sheikh Jemmal-Eddin is the best case of ethnic protest against religious conquest that one could cite.[83]

It is ironic that Renan saw Afghani as an ideal example of ethnic protest against the Islamic manacle, while he was a venerated pan-Islamist of the Muslim world. Renan further felt 'while I was talking with him, that I had before me, restored to life, one of my old acquaintances – Avicenna, Averroes, or another of those great infidels who represented for five centuries the tradition of the human mind'.[84] Renan's second point was that Islam was essentially hostile to science. This hostility was dominant during Arab rule and continued under the Turks, and was only temporarily and precariously overcome during the short period when the Greek and Persian influences were strong. Here again Renan harks back to his argument of Indo-European racial superiority and its contribution to the Islamic intellectual tradition, howsoever trivial that tradition was. Renan's hostility towards Islam should not be confused with his general atheism. He made it explicit that Islam, because it unites the spiritual and temporal realms and makes dogma rule in both, is 'the heaviest chain that humanity has ever borne'.[85] In a later article, Renan expressed another strong view:

> The human mind must be freed of all supernatural belief if it wishes to work on its essential work, which is the construction of positive science. This does not imply violent destruction or brusque rupture. The Christian does not have to abandon Christianity nor the Muslim Islam. The enlightened parties of Christianity and Islam should arrive at that state of benevolent indifference where religious beliefs become inoffensive. This has happened in about half the Christian countries, let us hope that it will happen in Islam.[86]

Did Afghani find all this criticism outrageous? Given his reputation as a pan-Islamist and a defender of Islam against the inroads made by Western imperialism he should have condemned outright Renan's rancour against Islam. On the contrary, Afghani agreed with most of Renan's criticism. However, he disagreed with Renan on two counts – first, the racist conclusion that Arabs by nature and temperament were inimical to science and philosophy and, second, that Islam as a whole was essentially hostile to science. Countering Renan's first point, Afghani began by saying that it was an undeniable fact that:

> . . . the Arab people, while it was still in the state of barbarism, rushed into the road of intellectual and scientific progress with a rapidity only equaled by the speed of its conquests, since in the space of a century, it acquired and assimilated almost all the Greek and Persian science . . . just as it extended its domination from the Arabian peninsula up to the mountains of the Himalaya and the summit of the Pyrenees.[87]

Afghani continued by saying that the Greeks and Romans had built great monuments to science and advanced the frontiers of civilization for many centuries, but that all that had collapsed and their most precious books been relegated to oblivion. The Arabs, ignorant and barbaric as they were originally, took up what had been abandoned by the civilized nations, rekindled the extinguished sciences, developed them and given them a brilliance they had never previously had. It is a historical fact that the age of Arabian learning lasted about five hundred years, and coincided with the darkest period of European history.[88]

Till recently, the Arabs had been credited with merely transmitting the Greek legacy to Europe, without introducing any significant epistemological advancement in what they had received from the Greeks. This period has commonly been spoken of as one of 'preservation' and 'safe keeping'. Islamic culture – itself a vast territory of peoples and cultures – is said to have 'rescued' the heritage of Greek science and held it intact, perhaps even making a few additions to it here and there, until the West was finally prepared to 'recover' it in full, as its rightful heir.[89] This nineteenth-century Orientalist and racist inheritance continued in the history of science till Joseph Needham (1954-), Roshdi Rashed (1984, 1986),[90] A.I. Sabra and many others intervened with their extensive researches in China and the Islamic world.

One could understand the use of racist categories in the legitimation of imperialism, but the post-colonial situation requires a cross-cultural and cross-civilizational perspective to comprehend the true character of modern science. Even in the 1880s, however, Afghani saw through the Orientalist programme when he countered Renan by saying that the Arabs, who usurped these sciences by right of conquest, 'developed, extended, clarified, perfected, completed and coordinated with a perfect taste and a rare precision and exactitude'.[91] He argued further that Byzantium and Rome were closer to the French, Germans and the English than they were to the Arabs, whose capital was Baghdad, yet all the scientific treasure remained buried underneath till the Arab civilization lit up with its reflections the summits of the Pyrenees:

> The Europeans welcomed Aristotle, who had emigrated and become Arab; but they did not think of him at all when he was Greek and their neighbor. Is there not in this another proof, no less evident, of the intellectual superiority of the Arabs and of their natural attachment to philosophy?[92]

While he rejected the racism of Renan's argument in the first case, Afghani had no major disagreement on the second point. He conceded that Islam did stifle the growth of science, but preferred to take an evolutionist view, saying that the modern Western intellectual climate was superior because Christianity had had an evolutionary head start on Islam:

> All religions are intolerant, each one in its way. The Christian religion, I mean the society that follows its inspirations and its teachings, and is formed in its image, had emerged from the first period to which I have just alluded; thenceforth free and independent, it seems to advance rapidly on the road of progress and science, whereas Muslim society had not yet freed itself from the tutelage of religion. . . .

In truth, the Muslim society has tried to stifle science and stop its progress.[93]

Afghani pointed out that Christianity had also stifled science in the past, and the Catholic church continued to do so, yet he was in full agreement with Renan that a believing Muslim was a slave to dogma and expressed himself much more strongly:

A true believer must, in fact, turn from the path of studies that have for their object scientific truth. . . . Yoked, like an ox to the plow, to the dogma whose slave he is, he must walk eternally in the furrow that has been traced for him in advance by the interpreters of the law. Convinced, besides, that his religion contains in itself all morality and all sciences, he attaches himself resolutely to it and makes no effort to go beyond. . . . What would be the benefit of seeking truth when he believed he possessed it all? . . . wherefore he despises science.[94]

Though Afghani rejected the racist side of Renan's argument and brought in an evolutionary thesis, he found it permissible to ask himself why the Arab civilization, after having thrown such light on the world, suddenly extinguished; why this torch had not been relit since, and why the Arab world still remained buried in profound darkness.[95] Close to a hundred years later, Lynn White Jr. expressed a similar view in his *Dynamo and Virgin Reconsidered*:

The Arabic-speaking civilisation knew what science was and was proficient in it. For four hundred years science was one of its major concerns. But a crystallisation of other values occurred in the late eleventh century which shifted the whole focus of Islamic culture. Science was abandoned, and abandoned deliberately.[96]

Aydin Sayili points out that Islam was remarkable for its achievements in the organization and systematization of education. The abundance of public libraries and schools, even of the *madrasas*, i.e. schools of higher education, bears witness to this attitude. However, apart from certain exceptional cases which occurred especially in the thirteenth and later centuries, the *madrasas*, as well as other institutions of instruction in Islam, were devoted almost solely to the cultivation and dissemination of the Islamic science. The *awail* sciences and philosophy were left out of the *madrasa* curriculum.[97] However, after highlighting the regenerative role of Islam in the cultivation of science and its subsequent abandonment and repression under the later Islamic regimes, Afghani concluded his response to Renan with a general statement, saying:

> Religions, by whatever names they are called, all resemble each other. No agreement and no reconciliation are possible between these religions and philosophy [read also sciences as Afghani uses the terms science and philosophy interchangeably]. Religion imposes on man its faith and its belief, whereas philosophy frees him totally or in part.[98]

Conclusion

We can see in these short accounts of Syed Ahmad Khan and Jamaluddin Afghani a deep divergence on political issues as well as a startling convergence on several points related to their perceptions of modern science. Both the divergence as well as convergence can be located in their respective political and social contexts. Syed Ahmad Khan was rooted in Indian politics and history and thus confronted the issue of science and Islam as an Indian citizen, bound by the constraints and demands of the country's politics and history. Afghani was a nomad in politics, with an equal eye on the politics of India, Egypt and Turkey, and wherever a substantial Muslim population was oppressed by British imperialism.

Syed Ahmad Khan avoided confrontationist politics in his dealings with the colonial government, believing that the Muslims in India could be redeemed only through cooperation with the British. For him, 1857 was:

> . . . the end of the medieval phase of Indian Muslim revivalism . . . the 'archaic' resistance had failed. . . . Sayyid Ahmad turned to 'futuristic' adjustment, to alignment with the dynamics of modernism and to rehabilitation within the opportunities provided by the unchallengeable foreign rule. This implied rejection of revivalism.[99]

Thus, his reconciliation of science with Islam was within a collaborative and reformative framework, and the consistency with which he pursued this policy 'widened the gulf between him and the neo-revivalist political consciousness of Indian Islam inspired by the political convulsions of the contemporary world of Islam'.[100] Afghani, on the other hand, represented these 'political convulsions', and his efforts at reconciling science with Islam were grounded in this framework. Being an anti-imperialist and pan-Islamist, the British to him were like 'a dragon which had swallowed twenty million people, and drunk up the waters of the Ganges and the Indus, but was still unsatiated and ready to devour the rest of the world and to consume the waters of the Nile and the Oxus'.[101] Afghani's political message caught the imagination of the majority of the Indian Muslim community, particularly the orthodox religious leadership of Dar-ul-Uloom and Nadwatul Uloom. His bitter denunciation of Syed Ahmad Khan's reformist modernism and reinterpretation of the Quran further strengthened these forces. Afghani expected 'the *Ulema* to arrive at a consensus of *ijtihad*, needed for adjustment with a world in which initiative of progress was in the hands of non-Muslims'.[102] He had great expectations of the *ulema*, and wanted them to come forward and meet the challenge of modern science. Syed Ahmad Khan, despairing of the capacity of the *ulema*, at least in India, to rise to the occasion, took the burden of *ijtihad* on himself. This was considered an encroachment by the religious leadership and made his reformist programme not only controversial but unacceptable to a large number of people.

There is one more point of convergence between Afghani and Syed Ahmad: both believed Islam to be capable of an evolutionary process in accord with the present and the future history of mankind. The difference between them, as always, is that 'the Indo-Muslim "modernist" was always concerned with the particular, the concrete, the detailed; while his adversary was concerned with the general, the generalised and the emotionally surcharged abstract'.[103]

Unfortunately, political Islam remained dominant in the nineteenth century and everything else was subservient to its political context. The future of science and civilization in Islam depends critically on whether the silent majority reasserts itself and snatches back control of civil society, or whether it buckles under the ferocious onslaught of nascent revivalism.[104] For the moment, all seems to be lost in the race to displace Eurocentrism in science with Islam-centrism,[105] which is as arbitrary and undemocratic as the former.

NOTES

1. Cited in W.T. Bary, *Sources of Indian Tradition*, New York: Columbia University Press, 1958, p. 743.
2 Cited in Nikki R. Keddie, *An Islamic Response to Imperialism*, Berkeley: University of California Press, 1968, p. 107.
3. Z. Sardar (ed.), *The Touch of Midas: Science Values and Environment in Islam and the West*, Aligarh: The Other India Press and Goa: Centre for Studies on Science, 1997.

4. Dhruv Raina and S. Irfan Habib, 'The Moral Legitimation of Modern Science: Bhadralok Reflections on Theories of Evolution', *Social Studies of Science*, 26, 1996, pp. 9-42.
5. Ibid.
6. B.M. Sankhdher, 'Mirza Abu Talib Khan', *The Quarterly Review of Historical Studies* 10, 4 (Calcutta), 1970-1, pp. 213-16.
7. Garcin, De Tassy, *Histoire de la Literature Hindui et Hindustaine* (2 vols), Paris: l'Ecole Imperiale et speciale des Langues orientales vivantes, 1870, p. 162.
8. Mujeeb Ashraf, *Muslim Attitudes Towards British Rule and Western Culture in India*, Delhi: Idarah-i-Adabiyat, 1982.
9. Muhammad Aslam Syed, *Muslim Response to the West: Muslim Historiography in India 1857-1914*, Islamabad: National Institute of Historical and Cultural Research, 1988, p. 38.
10. Pervez Hoodbhoy, *Islam and Science*, London: Zed Books, 1991, pp. 125-6.
11. The year in which Lord Clive defeated the Nawabs of Bengal and established British suzerainty over the whole of East India. The Muslims, in particular the aristocracy and the professionals associated with the courts of the Nawabs, took it as a personal and professional loss.
12. In 1857, a large number of Indian soldiers in the British army revolted against the Company and reinstated Mughal emperor Bahadur Shah as their ruler. This came as a shock to the British for several reasons, particularly because it reflected the combined strength of the Hindus and Muslims. While the Hindus did not take long to recover from the trauma of defeat at the hands of the *firangi,* the Muslims were much slower in recovering owing to the different treatment meted out to them by the British in accordance with their divide-and-rule politics.
13. David Kopf, 'The Brahmo Samaj Intelligentsia and Bengal Renaissance: A Study of Revitalization and Modernization in Nineteenth-Century Bengal', in R.I. Crane (ed.), *Transition in South Asia*, Durham: Duke University Press, 1970, pp. 1-48.
14. This was the conservative response of those Indian Muslims who, bereft of power and glory, sought refuge in religion. They believed that their present ruin was the result of their moving away from 'true faith', and that the revival of Islam as it flourished during the Prophet's time would restore to them their intellectual as well as political glory. For more details see A.F. Salahuddin Ahmad, *Social Ideas and Social Change in Bengal, 1818-1835*, Calcutta: Ridhi, 1976, pp. 20-1.
15. Some scholars put both Syed Ahmad and Afghani in the broad category of revivalists. This may seem appropriate to those who see any attempt to go back to tradition or indigenous sources of inspiration as an exercise in revivalism. Such a categorization is, however, flawed

on more than one count. Syed Ahmad looked for ways to synthesize modernity with tradition, and came under constant attack from the revivalists for betraying the cause of Islam and for being apologetic in his formulations. Afghani's is much too problematic and complex a profile to fit into any one category. A pan-Islamist, he was a heretic in Turkey, and an anti-imperialist in India where he attacked the views of Syed Ahmad Khan. He was a radical modernizer when confronted with the apathy of the entrenched orthodoxy and its opposition to modern science and technology, but appeared in different avatar in Paris during his exchanges with Ernest Renan.

16. Munshi Zakaullah was a product of Delhi College and the favourite student of Ramachandra, a well-known mathematician and teacher of science. Zakaullah himself was a mathematician and a scholar of Persian and Urdu who spent much of his life advocating the cause of modern science through the local language. He was deeply influenced by Syed Ahmad Khan's personality and programme, and was a front-line leader of the Aligarh movement.
17. Syed Amir Ali was one of those very few Muslim intellectuals of the late nineteenth and early twentieth centuries who had a grounding in modern education. A barrister trained in English, Amir Ali was an enthusiastic supporter of Syed Ahmad Khan's programmes. He wrote extensively to prove that true Islam is revolutionary, rational and progress-oriented. His *magnum opus The Spirit of Islam*, first published in 1891, was read avidly throughout the Muslim world.
18. J.M.S. Baljon Jr., *Sir Syed Ahmad Khan*, Lahore: Ashraf Press, 1964, p. 7.
19. The Indologist Garcin De Tassy translated this archaeological work into French. This attracted the attention of European scholars to his work, and Syed Ahmed was elected Honorary Fellow of the Royal Asiatic Society of London.
20. Syed Ahmad approached several people, including the famous Urdu poet Mirza Ghalib, to contribute to the introduction to his edited version of *Ain-i-Akbari*. Ghalib saw his work as futile wallowing in the past, and wrote thus to Syed Ahmad:

    'Look at the Sahibs of England. . . . They have gone far ahead of our oriental forbears. Wind and wave they have rendered useless. They are sailing their ships under fire and steam. They are creating music without the help of mizrab [plucker]. With their magic, words fly through the air like birds. . . . Cities are being lighted without oil lamps. This new law makes all other laws obsolete. Why must you pick up straws out of old, time-swept barns while a treasure-trove of pearls lies at your feet?' Q. Hyder and Sardar Jafri, *Ghalib and His Poetry*, Bombay: Popular Prakashan, 1970, p. 28.

21. Syed Ahmad's efforts were broadly similar to those of Rammohun Roy in the 1810s and 1820s. However, any attempt at reconciliation in the latter half of the nineteenth century was fated to clash with rising nationalist aspirations.
22. This famous saying of the Prophet has often been used in the past to encourage the community of believers to realize the significance of learning across religious boundaries. However, Syed Hossein Nasr, the famous Iranian scholar and chief proponent of Islamic science today, interprets the Prophet's call differently. According to him, the Prophet's call was limited to merely theological pursuits and did not extend to the search for secular (worldly) knowledge, pp. 1-48. It is strange that a believer in *tauhid* or Unity of Knowledge should attempt to make such a distinction.
23. Pervez Hoodbhoy, *Islam and Science*, London: Zed Books, 1991.
24. S.M. Ikram, *Rud-i-Kawther*, Karachi: Firoz Sons Publishers, 1958, pp. 424-6.
25. The seventeenth-century French traveller and physician Francois Bernier refers to Danishmand Khan's interests in modern science and philosophy saying: 'Astronomy, geography, and anatomy are his favourite subjects and he reads with avidity the works of Gassendy and Descartes.' F. Bernier, *Travels in the Mughal Empire, 1658-1668*, Delhi: Low Price Publication, 1989, p. 353.
26. K.A. Nizami, *Sayyid Ahmad Khan*, New Delhi: Publication Division, 1966, pp. 14-15.
27. S.A. Khan, *Maaqulat-i-Sir Syed*, vol. I, Lahore: Majlis-e-Taraqqi-e-Adab, 1962, pp. 97-8.
28. Hoodbhoy, *Islam and Science*, p. 56.
29. S.A. Khan, *Maqalat-i-Sir Syed*, Lahore: Majlis-e-Taraqqi-e-Adab, 1961.
30. C.W. Troll, *Sayyid Ahmad Khan: A Reinterpretation of Muslim Theology*, New Delhi: Vikas, 1978, pp. 168-70.
31. Hoodbhoy, *Islam and Science*, pp. 68-9.
32. Ekmeleddin, Ihsanoglu, Some critical notes on the introduction of modern sciences to the Ottoman state and the relation between science and religion up to the end of the ninteenth century. In Jean-Lousis Bacque-Grammont and Emeri van Donzel (eds.), *Comite international D'etudes Pre-Ottomanes et Ottomanes*, Istanbul: The Divit Press, 1987, pp. 235-51,
33. Alessandro Bausani, 'Islam is an essential part of Western Culture', in *Studies on Islam: A Symposium*, Amsterdam: North-Holland Publishing Company, pp. 19-36.
34. Ibid.
35. Ibid., p. 26.
36. J.M.S. Baljon Jr., *Sir Syed Ahmad Khan*, Lahore: Ashraf Press, 1964, pp. 138-9.

37. Hafeez Malik, *Sir Syed Ahmad Khan and Muslim Modernization in India and Pakistan*, New York: Columbia University Press, 1980, p. 274.
38. Aydin Sayili, historian of science of Turkish origin and author of the famous *The Observatory in Islam and Its Place in the General History of the Observatory* (1988), refers in detail to this failed reconciliation between Islam and Greek philosophy which surfaced as a battle between the Mutazilas and the Asharites, ending finally in the defeat of the former. In Christian Europe a reconciliation between Greek philosophy and religion was achieved, but not so in Islamic civilization. Clergymen, from their position in either society as social leaders, were the obvious candidates to digest Greek learning. So they did in Christendom, but not in Islam, where *awail* science were either ignored or actively opposed by orthodox theologians, despite the interest displayed by the Abbasid Caliphs.
39. Hoodbhoy, *Islam and Science*, p. 97.
40. Altaf Husain Hali, *Hayat-i-Javaid*, Delhi: Idarah-i-Adabiyat, 1979, pp. 247-71.
41. Ismail R. Al Afuqi, 'Science and Traditional Values in Islamic Society', in Ward Morehouse (ed.), *Science and Human Values in India and Pakistan*, New York: Rockefeller University Press, 1968, p. 25.
42. Why Syed Ahmad preferred Waliullah over others is clear from the following lines of an article published in *Islamic Culture* in 1947:

    He [i.e. Waliullah] was fully convinced of this fact, that once the conception of Muslims about the teachings of the Quran was put on a sound rational basis, all other reforms, economic or otherwise, would follow as the night follows the day. . . . He realised in his heart of hearts that in order to raise his decadent community a critical and intelligent study of Hadith was essential as a supplement to that of Quran . . . [he] denounced in strongest terms possible the Taqid Jamid, blind following, at any of the Madhahib-i-Arabia, the four schools of Islamic jurisprudence (cited in Baljon, *Sir Syed Ahmad Khan*, p. 141.
43. Abdul Khaliq, *Sir Syed Ahmad Khan on Nature, Man and God: A Critique*, Lahore: Bazm-i-Iqbal, 1993.
44. Sir Mohammad Iqbal, *The Reconstruction of Religious Thought in Islam*, Delhi: Kitab Publishing House, 1974, p. 126.
45. *Ijtihad* meant the interpretation of Islamic principles in the context of the times, contrary to *taqlid* which meant the tyrannical acceptance of tradition. Mutazilites followed *ijtihad* in their interpretation of Islam and were ultimately countered by an Asharite reaction in the eleventh and twelfth centuries, leading to the supremacy of *taqlid*. Ziauddin Sardar feels that since then 'Islamic science truly became a matter of history'.

Z. Sardar, 'Can Science Come Back to Islam?', *New Scientist*, 88, 1224, 1980, pp. 212-16.

46. Khaliq, *Sir Syed Ahmad Khan on Nature, Man and God*, p. 3.
47. Cited in Ross Masud, *Khutut-i-Sir Syed*, Badaun: Nizami Press, 1924, p. 55.
48. Nizami, *Sayyid Ahmad Khan*, p. 113.
49. Malik, *Sir Syed Ahmad Khan and Muslim Modernization in India and Pakistan*, p. 175.
50. It is ironical that Al-Biruni, an outstanding representative of Islam's excellence in science in the eleventh century, made a similar statement about Indians whom he called haughty, vain and reluctant to believe that they can learn from others.
51. Syed Ahmad Khan, *Taassub, Tahzib-ul-Akhlaq*, I Shawwal, 1870, pp. 1-2.
52. Munshi Zakaullah, *Tabiyat-Sharqi wa Gharbi ki Abjad* [Beginnings of the Eastern and Western Sciences], Delhi: Matbua Ahmadi, 1900, pp. 1-2.
53. Ibid., p. 6.
54. Ibid.
55. Syed Ahmad Khan, *Taassub, Tahzib-ul-Akhlaq*, pp. 1-2.
56. Aant Elzinga, 'Revisiting the "Needham Paradox"', in S. Irfan Habib and Dhruv Raina (eds.), *Situating the History of Science: Dialogues with Joseph Needham*, New Delhi: Oxford University Press, 1999, pp. 73-113.
57. Malik, *Sir Syed Ahmad Khan and Muslim Modernization in India and Pakistan*, p. 178.
58. See the work of Hungarian Islamist Ignaz Goldziher (1981) on the reaction of the religious orthodoxy to *ulum-al-awail*.
59. The characteristics of Western and Islamic science are being debated and compared with a great deal of fervour. I wonder which 'Islamic' science and which 'Western' science is being talked about or compared? Is it the science of the Islamic renaissance of the eighth-thirteenth centuries? So far we have little evidence of Islamic science being practiced today. What is being promoted in the name of Islamic science in Pakistan has been beautifully narrated by Pervez Hoodbhoy (1991).
60. Hoodbhoy, *Islam and Science*, p. 74.
61. Malik, *Sir Syed Ahmad Khan and Muslim Modernization in India and Pakistan*, pp. 275-6.
62. Ibid.
63. Hoodbhoy, *Islam and Science*, p. 59.
64. Nikki R. Keddie, *An Islamic Response to Imperialism*, Berkeley: University of California Press, 1968.

65. However, Ihsanoglu (1987) feels that there was not much conflict between religion and science during the first half of the nineteenth century. In the works of several Turkish scholars there is no mention of any religion *versus* science controversy: on the contrary, one comes across expressions to the effect that in the golden age of Islam, religion was the motivating factor in the progress of science. He even goes to the extent of saying that it is difficult to suppose the existence of anyone who defended the old sciences against physics, chemistry, astronomy and other branches of modern science.
66. Ibid., p. 42.
67. Albert Hourani, *Arabic Thought in the Liberal Age, 1798-1939*, London: Oxford University Press, 1962, p. 108.
68. Keddie, *An Islamic Response to Imperialism*, p. 55.
69. Cited in ibid.
70. Cultural nationalism is a fashion with a particular genre of scholars and politicians these days, involving the careful sifting of intellectual and cultural icons and ideas. Jamaluddin Afghani's formulation of cultural nationalism came close to what the Bengali *bhadralok* intelligentsia, such as P.C. Ray and Benoy Kumar Sarkar, found suitable a decade later in their attempts to articulate emerging nationalist aspirations (see Raina, 1997).
71 Cited in Keddie, *An Islamic Response to Imperialism.*
72. Aziz Ahmad, 'Afghani's Indian Contacts', *Journal of the American Oriental Society*, 89, 3, 1969, pp. 476-91.
73. Keddie, *An Islamic Response to Imperialism*, p. 60.
74. Ibid.
75. Ibid., p. 106.
76. Scott. L., Montgomery, 'Naming the Heavens: A Brief History of Earthly Projections, Part II: Nativizing Arab Science', *Science as Culture*, pp. 6, 26, 73-129
77. Today, Sardar (1980: 213) puts the same thing a little differently by constructing binary categories called *haram* science and *halal* science. Aydin Sayili, *The Observatory in Islam and its Place in the General History of the Observatory*, Ankara: Turkish Historical Society, 1988, p. 414.
78. Keddie, *An Islamic Response to Imperialism*, p. 107.
79. Ibid., pp. 130-1.
80. Hafiza as-Saut is an Arabic term meaning 'preserver of sound', which could refer to either the phonograph or possibly the telephone. Since both were invented in United States in 1876-7, and Afghani was writing in a princely state in south India in 1880-1, one sees the eagerness with which he followed modern Western inventions.

81. Edward Said observes that 'the number of travelers from the Islamic East to Europe between 1800 and 1900 is minuscule when compared with the other direction' (Said 1985: 204).
82. Cited in Edward Said, *Orientalism*, Middlesex: Penguin, 1985, p. 149.
83. Keddie, *An Islamic Response to Imperialism*, p. 92.
84. Cited in ibid., p. 92.
85. Cited in ibid., p. 17.
86. Cited in ibid., p. 93.
87. Cited in ibid., p. 184.
88. M.N. Roy, *Historical Role of Islam*, Bombay: Vora & Co., 1938, p. 69.
89. Scott L. Montgomery, 'Naming the Heavens: A Brief History of Earthly Projections, Part II: Nativizing Arab Science', *Science as Culture* 6, 26, 1996, pp. 73-129.
90. Roshdi Rashed, *Entre arithmetique et algebra. Recherches sur l' histoire des math-ematiques arabe*, Paris: Les Belle-Lettre, 1984.
91. Cited in Keddie, *An Islamic Response to Imperialism*, p. 185.
92. Ibid.
93. Ibid., p. 183.
94. Ibid., p. 87.
95. Ibid., p. 88.
96. Lynn White Jr., *Dynamo and Virgin Reconsidered*, Cambridge Mass: MIT Press, 1968, p. 99.
97. Aydin Sayili, *The Observatory in Islam and its Place in the General History of the Observatory*, Ankara: Turkish Historical Society, 1988, p. 414.

    The articulation of Islamic science today conveniently ignores the eleventh/twelfth-century binary categorization of Islamic sciences, meant to be theological and juridical in nature, and the *awail* sciences, including the Greek secular sciences that later came to be known as European sciences. Nasr's concept of *tauhid* or Unity of Knowledge is centred only around the former, leaving the *awail* sciences outside the purview of his definition of Islamic science today. This seems an interesting case of selective amnesia. In which one very important chapter of the history of Islam is deliberately overlooked to serve the contemporary political and psychological needs of some expatriate Muslim intellectuals.
98. Cited in Keddie, *An Islamic Response to Imperialism*, p. 187.
99. Aziz Ahmad, 'Sayyid Ahmad Khan, Jamaluddin Afghani and Muslim India', *Studia Islamica*, 13, 1960, pp. 55-78.
100. Ibid.
101. Ibid., p. 66.
102. Ibid., p. 60.
103. Ibid., p. 158.
104. Hoodbhoy, *Islam and Science*, p. 63.

105. Islam-centrism means looking at the history of science merely from the vantage point of Islam, ignoring or undermining the contribution of other civilizations and cultures to the corpus of scientific and technological knowledge. This is akin to Eurocentrism, which sees modern science as the product of the Greek miracle while all other cultures are reduced to insignificance.

REFERENCES

Ahmad, A.F. Salahuddin (1976), *Social Ideas and Social Change in Bengal, 1818-1835*, Calcutta: Riddhi.

Ahmad, Aziz (1960), 'Sayyid Ahmad Khan, Jamaluddin Afghani and Muslim India', *Studia Islamica*, 13: 55-78.

——(1969), 'Afghani's Indian Contacts', *Journal of the American Oriental Society*, 89, 3: 476-91.

Al Faruqi, Ismail R. (1968), 'Science and Traditional Values in Islamic Society', in Ward Morehouse (ed.), *Science and Human Values in India and Pakistan*, New York: Rockefeller University Press, pp. 12-28.

Ashraf, Mujeeb (1982), *Muslim Attitudes Towards British Rule and Western Culture in India*, Delhi: Idarah-i-Adabiyat.

Baljon Jr., J.M.S. (1964), *Sir Syed Ahmad Khan*, Lahore: Ashraf Press.

Bary, W.T. (1958), *Sources of Indian Tradition*, New York: Columbia University Press.

Bausani, Alessandro (1974), 'Islam is an Essential Part of Western Culture', in *Studies on Islam: A Symposium*, Amsterdam: North-Holland Publishing Company, pp. 19-36.

Bernier Francois (1989), *Travels in the Mughal Empire, 1658-1668*, New Delhi: Low Price Publications.

Bucalle, Maurice (1990), *The Bible, the Qur'an and Science*, New Delhi: Idara Isha'at-e Diniyat.

De Tassy, Garcin (1870), *Histoire de la Literature Hindui et Hindustaine* (2 vols), Paris: l'Ecole Imperiale et speciale des Langues orientales vivantes.

Elzinga, Aant (1999), 'Revisiting the "Needham Paradox"', in S. Irfan Habib and Dhruv Raina (eds.), *Situating the History of Science: Dialogues with Joseph Needham*, New Delhi: Oxford University Press, pp. 73-113.

Goldziher, Ignaz (1981) [1916], *Studies on Islam* (tr. and ed. Merlin L. Swartz), New York: Oxford University Press.

Hali, Altaf Husain (1979), *Hayat-i-Javaid*, Delhi: Idarah-i-Adabiyat.

Hoodbhoy, Pervez (1991), *Islam and Science*, London: Zed Books.

Hourani, Albert (1962), *Arabic Thought in the Liberal Age, 1798-1939*, London: Oxford University Press.

Hyder, Quratullain and Sardar Jafri (1970), *Ghalib and His Poetry*, Bombay: Popular Prakashan.

Ihsanoglu, Ekmeleddi (1987), 'Some Critical Notes on the Introduction of Modern Sciences to the Ottoman State and the Relation Between Science and Religion up to the End of the 19th Century', in Jean-Louis Bacque-Grammont and Emeri van Donzel (eds.), *Comite international D'etudes Pre-Ottomanes et Ottomanes*, Istanbul: The Divit Press, pp. 235-51.

Ikram, S.M. (1958), *Rud-i-Kawther*, Karachi: Firoz Sons.

Iqbal, Sir Mohd (1974), *The Reconstruction of Religious Thought in Islam*, Delhi: Kitab Publishing House.

Jameelah, Maryam (1977), *Islam and Modernism*, Lahore: Muhammad Yousuf Khan Publishers.

Keddie, Nikki R. (1968), *An Islamic Response to Imperialism*, Berkeley: University of California Press.

Khaliq, Abdul (1993), *Sir Syed Ahmad Khan on Nature, Man and God: A Critique*, Lahore: Bazm-i-Iqbal.

Khan, Syed Ahmad (1870), *Taassub, Tahzib-ul-Akhlaq*, I Shawwal, pp. 1-2.

——— (1961), *Maqalat-i-Sir Syed*, Lahore: Majlis-e-Taraqqi-e-Adab.

——— (1962), *Maaqulat-i-Sir Syed*, vol. I, Lahore: Majlis-e-Taraqqi-e-Adab.

Kopf, David (1970), 'The Brahmo Samaj Intelligentsia and Bengal Renaissance: A Study of Revitalization and Modernization in Nineteenth Century Bengal', in R.I. Crane (ed.), *Transition in South Asia*, Durham: Duke University Press, pp. 1-48.

Malik, Hafeez (1980), *Sir Syed Ahmad Khan and Muslim Modernization in India and Pakistan*, New York: Columbia University Press.

Masud, Ross (1924), *Khutut-i-Sir Syed*, Badaun: Nizami Press.

Montgomery, Scott L. (1996), 'Naming the Heavens: A Brief History of Earthly Projections, Part II: Nativizing Arab Science,' *Science as Culture* 6, 26: 73-129.

Nasr, S.H. (1968), *Science and Civilization in Islam*, Cambridge, Mass.: Harvard University Press.

——— (1978), *An Introduction to Islamic Cosmological Doctrines*, Bath: Thames and Hudson.

Needham, Joseph (1954), *Science and Civilization in China*, 17 vols., Cambridge: Cambridge University Press.

Nizami, K.A. (1966), *Sayyid Ahmad Khan*, New Delhi: Publication Division.

Raina, Dhruv (1997), 'The Young P.C. Ray and the Inauguration of the Social History of Science in India', *Science Technology and Society*, 2, 1: 1-401.

Raina, Dhruv and S. Irfan Habib (1996), 'The Moral Legitimation of Modern Science: Bhadralok Reflections on Theories of Evolution', *Social Studies of Science*, 26: 9-42.

Rasheed, Roshdi (1984), *Entre arithmetique et algebra. Recherches sur l'histoire des math-ematiques arabe*, Paris: Les Belle-Lettre.

—— (1986), *Sharaf al-Din al-Tusi* (Euvres mathematiques, Algebre et geometrie au xiie siecle), 2 vols., Paris: Les Belle-Lettre.

Roy, M.N. (1938), *Historical Role of Islam*, Bombay: Vora & Co.

Said, Edward (1985), *Orientalism*, Middlesex: Penguin.

Sankhdher, B.M. (1970-71), 'Mirza Abu Talib Khan', *The Quarterly Review of Historical Studies*, Calcutta, 10, 4: 213-16.

Sardar, Ziauddin (1980), 'Can Science Come Back to Islam?', *New Scientist*, 88, 1224: 212-16.

—— (1989), *Explorations in Islamic Science*, London: Mansell Publishers.

—— (ed.) (1997), *The Touch of Midas: Science Values and Environment in Islam and the West*, Goa: The Other India Press/Aligarh: Centre for Studies on Science.

Sayili, Aydin (1988), *The Observatory in Islam and its Place in the General History of the Observatory*, Ankara: Turkish Historical Society.

Syed, Muhammad Aslam (1988), *Muslim Response to the West: Muslim Historiography in India 1857-1914*, Islamabad: National Institute of Historical and Cultural Research.

Troll, C.W. (1978), *Sayyid Ahmad Khan: A Reinterpretation of Muslim Theology*, New Delhi: Vikas.

White Jr., Lynn (1968), *Dynamo and Virgin Reconsidered,* Cambridge Mass.: MIT Press.

Zakaullah, Munshi (1900), *Tabiyat-Sharqi wa Gharbi ki Abjad* (Beginnings of the Eastern and Western Sciences), Delhi: Matbua Ahmadi.

CHAPTER 3

Bhadralok Aspirations and the Quest for Technical Knowledge, 1830-1900

SUVOBRATA SARKAR

> We came to know that the Court of Directors approved the appeal of Lieutenant Governor of the North-Western Provinces Mr. Thomason to establish Roorkee Engineering College. Subjects like civil engineering, canal irrigation, bridge making, etc. would be taught there. Such an institution should be opened at Calcutta also. So that the local youth can learn subjects like civil engineering. We have heard that Lord Dalhousie has started considering the matter.
>
> *Sambad Prabhakar*,[1] 13 September 1852

> In the Bengal Engineering College at Shibpore the teaching of Chemistry, Physics, Geology, Metallurgy and Mining, on which the Science Industries are dependent is subservient to the requirements of a Civil Engineer, and is of a highly elementary character. All of these subjects are there taught by one and the same teacher—an arrangement of questionable efficiency even as regards the requirements of an ordinary Engineer. For *the successful industrial application of the sciences, however, the instruction must be far more advanced.* (emphasis added)
>
> P.N. BOSE, 'Technical and Scientific Education in Bengal', Pamphlet, 1886[2]

Nineteenth century was a very significant period in the history of modern India. It was during this period that the country witnessed the emergence of many intellectual currents in all aspects: religious, social, political, economic and cultural. For the colonial power, by the beginning of the nineteenth century, the empire had more or less been won. The job was to retain it, and to use it for profit. The Raj was founded on 'the right of conquest', but its continuance depended more upon how much acceptance it was able to draw from its subjects. The Raj was not only just the army or the bureaucracy; it represented a culture and a way of life which was very much different from that of the subordinated people. The intention of the British colonizers was to make this difference more clear in order to show 'the utility of one and the absurdity of the other'.[3] Education was an important tool in this project. It masked the intentions and controlled the results.[4] Since every European traveller and observer harped on the deficiencies of the native character, 'character formation' was projected as the main purpose of education and the content was expected to revolve around it.[5] The system led to the acquisition of literary rather than scientific knowledge.[6]

However, in the wake of the consolidation and extension of the British empire in India, training of the local youth in some useful branches of science became inevitable. Consolidation of the empire had brought in its wake certain building activities which in turn required a continuous supply of a less expensive but skilled and trained class of overseers, assistant engineers, mechanics, surveyors, and so on. Thus the introduction of Western science and technology involved the task of creating through English education a middle class which might act as an agency of colonial economy and administration.[7] Naturally, the government paid more attention to engineering than perhaps to any other branch of science. The kinds of technical education offered in the colonies, and to whom, depended on a complex mix of factors, including the level of indigenous technology and the goals of the British and the voice of the colonial subjects. Here of course the perceptions of the colonizers and the colonized differed sharply. From the rulers' point of view, administering a colony and increasing its production of profitable exportable commodities required new technologies and new forms of labour, hence a certain amount of basic technical education. Yet the colonial rulers also wanted to preserve the social *status quo*, which they feared was threatened by contact with the West. This apprehension led them to favour the teaching of crafts and agrarian skills over academic education.[8] The colonized, however, demanded an academic education based on higher level of science and technology rather than a training only in crafts.

The present paper seeks to find answers to the following questions: how did local knowledge(s) and communities re-shape colonial institutions and policies relating to technical education; and what was the response of the Bengali intellectuals towards state-sponsored technical education?

The Nineteenth-Century Cultural Bengal

The Bengali intelligentsia was the first Asian social group of any size whose intellectual world was transformed through its interactions with the West. In 1817, Bengal's social leaders took the initiative to establish the first institution of Western higher education in Asia.[9] By then, through trade and colonial government, Bengalis had had more than six decades of close contact with a European nation. In Bengal the agrarian changes, new economic opportunities, Western education, property laws, and a new spirit of individualism contributed to the growth of intellectual and social activities.

One of the major agents contributing to the changes brought about in Bengali society was Western education. Although the spread of Western education was desired by calculating colonial rulers who wanted to fill the lower levels of the bureaucracy with Indians, it was also eagerly sought by middle-class Hindus who perceived it as a vehicle for professional mobility and the means by which Indians could learn the secrets of the technologically superior Western world. One interesting feature of the colonial education system was that it produced political leaders, world-famous scientists, professional men, and intellectuals, not only office clerks. No simple model or statement will help us understand why colonial education had the kinds of effects it had. It socialized many into colonial values; at the same time, it turned many of its products against those values. As Krishna Kumar points out, the rejection of colonial education may not have been sustained for long periods, but the broader rejection of colonial rule was sustained and we cannot ignore the role of education in inspiring this rejection.[10]

The 1820s and 1830s were the optimistic decades for idealistic Englishmen and Western-educated Bengalis,[11] as were the 1840s and 1850s the decades of disillusionment. The Bengalis continued to be influenced by Western values and ideologies, but there began a criticism against the British government, the operation of British justice and the methods of British industrial and commercial enterprises.[12] Disenchantment with British rule was closely related to economic and professional frustrations. The educated class of Bengalis held high aspirations which could not possibly be met with the limited number of jobs in the colonial bureaucracy. They were further disappointed by the fact that high-salaried jobs were reserved for the Europeans.[13] The other professions open to Western-educated Indians – law, medicine, education and engineering – also favoured Europeans. These grievances were voiced through petitions, emanating from associational meetings and through Bengali journals which were rapidly increasing in number. For example, the editorial in *Sambad Prabhakar* on 8 June 1847, probably by Iswar Chandra Gupta, lamented the closing down of the Calcutta Mechanics Institute due to lack of public interest and noted that industry and technical skills were essential for a nation's development. It was of the view that by technical education and industrialization, the current unemployment problem could be solved.

The Western-educated Bengalis searched for new social and political models. While they were not rejecting aspects of Westernization to which their education had introduced them, their earlier desire to imitate Western social and religious institutions disappeared. The Bengali society moved towards a synthesis of the old and the new, the Indian and the Western. A new intellectual and moral maturity was becoming discernible.[14] The most important characteristic of mid-nineteenth-century Bengali thinking was an unprecedented emphasis on cultural synthesis. Numerous Bengali journals of the period like *Sambad Prabhakar, Tattobodhini Patrika,* and *Vividhartha Sangraha* claimed the same objective. The idea of cultural synthesis gave them the best of both worlds. It enabled them to absorb the cultural shock and also promised a possible opportunity to transcend the barriers imposed by colonialism.[15] Nineteenth-century Bengal thus remains a fascinating study of Bengali identity and nostalgia.

Technical Knowledge in the Colonial Context

Educational policy of the state, or of private institutions or individuals, has a number of different purposes in any social and cultural setting. The expansion of British political power in India was accompanied by the control, transmission, production and reproduction of knowledge.[16] In the imperial scheme, the production of knowledge is a function attributed to the metropolitan country ruling the empire, while the reproduction of that knowledge, its transmission and replication, is the function assigned to the education system created for the colonized people. The colonial system of education can therefore be viewed as a means of preservation and reproduction of colonial authority, not only cognitive authority but also political authority, among the 'natives' of the colony.[17]

The term 'technical education' covers a spectrum of activities, and its meaning has changed over time to cover every sort of work-oriented learning. P.N. Bose (1855-1934), a noted geologist and science-enthusiast, defined technical education as training for the industries.[18] P.C. Ray (1861-1944), an accomplished chemist, believed technological education was of great importance considering the stunted industrial development of India. The first technical college (Thomason College of Civil Engineering) in India was opened at Roorkee in the United Provinces in 1847[19] when Britain itself did not have a tradition of providing academic training to engineers.[20] In Bengal a survey department was started earlier in 1841 and a post of Professor of Civil Engineering was created at the Hindu College in 1843-4. Professorship in experimental and natural philosophy had already been instituted there.[21] Lord Dalhousie was keen that an engineering college each be set-up in Calcutta, Bombay and Madras. The College of Civil Engineering was started in 1856 at Calcutta with its temporary location at the Presidency College, which maintained its separate identity until it merged with the College of Civil Engineering in 1861.[22] Later on the engineering college was shifted to Sibpur, near Howrah, with extended workshop facilities.[23]

In India, engineering education was not introduced accidentally; it had definite objectives. It was intended to meet the needs and requirements of the colonial government. In 1854-5 a Public Works Department (PWD) was established, and with the expansion of its activities, the British administration required trained staffs in subordinate ranks on a large scale. To employ British engineers for lesser jobs was not economical. From the beginning, thus, the PWD influenced the growth of engineering education in India in several ways.[24] Most important among them were the courses which were structured to meet the immediate requirements of the department, rather than provide training for the higher ranks of the profession. For this reason civil engineering remained the favoured branch. Indeed, all the colleges opened during the nineteenth century were called 'civil engineering colleges'.[25] The other branches of engineering like mechanical, electrical and mining remained neglected until the 1930s.[26] Even in civil engineering, however, there was very little scope of development in the job hierarchy for Indian engineers as the PWD adopted a discriminatory policy of recruitment; it recruited its senior engineers from Britain[27] and restricted technical training in India to lower-level jobs. An expanding but not diversifying colonial economy needed craftsmen, skilled workers, and subordinate technicians, while the managerial and creative aspects of technology could safely be left to Europeans.

At the level of higher technical education there was an immanent connection between the scientific and technological instructions in India and the designs of the colonial capitalist state. The changing place of Britain in the international economy required that the colonial state be enterprising in founding formal technical institutes. The first engineering college was established in India in 1847, while the Imperial College, London, was founded in 1889. The shortfall of textbooks and teaching materials for engineering schools in England was initially met by the periodically revised lecture-notes, examples, drawings and college manuals circulated amongst students at Roorkee.[28] A number of institutions that were established at Roorkee (1847), Calcutta (1856), Poona (1854) and Madras (1859) were forerunners in the history of British technical education. As late as the end of the nineteenth century, England had no formal institution imparting technical education, and engineers received their training as apprentices. The engineering colleges established in colonial India thus provided the models for replication in England in the late nineteenth century, and colonial encounter contributed to the development of technical education in Britain.[29]

From the point of view of technical education, India is probably the most interesting of the colonies. Colonized earlier than other territories, India went through its colonial evolution sooner. The case of India shows more clearly than any other the dual nature of technical education: both as a response to a demand for technically trained people and as a means of developing the economy in the future. In a colonial setting, education responded to economic and political pressures from both the colonizers and the colonized. These pressures were not cumulative but often contradictory.[30]

A constant feature in the history of technical education in British India was the contrast between the government's oft-repeated policy of educating Indians in Western science and technology and its hesitation in carrying it out. They followed a policy of discrimination while recruiting Indians to various government jobs. Europeans held the managerial and higher technical jobs, Eurasians the mid-level skilled and supervisory positions, and Indians were at the bottom, in the unskilled jobs. Engineering and technical education thus had to remain confined to lower forms of instruction geared only to produce overseers, surveyors and mechanics of various hues, just as literary education produced clerks and pleaders.

Frustrated by the British educational policy, leading Indians took up the question of technical education because they thought it was a precondition for economic development. The second half of the nineteenth century saw education suddenly politicized in the struggle between British authority and an awakening Indian nationalism, with technical education as one of the issues. The belief of British officials, from the viceroys downward, was that technical education was only meant to meet existing demands, and anything more would only flood the society with unemployed graduates.[31] However, Indians had a much more positive view of technical education. Many nineteenth-century educationists of India veered round the view that the educational system must develop a technical-scientific bias for the industrial development of the land.[32]

Technical Education and Bengali *Bhadralok*[33]

The impartation of modern scientific knowledge in colonial India was not purely a question of diffusion. The transmission of science was certainly one component in the process of political and logistic domination, in which it was necessary 'to convince the colonised that knowledge, whether in the sphere of culture, science or technology, could be acquired only through the mediation of the colonial rulers'.[34] It is a situation in which 'A knows B more than

B either knows himself or A, and in which A tells B what he is or ought to be'.[35] The colonial discourse thus presents distinct categories and powerful hierarchies. Guns and sails could win territories but the empire could be sustained only by emphasizing differences and operating from a higher pedestal.

But Western science and technology, viewed as a cultural import, were actively redefined by the recipient culture. A close contact with a vibrant, though alien, culture could not have failed to produce ripples in the minds of the local people. The continued display of new and improved technology by the British, though mainly aimed at the consolidation of their power in India and to increase its productive resources, also evoked a considerable amount of interest among the Indians. Their response to the scientific and technical education arranged for them by the British testifies to their awareness of the new phenomenon. The *bhadralok* community of Bengal had become aware of the role of scientific and technical knowledge in transforming Indian society and it surfaced in various journals of the period. As the reputed journal of the day, *Tattobodhini Patrika* observed:

> The founders of the Hindu College were interested to incorporate technical education in the curriculum. This was certainly a great proposal. If the government officials followed the path, then it would definitely help the larger student community. Nowadays many students after passing from the college find it very difficult to get employment. Very few of them get the government jobs and the mediocre students mostly suffer. If technical education would form part of the college curriculum, then students could live respectable lives. It is very necessary to commence technical education at the Hindu College. The college authority should consider the matter.[36]

The intelligentsia started demonstrating their concern for the promotion of technical education in the Bengal Presidency and the lead was taken by Dwarkanath Thakur (1794-1846). Although he is famous for his contribution towards promotion of Western medical knowledge among the local youth, very few are aware about his efforts to promote engineering education. As *Samachar Chandrika*, a contemporary Bengali journal, reported on 18 July 1844: 'Babu Dwarkanath Thakur offered to defray the entire expense of sending two students of the Calcutta Medical College abroad for higher study. He conveyed his message to the Principal of the College. We are not aware yet about the reaction of the college authority.'

Bhabani Charan Bandopadhyay started this journal in 1822. It represented the conservative section of the Hindu community. In a letter to the Secretary to the Council of Education on 21 February 1844, Dwarkanath wrote:

> . . . instruction is required upon no subjects in this country more than upon Civil Engineering and architecture. I am anxious to be of some use to an institution in which I have ever taken the highest interest and for this purpose beg to place at the disposal of the Council of Education a sum of Co's rupees 150 per mensem upon the following conditions viz. that a chair of Civil Engineering be established in the Hindu College. . . .[37]

After ten years of his death, Dwarkanath's dream came true. The Calcutta College of Civil Engineering was established in November 1856. He envisioned a future India that was Westernized and industrialized; and realized the importance of higher technical education in it.

The most important characteristic of the mid-nineteenth century Indian thinking was an unprecedented emphasis on cultural synthesis. Almost all the interlocutors of Victorian India talked of a cultural synthesis for the simple reason that it gave them the best of both the worlds. The assimilation of modern science and technology naturally commences at the level of pedagogy. The standard tale informs us of the replacement of traditional pedagogy and curricula by new ones under the pressure of imperial dispensation. In reality 'science teachers had to contend with local cultural conceptions and knowledge forms as well as the need to mobilise existing teachers within modern schools'.[38] These contingent pressures opened up the gateways for a dialogue between modern science and the existing knowledge systems, a dialogue that produced interesting results which in turn enriched both.

In the nineteenth century a new regime of technology was introduced in India as part of the instrumentalization of the programme of empire on the part of the British. As for the adoption of these technologies by the Indian workmen, technology transfer under colonial relations offered very little scope for such a development.[39] In fact, almost all the machinery came packed from outside, often with technicians to handle it. Opportunities for Indians to advance in the colonial educational and scientific services were limited. Whatever information Indians gathered regarding the making of some new technology was, therefore, a result of their quest for it.[40] *Grambarta Prakashika*, a well-circulated Bengali journal in the *mofussil* areas, observed:

> We came to know that Babu Krishna Chad Bandopadhyay stood first in the final examination of the Roorkee College. He is the first person among Bengali students to achieve this distinction. Babu Umesh Chandra Mukhopadhyay who went to England to study medicine, secured the first place at the Glasgow College among two hundred British students. These are the proofs that Bengalis can also master European science and technology. But our government is still sceptical about the intellect of the Bengali students. The common argument is that due to caste prejudice, the Bengali people can not perform well in the arena of Western science and technology. But after the achievements of these students, the government is now saying that Bengali people are not efficient in various higher level jobs. Passing an examination does not lead to success in professional life where one has to deal with various kinds of responsibility. These are actually excuses on the part of the government to exclude Bengalis from the higher level jobs.[41]

Even in an unfavourable atmosphere, in the field of medical and engineering education, Bengal's performance on the whole was found impressive. The response was perhaps better in the field of engineering.[42] Even the high-caste youths were not unwilling to study practical engineering and undertake mechanical work.[43] But the prospects were hardly lucrative. Native subordinates, however intelligent they may have been in engineering matters, had little chance of rising above the subordinate grades.[44]

Bengali resentment of the preferential treatment Europeans received had grown since the second half of nineteenth century. This resentment was fostered by many highly publicized instances of transparent discrimination in appointments to the governmental services.[45] The resentment generated by this preferential treatment mainly on racial grounds had twin effects. On the one hand, it led to a call for greater self-sufficiency in scientific and technological training and research; and on the other, it increased the growing resentment of educated Bengalis towards British rule and hence helped the cause of Indian nationalism.[46] The government was well aware of this growing restlessness and sought to defuse it by clearing the lower decks for natives.

Mahendra Lal Sircar's (1833-1904) concept of self-help in the matter of scientific education and research in the growing atmosphere of nationalism in the last quarter of nineteenth century was a significant development in the history of modern India. He realized that science would never strike a deep root in this country under the tutelage of a foreign imperial power. What was needed was an institution for the generation of mass interest in science, for the training of scientists and for cultivation of science by Indians themselves under their own management.[47] Hence he wanted to establish an institution which would combine the character, scope and object of the Royal Institution (RI) and the British Association for the Advancement of Science (BAAS) of Great Britain. On 15 January 1876, Mahendralal established the Indian Association for the Cultivation of Science (IACS) with twin objectives. One was cultivation of and research in science by Indians and the other was popularization of science among the general populace.[48] Sircar thus set out his nationalist agenda – to build a culture of science in India through its practice and popularization.

The IACS was the first attempt at an institutional articulation of the relationship between nationalism and scientific research in colonial India. Initially, Mahendralal faced various oppositions in the establishment of his brain child, the IACS. Apart from inadequate funds, there were other, perhaps more formidable hurdles. The Lieutenant-Governor, Richard Temple, himself was inclined more towards technical education than original scientific research. This made the big zamindars reluctant to contribute to Sircar's scheme liberally. The India League, founded by Motilal and Sisir Ghosh, came out with a rival proposal of establishing a technical institute to be named after Prince Albert, consort of Queen Victoria who was then visiting India.[49] After realizing Temple's obsession for technical education, perhaps the zamindars of the India League hastened to call for the establishment of a big technical institute in Calcutta on the occasion of the royal visit. At the request of the League and the Director of Public Instruction, Dinanath Sen, a great educationist and headmaster of Dacca Normal School, prepared a proposal for the School of Industry or Practical Science.[50] Dinanath vividly described the necessity for such an institution, its objectives and mode of instruction in his proposal. According to him the reasons behind the backwardness of India in the industrial sector were 'the high pay necessary for employing European Engineers or Superintendents, the cost and risk of importing Europe-made machinery, and the difficulty of having machines, when out of order, cheaply and expeditiously repaired on the spot'.[51] Dinanath's prescription to solve the problem was to create a class of well-trained mechanical engineers and skilled workmen among the natives who would devote their energies to the discovery of cheap and suitable indigenous raw materials and chemical agents for manufacturing operations. The existence of such a class of men would give a great impetus to the introduction of scientific methods in manufactures and agriculture.[52] He was interested mainly in mechanical engineering, as for civil engineering there already existed the Bengal Engineering College.

After a few days of publication of Dinanath's 'A Scheme for the School of Industry or Practical Science', one Pratap Chandra Ghosh strongly protested against it. He raised his objection in the *Hindu Patriot* that educating the native artisan class was the crying need of the country, rather than creating a class of Western-educated engineers.[53] Dinanath replied through his letter published in the same journal.[54] According to him the skill of the native artisan class was acquired by a very long course of training as apprentice under the elders of their families. So their artisanal skill was the result of hereditary aptitude generated by the same occupations being followed by the same families from generation to generation. No school could teach them such skills. He rightly said, 'unless we could avail ourselves the two great advantages of European manufactures, first the extensive application of science to practical industry and second the adoption of the large system of production, and completely remodel our arts and manufactures on the European plan, there was no hope for the productive industry of this country'.[55] Dinanath lamented that the native workmen were familiar with only portions of any branch of study; being devoid of any knowledge of theoretical principles, they did not know-how to proceed further. India's great want therefore, he continued, was one of the educated engineers, who would be able to take charge of mills, manufactories and workshops and conduct them with the aid of country workmen and artisans. So he explained, the India League wanted to establish a 'European system of mechanical engineering and manufactures'.[56]

Such a great plan remained unheeded. The government did not want to spread technical knowledge beyond what was required for existing industries. It was more interested in the nuts-and-bolts aspect than in developing higher level of scientific and technological education and research. Mahendralal wanted 'pure-science learning and science teaching, with reference to the practical applications of science, so far only as are naturally and necessarily inferable while carrying on experimental investigations. The object is not to drill men in the arts which constitute the manual and the mechanical industries.'[57] This was diametrically opposed to what Temple and the League had in mind.

The IACS symbolized the search for a distinct Indian identity in the world of science. It encouraged Indians to engage in fundamental research in science and to develop their own hypotheses and arguments, thereby establishing themselves as citizens of a modern scientific nation. Sircar had underlined the need for 'applied science' and industry in 1890 while still insisting that it was in the laboratory that the industry's destiny was decided. He also made it clear that he was never against technical education and that the ultimate goal of his endeavour was to produce men who would use their training for practical ends. However, a broad scientific substratum had to be created first. Technical pursuits would stand independently on that solid base, without frequently looking to external intervention or imported expertise.[58] A famous Bengali journal of the day, *Somprakash* reported:

> We are sorry to say that all the initiatives of the government to impart education are confined mainly to the literary education. Science and technical education remain the step-child of the government's educational policy. The only effort for advanced level of science education has been taken by Dr. Mahendra Lal Sircar. After him nobody is interested in this regard. For the advancement in the field of science, rigorous scientific research is very necessary. But unfortunately there is no such scientific research conducted in this country.[59]

By 1900, Bengali intellectuals had developed a vigorous critique of the colonial discourse on scientific and technical education. In many cases, however, their criticisms were based on a number of equally restrictive assumptions, mirror images of the official ones. Thus the nationalists saw educational deficiencies as a problem of demand, rather than of supply, brought about largely by the policies of racial exclusion imposed by the colonial state and its allies in the expatriate business sector.[60] The deliberate policy of training PWD officials in Britain, the limited colonial agenda for tertiary education, and the problems of getting Indian labour hired by expatriate capital were all important here. Furthermore, most Bengali enthusiasts for technical education linked the issue directly to the larger one of India's industrial backwardness.

Education for Industrialization

In 1853 *Sambad Purnochandrodaya*, a contemporary Bengali journal, remarked:

> The people of our country are more or less conscious about education. In a civilized society education deserves special attention. But the job-oriented education remains neglected so far. Through technical education the problem of unemployment can be solved. Technical education leads to industrialisation which in turn maximises the wealth of the country. But unfortunately the bhadralok community is unable to overcome its aversion towards technical education so far.[61]

From the early nineteenth century, the spokesmen of the Bengali *bhadralok* community were searching for the causes of the industrial backwardness of their province. Throughout the century the timidity of Bengali entrepreneurs was a recurrent topic of the Bengali press. An important factor hampering the growth of industry in Bengal was the dearth of adequately trained technicians. Consequently, one of the important and oft-repeated demands of the Bengali leadership was for technical schools, colleges and research institutes in order to spread technical knowledge far and wide in the land.

A large section of the Indian intelligentsia was influenced by the Baconian programme with an optimism that scientific knowledge will bring wealth. They tried to revive the missing connection between science and industry. Pramatha Nath Bose, one of the first Indians to be recruited to the Indian Civil Service, superintendent of the prestigious Geological Survey of India, and later associated with the founding of Tata Iron and Steel Works, was probably the first to talk about science-based industries and the need to remodel the university curriculum accordingly. In 1886 he published a pamphlet on technical and scientific education in Bengal which attracted very wide notice and is said to have initiated the movement for technical education in Bengal.[62] He asked for the introduction of science at the intermediate level (FA) rather than later. He found the B.Sc.

course to be 'some sort of a compromise between the literary and the scientific courses' which he felt, like many such compromises, had to a great extent proved to be a failure. He wanted the science subjects to be taught with an eye to their application to industry. He was worried about the exploitation of Indian resources exclusively by Western enterprises, and called for some sort of higher technical education to enable Indians also to come up in the field. An Indian Industries Association was formed in 1891[63] and its principal members were P.N. Bose himself and Trailokya Nath Mukherjee. They arranged a series of popular lectures and also experimented with indigenous raw materials though without much success. Prafulla Chandra Ray endeavoured to make his science directly relevant to the immediate needs of the society. He started the Bengal Chemical and Pharmaceutical Works Limited (1892) which sought to put scientific knowledge to immediate industrial use. Ray felt the existing educational system was far removed from practical needs and driving students disproportionately towards clerical and legal jobs. But these favourite destinations too were becoming over-crowded, with receding scope for further absorption. For him the remedy was a close coordination between science, technology and industry.[64]

It was felt generally that scientific and technical education was a necessary precondition to industrial growth. The technical institutes were visualized as providing skilled workmen who would become the agents of industrial progress. The task was to initiate an 'industrial regeneration of India' by educating the 'Indian artificer' with the skills of modern science and technology.[65] *Somprakash* observed:

> Why are high level technological innovations like steam engine not taking place in this country? Why we are still depending on others for advanced technology? The common answer is that our country is still underdeveloped. But we think you are not trying to upgrade yourself, blaming the country is very easy. Many artisans of our country are making beautiful products. So, why are we still importing bulk of such products from foreign countries? We are confident that if proper encouragement and capital are provided to the artisans, they would definitely excel in their field. Locomotives can also be produced here. But it is due to lack of encouragement on the part of our countrymen that the situation is gradually worsening. Our students are getting academic degrees like M.A., B.A., etc. But if they study technical education, then nobody can stop us.[66]

The first decade of the twentieth century proved to be important for science and technology in Bengal from the point of view of institutional manifestation. By this time unemployment was a serious problem for the educated Bengali youths which affected the entire society. The partition of Bengal (1905) was like a final blow to the already discontented Bengali people. Combining these two, the *bhadralok* community started thinking in terms of self-sufficiency and freedom from the clutches of the colonial economy. They perceived modern industrialization as the final solution to their problem. Here technical education played a vital role.

The Dawn Society, established in 1902 by Satish Chandra Mukherjee (1865-1948), was formulating ideas in terms of a 'national' education in literary, scientific and technical subjects. Politically stimulated by the partition of Bengal, it was transformed into the National Council of Education (NCE) in November 1905. The council had support of the cream of the intelligentsia and the most prominent Bengalis of the time. It was intended to act as a national university, free from European control and aid, and aimed at a fusion between the best of the East and West. It formulated an ambitious scheme touching upon all aspects of education – literary, scientific and technical.[67] But soon cracks began to appear from within. Influential members like Taraknath Palit, Neelratan Sarkar and P.N. Bose wanted the council to confine itself only to scientific and technical education. This was not consented to by the majority of council members, so on the very day the NCE was officially registered, a second organization, its rival, made its way to the forefront (1 June 1906). This was the Society for the Promotion of Technical Education (SPTE). The SPTE went on to set up the Bengal Technical Institute (BTI) on 25 July 1906, while the NCE established the Bengal National College and School two weeks later.[68] From the point of view of institutionalization of technical education, the BTI played the most prominent role.[69] Its principal objective was to impart scientific and technical education to the Indians to further their industrial progress. The institute wanted to provide industrial education largely ignored by the University of Calcutta and the Directorate of Public Instructions.

An important feature of the ideological development of this era was that almost all the Bengali luminaries looked to Japan as the major source of inspiration. Contemporary vernacular journals propagated the idea of industrialization through technological advancement, pointing out the example of Japan. As *Education Gazette O Saptahik Bartabaho* reported:

> . . . machine-made products are cheap due to the blessings of technology. Here physical force is replaced by mechanical force and the products become cheap due to low labour cost. It is a totally wrong conception that many labourers of our country would be jobless due to rapid industrialisation like the West. Most of the population of our country depends on agriculture. Naturally the pressure is huge on the agricultural sector. Through industrialisation this gigantic pressure can be transferred to the industrial sector from agriculture. But unfortunately there is no sign of industrialisation so far in our country.
>
> At present there are only 351 industries in India. Among these 61 industries are situated in Bombay Presidency and 86 are at Calcutta and its adjacent areas. Although Russia is mainly an agricultural country, it has more than 500 textile industries. The poor state of industry is the proof of India's backwardness in science and technology.
>
> Japan is learning European science and technology very fast. They visit the European countries and America in a large number and learn the principles of various industrial arts. After returning home, they start their own industries by newly acquired Western science and technology. Unless we follow the Japanese and acquire technical education, India would remain backward in industrial sector. To overcome this situation we have to acquaint with Western science and technology.[70]

The recipient culture's redefinition of scientific and technical education and industrialization was shaped by the need for industrial development in the context of nineteenth-century Bengal. The major concern was the development of 'science-based' industries in the interest of India than that of Britian.[71] While addressing the issue of industrialization of India, P.N. Bose noted that the miseries of the world were largely due to the unbridled and thoughtless application of natural science to Western industrialism. At the same time he observed, 'at the present state of our industrial development, I have always understood its function to be chiefly the revival of our own practically extinct industries on modern lines'.[72] He was fully conscious of the manifold evils of modern industrialism, but, to quote his words: 'If I had choice, I would go back to the old ways. But there is none, at least under present conditions'.[73] Bose repeatedly suggested that to refuse to participate in the project of modernization would only limit the growth of the Indian economy and prove detrimental to the realization of sovereignty. Most interlocutors also felt that India could try to avoid the evils of modernization that had disgraced industrialism in the West. As remarked by V.G. Kale, a regular contributor in the contemporary journals, 'we cannot remain where we were or what we are. We must advance, we must imitate, we must assimilate.'[74]

Conclusion

The logic behind the metropolis-colony relationship was not to allow the latter to have a higher form of scientific or technical education in relation to the former. What India got was some sort of a hybrid system emerging out of a careless fusion between industrial and technical education. Education was no doubt an important segment of the whole colonial enterprise and was definitely meant to strengthen it. For the colonial administrators technical assistance (not expertise) from the Indians was more important. Proper scientific and technical education did not fit into the exigencies of the Raj. In Europe technical education was developed in order to facilitate the process of industrialization. In India there was no such imperative.[75] The numerous English journals of the period also echoed the same official version regarding technical education and industrialization. As the *Calcutta Review* remarked: 'For the development of her natural resources, India's most crying need is not higher technical education, but private enterprise and private capital.'[76]

Discrimination, it has been seen, was a major plank on which the British policy rested. But with the passage of time Indians were not likely to accept this without some amount of protest. The ground had already been prepared by the initiatives of the vernacular press. The campaign was begun as early as the 1840s.[77] The Bengali journals of nineteenth century started demanding the provision for technical education for the Bengali people. The growing problem of educated unemployment among Bengalis gave rise to questions concerning the relationship between higher education and business as a career. In the latter half of nineteenth century, the Bengali journals articulated the demand for a higher level of technical education, instead of the current plan which was training in a few technical skills to fill up the lower strata of various governmental jobs, specially the PWD. Realizing that the link between higher level of technical education and industrialization was vital and of utmost necessity for India's salvation from the existing disastrous condition, journals like *Sambad Prabhakar*, *Sambad Purnochandrodaya*, *Somprakash*, and *Tattobodhini Patrika* started propagating the new tenor among the Bengali people.

The 'apartheid' in scientific and technical education made the Indians react strongly to colonial policies during the last quarter of the nineteenth century. M.L. Sircar, P.N. Bose, J.C. Bose and P.C. Ray were the first rays of the new dawn. In the early 1880s P.N. Bose emerged as a link between India's demand for higher level of technical education and its fulfilment through the works of the Bengal Technical Institute's students in the second decade of twentieth century, who came to be referred to as the Jadavpur engineers and technologists. The British model was thus proved inadequate. The new icons were Japan and Germany, and the new watchword was science-based technology. The nationalists were largely instrumental in ushering in the modern capitalist era in Bengal in the first half of the twentieth century based on higher level of techno-scientific education.

Delivering the presidential address at the Bengal Industrial Conference as early as in 1891, P.N. Bose had remarked:

> The condition of the middle class is no better than that of the mass of the people; probably it is worse. The government services can offer only a few drops of water amongst thirsty millions; can afford relief only to an insignificant fraction of our distressed population. The only remedy that is likely to be of very wide application that is likely to afford substantial relief to all classes of our people, is the development of our industries. It is industries alone that can relieve the distress of the mass of the people by lightening the pressure upon land, it is industries alone that can relieve the distress of our middle classes by affording them openings other than clerkships.[78]

Nothing could describe the call of the time better than this.

NOTES

1. *Sambad Prabhakar*, a famous Bengali journal was started on 28 January 1831 with Iswar Chandra Gupta as the editor. Gupta was in favour of introducing modern technology in agriculture and was also an ardent supporter of development of technical institutions and modern factories in India.

2. P.N. Bose, *Essays and Lectures on the Industrial Development of India*, Calcutta: Newman & Co., 1906, p. 74.
3. Deepak Kumar, *Science and the Raj: A Study of British India*, 2nd edn., New Delhi: Oxford University Press, 1995, p. 113.
4. For more information see Gauri Viswanathan, *Masks of Conquest: Literary Study and British Rule in India*, New York: Columbia University Press, 1989.
5. As Mount Elphinstone reiterated, 'there is no way to improve the morals of the people, except by improving their education', T.E. Colebrooke, *Life of the Hon'ble M. Elphinstone*, vol. II, London: Parker, Son and Brown, 1884, p. 149.
6. As one civil servant noted, 'The study of physical and mathematical science is rendered more subordinate to the grand object of cultivating sound principles of practical morality and provident habits', 'A Treatise on Popular Education in India, by a Civil Servant', Calcutta, 1841, p. 122; quoted in Satpal Sangwan, 'Science Education in India under Colonial Constraints, 1792-1857', *Oxford Review of Education*, vol. 16, no. 1, 1990, pp. 81-95.
7. B.B. Misra, *The Indian Middle Class: Their Growth in Modern Times*, New Delhi: Oxford University Press, 1978, p. 152.
8. Daniel R. Headrick, *The Tentacles of Progress: Technology Transfer in the Age of Imperialism, 1850-1940*, New York: Oxford University Press, 1988, p. 306.
9. See Benjamin Zachariah, Subhas Ranjan Chakraborty and Rajat Kanta Ray, 'Presidency College, Calcutta: An Unfinished History', in Mushirul Hasan (ed.), *Knowledge, Power and Politics: Educational Institutions in India*, New Delhi: Lotus Collection, 1998, p. 307.
10. Krishna Kumar, 'Colonial Citizen as an Educational Ideal', *Economic and Political Weekly*, 28 January 1989, pp. 45-51.
11. The campaign was begun as early as the 1830s by 'Young Bengal', a group of Western-educated graduates of Hindu College (1817) given to measuring their countrymen by the yardstick of British achievement. Shibnath Shastri depicted a beautiful picture of the period in his book *Ramtanu Lahiri O Tatkalin Banga-samaj* (in Bengali), Calcutta: New Age Publishers, 1904.
12. T.W. Clark, 'Encounter and Growth in Bengali Culture', in E.C. Dimock (ed.), *Bengal Literature and History*, Michigan: Michigan University Press, 1967, p. 90.
13. In the entire civil service, having about 7,000 posts in 1857, the 900 'covenanted' positions went to Englishmen, and of the 5,298 lesser posts, 3,082 were filled by Englishmen, and only 2,846 by Indians. See B.B. Misra, *The Indian Middle Class*, p. 316.

14. B.B. Majumdar, *History of Indian Social and Political Ideas,* Calcutta: Firma KLM, 1967, pp. 84, 88-9.
15. Deepak Kumar, 'The "Culture" of Science and Colonial Culture, India 1820-1920', *The British Journal for the History of Science*, vol. 29, no. 2, June 1996, pp. 195-209.
16. See Nigel Crook, 'The Control and Expansion of Knowledge: An Introduction', in Nigel Crook (ed.), *The Transmission of Knowledge in South Asia*, New Delhi: Oxford University Press, 1996, pp. 1-26.
17. Sabyasachi Bhattacharya, 'The Contested Terrain of Education', in Sabyasachi Bhattacharya (ed.), *The Contested Terrain: Perspectives on Education in India*, New Delhi: Orient Longman, 1998, p. 7.
18. P.N. Bose divided the industries into two—'industries dependent upon science, or science industries, such as dyeing, tanning, sugar-refining, soap-making, glass-manufacturing, electro-engineering, mining, etc., and industries which have a very remote, if any connection with science and which may be called art-industries such as engraving, modeling, carpentry, shoe-making', Bose, *Essays and Lectures on the Industrial Development of India*, p. 59.
19. For an illustrated history of the college see K.V. Mital, *History of Thomason College of Engineering*, Roorkee: University of Roorkee, 1986.
20. Margaret Gowing, 'Science, Technology and Education: England in 1870', *Oxford Review of Education*, vol. 4, no. 1, 1978, pp. 3-17.
21. There arose a controversy whether the emphasis was to be put on pure science or applied science. One section of the Council of Education felt that 'the course of the Natural Philosophy would only be such as is considered necessary as a branch of general education without being specially adapted to or intended for professional men'. The other section thought that 'the course should be a combined experimental and mathematical course . . . without which it is quite impossible for the engineer, surveyor, navigator or mechanist to become proficient men in their several departments'; quoted in Deepak Kumar, 'Calcutta: The Emergence of a Science City (1784-1856)', *Indian Journal of History of Science*, vol. 29, no. 1, 1994, pp. 1-8.
22. S.P. Gupta, *Modern India and Progress in Science and Technology*, New Delhi: Vikas, 1979, p. 122.
23. *Sulav Samachar*, weekly Bengali journal published by Bharat Sanskar Sabha, reported on 13 April 1880: 'Calcutta Civil Engineering College has shifted from Calcutta to Bishop's College, Sibpur on 5 April. Those who want to take admission in civil and mechanical engineering, have to pass in the entrance examination. For overseer class, there will be a separate examination. The course is for five years.' This weekly

journal was published by the Bharat Sanskar Sabha (1870). Keshab Chandra Sen was associated with it.

24. Arun Kumar, 'Colonial Requirements and Engineering Education: The Public Works Department, 1847-1947', in Roy MacLeod and Deepak Kumar (eds.), *Technology and the Raj: Western Technology and Technical Transfer to India 1700-1947*, New Delhi: Sage, 1995, p. 216.
25. *Quinquennial Review on the Progress of Education in India, 1897-1902*, vol. I, Calcutta: Government Printing, 1904, pp. 248-9.
26. Until the 1920s, only civil engineering could be studied to degree level at the Bengal Engineering College. Teaching in electrical and mechanical engineering was introduced at the turn of the nineteenth century, but remained confined to diploma courses. Even then, these additions were made primarily because civil engineers employed by the PWD needed instructions in these fields. See Arun Kumar, 'Engineering Education and Public Works Department, 1906-1947', Ph.D thesis, University of Delhi, 1989.
27. For the recruitment of superior grades in government departments, there was an apex college at Cooper's Hill in England, established in 1869-70 by the Secretary of State without consulting the Government of India. The entire expenses of the college had to borne by India without the advantage of any Indian benefitting from this. The college, abolished in 1903, symbolized the supremacy of metropolitan institutions over colonial ones like Roorkee and Sibpur. Deepak Kumar, *Science and the Raj*, p. 140.
28. These books codified Indian engineering practices and were 'hailed as the most complete and satisfactory work on the subject in the English language'. See Mital, *History of Thomason College of Engineering*, p. 98.
29. Russel Dionne and Roy MacLeod, 'Science and Policy in British India, 1858-1914: Perspectives on a Persisting Belief', *Proceedings of the Sixth European Conference on Modern South Asian Studies*, Paris, 1979, pp. 55-68.
30. Headrick, *The Tentacles of Progress*, p. 306.
31. '. . . It may be conceded that the effect of these various influences (the extension of railways, the introduction of mills and factories, the exploitation of mineral and other products, the external trade, etc.) on an Asiatic people is very gradual, and that it would be premature to establish technical schools on such a scale as in European countries, and thereby aggravate the present difficulties by adding to the educated unemployed a new class of professional men for whom there is no commercial demand.' Government of India Resolution No. 199, 18 June 1888, paras. 22-5; quoted in B.V. Subbarayappa, 'Western Science in India up to the End of the Nineteenth Century A.D.', in D.M. Bose, S.N. Sen and B.V. Subbarayappa (eds.), *A Concise History of Science in India*, New Delhi: INSA, 1971, p. 551.

Education Gazette O Saptahik Bartabaho, contemporary Bengali journal, reported the convocation address of Lord Landsdowne, Viceroy (1888-94), delivered at the University of Calcutta on 25 January 1889. From this we can see the dilemma on the part of government regarding technical education. It quoted the Viceroy: '. . . Job oriented education is very necessary. The problem of unemployment can be solved by such kind of education. But such education should not hamper the progress of general education. Another conception is that the content of university education is very much literary which is far from real life situation. So people want to learn technical education and demand comes up to open technical schools. But incorporation of technical education in the University curriculum is not healthy. It will hamper the cultivation of literature which is very necessary for nation-building. The university authorities are aware of the problem, so they are reluctant to start technical education at the present format. But without hampering the current University education, I'm requesting them to consider commencing technical education separately.' This journal appeared first in 1856 with the financial assistance of the Education Department and Rev. O'Brien Smith was the editor. But most of the responsibilities of editing were in the hands of Rangolal Bandopadhyay. Bhudev Muhkopadhyay became the owner and editor of *Education Gazette* in 1868.

32. As *Sulav Samachar* reported on 31 May 1879, 'Recently government has declared that industrial schools will start at every railway station for the Europeans. A European teacher will instruct there with a salary of Rs. 200. Our government is very conscious about the Europeans. What about the Bengali people!'
33. The Bengali *bhadralok*, literally the 'respectable people', comprised the Western-educated middle class. For more information see John H. Broomfield, *Elite Conflict in a Plural Society: Twentieth Century Bengal*, Berkeley: University of California Press, 1968, pp. 5-20.
34. G.G. Joseph, V. Reddy and M. Searle Chatterjee, 'Eurocentrism in the Social Sciences', *Race and Class*, vol. 31, no. 4, 1990, pp. 1-26.
35. T.O. Ranger, 'From Humanism to the Science of Man: Colonialism in Africa and the Understanding of Alien Societies', *Transactions of the Royal Historical Society*, 1976, vol. XXVI, p. 126.
36. *Tattobodhini Patrika*, vol. IV, no. 86, 1850. This monthly Bengali journal was the mouthpiece of 'Tattobodhini Sabha', established by Debendranath Thakur (1839) to promote Brahmo religion but also many articles on science, archaeology, sociology, economy appeared in the *Tattobodhini*.
37. Quoted in Sidhartha Ghosh, *Kaler Shahar Kolkata* (in Bengali), Kolkata: Ananda Publishers, 1991, p. 71.

38. S. Irfan Habib and Dhruv Raina (eds.), 'Introduction', *Social History of Science in Colonial India*, New Delhi: Oxford University Press, 2007, p. xxxi.
39. For more information see Ian Inkster, 'Colonial and Neo-Colonial Transfer of Technology: Perspectives on India before 1914', in Roy MacLeod and Deepak Kumar (eds.), *Technology and the Raj*, pp. 25-50.
40. Satpal Sangwan, 'Indian Response to European Science and Technology 1757-1857', *The British Journal for the History of Science*, vol. 21, no. 2, 1988, pp. 211-32.
41. *Grambarta Prakashika*, 9 September 1876. Harinath Majumdar, headmaster of a Bengali *pathshala*, started this journal in April 1863 to make the government aware about the miserable condition of the poor villagers.
42. Even as early as 1840s, Radhanath Sikdar, a brilliant student of the Hindu College, was picked up for his talents in mathematics by Colonel George Everest and was in the service of the Trigonometrical Survey of India as the highest-paid Indian in government service before 1857. Radhanath suggested a mathematical method to Waugh, the Surveyor-General, through which the heights of all distinct peaks including Mt. Everest were measured. See Amitabha Ghosh, 'Colonial Constrains and Technology: Marginal Indian Attainments', in Arun Kumar Biswas (ed.), *History, Science and Society in the Indian Context*, Kolkata: The Asiatic Society, 2001, p. 162.

    The industrial art section formed the central feature of the Calcutta School of Art. The D.P.I. report recorded that the School had already attained a high standard and compared favourably with any school of art in England. See S.N. Sen, *Scientific and Technical Education in India: 1781-1900*, New Delhi: INSA, 1991, p. 400.
43. Deepak Kumar, *Science and the Raj*, op. cit., p. 186.
44. R.E. Fife considered the PWD 'singularly inimical to the native civil engineer'. R.E. Fife, *The Civil Engineering Profession in India*, London: n.p., 1879, p. 8.
45. Deepak Kumar, 'Racial Discrimination and Science in Nineteenth Century India', *Indian Economic and Social History Review*, vol. XIX, 1983, pp. 63-82.
46. Aparna Basu, 'The Indian Response to Scientific and Technical Education in the Colonial Era, 1820-1920', in Deepak Kumar (ed.), *Science and Empire: Essays in the Indian Context*, New Delhi: Anamika Prakashan, 1991, p. 131.
47. Mahendra Lal Sircar, *On the Desirability of a National Institution for the Cultivation of the Sciences by the Natives of India*, Calcutta, 1869, pp. 3-6.

48. Mahendra Lal Sircar, *The Indian Association for the Cultivation of Science*, Calcutta, 1877, p. 29.
49. Chittabrata Palit, 'Mahendra Lal Sircar, 1833-1904: The Quest for National Science', in Deepak Kumar (ed.), *Science and Empire*, p. 156.
50. Dinanath Sen, *A Scheme for the School of Industry or Practical Science Proposed to be Established in Calcutta, from Funds Raised by the India League, with Government Aid, Drawn Up, by the Order of the Director of Public Instruction*, Calcutta, 1876.
51. Ibid.
52. Adinath Sen, *Sargiya Dinanath Sener Jiboni O Tatkalin Purbobanga* (in Bengali), vol. 2, Kolkata, 1948, pp. 141-9.
53. Ghosh, *Kaler Sahar Kolkata* (in Bengali), p. 211.
54. *Hindu Patriot*, 6 March 1876.
55. Ibid.
56. Sen, *Sargiya Dinanath Sener Jiboni O Tatkalin Purbobanga*, p. 145.
57. Mahendra Lal received a spirited support from Father Eugene Lafont, who initiated advanced physical science education at Calcutta. To quote Lafont: 'The other association wants to transform the Hindus into a number of mechanics, requiring for ever European supervision, where as Dr. Sircar's object is to emancipate, in the long run, his countrymen from this humiliating bondage', quoted in Sircar, *The Indian Association for Cultivation of Science*, p. 106, n. 89.
58. J. Lourdusamy, *Science and National Consciousness in Bengal (1870-1930)*, New Delhi: Orient Longman, 2004, pp. 96-7.
59. *Somprakash*, 16 April 1883.
60. B.R. Tomlinson, 'Technical Education in Colonial India, 1880-1914: Searching for a Suitable Boy', in Bhattacharya (ed.), *The Contested Terrain*, p. 328.
61. *Sambad Purnochandrodaya*, 13 January 1853.
62. P.N. Bose, 'Technical and Scientific Education in Bengal', pamphlet, 1886, *Essays and Lectures on the Industrial Development of India*, pp. 59-74.
63. Deepak Kumar, *Science and the Raj*, p. 210.
64. For more information see P.C. Ray, *Life and Experiences of a Bengali Chemist*, vol. I, Kolkata: Chuckrvertty, Chatterjee and Co., 1932, pp. 112-23.
65. G. Subramanya Iyer, 'Our Artisans and Mechanics: or Indian Arts and Crafts', *The Dawn*, vol. VII, no. 9, April 1904, p. 272.
66. *Somprakash*, 30 July 1883.
67. R.K. Dasgupta, 'National Education', in *Concept of National Education in India, National Council of Education, Bengal*, Kolkata: National Council of Education, 1970, p. 10.

68. For more information see Dhruv Raina and S. Irfan Habib, *Domesticating Modern Science: A Social History of Science and Culture in Colonial India*, New Delhi: Tulika Books, 2004, pp. 83-147.
69. See Benoy Kumar Sarkar, *Education for Industrialisation: An Analysis of Forty Years of Jadavpur College of Engineering and Technology, 1905-45*, Kolkata: Chuckrvertty, Chatterjee and Co., 1946. Through this institute, Benoy Sarkar called for *mistrification* (training of the artisans), *factorification* and *industrialization.*
70. *Education Gazette O Saptahik Bartabaho*, 25 January 1889.
71. In locating the history of triple engagement of science, technical education and industrialization, Dhruv Raina and S. Irfan Habib point out three significant conceptual dimensions. The first is represented by a moral critique of Western science and industrialization; the second, by a pedagogical programme, accompanying the systematization of traditional systems of knowledge; while the third involved an acknowledgement of the importance of modern science and technology in effecting social transformation, but rejection of the Western model of industrialization in favour of an Indian alternative. Raina and Habib, *Domesticating Modern Science*, p. 85.
72. Bose, *Essays and Lectures on the Industrial Development of India*, pp. 68, 69.
73. Ibid.
74. V.G. Kale, 'The Present Economic Condition of India', *The Indian Review*, XI (5), May 1910, p. 346.
75. In Britain, Industrial Revolution saw the emergence of the millwright from the tradition of village carpenters, blacksmiths and wheelwrights. A similar pattern in a lesser scale can be drawn in Indian context from the career of Goluk Chunder, the first Indian 'engineer', Shiv Chunder Nundy of electric telegraph fame, etc. But this did not help the Indians as it did their counterparts in England, like Watt, Trevithick and many others who began their career as self-taught highly skilled artisans. Sidhartha Ghosh, *Karigari Kalpana O Bangali Udyog: A Case Study of Five Bengali Entrepreneurs and Scientific Workers* (in Bengali), Kolkata: Deys' Publishing, 1988.
76. *Calcutta Review*, 104, 1897, p. 238. It sums up succinctly the colonizers' point of view.
77. For instance, see *Sambad Prabhakar*, 22 July 1847.
78. Bose, *Essays and Lectures on the Industrial Development of India*, p. 7.

CHAPTER 4

Sanskrit Learning in Colonial Mithila
Continuity and Change

I.K. CHAUDHARY

Mithila, a cultural region in north Bihar, is traditionally known as a seat of Sanskrit learning. It had no organized ancient universities like Nalanda and Vikramshila. But through the ages it continuously attracted scholars and knowledge seekers and was famous for certain specialized branches of Hindu philosophy. Mithila flourished remarkably as a centre of Hindu learning in the medieval period. It declined under British colonial rule, yet its resilience could still be seen. This paper deals with the state of Sanskritic learning in Mithila under the British rule, with special reference to the episode of its freak revival, in the face of Anglicization of Indian education. Sanskrit knowledge was traditionally the domain of a particular class under the tenets of the *varnashrama*. In respect to educational change in our times, it has been observed: 'as distinct from the state dominance, there is a phenomenon of hegemonic potency in civil society, on the basis of caste, class, gender, criterion or criteria socially recognized and backed by social sentiments against infringement'.[1] Keeping this in view, the paper sees the nature of Sanskrit learning as a result of the colonial educational policies and its implications upon the local society of Mithila.

Traditional education and learning declined in colonial Mithila for several reasons as it represented conflict of ideas and interests of various groups. It faced challenge first from Persian education and then from English. There was also a pre-colonial development of linguistic bridging between the classical language and the language of day-to-day business. This gave rise to Tirhutia or Maithili as people's literary language. Thus, the sheen of Sanskrit learning was eroded in spite of it finding the favour of the powerful upper classes and patronage of the local ruler.

The Milieu

Before British colonialism, the system of organized higher education was generally sponsored by private grants of the aristocracy. This changed drastically under British colonialism.[2] The ruling zamindar of Mithila, the raja of Darbhanga, maintained the tradition of supporting Sanskrit learning but had to succumb to pressure from the rising popularity of Maithili and Persian education. So far as the munificence of the aristocracy was concerned, the Permanent Settlement of Bengal (1793) had an impact. In his minute of March 1811 Lord Minto observed:

> The principal cause of the present neglected state of literature in India is to be traced to the want of that encouragement which was formerly afforded to it by Princes, Chieftains and individuals under the native governments. Such a review would bring before us the liberal patronage which was formerly bestowed not only by princes and others in power and authority, but also by the Zamindars on persons who had distinguished themselves by the successful cultivation of letters at those places.[3]

There was, in general, a 'progressive state' of decay of science and literature during this time. The British government, in accordance with its policy of Orientalism, was seized of the matter:

> The immediate consequence of this state of thing is the disuse, and even actual loss, of many valuable books . . . and unless government interfere with a fostering hand, the revival of letters may shortly become hopeless from a want of books, or of persons capable of explaining them.[4]

To arrest the trend, the colonial government mooted to establish Sanskrit colleges at three principal seats of Hindu learning, viz., Benares, Tirhut (Mithila) and Nadia.[5]

The state of Sanskrit learning came under the purview of enquiry of indigenous education in Bengal by William Adam (1835-8). Sanskrit learning indeed became the matter of concern for several contemporary Europeans. Adam is one among them. Adam appreciated the importance of Sanskrit learning: it being the 'language of the God' and of influential and learned classes, and 'a large degree of respect and attention' associated with it. Besides, it was the 'source and origin of all the Hindu vernacular dialects, spoken and written through India and adjoining countries'.[6] Sanskrit education could this way be the base of moral education of the masses that the British mooted since Lord Minto's time.

Charles Grant, on the other hand, recommended English education as means to impart Western ideas. Thus, two approaches began to emerge right from the beginning of the nineteenth century – Anglicists and Orientalists. Among all these controversies Adam submitted his report on mass education. His reports were so well prepared that none could fail to appreciate them.[7]

Among all these diverse educational systems one aspect was very prominent. The British were in favour of promoting an educational system based on Western ideas. English education was one of their favourite agendas. The system of education in India was thus moulded in such a way that it did not have much scope other than producing men who could join ranks of various orders to serve the British masters.

The supercession of indigenous popular education by the official system has recently been explained as the imperialist 'political agenda of education'. Joseph Bara argues that social forces had been at work to shape the system of education both before and during the colonial period.'[8] Thus, an evaluation of continuity and changes between the pre-colonial and the colonial period may lead us to argue that colonialism was marked with major shift in Indian education. Mithila provides a suitable example for the arguments made above. Hetukar Jha remarks,

> this was the beginning of sad tradition in the history of learning in India in which education got only a subordinate status in relation to political institutions. Earlier, of course, there used to be court scholars, but there was no court scholarship. None of the faculties of learning such as *Nyaya, Navya-Nyaya, Vyakarna, Sankhya,* Buddhist philosophers, etc., ever related itself to any political way and hence each developed its independent intellectual tradition. But, unfortunately, British education at the very time of its inception in India got tagged with political interests and this inaugurated the process of colonization of education i.e. one way relationship between education and state.[9]

Structure and Stream of Learning

The Indian indigenous educational system was operating in and catering to a semi-feudal society. 'Like a stream which does not rise higher than its source, popular education could not go beyond the demand for education in the community'.[10] One may safely argue that when the British acquired control of this country they found four types of popular educational institutions sponsored by both community and the state. These were *chatuspathi* or *tol*, *pathshala*, *madrasa* and *maktab*.[11] The *tol* and *madrasa* were colleges of higher education, while *pathshala* and *maktab* were schools of elementary instruction. The Sanskrit school or college was called *chatuspathi* or popularly called *chaupari* which signified a place where four *shastras*, viz., grammar, law, *puran* (ancient Sanskrit text) and *darshan* (philosophy) were studied. It was only later on that they came to be called *tols*. The institutions for higher Sanskrit learning known as *chatuspathis* or *tols* thus continued to work even during the colonial period.[12] Adam also writes,

> these are called *tols* and consist of thatched chamber for the *pandit* and the class, and two or three ranges of mud hovels in which the students reside. *Pandit* does not live on the spot, but comes to the *tol* every day on which study is lawful at an early hour and remains till sunset.[13]

The classes were held mostly at the teacher's own residence. The number of pupils varied according to the reputation of a teacher and boarding and lodging facilities were often provided by him. Generally teachers took great pride in supporting the students at their own cost. In majority of the cases students were supported by comparatively well-to-do people of the village in which the school was established. We are informed that in most of the cases the house used as school and as place of accommodation for the students were separate from the dwelling house of the teacher, but built at his expense.[14] It has been observed that till the end of the East India Company's rule Sanskrit *pathshalas* depended on zamindars, small landlords and merchants for their support.[15] They patronized Sanskrit teachers. In the colleges where the number of students was very large, the teachers preferred to engage senior students to take classes. The relationship between the teacher and his pupils was very cordial, the Sanskrit teachers commanded respect in the society.

The *chatuspathis* or *tols* were maintained at different places. It should be noted here that the state of education in Bihar was first surveyed by Francis Buchanan from 1809 to 1812. He found that there were no less 79 *pandits* who had obtained the title of *adhyapakas* or professors of Sanskrit. He mentions that Jyotish and

Agam Shastras were practised. He mentions that the Darbhanga Raj paid attention to the education of *pandits*. According to him the number of proper *pandits*, including *adhyapakas*, was 247. Sanskrit study particularly flourished due to the patronage of the Darbhanga Raj. In Tirhut, as Buchanan notes, 'there were many teachers of high celebrity. Besides these teachers of higher branches of learning like literature, law, metaphysics and philosophy, there were many *pandits* who engaged themselves in teaching of the subsidiary subjects such as medicine, astrology, mythology, etc.'[16] In Tirhut there were 56 schools each run by one teacher. The number of students was 214. Both the teachers and the students were Brahmins. The subjects taught in these schools were grammar, lexicology, literature, rhetoric, law, logic, Vedanta, Mimamsa, Samkhya, medicine, mythology, astrology and Tantras.[17]

The survey made by Adam provides more useful information on the educational system of Tirhut. Adam visited over Tirhut on 26 April 1837 and returned to Calcutta on 1 July 1838. His report covers all relevant issues of Sanskrit education. J.S. Jha writes, 'it is somewhat surprising that Adam makes no mention of the Darbhanga Raj which has been famous for its patronage to Sanskrit learning. It is just possible that during his brief stay in Tirhut (May-June 1837) he could not contact the *pandits* of the Raj.'[18] Yet another scholar who assessed the ongoing system of Sanskrit education was Mahesh Chandra Nyayaratna.[19] He found 200 Sanskrit *tols* in Bihar. We find similarity in the reports of these two contemporary surveyors. The survey made by Francis Buchanan is equally important.[20] In fact, the contemporary colonial records provide important information on Sanskrit learning prevalent during the colonial rule in Mithila.

In Adam's report we find 27 Sanskrit schools in the district of south Bihar. The number of teachers was also 27. Four teachers were Maithil Brahmins out of the 27 in south Bihar. The ratio was almost double in Tirhut. There were 56 Sanskrit schools in Tirhut and the number of teachers was 50 Maithil Brahmins, 3 Saryupariya, 2 Kanyakubja and 1 Sakaldwipi.[21] Adam mentions that six teachers got no patronage, thus they managed their own resources. The rest categories of teachers received presents, endowments, annual allowance, and so on. These 56 teachers received an estimated income of Rs. 2,515, averaging to Rs. 50-4-9 per person per annum.[22] In 56 Sanskrit schools, there were 214 students, averaging 3.8 students per school. They were all Brahmins,

147 of them being natives of the villages in which the schools were situated and 67 natives of other villages. The majority of the students derived support from the resources of their own families. It was also a practice for the teacher to provide food to some students. However, it was not mandatory. We are also informed that only two schools had separate school houses for the accommodation of their students. The rest assembled their pupils in the varandahs of their own dwelling houses.[23]

The most popular subjects were grammar, lexicology, literature, law, logic, Vedanta, mythology and astrology. Adam provides a list of works read in the schools of Tirhut. However, none of teachers had distinguished themselves by written compositions.[24] The only exception to the Brahmanical monopoly of Sanskrit teaching were native physicians.[25] It has also been reported that Sanskrit learning to some extent was open to all classes of native society. This indicates the change in Sanskrit learning. The lower castes studied grammar and lexicology, poetical and dramatical literature, rhetoric, astrology and medicine. However, the study of laws, the writings of the six schools of philosophy and the sacred mythological poems still were monopolized by Brahmins.[26]

The Sanskrit teachers and scholars, popularly known as *pandits*, were of different hues:

> The pundits are of all ages, from twenty five to eighty two, some just entering upon life proud of their learning and panting for distinction, others of middle age, either enjoying a well-earned reputation and a moderate competence, or disappointed in their expectations and anxious representing future, some more advanced in years, possessing the heart-felt veneration of their countrymen, while others appear to be neglected and sinking to the grave under the pressure of poverty.[27]

The above remark leads us to believe that the general condition, especially the economic condition of the Sanskrit teachers was not satisfactory.

The colonial masters at times showed concern for the decaying condition of Sanskrit learning. Therefore on the basis of the report of the Hunter Commission, the Government of Bengal deputed Pandit Mahesh Chandra Nyayaratna, Principal of Calcutta Sanskrit College, to make survey of *tols* in Bengal, Bihar and Orissa in 1891.[28] He found 200 Sanskrit *tols* in Bihar. The general condition of the *tols* was not satisfactory. In Mahesh Chandra Nyayaratna's opinion non-availability of gifts of rent-free land to *pandits* was one of the important reasons for the decay of the *tols*. There was decline in the number of both recognized and unrecognized *tols*. In spite of some measures on part of the government, the general condition of *tols* could not improve.[29] It has been reported that the condition of *tols* deteriorated because of the establishment of Sanskrit primary schools where elementary instruction in vernacular was given along with Sanskrit. These were government aided schools. The result was that many *tols*, with a hope to receive aid, were converted into Sanskrit *pathshalas*. The stoppage of aid to *tols* which did not teach vernacular was considered an act of discrimination on the part of the government. The same rules were not applied to the *maktabs*. Further, the students of *tols* did not find their knowledge fruitful for service of any kind and they were not in a position to compete with the students of the modern education system.[30]

It is seen that apart from the support of the princely states, Sanskrit *tols* were patronized by the zamindars, petty landlords, and business community. This was not possible after the revolt of 1857. The British government decided to patronize vernacular language, science and English. Sir George Campbell's (Lieutenant Governor of Bengal) order made Sanskrit an optional subject as a student was given the option of learning either Persian or Hindi in lieu of Sanskrit.[31] There was resentment against this decision. This is in conformity with the opinion of Adam, who warned the authority not to neglect Sanskrit institutions, otherwise 'it may be feared that the hostility of the learned will be often incurred and that, through their all penetrating influence, they will raise serious obstacles to the spread of popular instruction'.[32] In fact, Adam was in favour of getting the support of Sanskrit scholars even in the field of popular education. The scholars who were consulted also showed interest in teaching European science and learning in their schools, provided that the works put into their hands were not to affect the subject of religion.

Examinations

It has been suggested that the system of teaching in Sanskrit *tols* actually obliviated the necessity of examination. In fact, the object of examination was fulfilled by day-to-day assignments. The success of a student determined the success of a teacher and also served the basic objective of education. The day a student succeeded in some *shastrarth* (scholastic dispute) and was declared fit to teach, he was conferred the title of *Upadhyaya*, and his teacher was known as *Mahopadhyaya*. Likewise when the *Upadhaya's* students became *Upadhyaya*, the *Mahopadhyaya* himself earned the title of *Mahamahopadhyaya* (henceforth MM).[33] In 1878 the operation of the education department was extended to Sanskrit education by the institution of title examination. This proved to be a popular measure. Apart from economic measures, the practice of giving the title of *Mahamahopadhyaya* on distinguished Sanskrit scholars was revived in 1893.[34]

In his book *Kavi Rahasya*, MM Dr. Ganganath Jha has referred to the prevalence of two types of examinations – one conducted by the king and the other by the public. According to him public examination was prevalent till about 200 years ago. It was called *Sadyantra*. MM Gokulnath Upadhyaya is said to have succeeded in this examination. From other sources also we know that a number of Gokulnath Upadhyaya's predecessors had obtained the much coveted title of *Sadyantra*. The *Sadyantra* examination continued even after MM Gokulnath.[35] Thus it is clear that the *Sadyantra* examination was in continuity since the medieval period. The second form of popular examination was *Dhoti.* MM Mahesh Thakur, the founder of Khandavala dynasty of the Darbhanga Raj, introduced this examination system which was since patronized by the Raj.[36]

Thus one may argue that till the nineteenth century two types of examinations, public and royal, were in practice. However, we do not find any reference to such examinations in Adam's report. As mentioned earlier, Adam has not discussed the academic activities of the Darbhanga Raj. It is quite possible that these two types of examinations which were in vogue since medieval period did not catch the notice of Adam. However, we get reference of *Sadyantra* and *Salaka Pariksha* for testing the merit of scholars in ancient Mithila. J.S. Jha has discussed various issues of *Dhoti* examinations on the basis of a book, *Darbhanga Vinoda*.[37] The book provides valuable information regarding the *Dhoti* examination organized by the Darbhanga Raj, which honoured scholars of proven merit by a pair of *Dhoti* (loin cloth). Known as *Dhautta Pariksha*, MM Mahesh Thakur instituted it to honour the distinguished scholars of his estate to mark his accession to the throne of Mithila. The earliest reference to this examination in government records is found in the Purnea report of Francis Buchanan, which is as follows,

> the Darbhanga Raja, being himself a Brahman of very high birth, pays some attention to the education of *pandits* on his estates. When any man, therefore, has finished his education, and wishes to assume the title of *pandit*, the assembly is held before the Raja who, when the new name is conferred, gives a dress and places a mark on the forehead of the candidate.[38]

It appears that higher-order Sanskrit texts were the basis of the examination. Vedas, Samkhya, Yoga, Dharmashastra, Vedanta, Mimamsa, Nyaya, Jyotish Shastra, Vyakarana, Kavya Sahitya and Hindi Kavya were the subjects on which the examination was organized. It has been argued that Mimamsa fell from favour in Mithila and Nyaya was given preference as this was the subject professed by Mahesh Thakur himself. The participants by and large were the natives of Mithila, although scholars from Kashi (Benares) and Vikrampur (Dhaka) also appeared at this examination from time to time. This indicates that the examination was popular even among scholars residing outside Mithila. Gradually the *Dhoti* examination became the hallmark of scholarship which was held in higher esteem than even the diploma of government Sanskrit College, Calcutta.[39] It would not be out of context to mention here that a contemporary scholar, who himself was a recipient of this award, raised questions regarding the credibility of this examination as it neither improved the financial position nor helped in getting official assignments even in the office of the Darbhanga Raj. 'An English knowing *Amla* (Raj employee) could very well sit on a chair in the presence of Maharaja, these *dhaut parikshottirna* had to content themselves with their seats on some carpet on the ground'.[40]

The concern for Sanskrit learning may also be seen among the people of this region. The awakening among the people for the revival of Sanskrit learning also influenced the government. In 1914 the Government of Bihar and Orissa appointed a committee to advise it on the various problems related to Sanskrit learning. As a result the Bihar and Orissa Sanskrit Association was formed. The association was to conduct examinations, distribute stipends and advise government on all questions connected with grants-in-aid to *tols*. Another important recommendation of the committee was to provincialize the Dharma Samaj Sanskrit School at Muzaffarpur.

Maharaja Rameshwar Singh of Darbhanga was made president of both the bodies. The Dharma Samaj Sanskrit School was upgraded and designated a college.[41]

In 1922-3 steps were taken to raise the standard of Sanskrit examination. The courses of study were revised. Accordingly, a common Prathama examination was prescribed. It was to be followed, after an interval of at least two years, by a Madhyama examination. The old title examination was replaced by the Acharya examination which was divided into four parts, each to be normally taken after an interval of one year. On passing the first two parts, a candidate was given the title of Shastri, and on passing all the four parts, the title of Acharya was conferred upon him.[42] The immediate result of the establishment of the Bihar and Orissa Sanskrit Association was a marked increase in the number of *tol* students appearing for examinations. However, this trend was temporary. It should be noted here that there was no Sanskrit school for girls. It has been reported that only five girls candidates appeared at various examinations between 1927 and 1932. The superintendent of Sanskrit studies also observed that Sanskrit learning would never make real progress as long as it remained confined to boys. Special *vidyalayas* (schools) for girls were opened in 1934 but did not continue for long.[43]

Sanskrit learning was also popular in Purnea, a frontier of Mithila. As stated earlier Buchanan made survey of education and learning then prevalent in Bihar. He also gave information regarding the indigenous schools of Purnea. He informs that some of the subjects taught were grammar, logic and law, astronomy and modern ritual. He informs that some students were inattentive and took long vacations. No *pandit* had more than eight scholars, and altogether there were less than two students for each teacher. The *pandits* in the district, including the professional teachers, amounted to 247. Buchanan also mentions another group of *pandits* which was distinguished from the former. They were 1,800 or 1,900 in number and were known as *Dasakarmas*. They officiated as priests for the higher order of lower castes of the society. The *Dasakarmas* could read and were able to pray from a book and had some knowledge of grammar and law. However, science was almost confined to a small region known currently as Saharsa (part of Kosi). There were not less than 33 teachers within a small space (west of Kosi). In spite of the patronage given by the Darbhanga Raj only eight *pandits* were well-versed in science and learning which they professed to teach, viz., one in logic and metaphysics, three in grammar and four in astrology. Buchanan writes, 'all these are Mithila pandits'.[44]

Patronage to Learning by the Darbhanga Raj

There is no doubt that Sanskrit learning was in a period of transition during the colonial period. The diversified nature of education and learning at times even diverted the attention of some of the rulers of the Darbhanga Raj. Still, Sanskrit was one of their favourite subjects and their patronage to some extent was natural. It was during the reign of Maharaja Chhatra Singh (1807-39) that a proposal was made to establish a Government Hindu College in Tirhut. The names of Darbhanga Raj and Bhaur figured much owing to the advantage of nearness of the residence of Maharaja Chhatra Singh. The scheme, however, could not materialize.[45]

Maharaja Maheshwar Singh, an ardent supporter of Sanskrit learning,[46] died on 20 October 1860, leaving two sons and a daughter. As the sons were minors the estate was placed under the Court of Wards (1860-78). Maharaja Lakshmishwar Singh assumed charge of his estate on 25 September 1879.[47] Though his reign was known for the progress of English learning,[48] Sanskrit education too enjoyed his favour. We are informed that every Monday the Maharaja held a meeting of *pandits* and awarded prizes to those successful in the scholastic disputations. From an account of MM Mahesh Chandra Nyayaratna we learn that the reputation of Sanskrit learning in the estate was still maintained. In 1881 the Maharaja donated to the government a sum of Rs. 5,000 for the establishment of a scholarship of Rs. 20 to be awarded to the most successful candidates at the Sanskrit title examination.[49] The principal of the Calcutta Sanskrit College was to administer the fund. MM Nyayaratna writes,

> The pandits of this country used to write prose and verse in Sanskrit only. They held the local dialect in scant regard and as such no important work was written in vernacular. The kings also were proficient in Sanskrit only; many of them avoided talking in vernacular. But at present there is Maharaja Lakshmishwar Singh, who is well-versed in many languages including Prakrit. Among the rules in his estate there is one of holding weekly meetings of distinguished scholars on every Monday for scholastic

discussions on different branches of learning, which he personally attends. In Nyaya he listens to the discussions on *Kusumanjali*, *Dravyaguna*, *Kiranavali*, *Padavakya Ratnakar*, etc. Discussions are also held of all ancient works of Maithil *pandits* of Nyaya, Vyakarana, Mimamsa, etc. He also wants the teaching of these subjects to be made according to traditional methods.[50]

The Maharaja had an intention to set-up a Sanskrit college at Darbhanga. The college, however, came into existence during the time of his successor Maharaja Rameshwar Singh and was designated as the Rameshwar Lata Vidyalaya. In the period of Maharaja Lakshmishwar Singh the *pandits* who had passed the *Dhoti* examination were considered as first-rate scholars and were given Rs. 50 the first time and Rs. 10 each as *Bidai* (reward) on subsequent visits, but, only once or twice in a year. The *pardeshi pandits* (foreign scholars) also got the same respect and remuneration.[51]

However, Maharaja Lakshmishwar Singh was also a champion of English education. The Raj School was upgraded in 1879 to teach up to the university entrance course. Besides, there were four other schools in Darbhanga district, all aided. These were at Tajpore, Madhubani, Roserah and Narham.[52] The benefit of English education was realized by the people soon. In the annual report of 1875 it was noted, that, 'Tirhootias, both Kayasth and Brahmins, who are as a rule averse to English education have began appreciating the same'.[53] This point was further emphasized in the annual report of the following year in which it was stated that even Brahmins of Tirhut attended English school. This was remarkable because hitherto they saw English education with distrust and suspicion.'[54] In fact, Maharaja Lakshmishwar Singh encouraged secular education. All branches of learning progressed under his patronage. O'Malley also notes in the beginning of the twentieth century 'though still backward, . . . [Darbhanga Raj] has made considerable progress in recent years'.[55]

Maharaja Lakshmishwar Singh, however, adopted Hindi for the conduct of business in Raj affairs in lieu of Maithili. Maithili lost its previous status of being the medium of vernacular education. Chanda Jha, a littérateur of high reputation, expressed his anguish at the decision of the Darbhanga Raj. As a consequence, Maithili got divorced from its script. Interestingly, a printing press of Hindi was established by the Maharaja of Darbhanga. The revival of the

Dhautta Pariksha by Maharaja Rameshwar Singh and the inclusion of Hindi as a subject of examination at the cost of Maithili reflected the pan-India zeal of the Maharaja.[56]

In the field of education, the foundation laid by Maharaja Lakshmishwar Singh was carried forwarded by his successor Maharaja Rameshwar Singh, a great patron of Indian culture and education and learning. His donation of Rs. 5 lakh to the Benaras Hindu University[57] and of the palatial Darbhanga building to the Calcutta University is indication of his special care of learning. Rameshwar Singh was a great patron of Sanskrit learning too. He established *chatuspathis* at several places and gave generous help to other such institutions in Mithila. Besides, he created a number of scholarships for the revival of the study of Vedas, Tantras, etc.[58] It was largely due to his efforts that the Government of Bihar and Orissa founded a Sanskrit Association at Patna to conduct examination and award of degrees in Sanskrit. As president of this Association, he was committed towards collecting valuable Sanskrit manuscripts. The Bihar Research Society took up this work in which the Maharaja, as its patron, took keen interest. The Maharaja writes,

> I trust that the relics will go to corroborate the glowing description of our civilization in the epics and the Puranas and show to the world that our Civilization was not only confined to the present four corners of India but it pervaded the greater part of the known world of those times. The discoveries may open up quite a new chapter in the history of mankind and might radically revolutionize the existing theories of *Ethnology*.[59]

The period of Maharaja Rameshwar Singh is a landmark in the history of Sanskrit learning in Mithila. He decided to endow a Vedic chair in 1909. This shows his eagerness for improving Sanskrit education in Mithila. He also created 20 scholarships for the revival of Vedic education.[60] The Dharma Samaj Sanskrit School was converted into a college which was to be managed by the members of a committee with the Commissioner of Tirhut as its president. The only other Sanskrit school entirely supported by the Raj till the close of twentieth century was at Rahika. Established in 1881, its students preferred to go to Kashi (Banaras) and Nadia for advanced study, specially in the field of Nyaya. However, the condition of the Rahika school was not satisfactory, therefore, the Maharaja established yet another school at Rajnagar. He also opened new schools in various parts of his estate. The study of Sanskrit was confined to Brahmins although there was no restriction on the people of other castes to join it. The Maharaja also revived *Dhoti* examination which was to be held on auspicious occasions. A Sanskrit college, i.e. Maharani Rameshwar Lata Vidyalaya was established on 12 July 1907.[61]

Rameshwar Singh was a great admirer of the *gurukul* system. In his opinion, education should aim at the cultivation of simple habits and tastes in consonance with the life of the people. Education should be broad based on national traditions and should be in tune with national aims and aspirations. Thanks to his interest, the Raj was then spending a sum of Rs. 18,700 a year on the encouragement of Sanskrit learning in the estate.[62]

Patronage to Sanskrit learning continued during the reign of Maharaja Kameshwar Singh (1929-62). The period saw the emergence and development of several colleges due to the generous aid. His contribution to the establishment of Mithila Sanskrit Mahavidyalaya at Farbisganj (Purnea) in 1943 is commendable. A new school was opened at Kapileshwar in 1930 and was named Rajmata Rameshwari Vidyalaya.[63] The Maharaja also contributed Rs. 10,000 for the establishment of a Sanskrit college at Rajnagar. The formation of Bihar Sanskrit Association was possible due to his contribution. He started the well-known Mithilesh Mahesh lectureship series in Sanskrit. Some of the prominent scholars who participated in this series were Sir Ganga Nath Jha and MM Harihar Kripala Dwivedi. He was also the president of the Bihar Sanskrit Re-organization Committee and responsible for laying the foundation stone of the Mithila Research Institute at Darbhanga on 21 November 1950. And, finally, he founded the Kameshwar Sanskrit University[64] at Darbhanga, which can be considered a landmark in the history of Sanskrit education in Mithila.

The services of both foreign and national scholars in the evaluation and propagation of Sanskrit learning cannot be ignored. Bihari Lal, one of the contemporary scholars, writes, 'Tirhut also known as Mithila in the subah of Bihar had been known as the seat of learning, tolerance and generosity'.[65] He also mentions that the *pandits* of Nadia (Bengal) and Benares held the *pandits* of Mithila in high esteem. Bihari Lal has provided a long list of scholars who excelled in different branches of learning during the colonial period. Most of them were patronized by the Darbhanga Raj. The description of Bihari Lal begins with 18 scholars of Vedas.[66] Some of them were the court *pandits* of Darbhanga Raj.[67] However, Bihari Lal has provided the names of only three scholars of Mimamsa.[68] It appears that the desire for studying Mimamsa was waning during the colonial rule.

In the medieval period a new dimension of Nyaya was given by the scholars of Mithila. Therefore, a distinct school emerged which was known as *Navya-Nyaya*. The scholars of Mithila continued to contribute to this branch of learning even during the colonial period. Bihari Lal has provided a list of 39 scholars who were the distinguished Nyaya experts of the period under discussion.[69] However, in due course of time Nyaya studies shifted to Navadvipa (Nadia) and Varanasi. The scholarly rivalry between Mithila and Bengal gradually subsided and the scholars of Mithila began to specialize in the works of Bengali 'Naiyayikas'. 'This was a temporary phase', writes Jha, and the works of scholars from Bihar are now receiving due attention in and outside Bihar.'[70]

In grammar also, the scholars of Mithila did not lag behind. Bihari Lal has provided a list of 56 grammarians.[71] He has also provided a list of 38 astrologers of Mithila. This indicates that astrology was also a favourite subject among the scholars of Mithila.[72] Bihari Lal lists 30 *vaidyas* (native physician) of Tirhut.[73] It appears that Darbhanga was the centre of eminent *vaidyas*, most of whom resided in Misartola, a prominent locality of Darbhanga town at present.

Bihari Lal in *Aina-i-Tirhut* mentions that both Maithil *pandits* and Maithil kayasthas used a common language and dialect, i.e. Maithili. It should be noted here that Bihari Lal has used the terms 'ganwari Hindi' and 'Tirhut Hindi' for Maithili, a language whose literary excellence had been continuous since the fourteenth century. Ayodhya Prasad 'Bahar' talks of *Tirhut ki Bhasa* in his *Maheshvani*. Buchanan in his survey of Purnea district (1809-10) has used the term *desh-bhasha*. Chanda Jha (1888), however, has used the term *Mithila bhasha* in his preface to the translation of *Purush Pariksha*.[74] It appears that George A. Grierson was the first to use the term 'Maithila' for the language of the people of Mithila, in 1882,[75] which is the legacy of the vernacular education move in Mithila.

Conclusion

Sanskrit learning could not get the respectable position as in the ancient and medieval periods. There was a sharp decline in the number of both recognized and unrecognized *tols*. The establishment of Sanskrit primary schools, where elementary instruction in vernacular was given along with Sanskrit, was a major factor for decline because many *tols*, with a hope to receive aid, converted into Sanskrit *pathshalas*. The stoppage of aids to *tols* which did not teach vernacular was a conspiracy against the traditional *tol* system of education. The same norm was not applicable to the *maktabs*.[76] Economically too, Sanskrit learning had no advantage The knowledge of Sanskrit was considered relevant only to religious rituals. A section of Brahmins had monopoly over this branch of learning and they preferred to get this kind of education.[77] Generally speaking, Sanskrit learning as a system of advanced learning had declined and even at chief centres, such as Benares, Tirhut and Nadia, this was in a decadent state.

The decline of Sanskrit scholarship in Mithila may also be assessed by evaluating the records of *panji* or genealogy of Brahmin families from the twelfth century AD until the present. These records are kept and maintained by *Panjikars*. According to the *Panjikar*, the number of scholars with the title of *Mahamahopadhyaya* declined sharply from the late eighteenth century to the first half of the nineteenth century. Sir Ganganath Jha observed with dismay:

> We have realized with somewhat like a shock that even in the home of intensive scholarship like Kashi, Mithila and Nadia, the deeply read scholar of whom there were large numbers 50 years ago, have practically disappeared and pandits who could be compared to these giants, even remotely be counted now on the fingers of one hand.[78]

The *tols* of Sanskrit learning had traditionally enjoyed support of local rulers, especially grants of land on which the teachers and the taught survived. The absence of it in the colonial system paved the way of its decline. British colonialism promoted English and Western knowledge system under the market economy and adopted English as the official language. Against this, the struggle of survival of Sanskrit learning in Mithila under the leadership of Darbhanga chiefs was an exceptional case. Before the powerful colonial culture of English, the struggle was bound to be a losing battle.

NOTES

1. Sabyasachi Bhattacharya, 'Introduction: An Approach to Education and Inequality', in Sabyasachi Bhattacharya (ed.), *Education and the Disprivileged*, New Delhi: Orient Longman, 2002, p. 2.
2. Kalikinkar Datta, *The Life and Thought of the People of Bihar*, Calcutta: Scientific Book Agency, 1967, p. 22.
3. Adam's reports on 'Vernacular Education in Bengal and Bihar', submitted to the government in 1835, 1836 and 1838 with brief review of its past and present condition (ed. J. Long), p. 308. Adam writes that the Minute dated 6 March 1811, ascribed to Governor-General Lord Minto, with the signatures of the Members of Council, G. Hewett, J. Lumsden and H. Colebrooke, possesses great interest because it bears Colebrooke's signature.
4. Ibid.
5. Ibid., p. 314. The college at Tirhut was finally abandoned in favour of a Sanskrit college to be established at Calcutta. From 1817-18 to 1822-3, estimates to the following amounts were made:

Nuddea @ Rs. 12,876 p.a. for 6 years	Rs. 77,256
Tirhoot @ Rs. 12,742 p.a. for 6 years	Rs. 76,452
Total	Rs. 1,53,708

6. Ibid., pp. 314-17.
7. Joseph Bara, 'Colonial and Educational Fragmentation in India', in Sabyasachi Bhattacharya (ed.), *The Contested Terrain: Perspectives on Education in India*, New Delhi: Orient Longman, p. 129.
8. Ibid., p. 22.
9. Hetukar Jha, *Colonial Context of Higher Education in India*, New Delhi: Manohar, 1985, pp. 35-6.
10. Bara, op. cit., p. 135.
11. *Tols* and *chatuspathis* were in existence till 1953. See Kalikinkar Datta and Jatashankar Jha, *Comprehensive History of Bihar*, vol. III, pt. II, Patna: KPJRI, 1976, p. 385.
12. Adam's reports on 'Vernacular Education in Bengal and Bihar' submitted to the government in 1835, 1836 and 1838, p. 51.
13. Ibid., p. 121. According to Adam, 'majority of the students derive their chief, many of their role, support from the resources of their own families', see p. 195.
14. K.K. Datta, *Studies in the History of Bengal Subah, 1740-70*, Calcutta: University of Calcutta, 1936, p. 1.
15. Datta, *The Life and the Thought of the People of Bihar*, op. cit., pp. 22-3 Also P.C. Roy Chaudhury, *Bihar District Gazetteers: Purnea*, Patna: Secretariat Press, 1963, p. 591.
16. Kalikinkar Datta and Jatashankar Jha, *Comprehensive History of Bihar*, vol. III, pt. II, pp. 359-60. According to Adam's the following works

were read in the schools of Tirhut. In grammar, *Subda Kaustubha, Siddhanta Kaumudi, Manorama, Sabdendu Sekhara, Laghu Kaumudi, Chandrica, Siddhanta Manjusha* and *Saraswati Prakria*. In lexicology, *Amara Kosha*. In literature, *Raghuvansa, Magha,* and *Kirata Kavya*. In law, *Sraddha Viveka, Vivaha Tattva, Daya Tattva, Ahnika Tattva,* and *Mitakshara*. In logic, the Jagdadisi commentary of *Siddhanta Lakshana, Samanya Lakshana,* and *Hetwabhasia, Abachedoktanirukti,* the Gadadhari commentary of *Vyapti Panchaka,* and *Pratyaksha Khanda, Pramanyabada,* and *Vyaddhikaranadharmavachhinnabhava*. In the Vedanta philosophy, the *Vedanta Sara*. In mythology, the *Bhagvata Purana*. In astrology, *Nilukanthia Tajaka, Laghu Tajaka, Vija Ghanta, Graha Laghava, Siddhanta Siromani, Sripati Paddhati, Sarra Sangraha, Surya Siddhanta, Ratna Sara, Brahma Siddhanta,* and *Bala Bodha*. For details see Adam's report, op. cit., p. 195.

17. Datta and Jha, *Comprehensive History of Bihar*, vol. III, pt. II, p. 364.
18. Ibid., p. 373. Mahesh Chandra Nyayaratna was principal of the Calcutta Sanskrit College.
19. Francis Buchanan, *A Account of the District of Purnea in 1809-10*, Bihar Research Society, 1928, pp. 174-6.
20. Adam's report, op. cit., pp. 191-4.
21. Ibid., p. 194.
22. Ibid., pp. 194-5.
23. Ibid., p. 194.
24. Datta and Jha, op. cit., p. 316.
25. V.A. Narain, *Jonathan Duncan and Varanasi*, Calcutta: Firma K.L. Mukhopadhyay, 1959, p. 172. In the context of Varanasi Duncan mentions that all the teachers except that of medicine were preferably to be Brahmins.
26. Adam's report, op. cit., p. 196.
27. Ibid., p. 119.
28. Datta and Jha, *Comprehensive History of Bihar*, vol. III, pt. III, p. 383.
29. Ibid., p. 385.
30. Ibid., p. 368.
31. Adam's report, op. cit., p. 317.
32. Datta and Jha, *Comprehensive History of Bihar*, p. 371.
33. Ibid., p. 378.
34. Ibid., pp. 371-2.
35. Parmeshwar Jha, *Mithilatattvabimarsh,* Patna: Maithili Ekadmi, 1977, p. 151.
36. Jatashankar Jha, *Darbhanga Vinoda* (*Dhoti* Examination of Mithila) *Pranya Bharti* (second year), Patna: KPJRI, 1982, pp. 145-81 for details.
37. Ibid., p. 146.

38. Ibid.
39. Ibid.
40. Datta and Jha, *Comprehensive History of Bihar*, p. 380.
41. Ibid., p. 381.
42. Ibid., p. 382.
43. Adam's report, op. cit., p. 81.
44. Jatashankar Jha, 'History of Darbhanga Raj', *Journal of the Bihar Research Society*, vol. XLVIII, January-December 1962, pts. I-IV, p. 68. Also extracts from a Minute of Lord Minto – 6 March 1811, Appendix 1 in Jha, *Colonial Context of Higher Education in India,* op. cit., p. 127.
45. Ibid., pp. 71-5. Also, Parmeshwar Jha, op. cit., pp. 186-7. Also S.N. Singh, *History of Tirhut*, Calcutta: The Baptist Mission Press, 1922, p. 114.
46. Ibid., p. 75.
47. Stephen Henningham, *A Great Estate and It's Landlords in Colonial India: Darbhanga Raj 1860-1942*, Calcutta: Oxford University Press, 1900, p. 86.
48. Jatashankar Jha, *Biography of an Indian Patriot: Maharaja Lakshmishwar Singh of Darbhanga*, Patna: Maharaja Lakshmishwar Singh Smarak Samiti, 1972, p. 125.
49. Ibid., pp. 122-3, also Jha, *Mithilatattvabimarsh*, pp. 192-4 for academic activities of Darbhanga Raj under Maharaja Lakshmishwar Singh.
50. Ibid., p. 125.
51. Jatashankar Jha, *Beginning of Modern Education in Mithila,* Patna: KPJRI, 1978, pp. 120 1.
52. Ibid., p. XVIII.
53. Ibid.
54. L.S.S. O'Malley, *Bengal District Gazetteer*, Darbhanga: Bengal Secretariat, 1907, p. 140.
55. Pankaj Jha, op. cit., pp. 167-8.
56. Upendra Thakur, 'Sanskrit Learning in Mithila under the Khandavala Dynasty'. *Journal of the Bihar Research Society*, vol. XLVIII, pts. I-IV, January-December 1962, p. 96. Also Henningham, op. cit., p. 102.
57. Stephen Henningham argues that 'one commentator has even suggested that Rameshwar Singh deserved equal credit with Pandit Malaviya for establishing the University, arguing that while Malaviya was responsible for most of the necessary fund-raising, the Maharaja, by announcing the first donation of Rs. 5 lakh to the Hindu University, did assuredly set an example, which the Hindu Ruling Chiefs had perforce to follow'. The Maharaja invariably advocated the necessity of combining secular education with religious training. Henningham, op. cit., pp. 102 and 106 for his grant to universities.
58. Jha, *History of Darbhanga Raj*, op. cit., pp. 97-8.

59. Jha, *Beginnings of Modern Education in Mithila*, op. cit., pp. XXI-XXII.
60. Ibid., pp. XX-XXII, The Maharaja also maintained a very good Sanskrit school at Benares.
61. Ibid., p. XXI.
62. Pankaj Jha, op. cit., pp. 164-5. The Maharaja also donated Rs. 1,20,000 towards the establishment of Patna University. See Henningham, op. cit., p. 136. From the Education circular No. 28, from G. Garden, Secretary to the Government of Bengal, to the Maharaja of Darbhanga it is evidenced that the Maharaja had promised to contribute Rs. 40,000 to the hostel fund of Ranchi College.
63. Jha, *History of Darbhanga Raj*, op. cit., p. 102. Maharaja Kameshwar Singh was the vice-president of the Bihar Research Society (Patna) for 30 years. He also donated Rs. 10,6000 to the Banaras Hindu University. See Henningham, op. cit., pp. 136, 154.
64. Bihari Lal 'Firrat', *Aina-I-Tirhut*, ed. Hetukar Jha, Darbhanga: Maharajadhiraj Kameshwar Kalyani Foundation, 2001, pp. 51-2.
65. Ibid., pp. 53-6.
66. Ibid. For details of Vedic scholars, see Datta and Jha, op. cit., pp. 459-62. Also S.N. Singh, *History of Tirhut*, Calcutta: The Baptist Mission Press, 1922, pp. 108-10 for Sanskrit scholars.
67. Ibid., p. 56.
68. Bihari Lal, op. cit., pp. 56-61.
69. J.S. Jha, op. cit., pp. 468-9.
70. Bihari Lal, op. cit., pp. 61-8.
71. Ibid., pp. 68-73. Also Surendra Gopal, *Urdu Histography in Bihar*, Patna: KPJRI, 2004, p. 50.
72. Bihari Lal, op. cit., pp. 73-8.
73. Ibid., p. 80.
74. Ibid.
75. Datta and Jha, op. cit., p. 384.
76. Jha, *The Colonial Context of Higher Education in India*, op. cit., p. 40.
77. Ibid., p. 41.
78. Adam, op. cit., p. 210.

PART II

INSTITUTIONAL SITES

CHAPTER 5

Higher Education and Christian Missionary Manoeuvres in India, 1818-1910

JOSEPH BARA

Christian missionaries in modern times adopted different approaches and strategies at different epochs to fulfil the urge of spreading the Christian faith, where the means of education was commonly present. Compared to other means, specially street preaching, the educational method, i.e. Christian knowledge and principles integrated in a structured capsule of instruction, was more organized. By education, a missionary was involved on a daily basis in 'implanting thoughts, deepening good impressions, uprooting the emerging errors, and shaping the habits' in his audience; thereby he prepared 'the good soil' where 'the Word of God' would fall and flourish 'hundredfold'.[1] Cases of missionary educational institutions becoming conversion sites or epicentres of spiritual formulation boosted the missionary belief.

India, facilitated by British colonialism's dilatory ways to use its machinery to educate the Indians, witnessed the rise of a sizeable structure of missionary education. In the early colonial phase, the missionaries made best use of the government encouragement to develop a network of Western schools,[2] qualifying the pre-1850 period as 'the age of mission schools'.[3] After the Educational Despatch of 1854, when the first Indian universities – Calcutta, Bombay and Madras – were established (1857) and the government policy favoured funding private enterprise in higher education, the missionaries opened a number of colleges in various parts of the country. This characterized the next 50 years as 'the great period of the Christian colleges' till the advent of the Indian University Commission, 1902.[4]

The missionary institutions, hurdled in various ways, regularly negotiated space for themselves under British colonialism, and later had to confront the burgeoning Indian nationalism. Yet, structurally speaking, they continued in post-Independence India almost intact.[5] Symbolizing their prominent presence, some of the Christian colleges today represent a kind of brand name in Indian higher education. Supposedly an outcome of an effort chiefly supported by British colonialism, the missionary managers had to actually, as the essay will show, tread a rocky path while running the institutions. Whether it was dealing with the colonial state or Indian nationalism, the bone of contention invariably was the missionary idea and purpose. Since the colleges addressed the upper classes and funnelled missionary agenda in a rigorous but refined manner, the missionaries had to be more careful and tactical at this level. This essay sets out to trace the rise of college education with the missionary idea from the founding of the Serampore College (1818), the first Christian college in India, by the British Baptists near Calcutta, and describes its buoyancy against uneven colonial socio-political terrain. The story then goes up to the World Missionary Conference, 1910, held at Edinburgh, by when the missionary idea of the Christian colleges was intensely interrogated by Indian nationalism and where the first missionary response was articulated.[6]

Complexities in Constructing the Colleges

Missionary college education was supposed to impact deeper spiritual formation in the recipients and the converts so obtained were to help in building an Indian church. Advantage apart, conducting such a Christian college in the colonial context stipulated deft dealing with the respective attitudes of the Indian social leaders and the colonial authorities.

The Christian colleges addressed the upper classes of the Indian society with the hope that they would lead the large masses to Christianity. But the projection hinged on the state of the Indian sentiments and could go awry. Right reading of the upper class sentiments was not always possible. In the fluid colonial situation, the upper class attitude and tastes frequently swung. Moreover, the cases of the attitude of one group differing from others' were not rare. A point in favour of the missionaries was the enamouring of Indians with English education. The missionaries, considered the first-hand agents of Western knowledge, were applauded in various ways, such as their being 'the great fathomless ocean of all imaginable excellencies',[7] and especially sought after. Interestingly, this was despite the missionaries' scathing criticism of Hindu religion and society. In the early nineteenth-century colonial Bengal, the missionaries were actually acceptable as 'reformers' of the Indian society.[8] By the turn of the century, however, some nationalist-minded organizations like the Arya Samaj labelled the missionaries as the arrowhead of Western cultural imperialism and lambasted the working of the missionary societies.

On the colonialists' front, the missionaries were advantaged by certain ideological commonness between colonialism and evangelicalism that ostensibly enabled, according to Carey, 'civilization and salvation walk arm in arm together'.[9] Since the mid-nineteenth century, both stood for 'civilization' of the 'backward' Indians on a Western model through English education.[10] But collaboration could backfire, for it bore the message of Western reinforcement against Indian religion and society. Since the late nineteenth century especially, the viability of collaboration based on certain common understanding was clouded by a suspicion of the colonial government that the missionary colleges harboured Indian nationalist activities. Some colleges were, in the eyes of the government, centres of 'disloyalty and sedition'.[11] The collaboration was not snapped because of this. But the relationship took the shape of business-model, both sides trying to realize maximum gain out of their respective agendas in the institutions.[12] This, at times, led to discord between the two, especially over doling out of the government grant-in-aid.[13] The vicissitudes of the colonialist and the Indian attitudes made the missionaries ever agile and forced them to change strategy in the interest of the missionary object.

The Serampore College began as a spearhead of an aggressive Christian mission to bludgeon the local beliefs and principles, and towards projection of the inherent superiority of Christianity. The approach was to yield abundance of Indian converts and would, out of them, raise local leaders to support the missionaries. After a few decades, the missionary attitude softened, opening, according to well-known historian of Christian missions, Stephen Neill, a crucial role for education.[14] Under the general missionary policy of evangelization, i.e. spread of Christian ideas and principles, the colleges now adopted 'dialogic' mode to achieve the missionary end.[15] The method, tested during the post-1860 decades, was in full play in the Christian colleges in the early twentieth century, even as the missionary idea and object interfaced with the Indian nationalist forces. Sustained nationalist inquisition restrained the Christian missionary idea. But the idea was defiant and ultimately blended as Indian Christian interest in the formative system of denominational interest in higher education, best represented by the Aligarh Muslim University and the Banaras Hindu University movements of that time.[16]

Despite the colleges representing Christian missionary interest in the largest chain of denominational institutions in India, their rise and progress rarely catches scholars' attention. Scholars' first choice, so far as the denominational interest in Indian education is concerned, is the Hindu or the Muslim interests, supposedly because of their more overt connection with Indian nationalism.[17] On the other hand, the Christian colleges' part, through chaste English education, is as that of a leading agent of Western imperialistic ideas; the case of some of them becoming the hotbed of nationalist politics is completely disregarded. The Christian colleges, thus, remain foreign agencies, and, since connected with the missionary societies from the West, are aptly presumed to be imperialist outposts.[18]

The Christian colleges are seen playing a somewhat sinister role, where the working of the missionary idea is contingent upon the changing nature of colonialism. With the rise of Indian nationalism, the idea is shown to be obliterated as a natural consequence.[19] Scholars at times locate the latent vigour of the idea in areas like Orientalist studies, scientific knowledge and Anglicization of Indian education, laying 'a stepping stone to Christianity'.[20] But the presence is shown as sporadic. Others see the idea as completely dormant.[21] There are even cases where scholars observe the idea being swept away by the incoming forces.[22] Not ignoring stray cases of individual missionaries, notably C.F. Andrews of St Stephen's Delhi, abandoning missionary pursuit in favour of a new role under the sway of local situation, the essay argues dynamic navigation of the missionary idea, where the reigning feature is its engaged dialogue with the colonial and nationalist forces.[23]

College for Conquering a Mission Field

The pioneering British Baptists – William Carey, Joshua Marshman and William Ward – teamed up as a 'Trio' at Serampore in Bengal (1799). While being an active preacher, Carey, the first comer (in 1793), joined the Fort William College, Calcutta (established in 1800), a government institution, as professor of Sanskrit and Bengali. A 'Non-conformist missionary' to the government, he was first offered tutorship which he accepted readily under the compulsion of bad financial condition of the Serampore mission.[24] In accordance with the British policy in the college, he followed Orientalist approach in his study and teaching, and wisely carved a space for his missionary agenda. His Protestant predecessor, Bartholomaeus Ziegenbalg (1683-1719), called 'the originator' of the various modern missionary activities (except medical), had pioneered, a century ago, oriental knowledge with Christian teachings in educational evangelization in south India; evangelization there was tuned to be a slow process.[25] Unlike this, Carey was anxious and aggressive. He fully exploited his Orientalist engagement, especially linguistic teaching, to complete some thirty-one translations of the scriptures in Indian languages. Amidst his devotion to teaching and translation, he 'strove all he knew to win his students and their Civil Service friends to Christ'.[26] Later, since 1828, he was seen using this link to extend the Baptist mission in the newly-annexed Assam region.[27]

These were fringe uses of higher education for missionary purposes under the constraints of prohibition of missionary activities in the East India Company territories. The missionary zeal was too strong to be content with such limited action. A welcome opportunity arose from the Company's Charter of 1813, which not only removed the ban, but also provided for 'the revival and improvement of literature and the encouragement of the learned natives of India, and for the introduction of and promotion of a knowledge of the sciences among the inhabitants of the British territories in India'.[28] Observing the growing interest of the Indians in English education, they assessed the possibility of its becoming 'a happy means of diffusing the gospel'.[29] Moreover, since 1811, they had made deft use of the monitorial system by importing a trained teacher in this method from Britain,[30] and following the Charter, they attempted to integrate the existing indigenous popular schools with the Western system.[31]

The successful effort in school education directed the Trio to advanced use of education. Carey was, from the beginning, aware of the limits of elementary schools for deeper impact. Thus, within three years of his coming, he conceived of college education, where he would teach Sanskrit, Bengali and Persian languages, along with the Bible and geography and philosophy.[32] The plan was too premature for execution. But since then the college agenda was fixed in the Trio's mind, which ultimately concretized in 1818. By now the Trio were seasoned hands, teaching some 10,000 children in 126 schools.[33] Serampore especially was surrounded by schools, and parents were desirous of advanced studies for their children.[34] The experience enabled them to design a comprehensive scheme, stated in a prospectus.[35] Serampore then being a Danish territory, the proposal was submitted to the Danish local governor, who heartily recommended for royal sanction from Denmark.[36]

The Serampore Trio conceived a vast mission arena. Acknowledged by Indians for their works in philology, printing, science and school education for the last two decades, they projected the concept of college for a promising mission. Somewhat like a modern university, the institution would admit students from the widest possible range of regions and cultures: '[Christian] Asiatic youth of all denominations, from every nation of Asia . . . from any of the provinces of Hindoosthan', or 'Native Youth from any part of India or Eastern Asia, therefore, whether Hindoo, Musulman, Sikh, Burman, Chinese, or any other nation'.[37] The urge of catering to the maximum number drove the Trio to set the college as one of 'the most economical Institutions to be found in the Christian world'.[38] A non-profit undertaking, it would bear the expenses of the Christian students fully.[39] With economy in mind, the Trio chose to locate the college at Serampore, an outlying settlement, so that 'nearly one half' of the expense of Calcutta could be saved.[40]

Such large missionary object motivated the Trio to make the college an advanced centre of training and learning. On the line of what the contemporary British Oriental institutions did, the college provided for varied and structured courses of studies, regular classroom teaching, reading and discussion for developing reasoning, and testing and awarding the students degree. Library was part of the original planning, and would contain works on various languages – from Sanskrit and 'popular dialects of India' to Persian and Arabic; Hebrew and Syriac; Greek and Latin; and French, Italian, Portuguese and English – and on various subjects – from divinity, history and philosophy to science.[41] As complementary aid to studies, even a museum was conceived.

The college bore a clear missionary slant of 'propagation of Christianity'.[42] The missionaries expected it to play a pivotal role in planting Christianity in India as a Halle institution did in Germany earlier in spreading Protestantism.[43] They believed that the object rested on the power of God 'alone'; but, as His wisdom's adaptation of means 'with infinite precision', they declared the college in 'unequivocal' terms 'the handmaid of evangelization'.[44] The college was to be primarily a teaching institution, but was simultaneously involved in literary production. Translation of the Scriptures was adopted as 'a duty paramount to all others . . . to produce a permanent and standard version' in different languages under a special 'Department for Translators', and also envisaged composition of original works once men were trained in Eastern and Western learning.[45]

The college adopted a two-pronged strategy to pursue the missionary agenda. First, as the Serampore College Act (1827) enshrined the object – 'to promote piety and learning particularly among the native Christian population of India'[46] – that partners from among the local Christians had be trained to lay a foundation of the mission.[47] The missionaries were convinced that exertions of a few Europeans 'in solitary and barren spots' would hardly yield results.[48] Not only were the European missionaries very few in number, their importation was not a right proposition in the given financial condition of the mission.[49] The missionaries, thus, believed boldly: 'If ever the Gospel stands in India, it must be *by native being opposed to native in demonstrating its excellence above all other systems.*'[50]

The priority of training of the local Christians was not at the cost of evangelization of the non-Christians. The college opened its gate to 'every Hindoo or Musulman youth', irrespective of caste or region on the condition of self-supporting and assumed the character of a general arts and science college.[51] It selected a few Christians for specific training for the ministry of the mission, but under general education, non-Christians students would be 'precisely on the same footing with the Christian youth', though one was free to skip a branch of knowledge, which he thought 'in any way infringe[d] on the cast [*sic*] or religion'.[52] The missionaries were once tempted to convert the college into an institution of divinity training, on the pattern of the contemporary Bishop's College, Calcutta.[53] But the idea of evangelization weighed against it and divinity training was made a faculty of the college.[54] Likewise another need – the normal school facility – was accommodated in the programme in view of the mission's 'School Plan throughout India'.[55]

According to the Serampore missionary schema, Christianity was to be planted in India on the vestiges of the demolished local faiths, best represented by Hinduism, and the college was to help in it. For momentous move the missionaries took into account the experience of 'the first promulgators' of the Gospel and realized the complexity of the Indian case.[56] The early Greco-Roman situation witnessed the expediency of the local dialects in the dissemination of Christian teachings. But in India, the missionaries found, Sanskrit, a sacred language, 'concealed' religious mysteries and doctrines; worse, it pervaded even the vernaculars. The missionaries decided to erode Sanskrit's hold by teaching its knowledge system, especially philosophy, by 'the ablest pundits', so that 'the most disadvantageous situation' that the local Christian preacher suffered before the learned Hindus was overcome. The curriculum would further include instruction in Arabic and Chinese – since former was the liking of many Sanskrit scholars and could connect many to the Hebrew and 'Syriac' works, and the latter was perceived as link to many other eastern languages and being the repository of several extant works of Sanskrit. The teaching of classical subjects was to be supplemented 'at pleasure' by related vernaculars, which the missionaries valued as the right medium of preaching.

Parallel to the teaching of the Eastern language and literature was the component of Scriptures and Christian doctrines. As accessory to Christian teachings, a course on Western science and English literature, including general history, chronology and geography was introduced; this would prove the darkness of the Indian beliefs and practices and the Gospel as the source of light. The whole programme was put into practice as follows, as J.C. Marshman describes:

The heathen students are all under my own care in the English department, and are classed with their Christian countrymen without any distinction. . . . All of them who are sufficiently advanced read and study the Scriptures two days in a week; and all their other studies, whether in science or history, are conducted after a Christian manner. At morning worship, indeed, the Christian students alone are required to attend . . . but the whole controversy between Christianity and idolatry and the whole contrast between religion and irreligion are before them continually, and we leave the result with God. What more can be necessary to make the college a religious institution?[57]

In such a missionary ethos of the college, the Serampore missionaries saw the making of a 'Christian Benares' that would tilt the whole balance of Sanskritic hold of India on the side of Christianity.[58] The missionary urge inspired the missionaries to experiment various modes at various stages of the college – English, Orientalist and vernacular education. The college was, both jurisdiction-wise and in technical terms, a Danish institution. Supposedly an internal affair of a neighbour, the scheme, because of its strong missionary features, alarmed the British big-brother imperialists, who 'apprehended the most dangerous consequences'.[59] The Trio tried to assure them of its liberal side, especially the space of freedom allowed to the non-Christian students on what lecture to attend or what not. But the fear of an untamed missionary zest was hard to let go.

Missionizing Western Education

Meanwhile, as Serampore College progressed, an Anglicist movement professing the teaching of advanced Western science and English literature through the medium of English arose since 1830. In this atmosphere another distinct employment of higher education for the missionary end was carried out by Scottish Presbyterian, Alexander Duff, 'a man of rare ability, tremendous energy and indomitable will'.[60] Duff initiated experimentation in his General Assembly's Institution of Calcutta that earned him the credit 'beyond all question' of being 'the founder of the modern Educational Mission'.[61] From his Scottish background, Duff was an inborn Anglicist,[62] who expounded English education in India with the following reasoning:

The English language opens up a whole world of new ideas, and examples of success in every department of success in every department of science; and the ideas so true, and the examples so striking, work mightily on the susceptible minds of native youth, so that by the time they have acquired mastery over the English language, under judicious and enlightened instructors, their minds are almost metamorphosed into the texture and cast of European youth, and they cannot help expressing their utter contempt for Hindoo superstition and prejudices.[63]

An equally avowed evangelist, he forged an 'inseparable combination' of Western knowledge with Christian faith and doctrines. In his scheme, religion, while serving as the base of the superstructure of all useful knowledge, would become '*the animating spirit which was to pervade and hallow all*'.[64]

In his Anglicist faith Duff differed from the Serampore Baptists. When he mooted the Institution, the Serampore College was in a flux. The Trio patriarchs had given way to younger men – J.C. Marshman and John Mack (a Scot who joined in 1821) – in conducting the college.[65] Educated in the university system, unlike the self-taught Trio, they felt, within a decade, that the task of vindication of the errors of Hinduism through the mastery of Sanskritic knowledge was greatly achieved.[66] They, therefore, wanted reduced time on Sanskrit study. Already staunch 'Anglicists', especially upholding the superiority of Western science,[67] when Governor-General William Bentinck issued a resolution on the government policy for English education (1835), they welcomed it. But, unlike Duff's outright condemnation of the whole learning system of India, they wanted continuity of encouragement to it, since they still saw some scope of the learned Indians taught the Gospel precepts through the classical languages in a natural way. More importantly, they wanted to combine English education with 'a widely extended and judicious plan' of popular education through the vernaculars, so that the missionaries were connected with the masses.[68]

The vernacular-English divide between Duff and Serampore actually reflected a difference of missionary perception and approach on the Indian society. The Baptists believed that the institution of caste was malleable by the force of Christianity, and an Indian Christian leadership was possible from any caste group, including the lower castes, which had actually been more responsive to the missionary preaching. Duff, on the other hand, noted the hold of the upper castes, led by Brahmins, over Indian society, whose leadership in any Christian conversion movement could not be written off; English education, to which they were already inclined, would, therefore, be the right means for a conversion movement.

Before Duff appeared in the Indian scene, the Serampore Baptists had firmly established themselves, and their experience and views were reckoned with in the missionary circle. Besides theirs, there was another missionary viewpoint that concurred, on the basis of past experience, with Duff's assessment of the Brahminical clout upon the Indian society.[69] But their 'decided opinion' was that there was 'no human possibility of converting the Hindoos (meaning high castes) to any sect of Christianity'.[70] The view of the 'missionary' Bishop Reginald Heber in 1823 that the Brahmins were 'our chief hindrances' re-affirmed it.[71] Moreover, just before Duff's appearance, the development of deistic and atheistic tendencies among the students of the Hindu College, Calcutta (est. 1817),[72] made the missionaries to associate superior English education with 'infidelity'.[73]

Unfazed, Duff embarked upon the task of turning the Brahmin mind to Christianity by replacing the conventional missionary methods, supported by stereotyped vernacular or English elementary schools. The Hindu College episode convinced him of the need of advanced offensive by a rival 'intellectual gymnasium' that would imbue minds with 'the enlightened spirit of modern science', but regulated by the principles of 'true religion and sound morality'.[74] He set out to canvass his idea, visiting 'every missionary and mission station' around Calcutta.[75] The old veterans, sceptical about it, feared that the proposed institution would freshly 'deluge Calcutta with rogues and villains'. An exception was William Carey who gave him 'the most earnest encouragement'.[76] Outside the missionary fraternity, Duff received valuable support from Raja Rammohun Roy, the local reformist leader, who had pleaded the British government for the promotion of Western learning in 1823. By a reconnaissance of the Bengal social situation, Duff discovered that the city of Calcutta, while being the intellectual nerve-centre of India and 'the brain of Hinduism', was rife with 'so general a *laxation* of ancient inveterate prejudices, more especially among the upper classes' than any other city or district.[77] After a quick but scrupulous planning, he launched his Institution there in July 1830.[78] His first test was to counter the Hindu College-bred anti-religion virus. This he did by public lectures 'with pleasing effect', even upon Hindu College students.[79]

While pursuing his college project, Duff adopted a high profile public life. Among others, Bentinck and Charles Trevelyan, a high ranking British official and the leader of the Anglicist movement inside the government, became his personal friends. Already a diehard Anglicist, this propped him up as the leading figure of the movement.[80] Once Anglicism triumphed in 1835, he came out to hail the government resolution as 'the greatest master-stroke of sound policy' and Bentinck personally for his 'moral intrepidity'. To him, it was the victory of 'true literature and true science' over 'false literature, false science, and false religion' of India.[81] By now, by hard work he was able to raise a group of men, who, as a result of new intellectual training, could form independent and rational views on socio-religious matters.[82]

Under Anglicist garb, Duff always coveted his missionary object with the conviction that the 'grand and only adequate remedy for the miseries of India, temporal and spiritual, [was] the Gospel of Salvation', and his whole effort would be 'one focus of concentrated light'.[83] His championing of the English education, and supporting the scheme under the well-known minute of T.B. Macaulay (1835),[84] therefore, could not be 'unreserved' as scholars have viewed.[85] For the missionary cause, he would not spare even the criticism of his Anglicist friends. Aware of Macaulay acceding to the Indian sentiments and promising to 'always abstain from giving any public encouragement' to conversion by missionaries,[86] he pointed out to the government that the projected fall of 'false religion' was not filled by any provision of the 'only true religion – Christianity'.[87] In the line of what Charles Grant (1746-1823), the early British colonial theorist, propounded, Duff cautioned the rulers that to give the people knowledge without religion would be 'the greatest blunder'.[88] He went on to cajole the conscience of the 'Christian government': 'Our maxim has been, is now, and ever will be this: *Wherever, whenever, and by whomsoever Christianity on the altar of worldly expediency, there and then must the supreme good of man lie bleeding at its base.*'[89]

The realpolitik of colonial governance would not allow the government to concede to Duff. But that did not deter Duff to lead a campaign for Christian instruction in the government institutions. Constantly on the lookout for some missionary way, he was pragmatic too. Without waiting for the government heart to change, he deftly found space for the missionary agenda in the existing government policy of religious neutrality. He exhorted his missionary colleagues:

> But if we are wise in time, we may convert the act of the Indian government into an ally and a friend. . . . Whenever a government seminary is founded, which shall have the effect of battering down idolatry and superstition, let us be prepared to plant a Christian institution that shall, through the blessing of heaven, be the instrument of rearing the beauteous superstructure of Christianity on the ruins of both.[90]

Duff had launched his project of General Assembly's Institution against a hostile Indian psyche. The Bible was detested as 'the most infamous of all books . . . *expressly* written by the *Mlech'has*, the "polluted and unclean" . . . for the express purpose of abusing and vilifying the pure and holy religion of Brahma.'[91] To overcome this, he solicited local support and won the confidence of 'a native of rank and influence' in Raja Rammohun Roy. This was a deviation from the Serampore Trio, who did not enlist any such local support. After 'a long pleasing colloquy' with the five boys recommended by Rammohun Roy, Duff attracted, within three days, 80 students from the upper castes.[92] Later, in five years, his impressive pedagogy, starting from the basics to the highest level of intellectual discourse, multiplied the student size to 500.[93] By his intelligent approach, he made Bible studies a distinct feature of the Institution education. Each day's work began with Bible class, which was approvingly witnessed by the students' guardians.[94]

Duff left Calcutta within a decade for health reasons, but was, in a short period, able to demonstrate that his missionary stratagem was workable. The depth of impact of his effort was clear from the conversion of a number of students and especially from the exclamations of the first converts. Mohesh Chunder Ghose, for instance, declared: 'A twelve-month ago I was an atheist, a materialist, a necessitarian; and what am I now? – A baptized Christian. A twelve-month ago I was the most miserable of the miserable, and what am I now? – In my own mind the happiest of the happy!'[95] This and similar other testimonies by Krishna Mohun Banerji, Gopeenath Nundi and Anando Chund Mozoomdar gratified Duff because from such ideal recruits he wanted to have the pillar of the future church.[96] With quality and single missionary end in mind, he spurned the suggestion of friends to open the Institution's replicates elsewhere, and instead wanted just one 'Central Institution', open to all denominations.[97]

Duff returned to India in 1840 for a decade to mentor the Institution he had assiduously built. Even after departure, his heart was moored to the Institution.[98] In the following decades, the legacy of the Institution was clear in the presence of its students in church leadership. Duff's individual charisma had won some 40 converts between 1831 and 1857 at the Institution.[99] The descendants of these converts formed the nucleus of the church management. The Christian Higher Education Commission of 1930 found 'the grandsons and great grandsons' of Duff's 'early Brahman converts' holding key positions.[100]

Trials and Tribulations of the Duff Idea

The thrust of winning converts and raising leadership, endeavoured by Serampore College and Free Church Institution, met with challenge from certain developments after 1850. The government policy and action, while helping in the expansion of Christian higher education, also brought in adversities to the missionaries. The encouragement to English education and material value attached to it suggested students to pursue education with secular features. There was, thus, the danger of the end being superseded by means in the missionary colleges.[101] Even when sections of missionary educators were earnest about religious instruction, their moves were defeated by university regulations.[102] Under pressure from these, the Serampore College, already orphaned by the death of Joshua Marshman, the last of the Trio, in 1837, and not adopted by the Home Committee of the British Baptist mission until 1856, found it tough to cope with.[103] The College was affiliated with the Calcutta University (1857), but with weak English teaching, it closed down, in 1883, its general arts education. This left the college as a mere 'Vernacular Native Christian Training Institute'.[104]

The English mania in higher education, now institutionalized and complicated by a degree culture, did not go down well with the Free Church Institution as well. Neither was Duff's spirited leadership to generate interest in Christianity available, nor was students' interest on Christianity coming spontaneously. In the

Protestant missionary conference at Liverpool in 1860, a colleague of Duff rued that the positive attitude of students on Christianity at high school level evaporated as one of indifference in the college.[105] After the reaping of the first fruits by Duff, conversion in the college campuses had become infrequent. Earlier the missionary educator could afford to concentrate on religious instruction, but now the demand was to equip the students for passing examinations for a degree.[106] This severely encroached upon personal talks of the missionaries with students behind cloisters that used to prepare many for conversion.[107] Worse still, the ambience of social reform worked against the missionary interest. Not only was it infested with reaction against missionaries, there were even efforts by movements like Brahmo Samaj to graft Christian principles and morality on Hinduism.[108]

Against unfriendly atmosphere, the British government's landmark educational policy of 1854 was announced where the policy of promotion of Western knowledge and the system of grants-in-aid were confirmed. The grants-in-aid proviso qualified the missionaries as a beneficiary private agency subject to government inspection. While wanting the missionaries to impart secular education, the government claimed 'entire abstinence from interference with the religious instruction' that the missionaries might conduct in extra hours.[109] The government even promised to transfer the responsibility of running higher education to private agencies as the system of grants-in-aid matured.[110] The missionaries construed these as the right government signal and looked forward for furtherance of the Duff model of Christian college.

But in the meanwhile the Indian Mutiny (1857) broke out. The Mutiny afforded the missionaries an opportunity to reiterate the necessity of Christian teaching of the Indians and impress upon the government for a more prominent role of missionary education. Duff, who was in Calcutta during the Mutiny, wrote graphic details of the sequence of the event and reminded the British government of its 'accountability to the great God for the amazing trust committed to them'. For 'permanent peace', he insisted, 'mere secular education, sharpening the intellect, and leaving the heart a prey to all the foulest passions and most wayward impulses' would not do.[111]

Duff seized it as an opportunity to reiterate the demand of Bible teaching in government institutions, which he had advocated earlier in evidence before the Committee of the House of Lords.[112] The moderate Bishop of Calcutta and Metropolitan of India, George E.L. Cotton, who took over just after the Mutiny, came to support him. Bishop Cotton pointed out that 'the grand defect' of government education was 'the necessary exclusion of all Christian teaching'.[113] Though he conceded that the exclusion was 'unavoidable' in the 'peculiar position' of the British rule, he wanted the gap made up by the teachers' freedom to hold Bible classes beyond class hours. But he regretted 'the needless interference', like one by the government of Bengal in 1862, that banned voluntary Bible classes in the institutional premises.[114]

The government was, in the Despatch of 1854, wary of 'considerable misapprehension' in Indian mind in respect to Christian religious teaching in the government institutions, and had pledged to guard against 'the slightest suspicion' in this regard.[115] The event of the Mutiny rendered the trepidation real. Contemplation on the causes convinced the government of soundness of the stated educational object of 'raising the moral, intellectual, and physical condition' of the Indians.[116] The government, however, was pushed to find ways for easing the heightened Indian distrust. A simplistic way would be to accede to the Indian sentiment. But the government found it 'peculiarly embarrassing' to bring any modification to the existing condition of religious neutrality; the plea was the Queen's post-Mutiny declaration (1858) in that line, but understandably the consideration was to respect the missionary viewpoint.[117] Seemingly settled, the question of government neutrality was at stake again at the forum of the Indian Education Commission (1882), when a demand for equal facility for instruction on all religions in government colleges surfaced. The Commission was unable to recommend any thing, but suggested to make profitable use of the grants-in-aid system to set up appropriate institutions.[118]

Objectively speaking, the *status quo* favoured the missionaries. Yet, given the background of controversy, the limited available scope in the government institutions was least expected to serve the missionary purpose, more so when a strict regime of inspection was now in force.[119] In such circumstances, it was the domain of Christian colleges that promised certainty and better scope, since the government discreetly spared the colleges freedom to teach Christianity. But even this could not escape the cautious eye of the government. The post-Mutiny review discerned a 'jealousy . . . excited by the assistance indirectly extended, through the medium of grants-in-aid, to missionary teaching', and the government wanted to examine the working of the system of grants-in-aid with a view to bring change, if necessary.[120] Alarmed by this, the missionaries were set to defend and expand the Christian college realm.

While hesitating to withdraw from direct management of higher education, the government wanted to convey the impression that the proposition of gradual transfer was not a ploy for evading the state responsibility for higher education.[121] Nonetheless, the wavering in the 1859 review was a bad omen to the missionaries. In the following years, the government faced the Indian criticism of denying avenues of higher education; a leading example of this was the protest of the powerful middle class in Bengal in 1870-1 against the government decision of appropriating funds from higher education for primary education.[122] Such situation left the government vacillating.

The missionaries on their part would not be considerate on the government compulsion. An outcry, led by Bishop Cotton, followed. Explaining the omission of Christian religious element in the system, he referred to the 'footing' prescribed in the Despatch of 1854 and wanted the state 'gradually to retire from the position of actual instructor of the people, and retain only the function of aiding, promoting, inspecting, and rewarding education'.[123] Since then the criticism took the shape of a campaign.[124] The government was blamed for reneging on its promise of withdrawing itself from direct participation in higher education; instead, the government colleges were extended, and the aided Christian colleges discouraged and reduced.[125] The missionaries allayed the fear of Indian reaction against Christian teachings by pointing out that the Christian colleges, where Bible teaching was regular, were more popular than the government colleges.[126] By the time of the Education Commission, the subject of government withdrawal had become most contentious. The indigenous private effort being in its 'infancy', the Commission felt that the time for state withdrawal was 'still distant'; withdrawal would throw the field into the hands of the missionaries.[127] Despite the atmosphere of a general desire for religious instruction, the government could ill-afford to lean to the missionary enterprise so openly.

Advanced Evangelization: Diffusion by Dialogue

While asserting for wider space for Christian higher education, the missionaries pondered over the issue of rising disinterest of students in the Christian colleges. The concern was how to retain college education as subservient to missionary object. The loss of glory of the Duff days was least a consideration for closure of the colleges. The colleges were too institutionalized in the Indian colonial society to be demolished. The question then was how to discover new relevance and effectiveness by new educational method. Retrospection convinced the missionaries that the problem behind youth's disinclination on Christian teachings lay on the receiving 'soil', i.e. the audience, and not on 'the seed of the word'.[128]

Under this conviction, 'on no question were [British] good men's minds more exercised', in the post-Mutiny years, 'than on the subject of Missions and Evangelisation'.[129] In this aura, Bishop Cotton disapproved 'Bazaar preaching' and wanted Bible instruction only by 'strong and well-educated Christian' and in organized manner 'in some quite hall, as St. Paul did in the school of one Tyrannus'.[130] But mere reinvigoration of the Duff method was unlikely to work. Thinking about alternative led some to the idea of missionary higher education acting 'chiefly' as a conduit for 'extensive diffusion of knowledge of the gospel'.[131] Accordingly, the colleges would be, as an exponent of this viewpoint put, the 'chief instrument . . . to convince to the world . . . of sin, of righteousness, and of judgement, and thus to prepare the way for the perfect establishment of the kingdom of heaven upon earth'.[132] Much of the hassles would be avoided by this option, since aided colleges were left a free zone for religious education, even after the Education Commission. The presence of other denominational colleges since the foundation of the Mohammedan Anglo-Oriental College (1875) validated the case of the Christian colleges.

Rethinking led a group in Britain to believe that universities like Oxford and Cambridge were 'providentially fitted to train men who shall interpret the faith of the West to the East'.[133] This gave birth to the Cambridge Mission which headed for Delhi and opened St. Stephen's College (1882) after close survey of the local situation and negotiation with the government over freedom for religious education.[134] The focus now being on dissemination of Christian influence, conversion was a secondary aim. Bishop Alfred Lefroy's words capture the new missionary priority when he wrote to St. Stephen's Principal, S.S. Allnut:

> They (the boys) are, of course, in a very curious kind of position, neither Hindu nor Christian. It is not satisfactory one, and yet I am sure it is by producing such that we are most of all preparing the way for the wide reception of the Faith. There is, at least, a congenial soil being made. . . . At present we lack the quickening fire of the Holy Spirit, or see it only in very rare cases.[135]

Under the idea of Christian higher education for evangelization, the missionaries retained Duff's basic belief in the efficacy of Western education for missionary object. Vernacular schools and vernacular literature were, therefore, tagged to the Western system, and the Orientalist education was conspicuously kept away.[136] Falling in line with the trend, an institution like Wilson College, Bombay (est. 1835), another Scottish missionary venture, which hitherto concentrated on vernacular languages and classical learning, now laid emphasis on English education.

Within the mode of Western education for evangelization, missionary educators adopted different ways. Of the two distinct experiments, one was conducted by the Roman Catholics, represented by the Belgian Jesuits of the Bengal Mission and led by Eugene Lafont, at St. Xavier's College, Calcutta since 1867. To the Roman Catholics, who entered the field slowly, college was primarily meant for 'the education of the Catholic students, the remote preparation of a Catholic priesthood and formation of a Catholic elite', in other words, training the community and community leaders.[137] The 'first' Catholic college at Nagapatnam was exclusively for the Catholics. Even St. Xavier's Calcutta, at its opening in 1862, was meant for the Catholic youth.[138]

In fact, 'for 25 years no strenuous efforts' were made by St. Xavier's to attract non-Catholics.[139] The idea of *preparatio evangelica* evolved gradually, paving the way for the non-Christians' admission. To begin with, the college admitted Protestants, Jews and Armenians.[140] Lafont played a major role in the change of the Catholic attitude with the instrument of science education. At a time when, in the name of Western education, only the subjects of English literature, history, philosophy and law thrived in various government and missionary colleges, he pushed for science education, initiated by John Mack at Serampore College, as a subtle method of evangelization.[141] His focus was on advanced physical science, the progress of which was reported by St. Xavier's:

> This subject has, for some time, already attracted the attention of the public. . . . Three times a week lectures on this attractive and useful science are delivered to all the students of the College Department by the Rev. Fr. Lafont. The lectures illustrated with experiments form a complete course quite distinct from, though parallel to, the mathematical study of the subjects required by the University Examinations.[142]

Soon, as Lafont's initiative elicited 'praiseworthy thirst for knowledge' in the city of Calcutta, evening public lectures were started.[143]

Lafont's passionate pursuit of Western science education produced a 'science movement' in India that seemingly overshadowed the Jesuit evangelization object.[144] Lafont himself was reticent, speaking rarely and only to close colleagues, on the relationship of his science effort with the missionary object. Whatever little he spoke reveals his belief that scientific knowledge and Gospel teachings went hand in hand:

> What barometer, thermometers, etc. are to science, the crucifix, reredos, stoles etc. are to religion; these testify to the existence of religious feelings, those stand witness to really scientific investigations. A man, who laughs at both, betrays an ignorance in religion and science . . . our barometers are suggestive to meteorologists of truths as plain and positive as those that are to a Christian by a mere glace at the crucifix.[145]

Lafont opened his missionary mind in his response to fellow-missionaries' compliments for various honours he received. He wittily stated that what he was doing at Calcutta was actually meant for tribal Chhotanagpur, where, since 1885, the Belgian Jesuits had begun a massive conversion movement.[146] Lafont though did not qualify how. His science preoccupation never spared him to go to the conversion field, nor was he fit to be a countryside preacher to a tribal audience. But the statement indicated his ardent missionary mind. He not only believed in silent evangelization among the upper classes, but wanted the evangelized Indian mind to proxy a mass conversion movement.[147] The object seemed to be working. St. Xavier's Jesuits reported in 1872 with a sense of fulfilment that the Calcutta intelligentsia especially wanted the 'self-denying' Catholic missionaries to work among the 'poorer classes' of Calcutta.[148]

During the same period as Lafont's, William Miller from Duff's mission, spectacularly demonstrated the potency of higher

English literature for evangelization at the Madras Christian College. Like Lafont, Miller was a talented and committed teacher, and also an avowed evangelist. But unlike Lafont, he expressed his evangelization idea freely ever since he enunciated it at the General Missionary Conference, Allahabad in 1872. Miller wanted 'the light of Christ reflected from poetry, the philosophy and the history of church land'.[149] Especially in the missionary educational growth of south India, he discerned 'boundless opportunity' for evangelization works.[150] Reading a right climate, he raised the college, in 1865, from the erstwhile General Assembly's English school, started by John Anderson three decades ago,[151] and shaped it single-handedly as an efficient 'central' institution of a number of Protestant missions. The most important of all subjects of college study, according to him, was the Scriptures, especially the words of Christ; the Scriptures were the 'spearhead', to which all other knowledge were just a 'well-fitted handle'.[152] This he practised in his brilliant lectures in and outside the college classes.

From his college-mediated evangelization task, Miller obtained very few converts. His priority was the 'great preparatory work' for Christian India. Here he differed with his own colleagues in the Free Church of Scotland, who took it as too idealistic and deviating from the Duff approach. Miller also differed with other fellow-missionaries, who wanted the college to convert and produce Christian leaders.[153] Direct conversion was, to Miller, only a 'side product' to preparatory evangelization, whereas training of Christian leadership a 'secondary' function. In the existing obsession of the Indians for higher English education, he apprehended that the dream of conversion and the rise of local church leadership would go astray and the church would rather turn into 'a guild for the worldly welfare of its sons'.[154] The best way to avert this and make English education expedient for missionary object was, he suggested, advanced input of Christian ideas and principles and make it incisive by efficient teaching.

At the turn of the nineteenth century, the Calcutta Jesuits' earnestness and zeal for science education co-terminated with Lafont's demise (1907). The show of the magic of scientific knowledge was subsequently stolen by his students and colleagues outside St. Xavier's,[155] and the college was left to continue as a general Christian institution of Western higher education. The same year Miller departed from India due to ill-health. But the ideals of evangelization by advanced Western education that they exemplified were emulated by many missionary educators in a string of Christian Colleges across the country. The Indian middle-class audience, drawn from the upper castes, was comfortable with it, since evangelization essentially meant just an intellectual appeal for considering Christian teachings. To many Indians, individual missionaries were great teachers and missionary colleges the best embodiment of Western education.

Nationalistic Questions and Missionary Answers

As advanced Western education and Christian teaching combine appeared settled in the missionary colleges, a slew of developments afforded by nationalistic upsurge unsettled the college-mediated concept of evangelization mission. From the late nineteenth century, the social reform movement was steadily sheltered by Indian nationalism. The convergence gave rise to educational movements like Dayanand Anglo-Vedic College and the Deccan Education Society. The movements founded a number of Western-type colleges, which, while claiming to be national, were modelled on the Christian colleges in terms of quality and efficiency.[156] The Deccan Education Society members, for instance, were awed by Jesuit professionalism and called themselves 'Indian Jesuits'.[157] Besides, there were movements for individual denominational colleges like the Mohammedan Anglo-Oriental College, Aligarh and the Central Hindu College, Benares (est. 1898).[158] There were even individual efforts, for instance, by the nationalist S.N. Banerjee who founded the Ripon College, Calcutta (1882) and by some philanthropists in Delhi who started the Hindu College (1898). Many of these were inspired by, what J.N. Farquhar termed, 'counter-reformation', i.e. opposition to missionary teachings accompanied with alternative Hindu preaching.[159] The movements, thus, depicted 'deliberate attempts' of using the missionary models to contest the missionary upper hand.[160]

The foundation of the structure of missionary higher education was too strong to be dislocated by competition from new Indian institutions. There were hardly any deserters from the missionary colleges. The colleges rather continued to attract the Indian middle class as earlier. In this respect, the missionaries especially noted a case of Madras where a rival institution opened by funds from a

Brahmin to supplant a successful missionary school actually turned to supply 'the large proportion of the students' to the Madras Christian College.[161] Notwithstanding that, the message was clear that imparting quality English education outside the government agency was no longer the monopoly of the Christian missionaries.[162] Overwhelming response of the Indians to the Education Commission with numerous petitions and depositions, manifested that subject of education was their special interest. Under the Swadeshi Movement in Bengal (1906), the interest changed into the slogan of education 'on National lines and exclusively under National control', concerning especially higher education.[163]

The nationalistic developments of the time brought in a bogey of another challenge to the missionaries. The wave of concern for the lower classes raised by the social reform organizations, especially the Arya Samaj and Satyashodhak Samaj, reached the shores of Indian National Congress. An intra Congress forum called 'Social Conference' regularly discussed the problems of the 'depressed classes'.[164] This way the conscience of the missionaries was stirred, since there existed in the church courtyard a large mass of lower class Christians, as backward and uneducated as any other lower class. Their presence flashed the dark side of the Christian colleges. A stark truth was that while the upper class, including the upper class Christians, were given the boon of English education, the lower classes were untouched by this. This was what the infamous feature of the colonial system of government education was.[165]

The first response of the missionaries to these developments was to shed the ingrained stigma of foreignness and colonial connection. In 1894, a leading local Christian opened the issue in a broad manner when he suggested Indianization of Christianity.[166] The thinking materialized in the formation of the National Missionary Society of India (1905) with the motto, 'Indian men, Indian money and Indian management'.[167] The adherents were asked to abjure identification of the profession of Christianity with the English nation.[168] The idea reached the World Missionary Conference, 1910 at Edinburgh which, in deference to general missionary opinion, endorsed the proposition of 'national' churches in the colonial countries. As a follow-up, a 'Continuation Committee' was instituted in India to work out the modality and the National Missionary Council (1914) came into being, which finally changed into the National Christian Council (1923). Along side nationalistic face-lifting, there was marked change in the missionary outlook on Hinduism. Earlier the missionaries indulged in denouncing Hinduism on the basis of certain elementary knowledge on it. Such 'ignorance and mistakes' would, it was now realized, yield 'harmful results' than doing any good.[169] The new attitude, therefore, was sympathetic understanding of Hinduism.

In their assessment of Indian nationalism, the missionaries perceived not just one national movement of India, but 'many movements', of which many were 'by no means accordant'; the mainstream movement was fraught with 'eddies and backwaters'.[170] One such strand was Muslim minority politics in the beginning of the twentieth century. A psychology of fear from the majority Hindus inspired the Muslims to seek special safeguards for the community. This led to the formation of the Indian Muslim League (1906) and subsequently the first political extraction of the provision of separate Muslim representation in the legislature from the government (1909). The development impinged upon the missionaries a minority syndrome. Thus, they discovered, behind the screen of Extremist Congress, a resurgent Hinduism and feared the face of an 'old enemy'.[171] The Arya Samaj programme of *shuddhi*, aiming to reconvert the Christian converts to Hinduism, and 'conscience clause' attached to the government grant to missionary institutions were perceived as the stretched arm of dominant Hinduism. The 'clause', a nineteenth-century legacy that provided freedom to unwilling non-Christian students of missionary institutions to avoid Bible classes as a condition for government grant, suddenly became a subject of debate since 1915. There was, thus, a rising sense of insecurity among the missionaries.[172]

Under hue and cry over these, many missionaries were actually sure that neither *shuddhi* nor conscience clause was, in substance, any threat to the missionary interests.[173] The sense of insecurity, however, underscored the need for building a compact Christian community which broached the backward condition of the lower class Christians. Abysmal plight of these Christians stimulated a missionary humanitarian concern leading to an internal movement for their cause, spearheaded by some key church functionaries like Henry Whitehead, the Bishop of Madras. Hitherto a dominant missionary view assigned low spiritual value to these Christians, since they were obtained from the spurt of 'mass movement' to Christianity, driven chiefly by secular impulses. The protagonists of the lower class Christians contested this: 'Ought we to devote the whole of our strength to those we can reach, or to those Brahmins who steal their hearts against Christianity? . . . we have not done anything like what we ought to have done for the lower classes.'[174] The advocates argued for separate treatment of these classes – the lower castes, outcastes and tribes – since they were 'very slightly influenced by Hinduism'.[175]

The pro-lower class Christian stance was upheld by the Edinburgh Conference. The Conference took mass conversion with secular motive as a step towards actual spiritual transformation of individuals and urged for a cohesive 'strong Christian community'. One way of community building was 'development in numbers', perhaps directed by the realization that the number of registered bold believers mattered more than the intangible Christian-minded ranks that the college evangelization mission stood for. The other was 'development in intellectual power – the elevation of the community, morally and religiously, individually and socially'.[176] This suggested making up the arrears of action in respect to the status of the lower class converts.[177] Discussions fructified a project of 'rural reconstruction' under the stewardship of K.T. Paul, an Indian Christian.[178] Adjunct to it, the urgency of schooling of these masses was realized and a Village Education Commission (1919) was instituted. The recommendations of Commission, after wide discussion, resulted in a scheme of 'community middle schools'.[179] The atmosphere of awareness on lower class Christian issue gripped even the Roman Catholic church, and the cases of initiative of developmental cooperative and school projects were evident in its mass movement regions.[180]

Meanwhile, with 'mass movement' now accepted as an alternative missionary mode, the humanitarian missionaries wanted the lower class Christians to form the core of the Indian church. Bishop Whitehead advocated this in 1907:

> . . . that instead of looking forward to the spread of Christianity first among the higher castes and then to the conversion of the masses through their agency, we ought to look forward to the foundation of the church among the poor and the outcastes in the village districts and direct our energies mainly to that end.[181]

In Whitehead's estimation, the Christian colleges were, in the then circumstances, 'less and less possible means' of Christian influence.[182] The view, a clear rebuttal of the Miller model, reached the Edinburgh Conference. A critic there suggested that the prime duty of missionary education was 'not the leavening of non-Christian population but the development of the latent energies and possibilities of the Christian church itself'.[183] Such shift was seen among the Roman Catholics as well. In their questioning, the Catholics found the college impact on non-Christians negligible; the high schools rather offered 'more promising ground' for the missionary purpose.[184]

The Christian college-mediated evangelization mission looked poised for condemnation to disuse and its substitution by mass conversion approach. But the Indian nationalism that bought this wind of change also imposed other exigencies upon the quasi-national church. If the church were to survive the storm of Indian nationalism, it was imperative that the community members took active part in the national life. A view in this connection was:

> Christians, because they are Christians, ought to be a power in the land, and in all matters affecting the moral, and even physical, well-being, prove the sagest counsellors and the bravest workers. . . . Just as in England we desire to see many strong Christian men as Members of Parliament, and in other public positions, and to find every man faithful to his duty towards the state, so it is most desirable that the Indian Christians should rise to their responsibilities, and become as *light*, and *salt,* and *leaven* in the national life.[185]

A recast of the missionary idea, this stipulated more active and persuasive missionary role. The Christian college educators were, accordingly, not only to train Christian men, but also orient the Indian intelligentsia in Christian principles and morals. They had to be an agent of close interaction between Christian and non-Christian students in the college.

The Continuation Committee of the Edinburgh Conference sought to harmonize the viewpoints of evangelization and mass conversion. The Committee accepted the 'heavy responsibilities' of educating the depressed class Christians and adopted a new evangelization agenda for a 'profound Christian impression rather than a diffused Christian influence'.[186] The composite aims of missionary schools and colleges, outlined by the Committee, were the following: 'a) The upbuilding of the Church through the training of children and youth of the Christian community; b) the conversion of individual students; c) the diffusion of Christian ideas as a preparation for the large influx of converts, which we believe is coming into the Christian church.'[187]

Under the coalescence, the emphasis was on 'the fullest Christian efficiency' of the Christian education. For this, the Committee wanted 'more carefully revised and graded system of Bible teaching', and large increase of the Christian college teachers with 'more thorough religious and Biblical training'; this would free the teachers from the over-burden of teaching duties and allow them to maintain close contact with their present and past students.[188]

Conclusion

Christianity, organically a missionary religion, was injected with fresh missionary ingredients in the modern West. Under the revived missionary spirit, the Western missionaries made profuse use of the means of education. In the century-long rather random survey of the missionary agenda of Christian higher education in India, the essay has shown multifarious employment of this means. The early two experiments by the Serampore Baptist Trio and Alexander Duff, thus, differed strikingly from each other in terms of approach and mode. The Serampore Trio's priority was to win large groups of converts and raise local missionary helpers in a sprawling area by the method of Oriental and vernacular education. Duff's strategy, on the other hand, was to recruit select converts through Western education and train future church leaders. Irrespective of difference, both were conduit of an arrogant missionary idea, operating in the nature of a monologue upon the Indian society. The characteristic colonial cultural milieu of the early nineteenth century let this work almost unchallenged.

After 1850, the pompous missionary character of the Christian colleges was restrained by the excess Indian taste for secular English education. Simultaneously, the missionary idea was interrogated by Indian social reform movement and later by Indian nationalism. This afforded close interaction between the missionary idea and the Indian reformist ideas. Since the turn of the nineteenth century, when the reformist ideas were harboured by Indian nationalism, the intensity of interaction made the missionary colleges cultural interlocutors. As a result, especially on Hinduism, some of the best missionary writings appeared during this phase. A notable feature of the dialogue that took place was intense quizzing of the missionary idea by the nationalist forces and equal dynamism of the missionary idea.

The nascent national church always wanted to retain elements of the ingrained missionary idea in the Christian colleges, which was curiously facilitated by shaping denominationalism under the democratic secular ethos of India. Thus, as the Indian Independence became imminent, in 1930, the Commission on Christian Higher Education in India was concerned with 'the value of the mission college as a missionary method', and 'a higher standard of education and missionary efficiency'.[189] The same year, the Jesuit educators, in a meeting at Madras, recalled 'promotion of the religion of Christ' as 'the sole reason' of their coming to India, and asked themselves whether the Jesuit colleges served the purpose 'in a manner proportionate to the number of men and means employed'.[190]

Reservation of the nationalists, led by Mahatma Gandhi, on traditional missionary character of the Indian church precluded any rehabilitation of the earlier missionary arrogance. The missionary method of Christian influence by dialogue, practised by Christian colleges, this way gained more importance. The dialogic verve of the colleges also salvaged the missionary educators from becoming 'additional [teaching] members of the Indian Educational Service' under the nationalist impact.[191] Today, Christian colleges, a craze of the Indian middle class, maintain traces of the missionary idea. Various college prospectuses commonly state inculcation of Christian values as the primary object of the colleges, which is acceptable with least rancour to the Indian society.

NOTES

1. World Missionary Conference, 1910, *Report of Commission III: Education in Relation to the Christianization of National Life*, Edinburgh: Oliphant, Anderson & Ferrier, 1910, Chapter II, p. 16.
2. The initiative began from the East India Company Charter Act, 1813 and took the form of government aid to missionaries and other private agencies. This was formalized and widened by the well-known Educational Despatch of 1854.
3. M. Mohur Ali, *Bengal Reaction to Christian Missionary Activities 1837-57*, Chittagong: Mehrub Publications, 1965, p. 68.
4. A.D. Lindsay, *Report of the Commission on Christian Higher Education in India*, London: Oxford University Press, 1931, p. 65. Some of the famous institutions that came into being during this period were: St.

Xavier's, Calcutta (1862, Jesuits), Madras Christian College (1862, Scottish mission), Forman College, Lahore (1864, American Presbyterians), St. Xavier's, Bombay (1869), St. Aloysius, Mangalore (1880, Jesuits), St. Stephen's, Delhi (1881, Cambridge University Mission), Hislop College, Nagpur (1883, Scottish mission), Isabella Thoburn, Lucknow (1886, Methodist mission) and Ewing Christian College, Allahabad (1902, Presbyterian).

5. Dickinson mentions the presence of 130 Christian colleges in 1966, which was less than 5 per cent of the total number of colleges in India. But they taught one-tenth of the number of students in higher education in the country. Richard D.N. Dickinson, *The Christian College in Developing India: A Sociological Inquiry*, London: Oxford University Press, 1971, p. 69.
6. Against growing nationalism, a wider response came in the Commission on Christian Higher Education in India (1930), popularly known as Lindsay Commission after its chairman. Lindsay, *Report of the Commission on Christian Higher Education in India*.
7. Alexander Duff, *India and India Missions*, Edinburgh: Johnstone Hunter Square, 1839, p. 551.
8. K. Ingham, *Reformers in India*, Cambridge: Cambridge University Press, 1956.
9. George Smith, *The Life of William Carey D.D.: Shoemaker and Missionary*, London: John Murray, 1885, p. 380.
10. Eric Stokes, *The English Utilitarians and India*, New Delhi: Oxford University Press, Indian edition, 1982.
11. Hugh Tinker, *An Ordeal of Love: C.F. Andrews and India*, New Delhi: Oxford University Press, 1979, p. 39; E.P. Thompson, *'Alien Homage': E.J. Thompson and Rabindranath Tagore*, New Delhi: Oxford University Press, 1993, p. 10.
12. The standard missionary attitude was: '[F]urther the Government goes in any country in supplying education, the more decisively must it be the policy of missionary bodies to concentrate their effort, especially in secondary and higher education, on certain centres where first-rate education on a Christian basis, and under Christian influences, can be supplied.' World Missionary Conference, 1910, *Report of Commission III*, p. 8.
13. The missionaries resented a 'growing tendency to discourage, if not destroy, the aided [missionary institution] as rival to those of Government' under the provisions of the Despatch. James Johnston, *Our Educational Policy in India*, Edinburgh: John Maclaren & Son, 1880, p. 50.
14. Quoted in Udayan Namboodiry, *St. Xavier's: The Making of a Calcutta Institution*, New Delhi: Viking, 1995, p. 27.

15. Hayden J.A. Bellenoit, *Missionary Education and Empire in Late Colonial India,* London: Pickering & Chatto, 2007.
16. For the notion of denominational universities see S.C. Ghosh, ed., *Development of University Education in India 1916-1920*, New Delhi: Jawaharlal Nehru University, 1977, introduction.
17. See Reah Renold, *A Hindu Education: Early Years of Banaras Hindu University*, New Delhi: Oxford University Press, 2005; Mohammad Talib, 'Jamia Millia Islamia: Career of Azad Talim', and Mushirul Hasan, 'Negotiating with its Past and Present: The Changing Profile of the Aligarh Muslim University', both in Mushirul Hasan, ed., *Knowledge, Power & Politics: Educational Institutions in India*, New Delhi: Lotus Collection, 1998.
18. Gerald Studdart-Kennedy, *Providence and the Raj: Imperial Mission and Missionary Imperialism*, New Delhi: Sage, 1998.
19. A. Mathew, *Christian Mission Education and Nationalism: From Dominance to Compromise*, Delhi: Anamika Prakashan, 1988.
20. Sujit Sivasundaram, 'A Christian Benares', p. 140; M.A. Laird, 'The Contribution of the Serampore Missionaries to Education in Bengal, 1793-1837', *Bulletin of the School of Oriental and African Studies*, vol. 31, no. 1, 1968, p. 112.
21. D.H. Emmott, 'Alexander Duff and the Foundation Modern Education in India', *British Journal of Educational Studies*, vol. 13, no. 2, May 1965.
22. David Baker, 'St. Stephen's College, Delhi, 1881-1997: An "Alexandria on the Banks of the Jamuna"?', in Hasan, *Knowledge, Power & Politics.*
23. The article is concerned mainly with the Protestant groups, though also refers to the Roman Catholic missionary efforts occasionally.
24. S. Pearce Carey, *William Carey DD, Fellow of Linnaen Society*, London: Hodder and Stoughton, 1924, 3rd edn., pp. 205-6.
25. Brijraj Singh, *The First Protestant Missionary to India: Bartholomaeus Ziegenbalg (1683-1719)*, New Delhi: Oxford University Press, 1999, chapter V: Ziegenbalg, Educator.
26. Carey, *William Carey DD*, p. 210.
27. Smith, *The Life of William Carey*, pp. 408-9.
28. 'East India Company Act of 1813, Section 43', H. Sharp, ed., *Selections from Educational Records, Part I, 1781-1839*, Delhi: National Archives of India, 1965, rpt., p. 22.
29. Smith, *The Life of William Carey*, p. 378.
30. The system made use of the senior students or monitors to instruct junior boys. It was devised in India by Andrew Bell, a chaplain at Madras in the late eighteenth century, and, simultaneously, in Britain by Joseph Lancaster. On Serampore missionaries' request, Lancaster sent to them James Penny, an experienced hand. See detail on the experiment in Jana Tschurenev, 'Diffusing Useful Knowledge in

Madras, London and Bengal, 1789-1840', *Pedagogica Historica*, vol. 44, no. 3, June 2008, pp. 245-64.

31. Laird, 'The Contribution of the Serampore Missionaries to Education in Bengal, 1793-1837', pp. 99-100.
32. Ibid., p. 98.
33. Smith, *The Life of William Carey*, p. 378.
34. George Howells and A.C. Underwood, *The Story of Serampore and its College*, Serampore and Calcutta: Baptist Mission Press, 1918, p. 23.
35. *College for the Instruction of Asiatic Christian and Other Youth, on Eastern Literature and Science at Serampore, Bengal*, London: Black, Kingbury, Parbury, and Allen, 1819. Though a joint effort, the details were drawn out by Joshua Marshman, who only had the experience of higher education in Britain.
36. Ibid., pp. 25-7. The Danish King, besides granting funds, accorded approval by a Royal Charter in 1827. In 1845 when Serampore was transferred to the British government, the Royal Charter was not interfered with; see Government of West Bengal, Legislative Department, *Bengal Act IV of 1918: The Serampore College Act, 1918*, Alipore: Government Printing, West Bengal Government Press, 1951, p. 1.
37. Ibid., pp. 13-14. To start with, this was broadly implemented by admitting nineteen Christian and eighteen Hindu students. Smith, *The Life of William Carey*, p. 384.
38. *College for the Instruction of Asiatic Christians and Other Youth*, p. 23.
39. Ibid., pp. 22-3.
40. Ibid., p. 22.
41. Ibid., pp. 11-12.
42. Ibid., p. 1.
43. Ibid., p. 21.
44. Ibid. The last phrase is quoted from J.C. Marshman, *Life and Times of Carey, Marshman and Ward*, vol. II, London: Longman, Brown, Green, Longman, & Roberts, 1859, p. 168. Young Marshman, son of Joshua Marshman, was Recording Secretary and Examiner of the college on its beginning, and, later, a core member of the management.
45. 'To all those who encourage the Translations of the Sacred Scriptures into the Languages of Eastern Asia', *College for the Instruction of Asiatic Christian and Other Youth*, pp. 28-33, esp. pp. 19-20.
46. The Government of West Bengal, *Bengal Act IV of 1918: The Serampore College Act, 1918*, Schedule I: 'Charter of Incorporation of the Serampore College', dated 23 February 1827, p. 6.
47. Letter dated 15 November 1827 from William Carey and J.C. Marshman to the Home Committee, Baptist Missionary Society, reproduced in Smith, *The Life of William Carey*, p. 395.
48. Ibid., p. 397.

49. Ibid., p. 396.
50. *College for the Instruction of Asiatic and Other Youth*, pp. 5-6 (emphasis original).
51. Ibid., p. 10.
52. Ibid., pp. 11, 14.
53. Bishop's College, established in 1820, primarily trained converts as preachers, catechists and school teachers, and instructed few others on little English knowledge.
54. Smith, *The Life of William Carey*, p. 409.
55. *College for the Instruction of Asiatic Christian and Other Youth*, p. 20.
56. Ibid., pp. 3-7.
57. Letter dated 23 September 1835 from J.C. Marshman to Scottish missionary, John Wilson of Bombay, quoted in Henry Huizinga, *Missionary Education in India*, Ongole: Author, p. 12.
58. *College for the Instruction of Asiatic Christian and Other Youth*, p. 20.
59. Marshman, *The Life and Times of Carey, Marshman, and Ward*, vol. II, pp. 174-5.
60. H.V. Hampton, *Biographical Studies in Modern Indian Education*, Madras: Oxford University Press, 1947, p. 85.
61. Earlier, in 1824, a Scottish college was conceived, but the plan, chiefly a product of 'sectarian hostility' to the Bishop College, was still-born; ibid., pp. 85, 87.
62. Duff wrote in the early 1830s: 'As a native of the Highlands I vividly realized the fact that the Gaelic language, though powerful for lyric and other poetry and also for popular address, contained no works that could possibly meet the objects of a higher and comprehensive education'; quoted in George Smith, *The Life of Alexander Duff, D.D., LL.D.*, vol. I, New York: A.C. Armstrong & Son, 1879, p. 189.
63. Quoted in C.E. Trevelyan, *On the Education of the People of India*, London: Longman, 1838, Appendix, pp. 218-19.
64. Smith, *The Life of Alexander Duff*, vol. I, p. 110 (emphasis original).
65. Another young Scot, John Leechman joined the college in 1832.
66. Laird, 'The Contribution of the Serampore Missionaries to Education in Bengal, 1793-1837', pp. 107-8.
67. Ibid., p. 108; Sivasundaram, 'A Christian Benares', pp. 135-6.
68. Ibid., p. 107.
69. The examples cited were of the problems faced by Jesuits, led first by Francis Xavier and later by Roberto de Nobili, and the Moravians of the Lutheran fold from sixteenth century onwards. See Abbe J.A. Dubois, *Letters on the State of Christianity in India*, ed. Sharda Paul, New Delhi: Associated Publishing House, 1985, rpt., Letter I (7 August 1815), pp. 1-27; I.G. Zupanov, *Disputed Mission: Jesuit Experiments and Brahmanical Knowledge in Seventeenth-century India*, New Delhi: Oxford University Press, 1999.

70. Dubois, *Letters on the State of Christianity in India*, p. 1.
71. See letter dated 16 December 1823 from Heber to the Dean of St. Asaph, Fort William, in Reginald Heber, *Narrative from a Journey through the Upper Provinces of India*, vol. III, Delhi: B.R. Publishing Corporation, 1985, rpt., p. 19.
72. The most radical upsurge began in 1829 with the beginning of professorship of a young Eurasian, Henry Derozio, that led to the formation of a group called Young Bengal.
73. Duff, *India and India Missions*, p. 545.
74. Ibid., p. 546.
75. Smith, *The Life of Alexander Duff*, vol. I, p. 104.
76. Hampton, *Biographical Studies in Modern Indian Education*, p. 86; Smith, *The Life of William Carey*, p. 421.
77. Duff, *India and India Missions*, p. 529 (italics original).
78. The General Assembly's Institution became Free Church Institution or simply Duff College since 1843 when the Scottish church was divided. The details on its rise and development are available in Duff, *India and India Missions*, pp. 530 50; and Harashanker Dutt, 'On the Rise, Progress and Objects of the Free Church Institution in Calcutta', in *Transactions of the Proceedings of the Bethune Society*, Calcutta: Bethune Society, 1870.
79. Duff's letter dated 9 January 1832 to Rev. Ferrie, extracted in Smith, *The Life of Alexander Duff*, vol. I, p. 173.
80. Trevelyan acknowledged his leadership: 'The example of his success and the stimulus given by him to the popular demand for English education entered largely into the causes which brought about the Resolution of the government of the seventh of March, 1835'; Even Bentinck, who, as head of the government, hitherto reserved his appreciation of Duff's 'such unparalleled success' could not resist letting it out of the bag on his demitting Governor Generalship. Smith, *The Life of Alexander Duff*, vol. I, pp. 31, 195-6. Even later, some see Duff, along with J.C. Marshman, putting words in the mouth of Charles Wood, the architect of the Court of Director's well-known Educational Despatch of 1854 that recognized the role of the missionaries in Indian education. Smith, *The Life of Alexander Duff*, vol. II, Toronto: William Briggs, 1882, p. 245. Later, because of all these, it was all in fitness of things that Charles Trevelyan, on being offered the first Vice-Chancellorship of the Calcutta University (1859), gestured to vacate the honour in favour of Duff. D.H. Emmott, 'Alexander Duff and the Foundation of Modern Education in India', *British Journal of Educational Studies*, vol. 13, no. 2, May 1965, p. 167.
81. Duff's pamphlet 'New Era of the English Language and English Literature in India' (1836), extracted in Smith, *The Life of Alexander Duff*, vol. I, pp. 200-1.

82. For instance, when the founding of the Calcutta Medical College was bogged down by a contention that Hindu scriptures disallowed touching of a dead body, his students rescued the government by testifying against it; Emmott, 'Alexander Duff and the Foundation of Modern Education in India', p. 163.
83. Duff, *India and India Missions*, pp. 390-1.
84. Macaulay wrote the minute as Law Member and in charge of education in the Governor-General's Council. The minute was the background note to Bentinck's resolution.
85. Laird, 'The Contribution of the Serampore Missionaries to Education in Bengal, 1793-1837', p. 108.
86. 'Minute by the Hon'ble T.B. Macaulay, dated the 2nd February 1835', in H. Sharp, ed. *Selections from Educational Records*, pt. I, *1781-1839*, Delhi: National Archives of India, 1965, rpt., p. 115.
87. Duff's pamphlet 'New Era of the English Language and English Literature in India' (1836), extracted in Smith, *The Life of Alexander Duff*, vol. I, p. 201.
88. Hampton, *Biographical Studies in Modern Indian Education*, p. 111.
89. Duff's pamphlet 'New Era of the English Language and English Literature in India' (1836), pp. 201-2 (emphasis original).
90. Ibid., p. 202.
91.. Duff, *India and India Missions*, p. 558.
92. Ibid., p. 549. Rammohun Roy also secured Duff the premise for the Institution, and explained the students, at the Institution's inauguration, its object and encouraged them to study the New Testament there.
93. Emmott, 'Alexander Duff and the Foundation of Modern Education in India', p. 162.
94. Duff, *India and India Missions*, pp. 561-6.
95. Extracted in Smith, *The Life of Alexander Duff*, vol. I, p. 159.
96. Duff's letter dated 9 January 1832 to Rev. Ferrie, extracted in ibid., p. 175.
97. Ibid., pp. 173-4.
98. In a letter dated 2 April 1853 to his former students and teacher colleagues, he wrote: 'Oh no! though separated from you in body I am constantly with you in spirit; in the Institution and among your classes. If I am remaining in this country longer than I had expected, it is only for the sake of India's welfare', extracted in Smith, *The Life of Alexander Duff*, vol. II, p. 233.
99. M. Vermeire, 'Anent the Lindsay Commission' (undated, mimeo.), p. 1, Vermeire Papers: Education File, Jesuit Archives, Ranchi.
100. Lindsay, *Report of the Commission on Christian Higher Education in India*, p. 61.

101. 'Dr. Miller's view of the function of the colleges', Lindsay, *Report of the Commission on Christian Higher Education in India*, p. 22.
102. So disgusted were they that they drifted to think of an 'independent Christian University' by the time of the Commission on Christian Higher Education. Ibid., p. 16.
103. In 1837, the Bengal Baptist mission was owned by the Home Committee after longstanding dispute with the Trio, but the college was left out; Howells and Underwood, *The Story of Serampore and its College*, p. 29.
104. Ibid., pp. 33-4. Discontinuing arts education meant disaffiliation from Calcutta University, which was restored in 1911 with the re-starting of it.
105. Statement of Rev. Thomas Gardiner, *Conference of Missions Held in 1860*, London: James Nisbet & Co., 1860, p. 145.
106. Ibid., p. 146.
107. The report of the deputation of the Free Church of Scotland, 1889-90, summed up in Lindsay, *Report of the Commission on Christian Higher Education in India*, p. 23.
108. J.N. Farquhar, *Modern Religious Movements in India*, New Delhi: Munshiram Manoharlal, 1977, rpt.; Mohar Ali, *Bengal Reaction to Christian Missionaries 1837-57*, p. 24.
109. 'Despatch of 1854', J.A. Richey, ed., *Selections from Educational Records,* pt. II, *1840-1859*, New Delhi: National Archives of India, pp. 378-9.
110. Ibid., p. 381.
111. Alexander Duff, *The Indian Mutiny: Its Causes and Results*, New York: Robert Carter & Brothers, 1858, p. 109.
112. Letter dated 28 April 1858 from A. Duff to Mr. Young, Director, Public Instruction, Bengal, in Richey, *Selections from Educational Records*, pt. II, p. 142.
113. Mrs. Cotton, ed., *Memoirs of George Edward Lynch Cotton, D.D., Bishop of Calcutta, and Metropolitan: With Selections from his Journals and Correspondence*, London: Longmans, Green, and Co., 1871, p. 391.
114. Ibid., pp. 392-3
115. 'Despatch of 1854', Richey, *Selections from Educational Records*, pt. II, pp. 388-9.
116. 'Despatch of 1859', ibid., p. 450.
117. Ibid., p. 448.
118. Education Commission, *Report of the Indian Education Commission, 1882*, Calcutta: Superintendent of Government Printing, 1883, pp. 295-6.
119. Ibid., pp. 441-2.

120. Ibid., p. 447.
121. 'Despatch of 1854', p. 381.
122. Archana Mandal, 'The Ideology and the Interests of the Bengali Intelligentsia: Sir George Campbell's Education Policy 1871-74', *Indian Economic and Social History Review*, January-March 1975.
123. Cotton, *Memoir of George E.L. Cotton*, p. 392.
124. The issues of the *Church Missionary Intelligencer*, vols. IX (1858), XII (1861), and XIII (1862) are some of the representative writings in this respect.
125. Johnston, *Our Educational Policies in India*, pp. iv-v.
126. J. Johnston, *'Abolition' or 'Transference' of Government Colleges and High Schools in India, as Required by the Despatch of 1854, Illustrated by the State of Education in Madras*, London, 1880, p. 4.
127. *Report of the Indian Education Commission, 1882*, p. 452.
128. The report of the deputation of the Free Church of Scotland, 1889-90, summed up in Lindsay, *Report on Christian Higher Education in India*, p. 24.
129. Eyre Chatterton, *A History of the Church of England in India: Since the Early Days of the East India Company*, London: Society for the Propagation of Christian Knowledge, 1924, http://anglicanhistory.org/India/chatterton1924//16.html, p. 2.
130. Ibid., p. 3.
131. 'Minute on Missionary Education', *Conference of Missions Held in 1860*, p. 150.
132. William Miller quoted in World Missionary Conference, 1910, *Report of Commission III*, pp. 20-1. William Miller steered the Madras Christian College for over four decades. An outstanding educationist and public person, he was member of the Indian Education Commission, 1882 and of Madras Legislative Council four tomes since 1893. In 1901, he was appointed Vice-Chancellor of Madras University.
133. Lilian, F. Henderson, *The Cambridge Mission to Delhi: A Brief History*, Westminster: The Offices of the Mission, 1931, http://anglicanhistory.org/india/henderson1931/01.html, p. 3.
134. F.F. Monk, *A History of St. Stephen's College, Delhi*, Calcutta: YMCA Publishing House, 1935, p. 10.
135. Letter dated Cawnpore, 26 October 1893 from Bishop G.A. Lefroy to S.S. Allnutt, in H.H. Montgomery, *The Life and Letters of George Alfred Lefroy, D.D.: Bishop of Calcutta and Metropolitan*, London: Longmans, Green and Co., 1920, http://anglicanhistory.org/India/lefroy_montgomery/10html, p. 9.
136. Ibid., pp. 150-1. The Orientalist education was also omitted by the Bengal Missionary Conference at Calcutta in 1855. 'Appendix I: Previous Conferences on Missions by Rev. Joseph Mullens', *Conference of Missions held in 1860*, p. 372.

137. Vermeire, 'Anent the Lindsay Commission', p. 1.
138. Ibid.
139. Ibid.
140. Namboodiry, *St. Xavier's*, p. 61.
141. Sivasundaram, 'A Christian Benares', pp. 135-6.
142. 'St. Xavier's College Report 1869-70', *The Indo-European Correspondence*, 30 April 1870, p. 245.
143. 'Lectures at St. Xavier's College', *The Indo-European Correspondence*, 28 May 1870, p. 307.
144. Arun Kumar Biswas, ed., *Collected Works of Mahendralal Sircar, Eugene Lafont and the Science Movement (1860-1910)*, Kolkata: Asiatic Society of Bengal, 2003.
145. Lafont's letter on hypothesis and induction to editor, *Indo-European Correspondence*, 16 October 1869, reproduced in, Arun Kumar Biswas, *Father Lafont of St. Xavier's College, Kolkata and Contemporary Science Movement*, Kolkata: The Asiatic Society, 2001, p. 182.
146. Arun Kumar Biswas, *Father Lafont of St. Xavier's College, Kolkata and Contemporary Science Movement*, Appendix XLVIII: Adelin Grignard S.J., 'Le Pere Eugene Lafont' (1908), pp. 309-10.
147. Namboodiry, *St. Xavier's*, p. 27.
148. *The Indo-European Correspondence*, 20 April 1872, p. 213.
149. 'Dr. Miller's View of the Function of the Colleges', p. 22.
150. Ibid.
151. Anderson was incidentally under the spell of Duff in Edinburgh in 1837, when Duff delivered a few lectures from his sick bed; Huizinga, *Missionary Education in India*, p. 47.
152. 'Dr. Miller's View of the Function of the Colleges', p. 23.
153. 'The Report of the Deputation of the Free Church of Scotland', Lindsay, *Report of the Commission on Christian Higher Education in India*, pp. 23-5.
154. 'Dr. Miller's View of the Function of the Colleges', pp. 22-3.
155. Noted twentieth-century scientists, J.C. Bose and P.C. Ray were Lafont's students.
156. See the objects and principles of the DAV College, in Lajpat Rai, *The Arya Samaj: An Account of its Origin, Doctrines Activities*, Delhi: Renaissance Publishing House, 1989, rpt., pp. 185-90.
157. B.G. Tilak's letter of resignation dated 15 December 1890, in S. Bhattacharya et al., eds., *Educating the Nation: Documents on the Discourse of National Education in India, 1880-1920*, New Delhi: Kanishka Publishers, 2003, Document No. 2.
158. The two institutions eventually became the nucleus of the Aligarh Muslim University (1920) and the Banaras Hindu University (1915) respectively.
159. Farquhar, *Modern Religious Movements in India*, p. 26.

160. The report of the deputation of the Free Church of Scotland, 1889-90, summed up in Lindsay, *Report of the Commission on Christian Higher Education in India*, p. 24.
161. Johnston, *'Abolition' or 'Transference' of Government Colleges and High Schools in India*, p. 3.
162. World Missionary Conference, 1910, *Report of Commission III*, Chapter II, p. 15.
163. 'Memorandum of Association of the National Council of Education, Bengal dated 23 May 1906', Bhattacharya et al., eds., *Educating the Nation*, Document No. 4, p. 9.
164. The initiative led to the formation of a Depressed Class Mission two decades later.
165. Joseph Bara, 'Christian Missionaries and Popular Education in India, 1910-40', *Indian Social Science Review*, 2, 2 (2002).
166. P.C. Mozoomdar, *The Oriental Christ*, Boston: Geo. H. Ellis, 1894.
167. V.S. Azariah, *The Christian Movement in India*, Madras: The Christian Literature Society for India, 1936, p. 73.
168. Rev. Edwin Greaves, 'The Indian Christian Church and the National Movement', *Harvest Field*, vol. XXX, no. 1, January 1910, p. 13.
169. World Missionary Conference, 1910, *Report of Commission IV*, Edinburgh: Oliphant, Anderson & Ferrier, 1910, p. 158.
170. Greaves, 'The Indian Christian Church and the National Movement', p. 6.
171. Eric Sharpe, *The Universal Gita: Western Images of the Bhagwat-Gita*, London: S.C.M. Press, 1985, p. 84.
172. Heike Liebau, '"Indianization" and Education: Reaction from Protestant Christians of the Madras Presidency to the Lindsay Commission Report', in Krishna Kumar and Joachim Oesterheld, *Education and Social Change in South Asia*, New Delhi: Orient Longman, 2007, p. 59.
173. Bara, 'Christian Missionaries and Popular Education in India', p. 313; 'Minutes of the Educational Conference Held at Loyola College, Madras, 27-30 December 1930, pp. 11-14.
174. Discussion of the report by Rev. J.A. Sharrock, Principal, SPG College, Trichinopally. World Missionary Conference, 1910, *Report of Commission III*, p. 418.
175. World Missionary Conference, 1910, *Report of Commission IV*, p. 157.
176. Ibid., *III*, pp. 54-5.
177. Ibid., *II*, p. 86.
178. Ibid., H.A. Popley, *K.T. Paul: Christian Leader*, Calcutta: YMCA, 1938.
179. Bara, 'Christian Missionaries and Popular Education in India'.
180. Joseph Bara, 'Schooling "Truant" Tribes: British Colonial Compulsions and Educational Evolution in Chhotanagpur, 1870-1930', *Studies in History*, 26 (2), pp. 157-9.

181. H. Whitehead, *Our Mission Policy in India*, Madras: Society for the Propagation of Christian Knowledge, 1907, p. xi.
182. Ibid., p. 9.
183. Discussion of the report by Stephen S. Thomas, Baptist Mission, Delhi. World Missionary Conference, 1910, *Report of Commission III*, p. 415.
184. Vermeire, 'Anent the Lindsay Commission', p. 2.
185. Greaves, 'The Indian Christian Church and the National Movement', pp. 14-15 (italics original).
186. 'Edinburgh Continuation Committee Conferences: Education', *Harvest Field*, vol. XXXIII, no. 5, May 1913, pp. 188-9.
187. Ibid., p. 189.
188. Ibid.
189. Lindsay, *Report of the Commission on Christian Higher Education in India*, p. 2.
190. 'Minutes of the Educational Conference held at Loyola College, Madras, 27-8 December 1939, p. 2; Vermeire Papers (Jesuit Archives, Ranchi).
191. Bishop of Bombay, 'Religious Education under a Neutral Government', *International Review of Missions*, vol. 9, 1920, p. 44.

CHAPTER 6

Politics of Patronage and the Institutionalization of Language Hierarchy in Colonial Western India

DILIP CHAVAN

There is no dearth of studies on the history of modern education and the development of educational institutions in colonial India. However, as Veena Naregal has argued, many such studies only trace the events chronologically and outline 'the contributions of modern education to the emergence of nationalist consciousness'.[1] More recently, Naregal argues, scholars trained in English have taken a critical note of colonial literacy and its ideological underpinnings.[2]

There are many studies devoted to the history of individual institutions. Such studies remain lopsided as they concentrate only on one institution. The historical scholarship on modern India, however, has paid little attention to the development of the educational institutions and language policy pertaining to them in comparative mode. The colonial state implemented differentiated language policy with regard to different institutions. This differentiated language policy can be understood if such institutions are studied comparatively. In western India, the Sanskrit Pathshala in Pune (also called the Poona College) and Elphinstone Institution in Mumbai were established in the second and third decades of the nineteenth century respectively, with apparently different and contradictory objectives. Cultivation of Sanskrit was the primary preoccupation in Pune and the dissemination of English education was the professed aim in Bombay. Both of these institutions were of tremendous prestige and distinction and were very much instrumental in the cultivation of the literary culture, intellectual trends and intelligentsia of the colonial times. This article aims to study the differentiation in language policy and shifts in the patronage offered by the British to these institutions in western India.

The British Orientalists' discovery of Indian culture remained very vital to the revival and institutionalization of Sanskrit, the skewed development of education and institutionalization of the hierarchical language policy. Romila Thapar has rightly argued that the search for or discovery of the Indian past resulted in a number of interpretations of the past. Thus, for example, William Jones[3] (1746-94) in the late eighteenth century and Fredrich Max Müller[4] (1823-1900) in the nineteenth century had delineated a glorious picture of the ancient past. Warren Hastings' ambition to reconcile the British rule with the Indian institutions paved the way for patronizing Oriental learning towards the end of the eighteenth century.

Accumulation of information about Indian culture, religions, race, literatures, etc., had become a politically expedient task. Gauri Viswanathan rightly observes that behind Orientalism's exhaustive enquiries lay interests that were far from scholarly. It has frequently been observed that Orientalist research often furthered the pursuit of power in projects that represented themselves as the pursuit of truth. For Hastings, Orientalist knowledge was a specific aspect of 'state power' which could reduce the weight of 'subjection' for Indians, produce 'the sense and obligation of benevolence' in Englishmen and more generally be 'a gain for humanity'.[5] Kumkum Sangari argues that the Orientalists who either held or rose to important positions in the government were committed to preserving British power.[6]

Though quite aware of the utility and futility of the Orientalist knowledge, Hastings spelled out his position on Orientalism.[7] According to Sangari, the need for intermediary groups and the desire to replace existing structures of patronage resulted in the establishment of Sanskrit. Sanskrit, along with Persian and Arabic, was one of the first recipients of state patronage.[8] Hastings' *madrasa* in Calcutta was formed on local demand to train Muslim men through religious instruction for gaining subordinate position in civil and criminal courts. Arguing along the same line, Jonathan Duncan (1756-1811), the Resident at Benares, followed the example set by Hastings and recommended the establishment of Hindu college, which became known as Sanskrit College at Benares.

Duncan's long stay in India is significant with regard to the development of Orientalism and the early institutions of higher education. He recognized the special position of the Brahmins and gave them encouragement.[9] His respect and regard for their customs and institutions and his partiality towards them led people to declare that he was Brahminized by his long residence in India.[10] One of the objectives of establishing the Sanskrit College in a town having numerous private seminaries was 'endearing our Government to the Native Hindus, by exceeding in our attention towards them and their systems'.[11]

The Charter Act of 1913 marked an important stage in the later history of the East India Company in India. The Act had two goals: (1) 'the *revival* and *improvement* of literature, and the encouragement of the learned natives of India' and (2) 'the introduction and promotion of a knowledge of the sciences'.[12] Some scholars have rightly noted that the 1813 Act fostered two seemingly different goals at once: the revival of traditional learning as well as the introduction of Western science.[13]

The foundation of the Sanskrit College and the *madrasa* in the late eighteenth century in Bengal exemplifies the collaborative mode in which the colonial state chose to operate in the early phase of colonialism. Such collaboration entailed heavy patronage to the traditional institutions of the upper caste Hindu and Muslim elites. Unlike Bengal, which was ruled by the Muslim rulers before it was conquered by the British, the Pune region in western India was being ruled by the indigenous upper caste. As compared to Gujarat, where Brahmins were divided into 80 different local divisions or sub-castes, the Brahmins in the Poona-Bombay region were less fragmented.[14] Again in contrast with Bengal, where Brahmins shared predominance with Kayasthas and Baidyas, the Brahmins in the Poona-Bombay region had solitary preeminence.[15] Different structures of patronage were operative in these regions. Deeply institutionalized structure of patronage to Sanskrit learning in Pune during the Peshwa regime led to a stringent policy of conciliation through patronage during the early period of colonial rule.

I. Sanskrit College: Continuity in Change

During the Peshwa regime, the fate of a large number of Brahmins rested largly on the patronage granted to them by the Peshwas. Thousands of rupees used to be distributed among the Brahmins in the month of Shravana.[16] The Peshwa regime, which was one of the most tyrannical regimes in India, did not have any kind of legitimacy. The regime could gain legitimacy only through the Brahmins. The Peshwas had to win this by bestowing lavishly a huge amount of donation on the Brahmins.

When Mountstuart Elphinstone (1779-1859) became Commissioner of the Deccan, the peculiar structure of power and patronage existing there for a long time posed many difficulties to him. However, Elphinstone's long stay in the Deccan, his intimate knowledge of the social life under the Peshwa regime and his firm belief in 'morality rather than expediency as the basis of politics'[17] helped him tremendously in dealing with the new problems.

Though Elphinstone was influenced by the French Republicans in his early life, he remained all his life a Whig of the old school, who saw statesmanship of the highest quality in the politics of moderation rather than in hasty reforms.[18] He was not a blind opponent of change. He believed that innovation and reform were essential parts of social process. However, his progressivism regarding the social structure did not presuppose any break with tradition.[19] According to him, reform should not presuppose a total upheaval in the social structure. Instead, reform should reconcile and synthesize the conflicting principles and should have a soothing effect on the society. After the defeat of Bajirao II in 1818, Elphinstone had decided to retain the structure of the revenue administration.

Elphinstone's policy of constrained and cautious reform was best evident in the continued prevalence of the institutionalized practice of *dakshina* even after the fall of the Peshwa regime. He was quick to realize the significance of *dakshina* as a means of satisfying the Brahmins, who were affected most by the collapse of the Peshwa regime. He had no illusions about the utility of the knowledge that the Brahmins possessed. He took the decision of continuing *dakshina* out of political exigency rather than any sentimental concerns. Many of these existing donations were almost indiscriminate and were regulated more by caprice and interest than by any other principle.[20] He desisted from abolishing it, even though the institution held no 'moral' significance for the political system which was introduced in the 'Poona-territories under the aegis of the British'.[21]

One of the chief defects of Elphinstone's policy on education was the limited scope it had for the universalization of primary education. W. Meston's view that 'Elphinstone was keenly interested in higher education, his thought constantly turned to the education of the Great masses of the people'[22] should be accepted very cautiously. In fact, Elphinstone had made it quite clear that he intended to provide elementary education principally to the sons of the better classes and that 'a mixture of ranks' would prevent high-caste Hindus from sending their children to school. He detested the missionary intervention and refused to seek their help for they found the lowest castes their best pupils and he feared that if the government were to encourage men 'of that description', schools would be boycotted by upper and middle castes-classes, whom he wished to conciliate.[23]

Occasionally, Elphinstone mentioned the necessity of educating the peasantry. However, it was not more than paying lip service. He seemed to believe that education for the peasants was not endowed with high function and the colonial state disowned the responsibility of financing the village schools as the expense for this was to be met from the *gram kharch* (village expenses).[24]

The cultural and intellectual hegemony which the Chitpavan Brahmins exercised by virtue of their caste under the Peshwa rule had no parallel in the rest of India. This hegemony was expressed in the institution of *dakshina*. *Dakshina* represented, according to Ravinder Kumar, an informal alliance between the Chitpavans and the state.[27] The recipients of *dakshina* looked at it as an important institution which they could not afford to lose. Predominance of the Brahminical caste groups in the pre-colonial Poona region and their continued prevalence in the colonial era through new patterns of negotiation with the colonial rulers entailed differentiated patterns of patronage.

Dakshina: *Institutionalization of Discrimination*

Poona flourished as a seat of Brahminical education during the Peshwa regime. The Peshwas had supported *pathshalas*, which were run exclusively for the high-caste children, and they imparted religious education to the students. There were 164 *pathshalas* in Poona which imparted instruction in Sanskrit.[26] The Brahmins were considered to be the most eligible persons, in some cases the only eligible persons, to receive donations. The occasions on which the Brahmins were to be given charities were numerous and varied. The types of donation which were offered to the Brahmins included *tuladan*,[27] and *bhumidan*.[28] *Dakshina* means a present or a gift to the Brahmins. It was through *dakshina* that the Peshwas extended them support in preserving and propagating the values of Brahminism. The most notable instance of this lavish distribution of charity was that of Shravana *masa*.

The Orientalist phase had started much before the formal establishment of the colonial rule in India. Hastings had established a *madrasa* for the Muslims in Calcutta and a Sanskrit College for the Hindus in Benares. Though one of the avowed objectives of these colleges was the cultivation of the classical languages, they were also aimed at conciliating the Muslim elites in Bengal, who had ruled Bengal for a fairly long time, and the upper caste Hindus in Benares, whose prerogative had remained unchallenged even during the medieval rule. It was mentioned repeatedly in defence of these colleges that the objective of their establishment was to win the loyalty of the Muslim *maulvis* and Hindu *pandits*.[29] This defence was a case of political expediency. The colonial rulers could not afford any kind of threat to the 'precarious' balance of power.

Elphinstone could foresee the danger in encouraging the missionaries. So in western India, he discouraged the missionaries. The missionaries were discouraged also because they were working among the lower castes and similar sections of the society. As part of the conciliatory measures, he had planned to establish two colleges at Nasik and Wai, which were the traditional seats of Brahminical learning. However, he had to abandon this idea in order to utilize the resources more systematically for the distribution of *dakshina*.

Elphinstone was doubtful about the possibility of a widespread demand for English in the country at large. He was the first officer to introduce Western education in Bombay. He had little hope of diffusing knowledge of the English language and European literature.[30] Realizing the volatile basis on which the British empire rested, Elphinstone gave less importance to English and tried his best to strengthen the landed aristocracy and Brahminical castes.[31] The foundation of the Sanskrit College was a logical outcome of the policies that Elphinstone had been implementing. The college was established shortly after his accession to governorship. The idea and plan of the college were submitted to the government by William Chaplin, the Commissioner of the Deccan. The immediate political motive behind the establishment of the college was more political than educational - namely, to conciliate the learned Brahmin class who had suffered severely by the change of government following the overthrow of the Peshwa by the British in 1818.[32]

The foundation of the Sanskrit College was not merely an Orientalist design. Its dual function was, first, to encourage and improve the useful part of Hindu learning and, second, to introduce as far as possible the means of communicating European knowledge to the new subjects.[33] The idea of the Sanskrit College originated out of the combined interests of the indigenous elites and the colonial rulers. In his plan, Chaplin said:

> . . . to direct the attention of the College principally such parts of their own Shasters as are not only most useful in themselves but will best prepare their minds for the gradual reception of more valuable instruction at a future time. When we have once secured their confidence, but not only then will be the time to attempt the cautious and judicious introduction of those improvements in the education of those Hindoo subjects by which alone joined with good Government, we can hope to ameliorate their moral condition.[34]

It was also argued that the college would contribute very much to preserve the attachment of the learned Brahmins, a class of people who had suffered most 'severely by the change of Government', to the colonial state.[35]

In order to make the college popular among 'the Hindoo community', the appointment of teachers in all the branches of learning was proposed. The initiative towards the foundation of the college was taken despite the founders' awareness that many of the branches of learning were 'worse than useless'. It was also hoped that the establishment of the college would attract the 'Hindoo subjects' to the colonial empire and would facilitate the amelioration of their moral conditions. With a view to preserving the ancient literature of the Hindus, the British government had resolved on establishing a Hindu College in Poona.

Defence of Sanskrit College and Claims over Dakshina

The officials of the East India Company, who were manipulating the affairs while being in their home-country, could not recognize precisely the political expediency of the establishment of an educational institution like the Sanskrit College. The lack of understanding of the London-based officials was perhaps because they did not have primary and first-hand experience of the situation in the colony. Their understanding of the social structure of the Indian society and the appropriate measures of conciliation required was very weak and sometimes erroneous. Therefore, many England-based authorities were critical about the educational institutions which were opened to conciliate the upper castes/classes in the Hindu and the Muslim societies. They deemed such attempts, initiated by the administrators of the East India Company in India, as waste of resources.

The Bombay government had suspended the plan of Bombay College and preferred the establishment of Poona Hindu College (Sanskrit College) on the ground that the Supreme Government had sanctioned an expenditure of Rs. 2 lakh a year 'for the support of native literature in the Deccan' and on the assumption that 'the faith of the Government' seemed to have been pledged to the 'learned classes of our own subjects in the Deccan'.[36]

Elphinstone's proposal for establishing a Sanskrit school in Poona, though appreciated by William Chaplin, the local Commissioner, was not welcomed by the Court of Directors of the East India Company. They were unprepared to receive a proposal of this kind and rebuked the founders of the college in their dispatch dated 11 June 1823:

> Thus far you have left to us the power of determining what it is or is not expedient to perform. In regard to the other important part of the subject you have acted in a different manner and have proceeded to execute the measure of establishing a College for the Hindoo learning at Poona without waiting for the communication of our sentiments.[37]

The authorities in England expressed their resentment over the foundation of the Sanskrit College in Poona and not pursuing the Utilitarian policy. The Utilitarians representing the East India Company in England were equally critical about the colleges which were started in Benares and Calcutta. They quoted their dispatch had been expended for the encouragement of learning that was not already required to prevent popular discontent. Elphinstone himself was quite aware of the need of super-intendence in the college. In 1823, he had felt that 'the want of superintendence' was the greatest difficulty which he had to face – greater even than the want of money.[40] However, the college was not without a purpose. The educational policy in the early nineteenth century was a logical derivative of an astute understanding of the need of conciliatory measures to be adopted by the pre-British state towards the Brahmins. With the growing importance of Utilitarians among the policy makers, newer challenges were posed before the Sanskrit College. J.H. Baber, the Principal Collector of Poona, found that the college had moved far away from the ideals set by Elphinstone and had become 'a refuge for idlers and drones'.

However, Robert Grant, the Governor of Bombay, refused to take such a stiff action as he thought that though the institution 'preserves and cherishes the old brahminical interest, which is anti-British in all its tendencies', abolishing the college would be highly offensive to the Brahmin community.[41] Grant thought that an immediate abolition would be a breach of faith on the part of the government, as regards to the present students and therefore a measure inexpedient to be adopted.[42] As political considerations ruled out the idea of the abolition of the college, Grant thought that the only solution open to the government was to modify the courses offered.[43]

J.H. Baber, the Principal Collector of Poona, had already warned that the distribution of *dakshina* hardly promoted any of the objectives envisaged by Elphinstone. Finally, the arbitrary practices about it were dismissed and rules for admission to it were made more rigorous than before.[44] Such a move by the British was bound to be responded to by the Brahmins aggressively. Ravinder Kumar rightly argues that the Brahmins did so because *dakshina* not only provided the means of subsistence to impecunious but scholarly Brahmins also represented the predominance of Brahminical values over the community, and the acquiescence by the state in this predominance.[45] The Brahmins considered this decision a challenge to their hegemonic position and submitted a petition signed by 800 '*shastris, pandits* and *puraniks*'. One of the rules stated that no 'new candidate to be hereafter admitted' to *dakshina*. The petitioners to the Supreme Government in which they critici of pursuing Oriental learning. They condemned such colleges as 'originally and fundamentally erro dispatch, they scorned the traditional Oriental learni

> With respect to the sciences, it is worse than a waste of persons either to teach or learn them, in the state in which in the Oriental books. As far as any historical documents m the Oriental languages, what is desirable is that they should and this, it is evident, will be best accomplished by Europe acquired the requisite knowledge. Beyond these branches, in Oriental literature is poetry, but it has never been though establish Colleges for cultivation of poetry. . . .[38]

The Court applied the same criticism to the Sanskr Poona and its tone was harsher as the Bombay governn only established the college but also laid down its syllabu we see nothing to which we can attach almost any of utility'. The Court of Directors objected to both the education provided at the Sanskrit College and also to its lack of purpose. It cited the examples of the colleges at C Benares and pointed out that these colleges produced no effect' or 'beneficial impression'. They argued that their not have been 'to teach Hindoo learning or Mahomeda but useful learning'. What was important for them w language of instruction but its content. In regard with the Poona, the Governor-in-Council defended his position:

> In the case of the College at Poona the fact can scarcely be cont of the principal objects of the Paishwa's Government was the m of the Brahmins. It is known to your Honorable Court that h distributed five lacs of Rupees among that order, under the na Dukshna, but it must be observed that the Dukshna formed b portion of his largesses to Brahmins; and the number of persons Hindoo learning, and religion who were supported by him excee would readily be supposed.[39]

Elphinstone further argued that the college would be e useful in view of the enemies of the British who were inc the opinion that the latter were changing the religion and r of the Hindus. In self-defence, he also argued that the whole of the college had been saved out of *dakshina*, and not on pointed out the pernicious consequences that were to emanate from the discontinuation of *dakshina*.[46]

The petitioners argued that the decision was a source of much grief to both old and young Brahmins and would tend to the diminution of that learning which was essential to mercantile concerns. The practice of *dakshina*, the petition pointed out, had been the means of making the Brahmins apply themselves industriously to the cultivation of sciences. They further argued that this practice, despite the amount of *dakshina* being small for the government, had benefited 'a great multitude of people' and also protected the interest of the rulers as the beneficiary Brahmins offer 'prayers for the welfare and prospering of the Kingdom'. The petitioners further pointed out that the safety of the government lay in refraining from the decision of discontinuation as it would cause anarchy and political disintegration:

> We therefore entreat that the Sircar will take the whole of these cir cumstances into serious considerations, and make such arrangements as to cause all such balances as will have remained in hands after the distribution to the ensuing *Dakshina* on account of the absent Brahmins to be distributed to all new candidates who may be admitted after passing the usual examination. This will be the means of disseminating the learning and the people moreover be happy and it will greatly tend to honour of the Government but should be otherwise both science and Religion will be lost and ruined and people will not act uprightly in their dealings and every one will suffer extremely. . . . By the present arrangement both the Brahmins and the Sircar will not be exposed to much trouble.[47]

However, the state did not concede to the pressure of the Brahmins and pointed out that 'the whole of that allowance should continue to be made available to the general purpose of promoting education and rewarding those who 'distinguish themselves in the acquisition of science' and 'the preservation of useful knowledge'.[48]

As the government refused to retreat from its decision, the dissidence among the Brahmins in Poona 'persisted with unabated vigour' and even spread among their caste-men of 'Waee, Sattara, Pundurpoor, Kurad, Maholee, Carnatie, Konkan and Khandesh'. This petition was submitted a year after the petition of the Poona-based Brahmins and it also exhibits a well-articulated pragmatism. This long document begins with a detailed history and advantages of *dakshina*. The petitioners complained against the decision of the establishment of the Hindoo College and diversion of some amount of funds reserved for *dakshina* to the maintenance of the college. After the establishment of the Hindoo College, the provision for the *dakshina* was reduced to Rs. 30,000 only. Thereafter, a committee of *pandits* was established to deal with the matter pertaining to the distribution amount. However, the functionaries of the committee disputed among themselves continuously. Thereupon, a committee of the European officers was established with a view to restore 'peace and harmony.' The *pandits* complained against the recommendation of the committee not to admit any new candidates whereupon the whole of the Brahmins jointly petitioned the committee of management against this clause. Then the committee obtained an order from the Governor-in-Council 'that the surplus funds which shall remain after the distribution of the *dakshina* to the old incumbents should be distributed among the new candidates'.[49]

The state refused to acquiesce to the demands of the conservative Brahmins because there was already a class in the offing which was asking for and being provided with English education in Poona. The state was quite awake to the cleavage in the Brahmin caste. A section of the Brahmins was aware of the fact that their arrival in the portal of colonial employment was possible only through English education. The colonial state was also equally conscious of the fact that the mere Orientalist language policy could not ensure the creation of personnel having acumen required for colonial bureaucracy. By the mid-nineteenth century, the state had started employing the English-educated natives.[50]

By 1850, a new class of English educated had arisen in Poona and this class claimed an equally legitimate right on *dakshina* fund. They argued that Sanskrit students could no longer 'claim a monopoly to official patronage'. In a petition submitted to the government, the students of English School presented their rationale for *dakshina*. They distanced themselves from the Sanskrit-educated Brahmins without breaking the lineage of their 'common Brahminical background'. This petition was submitted at the time when the Agents of Sirdars in Deccan were about to allot life and sinecure premiums from the Rs. 3,000 of the *dakshina* fund lately sanctioned by the government to the students of Sanskrit and that each premium was to be about Rs. 25 so that the whole number of sinecure life grants might be expanded.

The petitioners, in order to legitimize their claim, reminded the government that when the rules of *dakshina* were changed in 1837 with a view to making it available to the more useful branch of knowledge, there were 'few or no English students to compete' with the traditional Sanskrit-educated Brahmins. These circumstances, however, changed and now there were many Brahmins who could write vernacular books on the most useful subjects such as the natives urgently wanted. The petitioners requested the government to allot some of the premiums from the *dakshina* fund. They insisted that the Sanskrit students, who were taught at the public expense, should have the same condition of promoting useful learning and moral and liberal ideas as they would be having. They further argued that the fund reserved for *dakshina* should not be used for promoting 'idleness, pride and the most baneful prejudices'.[51]

In order to distance themselves from the traditional Brahmins, the English-educated Brahmins had to come to terms with the colonial notion of education. As the controversy over *dakshina* reached its climax around 1850, Major Candy, who was working as the Superintendent of the Sanskrit College and whose opinion on the issue was sought by the government, wrote several minutes, which exhibit his shrewd understanding of the new structure of Sanskrit and English: 'In 1848, Candy had reported to the government that though cultivation and preservation of Sanskrit was the only good to be achieved through Sanskrit College, this was a good not to be esteemed lightly.'[52] Unlike Chaplin, who had seen the college as merely a political expediency and stamped the Sanskrit knowledge as 'worse than useless', Candy realized the importance of Sanskrit in the improvement of the vernaculars. He wrote that Latin was not more useful in the improvement of English than Sanskrit may be made in improving Marathi.

In pursuing his efforts to increase the efficiency of the college, Candy had already suggested the introduction of the study of the vernacular, the establishment of the lithographic press department and the introduction of the study of English combined with the study of Sanskrit and Marathi. Candy's policy caused linguistic shift in the college, turning it into a modern institution having a Sanskrit, a vernacular, an English-vernacular department, a lithographic press and a depository department. Candy then submitted several suggestions for increasing the efficiency of the college and making it extensively useful as a seminary for translators and an institution for training masters for the vernacular schools. The proposed changes unfold a plan of modernizing the college and making it more useful. His suggestions included:

> . . . 1st, the appointment of a European gentleman to the College, who should study the vernacular and Sanskrit languages to qualify himself for eventually becoming Superintendent and we should in the meanwhile discharge the duty of Professor of English literature and science; and 2nd the appointment in the English department of a Professor of the vernacular, who should be able to give to the students a critical knowledge of their own language in connection with the study of Sanskrit and English; 3rdly, the establishment of two or three translation scholarships or exhibitions, the holders of which should be required to produce periodically a translation or an original composition, 4thly, the formation of a schoolmaster class.[53]

However, this shift in the language policy with regard to the Sanskrit College was not to cause any harm to Sanskrit. Candy advised the government to assure the petitioners that the government entertained no views injurious to the college and their 'desirability of preserving and encouraging the study of Sanskrit' would be acknowledged and the Sanskrit Department of the college be kept *efficient*.[54] The new English-educated elites' avowed progressivism and their readiness to become bearers of 'useful' skills to promote 'general enlightenment' was to transcend the caste boundary. They were also to be a minuscule group which would work as a mediating class and prove its worth by disseminating new knowledge and true science 'among all classes of the Hindoo nation'.

Though the Sanskrit College was thrown open to the non-Brahmin students in 1850, every care was taken to ensure the enrolment of the upper-caste students. Before it was opened to the non-Brahmin students, Major Candy had delivered a speech to the 'Nobility and Gentry of Maharashtra' with a view to informing the sons of the noble families of the liberal policies of the government which could potentially benefit the lower castes and thereby challenge the authority of the upper castes. The speech showed acute realization on the part of the colonial rulers of the importance of this group in running the state machinery. Candy touched a raw nerve by referring to their enemies and also assured them that he would side with them in this conflict: 'But you have enemies which seek to rob you of your high station, your wealth and dignity. I need not specify who these enemies are, but I beg of you to be on your guard against them.'[55] Candy informed them that the government had made provision of the Sanskrit College for instructing the children of the nobility and gentry in the English, vernacular and Sanskrit languages and several had already joined the classes.

By citing the example of the nobility of ancient Europe, who slighted study and thought only of the pursuit of arms and of sensual pleasure and then considered it reproach to be without education, Candy advised them to take the benefit of the facilities that the state was ready to shower on them. He also warned them against the rise of the lower castes which was to ensue:

> Surely I need not labor to show that learning which enriches and ennobles even the poor and mean must be beneficial to you! I will illustrate the benefit of learning by the case of a peon's son whom his father sent to school. He first attended a vernacular school, where he became proficient in reading, writing and accounts; he then went to the English school and studied for some years. The learning which he thus acquired procured him a situation in the service of Government. . . . Government has notified its intention of employing in the public service those who qualify themselves for it by a good education; so that qualified persons of whatever cast[e] they be will get situations. How will it grieve you to see persons of low origin provided for, while your children remain as they are.[56]

Candy's speech reveals that the state policy of liberalism towards the lower castes was only a symbolic gesture. The state did not intend to extend this to the extent of breaking the caste structure. The loss of the upper castes as the indigenous allies of the Raj and the consequent threat that the shift in education policy could potentially cause was to be mended by encouraging the 'nobility and gentry' to monopolize English education. This elucidates that the early educational institutions had become the sites wherein the class interests of the elites of India were to be generated, promoted and safeguarded. George Thompson, who worked as agent of the Landlords' Society of Bengal in the British Indian Society in London, had delivered a similar speech in Hindu College in Calcutta, on 'the art of agitation' and called for a new political association.

Care was also taken through fee hike to restrain the flow of undesirable students to the college. W. Wordsworth, the Principal of the College, openly acknowledged this in the Report of the College for the year 1866-7:

At the beginning of the present year the fee for attendance at the College was raised from two to five rupees. The effect of this has not been to check admissions which have been more numerous this year than last. There were 29 admissions in January 1866 of whom 22 are now paying students and 7 free students or scholars.[57]

English education in India followed the uneven trajectory of the formation of an urban upper-caste middle class and the reconstitution and rise of elite. The introduction of English was primarily for the benefit and consolidation of British power but it also afforded distinct opportunities for certain sections of the Indian population.[58]

The elitist policy ultimately resulted in the rise of a new English-educated intelligentsia, having a very narrow caste base in western India. In the Sanskrit College, which later became Deccan College, more than 97 per cent of the students were Brahmins, whereas this caste constituted only 4 per cent of the total population of the region.[59]

The Sanskrit College: Modernization of Tradition

Kumkum Sangari has rightly pointed out that the British Orientalists' rediscovery of Indian culture was the ideological counterpart of Warren Hastings' project of rule after 1772. Hastings' ambition to reconcile British rule with Indian institutions was partly modelled on the Roman empire.[60] Romila Thapar points out that the ancient Indian past was virtually perceived as 'a lost-wing' of early European culture, as for instance, in William Jones' discovery of the affinity between Sanskrit and Greek and Latin.[61]

The Orientalist field, at least initially, could only be established with local collaboration. Accumulation of the knowledge about India was a politically and ideologically motivated programme aimed at the subjugation of the colony. The foundation of the religious seminaries and colleges towards the end of the eighteenth century in Benares and Calcutta and early nineteenth century in western India was aimed at structuring the modalities through which the colonial state could accumulate knowledge about the Orient,[62] translate the religious texts,[63] reduce the weight of 'subjection for Indians'[64] and conciliate a class. These institutions provided an ad-hoc field which was further enlarged, shaped and systematized to yoke them to the imperial interests.

Redefinition of tradition by the Orientalists also presupposed the creation of an altered field of new social formation, new alignments and new structures of patronage. The foundation of new institutes created such sites where these new alignments could materialize. Sangari argues that the power of Orientalism lay in the methodological field itself, which, among other things, offered a *relationship* with the 'West'. These institutes became potentially hegemonic *only* when they became modes of self-identification for members of the Indian middle class.[65]

The recurring official emphasis on patronage was replete with Orientalist assumptions – the decline of science and literature caused by the absence of aristocratic patronage partly explained the present condition of India.[66] Such a flawed but politically correct understanding of the Orientalists authored the policy whereby Sanskrit was to be revived, reinvigorated, cultivated, preserved and reintroduced through a curricula. The Orientalists lamented over the potential threat to and loss of the rich treasure of Sanskrit because of the apathy the colonial state was showing. Lord Minto lamented that Britain ('distinguished for its love and successful cultivation of letters') had failed 'to extend its fostering care to the literature of the Hindus, and to aid its opening to the learned in Europe the repositories of that literature'.[67] Lord Minto, in his minute of 6 March 1811, had contemplated 'much higher' objects for observing the decay of science and literature among the natives, and attributed the loss of it to the British rule, and proposed that the government should 'interpose with a fostering hand to aid in the revival of letters'.[68]

As one of the avowed objectives of the Sanskrit College was to establish a channel through which the colonial state could mediate, it became imperative to do away with some of the traditional methods of learning which were prevalent in the Brahminical education system. As creation of a rational individual was never an objective of the Brahminical education system, rote-learning, which is devoid of comprehension, was the method followed. Formation of a class of intelligentsia, which was to be capable of carrying the modern knowledge and function as mediators between the colonial state and the colonized state, could not have been possible if the traditional method of teaching had been continued.

Though vernacular education was rationalized in the name of its potentiality of wider circulation of ideology and diffusion of knowledge, vernacular education was never to be a democratic enterprise. The dichotomy between English education and vernacular education as representing the elitist agenda and mass programme respectively was not true to its core. The Company officials were very keen on nurturing a few than many. The Board of Education clearly acknowledged that the idea of national education was in its infancy even in Europe and its implementation in India posed newer challenges.

A similar argument about vernacular education was also made in the 1843 Report of Board of Education, Bombay:

> The tendency of our proceeding in regard to Vernacular Education, has evinced our conviction that the primary instruction of the people should be conducted exclusively in the vernacular language of the respective Provinces, and that it is essential to permanent and real success, that exertions of Government should be responded to by that degree for cooperation on the part of people, which will suffice to give evidence of a sincere desire on their part, to avail themselves of the benefits of education – it is with this better view, that we have attached so much to the constitution of Local School Committees consisting of representatives of the different classes of the community. . . .[69]

Elphinstone had proposed that a college should be established in Bombay on the model of the college at Fort William. However, this college was to aim at the training of young Indians who were considered suitable for employment in the higher ranks of government service and not solely for the training of junior civil servants from England.

Linguistic Modernization of the Sanskrit College

The attempt to introduce Western courses in the traditional institutes resulted in violent responses in Maharashtra and Bengal. In the Sanskrit College, Poona, the orthodox Brahmins reacted violently when new courses and language were to be introduced. Unlike the Maharashtrian elites, who had hailed largely from only one caste, the Bengali elites had come from a relatively wider social base of the community. They were quicker to recognize the fruits that the new education could potentially promise. Therefore, they were more prepared to accept European knowledge.

In 1851, it was decided that Sanskrit should be taught to the non-Brahmins in the Sanskrit College. This created a wave of shock in the city. Two teachers - Narayan Shastri Abhyankar and Gopal Shastri Gokhale - agreed to teach Sanskrit to youths of all castes without distinction. Their act of teaching Sanskrit to Sonars, Shimpis, Prabhus, Parsis and various Shudra castes created indignation among the Brahmins. Even while achieving linguistic modernization of the Sanskrit College, the idea of the continuation of Sanskrit was not lost sight of. Moreover, it was argued that Sanskrit should continue to be deployed to cultivate Marathi.[70]

Though Candy was inspired to achieve modernization of the college and committed to achieving qualitative overhaul, he could not earn the favour of the Poona Brahmins by diminishing the importance of Sanskrit. This could have been even dangerous, given that the colonial authority had already initiated substantial abatement in *dakshina* fund. Candy rationalized the differentiated principle of patronage and also suggested an outline for the development of Marathi.[71] The Brahmins in Poona also responded to the change in policy with regard to the college. They were not opposed to English. However, they did not want the importance of Sanskrit to be diminished. Pointing out the similarity between the roles played by Latin in Europe and Sanskrit in India, they argued in the petition that the vernaculars of India could be cultivated and improved only with the help of Sanskrit. The petition exhibits shrewd understanding of the significance of Sanskrit and English, the former being a traditional apparatus of hegemony and the latter being a new mode of dominance for the traditional elites. The petitioners wrote: 'While then in the present circumstances of the country, the English is necessary to furnish ideas to the native mind, the Sanskrit is equally necessary. . . . The question before us, however, is how far does the College at Poonah, tend to promote the object in view, the promotion of Sanskrit Literature.'[72]

Linguistic modernization of the Sanskrit College entailed many shifts in the teaching of language. The changed situation demanded Anglicization as well as vernacularization of the college and enhancing its utility and efficiency. The expansion and further infiltration of the colonial state demanded more informed and linguistically modernized class of intelligentsia. This class was endowed with the function of mediating between the colonial state and the colonized subjects. Moreover, this class also had to retain its hegemonic position in the caste-society, which had demanded for more opportunities of employment in the spreading network of bureaucracy. The traditional intelligentsia had also begun to realize the importance and necessity of learning English.

While it was difficult to introduce English education in Poona, it was observed in and around Bombay that there was a great demand for English. In Poona, the state had to take initiative for introducing English; in Bombay, the native intelligentsia pined for it. Having realized the growing demand for English education among the Indians, the British began to press upon them to raise funds for English schools. A letter expressing this sentiment of the state was attached to the Report of Board of Education.[73] The report stated that the state would shoulder the responsibility of introducing English to the Brahmins and, thus, ensure their smooth entry as English-educated intelligentsia in the mould of colonial machinery:

> Subsequently, the whole subject of the College has been under our consideration with a view to remodel it. The object of our plan is to combine the Sanskrit College with the English school *so as to enable the Brahmin youths* who have hitherto devoted to many laborious years to the study of Sanskrit literature to enter the field of competition with their young countrymen, whom we are endeavouring to impregnate with the results of European knowledge.[74]

Francis Warden mentioned in his Minute of 24 March 1828 'the eagerness the natives had displayed to obtain a knowledge of the English language' and 'the proposition having been made to the colleges at Poona and Surat to open a branch for teaching the English language'. The initiative displayed by the natives regarding English provided Warden an opportunity to debate the language issue in the Bombay Council. In this Minute, he maintained that the objective of that policy should be 'diffusion of a knowledge of English language as best calculated to facilitate the intellectual and moral improvement of India'. He had advocated the expediency of making the study of English a primary object and had contended that it was better and safer to commence by giving a good deal of knowledge to a few than a little to many. However, he felt that such a selective distribution of English at the higher level also required wide distribution of English at the elementary level.[75]

He hoped English to become 'the lasting monument of our dominion' and thereby the Indians could rival the rest of the civilized world. He considered that 'there was nothing chimerical in laying the foundation of a good edifice for teaching what the higher classes of natives are anxious to learn, a knowledge of English'.[76] A clear indictment with regard to the elitist nature of English education is evident in the Report of the Board of Education:

> We have before intimated our deliberate opinion of the necessity of imparting a higher education than vernacular schools can supply, *to all those who are in a position of life to demand it*. . . . With these views we have carefully examined the means of our disposal for promoting a zeal and supplying a demand for English Education. We should have desired, if the funds at our command would allow it, to locate a good English School at every Zilla town in the Presidency and at such large towns also as would be likely to present a demand for superior education.[77]

Warden saw such an elitist view of English education and determined an asymmetrical fee structure for vernacular education and English education. Access to English education was controlled through a stringent fee structure whereas moderate fee structure was designed for vernacular education.[78]

It is not that the Court of Directors was opposed to the idea of patronizing indigenous education in India. In the early decades of the nineteenth century, they admired Sanskrit literature, and the pre-colonial regimes which patronized them:

> The mode of encouraging in India prevailed for many years, and the theory on which it is based is clearly traceable in the views promulgated by Mr. Chaplin, the Commissioner in the Deccan, on his founding the Hindu College in Poona. The Court of Directors indeed in the first instance gave it express encouragement. In their public dispatch to Lord Minto of June 1814, they observe, 'We are informed that there are in the Sanscrit language many excellent systems of ethics, with codes of laws and compendiums of the duties relating to every class of the people, the study of which might be useful to those natives who may be destined for the Judicial Department of Government.'[79]

Therefore, introduction of English in the traditional institutes of education cannot be equated with democratization of education. English was introduced in such institutes out of political exigency. However, while doing so, care was taken to ensure that the new language did not cause vertical alteration in the existing social structure. Like Sanskrit, English also became an arena of negotiation and manipulation.

English in the Sanskrit College

The Anglicists had astutely tapped that there was a small but visible class of elite who were clamouring for English to the neglect of vernacular schools. The Board of Education ratified the Anglicist claim that it was impossible to undertake a gigantic scheme as the education of the masses of India, and even if the necessary funds were made available the 'national mind' was not ripe. Disqualifying the possibility of educating the whole of the population, they pointed at the inadequacy of the machinery at hand, in terms of either literature or teachers for the introduction of systems which would embrace all orders of the community.

A school was established in Poona in 1823 to teach English to the Indians. However, owing to the absence of students aspiring to learn English, the school was dissolved.[80] Elphinstone's proposal for English education in Poona came under minute scrutiny of the provincial government in Bombay. Some members of the committee, appointed to study the proposal, had felt that the eventual aim of spreading European knowledge to the Indians, will have a higher rate of success, if the college would be located not in Poona but in Bombay, which was emerging as an industrial site. However, Elphinstone, in favour of Poona, pointed out that the most eminent Hindu *shastris* would never leave Poona and yet the government was obliged to provide some compensation to them for the *dakshina* they used to receive previously.[81] It was difficult to arouse interest for English in Poona even after the fall of the Peshwa regime, which had patronized the cultivation of Sanskrit so liberally, as the city had continued to be predominantly orthodox. The continued prevalence of orthodoxy in the post-Peshwa regime can partly be attributed to the differentiated educational policy initiated by Elphinstone for Bombay and Poona.

In 1825, the Sanskrit College witnessed a major shift with regard to language policy. Francis Warden planned to introduce English in the Sanskrit College.[82] The amount of Rs. 15,250, which was spent on the college, was increased by Rs. 960 in order to provide a classroom for the study of English. As the circumstances changed tremendously and rapidly, the demand for English increased further around 1832. The colonial state was waiting for this to happen. This provided the state an opportunity to intervene in the affairs of the Poona College and introduce English in it. The Junior Principal Collector unmistakably tapped this opportunity and wrote to the

Secretary to the Government of Bombay, recommending the introduction of English in Poona Sanskrit College. He persuasively wrote:

> I have no doubt that at present there would be many desirous of learning the English language, and I should certainly recommend this branch to be added to the College studies, a knowledge of the English language would I humbly conceive tend greatly to the improvement of the Natives generally the higher walks of literature and science would naturally soon follow and a field would be open to many which otherwise for a length of time must remain closed. I should also say that the knowledge of the English language would become a link between the natives and their rulers, it is decidedly a gift which would scarcely be forgotten in consideration of the valuable works in it.[83]

The Junior Principal Collector recommended reduction in the number of professors for Hindu literature and addition of some for English and Persian. Questioning the very utility of the courses taught in the college, he hoped that introduction of English would increase its utility. The Brahmin professors in the college were bound to respond fiercely to such a move. The British officials could also anticipate this. The real cause of dissent among the Brahmins was the potential threat that English could cause to their existence and the consequent displacement. The arrival of English was seen as a threat to their prerogative to dominate the positions in the college. The Junior Principal Collector presupposed this: 'I think it probably the introduction of a professor in the former language [English] into the College would give offence, if he were to displace any of the present incumbents – more particularly if he were not a high caste Brahmin.'[84] The introduction of English in the Sanskrit College was not to achieve any democratizing effect. In fact, it added a new dimension to hierarchization of language education which was emerging in Poona.

Institutionalization of Language Hierarchy: Vernacularism vs *Anglicism*

The purpose of the vernacular medium was not, even for the Vernacularists like Colonel George Jervis (1794-1832), to invigorate vernacular literature or strengthen vernacular languages exclusively. Vernaculars were seen more as a facilitating media for the diffusion of the 'positive information of Europe'. Both the Anglicists and the Vernacularists agreed upon the view that only European knowledge was a panacea to the Oriental despotism; they only differed on the ways to be used to achieve them. As the conflict between the Anglicists and the Vernacularists reached the climax around 1845, the latter argued hard to establish that a vernacular language had more advantages over English with regard to the view of the diffusion of European knowledge.

Assuming the utility of European knowledge in the perpetuation of the empire, the Vernacularists verbalized serious concern about it. They were dubious about the availability of sufficient teachers of English. They argued that a competent teacher of vernacular will more effectively 'indoctrinate his [a competent teacher's] class with the elements of any branch of science through the medium of their mother tongue, in an infinitely shorter period than if he is compelled to address them in a very difficult foreign language.'[85] Challenging the very ability of English to indoctrinate, they cautioned that English education had been to produce a set of *purvoes* or copying clerks, with little but parrot-like information. This view of the Vernacularists not only suggested the practicability of the vernacular tongue but also challenged the claim which the Anglicists had been making so vigorously since the late eighteenth century. Eliciting consent to the utility and relevance of European knowledge, which was allegedly stored in the canonical texts, the Vernacularists recommended the production of translations of the 'standard works of Europe' into the languages of India. According to this scheme, these translations were to be used to achieve the growth of Indian literature.

The difference between the positions of the Anglicists and the Vernacularists symbolically stood for the ideologically differentiated motives. The Vernacularists claimed to have in their purview the whole Indian populace which they estimated at 120 millions, and the Anglicists, since the beginning, were arguing in favour of the creation of a minuscule class through which the colonial state could achieve ideological initiation.

Apart from the Sanskrit College, other institutions were also established with a political purpose. Teaching through vernacular aimed at training the students to fulfil the necessity of discharging subordinate duties and save the expenses of the government. Captain Jervis writes:

> The primary object... of these institutions was the instruction of native and half-caste youths, so as to render them competent to discharge subordinate duties in the Engineer and Quarter Master General's Departments, in an economical and efficient manner; thereby avoiding the necessity of having those duties performed by officers of the line, to the detriments of the Regiments to which they belonged, and at a very serious expense to the Govt. They are subsequently enlarged by the admission of a member of native youths from the Deccan – sons of respectable parents deprived of employment on the subversion of the *Peshwa*'s authority; and this measure was adopted on the one hand as a *means of conciliation towards the conquered people*, and on the other with a view to obtaining natives properly qualified for the branches of the service.[86]

Jervis' letter clearly manifests the imperial agenda of Indian education in the early phase of colonization. Jervis clearly states the conciliatory function that education had to serve and the necessity of recruiting the subordinate personnel from the Indian upper castes with a view to curb the expenses.

Sanskrit College and the Vernacular Department

Major Candy's appointment as the Superintendent of the Sanskrit College was a pragmatic move and was intended at achieving a desirable change in the college. His attempt to effect changes in the functioning of the college remained constrained due to his ignorance of Sanskrit. He frankly confessed in his report that the efficiency of his superintendence was necessarily limited by his little knowledge of Sanskrit.[87] He felt it necessary to read the books that were taught in the college. However, he had to depend on the principal and the *pandit* who were appointed to assist him. Realizing his limitation with regard to reforming Sanskrit education in Sanskrit College, Candy began to pay more attention to the Vernacular Department. He was doing this with 'a conviction of its [Marathi's] very great importance'. He had assumed that it was necessary to teach English liberally to more number of people. Then, obviously, it became imperative to train the students in their language and, thus, make them more eligible arbitrators.

Candy recognized the importance of training the teachers to teach Marathi. As there was no tradition of studying or teaching Marathi, the state of Marathi in general was very precarious. The students, who were so eager to learn Sanskrit and later on English, were least interested in learning Marathi. Candy took the practical and sensible decision of using the college to train the teachers of Marathi:

The present Acting teacher [of Marathi] will, I hope, prove a good one. I am more and more convinced of the importance of this [Vernacular] of the College. Without it the major part of the students would leave the College unable even to read or write a letter in the common written character of their mother tongue, and destitute of qualifications for any offices, except those few which belong exclusively to Pundits.[88]

One of the reasons for choosing Sanskrit College for training the teachers in Marathi lay in the assumption that achieving proficiency in Marathi was seen as inextricably linked with achieving proficiency in Sanskrit. Rather, being proficient in Sanskrit was considered indispensable for becoming eligible to teach Marathi. Candy assumed that the present vernacular schoolmasters, for their 'want of acquaintance with Sanskrit' were ignorant of the exact power and meaning of many words that were in use in Marathi and hoped that the students of Marathi from Sanskrit College would be free from this defect.

The appointment in the college of the teacher of the vernacular language, which was attributed to Candy, was seen as the most useful measure. The Report of the college clearly acknowledged that the students who were being educated at the Sanskrit College used to leave the college with contempt for their mother tongue and without developing the ability to write in it with propriety. Such disability used to make them ineligible for colonial bureaucracy and bereft them of the opportunity to enter any department of public service. The colonial state could not afford the creation of such a handicapped intelligentsia. The Sanskrit College had already become an object of criticism and its utility was seriously doubted by the utilitarians.

The introduction of Marathi also entailed an ideological function of the creation of the literati, which was one of the important objectives of colonial education. This class of literati was to function as a mediating agency between the colonial state and the indigenous subjects. Candy expressed this thus:

. . . Karkoons make no pretensions to learning, and Pundits are useless as men of business. But now we may look forward to many leaving the College whose learning will entitle them to respect among literati, and whose attainments in the ordinary branches of education, will fit them discharge with credit the duties of situation, which they may obtain.[89]

Thus, the Vernacularists and the Anglicists differed on the issue of means of instruction and the extent of spread of education; however, they shared the view that both language and education were to be used to strenghthen the empire. These seemingly contradictory views of the Vernacularists and Anglicists were different expressions of the ideology of the empire.

II. Elphinstone College: Differentiated Language Policy

When Elphinstone left Bombay in 1827, some of the leading Indian citizens like Jamshetji and Framji Kawasji formed themselves into a committee with the aim of raising funds to endow in his memory professorships under the Native Education Society. They explained to the society in December 1827 that they hoped to secure at least three professors from England to teach English language and also 'the arts, sciences and literature of Europe.' The growing interests of the Indians in English education found expression in the desire they expressed at the time of farewell to Elphinstone. At the same time, they were careful to emphasize that they had no intention of superseding the vernaculars by English in the education of the people but only of teaching English as a classical language to the few who would, in turn, diffuse European arts and sciences by translation.[90]

Fundamentally, Elphinstone regarded education as a duty of the government because it was to achieve moral influence. In the report, which he wrote on leaving the Deccan in 1819, he declared that there was no way to improve the morals of the people except by improving their education. He elaborated upon this theme in Benthamite terms in the course in his lengthy Minute in 1824,

> It is now well understood that in all countries the happiness of the poor depends in a great measure on their education. It is by means of it alone that they can acquire those habits of prudence and self-respect from which all other good qualities spring; and if ever there was a country where such habits are required, it is this. . . . If there be a wish to contribute to the abolition of the horrors of self-immolation, and of infanticide, and ultimately to the destruction of superstition in India, it is scarcely

necessary now to prove that the only means of success lie in the diffusion of knowledge.[91]

Conscious of the 'slippery foundation' of the colonial rule, Elphinstone was thus concerned with the education both of the learned classes and also of the peasantry. The peasants, it might be thought, would have little opportunity to read even if they had once learned how to do so. He was, however, anxious not only to eradicate 'superstition' by the spread of Western knowledge, but also to teach the peasants to read so that they might understand the declarations of the government, decipher their own revenue certificates (*pattas*) and work out their own accounts. Under the *rayatwari* system, each peasant would have at least this much of immediate personal concern to read. Elphinstone's policy on education was not merely a product of a certain ideology in the West. Instead, it was deeply informed by local expediency. With the increased familiarity with the situation in western India, he was unhesitant in changing his views on education.[92]

The East India Company had decided to establish a college in Bombay to train the administrators in the native languages. This college was to be modelled on the Fort William College in Calcutta. What distinguished the notion of this college from the Sanskrit College in Poona was that it was expected to have more utility and it was infused with a relatively more secular notion of education. In a letter to Francis Warden, the Agent writes about courses to be taught at the college: 'Of the sciences to be taught at the College, the most useful would certainly be the Regulations of Government and the portions of the Hindoo and Mohamedan Law that are actually in force in our dominions.'[93]

One of the recommendations of the sub-committee of the Bombay Education Society had been the establishment in the Presidency of an English school where English may be taught classically. This proposal was supported by Warden and Elphinstone equally, barring their differences. Elphinstone realized that the establishment of such a school would help conciliate advanced public opinion. Without waiting for the approval of the Court, he sanctioned on his own responsibility the opening of the Society's Central School.[94]

On Elphinstone's retirement from Bombay governorship, the institution of Elphinstone Professorship by the Native Education Society was spontaneous and the business magnets, who had contributed towards the donation, had no clear idea of the purposes of the Professorship.[95] In the farewell address to Elphinstone, the wealthy natives of Bombay spoke of the necessity of the Professors teaching the English language and the Arts and Sciences and Literature of Europe. However, as Naheed Ahmed points out, 'the Shetia subscribers expressed the desire for professorship more as a personal genuflection to Elphinstone than an actual commitment to English education on their part'. This respectful approach of the trading community in Bombay towards Elphinstone shows the ties the *shetias* had developed with the colonial state. Though the contributors towards the fund were predominantly from Bombay, a sizeable number of contributors were the Rajas and *Jagirdars* of the Maratha country and the Brahmins of Poona, where Elphinstone had been posted as the Commissioner.[96]

Unlike in Calcutta, which was the hub of East India Company's rapidly expanding administrative machinery, Bombay continued to be a traditional commercial town. The class of employers in Bombay did not insist on knowledge of English. Resultantly, there were no students for English in the early years of Elphinstone College.[97] Poona remained an orthodox town even in the early phase of colonial rule because of the *status quo* orientation of the company's rule under Elphinstone. Though Bombay had come under the colonial rule much before the fall of the Peshwa rule and it was predominantly a commercial town; it was not free of caste prejudices. Umesh Bagade has shown that various upper caste groups in Bombay, in the wake of upward mobility, were becoming more conservative in the mid-nineteenth century.[98] The education policy could not remain uninfluenced by caste prejudices. In Bombay, both Elphinstone and Sir John Malcolm, favoured the Brahmins for English education:

> While I can quite understand the facility with which sons of Europeans brought up at the national school, and similar charitable establishments, can pursue their studies by the aid of English books and English masters, I am convinced that limiting this course of instruction to that language would be to exclude almost all the natives from advancement in a line it is most desirable they should pursue, and for which some classes of them, particularly the Brahmins, are singularly well prepared by previous education.[99]

Malcolm, like Elphinstone, believed that the Brahmins were the most displaced caste and, hence, they required to be co-opted into the new structure of power. Referring to educated Indians' employment in respectable positions, Malcolm wrote in his Minute: 'I value this, as it relates this to every class of our subjects, but particularly the Brahmins, who I am pleased to see from the greatest proportion of the students, amongst all the natives of this class, who have suffered most from the establishment of our dominion.'[100] Both of them felt education should fulfil two needs of the empire – first, it should man the colonial bureaucracy with technical acumen and secondly, it was to substantiate the colonial empire by collaborating with the Brahmins. Malcolm frankly acknowledges this objective of the empire: 'One of the chief objects I expect from diffusing education among the natives of India is our increased power of associating them in every part of our administration.'[101] The diffusion of English could be of immense use for the study of European sciences. The first step was an English school in Bombay, where English was to be taught classically. This type of education was to be given to the sons of wealthy natives and to the boys with a promise of talent. When well established, a separate class for the lower orders was to be instituted.[102] In the early phase of its history, admission to Elphinstone College was denied to the lower-caste students.

Elphinstone College was a natural outcome of the demand for English education in Bombay, though this demand was not articulated for long. Elphinstone himself was not opposed to English education, provided that there was a genuine demand for it. 'If English,' he said, 'could be at all diffused among the persons who have the least time for reflection, the progress of knowledge, by means of it, would be accelerated in a ten-fold ratio.'[103] He readily admitted that there was a growing demand for English in Bombay though it was limited to a small number of people who hoped that proficiency in the language, would help them either in their business pursuits or for government employment.[104] Francis Warden recorded in his dissenting Minute of 29 December 1823, the rapidly increasing desire for English education.[105] Very soon, English was to become in Bombay a marker of class privilege and a terrain of struggle among the elites.

Elphinstone realized that there was much force in Warden's argument that the wealthy natives of Bombay would like their children to be educated thoroughly in English. He also remained unhesitant in approving the establishment of an English school at the Presidency where 'English may be taught classically'. One of the reasons why Elphinstone felt the need of English education was his desire to 'man the public services with highly educated recruits'.[106] The Indian members of the Bombay Native Education Society, all of them commercial magnates, suggested the study of English language 'as a branch of classical education to be esteemed and cultivated in this country as the classical languages of Greece and Rome are in the Universities of Europe'.[107] They also proposed that the sphere of one professor should be Languages and General Literature; of the other Mathematics and Natural Philosophy, including Astronomy, Elementary and Physical; of the third (Professor) Chemistry, including Geology and Botany. The English members, in 1832, proposed a more pragmatic syllabus with an emphasis on mathematics, architecture, hydraulics and mechanics.[108]

As Naheed Ahmad has pointed out, there was a marked discrepancy between the expectations of the British officials and the actual support given to English education by the poor but high-caste youths. The Court of Directors had already urged, in their letter of September 1830 to Madras government, that the improvements in education, which most effectively contributed to elevate the moral and intellectual condition of people, were those which concerned the education of the higher classes.[109]

Despite that the British deliberately oriented their education policy towards a minuscule class of Brahmins, they hardly showed any interest in Western education in the early years of Elphinstone College. A list of the students who left the higher classes of the Elphinstone Institution between 1827-42 affirms the dominance of not the Brahmins but the Pathare Prabhus among those seeking education. There were 71 Prabhus out of a total of 161 students for the period, followed by 28 Parsis, 16 Brahmins and 12 Saraswat Brahmins. Contrary to the expectation of the British, the Prabhus rather than the Brahmins gave greater recognition to English education.[110] Prabhus had a long tradition of writing as they worked as scribes and copyists in the courts of the Maratha *sardars*, Muslim rulers and the Portuguese courts.

The absence of Brahmins was seen as a major cause of the 'poorer performance' of the Elphinstone College at the examinations. In 1884, the principal of the Elphinstone College expressed the concern that the proportion of failures in the first year B.A. course was 'nearly twice as high in this college as in the Deccan College'. The principal reasoned: 'The Brahmanee element in the Deccan College constitutes, I understand, more than 90 per cent of the total; in this college the same element constitutes scarcely 40 per cent. . . . The Brahmins who fill the lecture room at Poona have generally more developed intellectual tastes, and much more application.'[111] Such understanding led the administrators to formulate a policy whereby the number of Brahmin students was to be increased systematically. In 1851, the government stated that the most promising and influential pupils to whose education the principal efforts of the Board should be directed were the children of the indigent Brahmins; on the other hand, the participation of the Mahar and Dhers should be disregarded.[112]

This policy began to bear fruit after 1860. The Brahmins became the single largest Hindu caste at the College from 1867. They had effectively replaced the Pathare Prabhus who dominated English education in the 1840s. The Brahmins averaged 43 per cent of all college students before 1885 and the Prabhus constituted only 4 per cent. In 1890, out of a total number of 218 students, there were only 12 Prabhus but Brahmins 65.

The intelligentsia in Poona showed ambivalent response to the arrival of the English language in the city in the third decade of the nineteenth century. Though the conservative Brahmins of Poona looked upon English as a potential threat to their culture, there certainly had arisen a new class of intelligentsia who could foresee the material gain that English could offer. The Brahmins in Poona had started to submit petitions begging for English education. One such petition was submitted by Janardhan Appa who appealed to the British to add an English branch to the Poona College as 'there would be many desirous of learning the English language':

> A knowledge of the English language would I humbly conceive tend greatly to the improvement of the Native generally, the higher walks of literature and science would naturally soon follow and field would be open to many which otherwise for a length of time must remain closed; I should also say that a knowledge of the English language would become a link between the natives and their rulers, it is decidedly a gift, which would scarcely be forgotten in consideration of the valuable works in it. [113]

Thus, from the studies of these educational institutions, it can be inferred that the language policy was predetermined to be selective. This differentiated language policy resulted in the uneven distribution of English education. Students in English colleges in the Poona-Bombay region consequently remained socially preselected. As Anil Seal argues, Elphinstone's policies might have possibly saved British dominion in western India; however, they certainly postponed the decline of Brahminical preeminence.[114]

The colonial rulers did not favour English at the neglect of Sanskrit or Marathi altogether. When the social life in western India was still very slow and relatively less affected by the socio-cultural onslaught of colonialism, they took the strategic decision of not imposing English or allowing it to replace Sanskrit or Marathi so quickly. Language policy shows some apparent contradictions. Viewed carefully and closely, these contradictions do not represent any flaw in the colony policy. Instead, they represent the contradictory exigencies that the colonial rulers' alliance with the dominant castes had created. The strong urge that the dominant castes had displayed in order to continue their hegemonic position was one of the early predicaments that the colonial rulers had to engage with. Policy on language and education exhibits the exceptional brilliance and uncommon acumen that the colonial rulers possessed to deal with such predicaments. There is a thread of commonality underlying the seemingly contradictory policy and the variety of ideological trends which surface above the commonality were the different expressions of the ideology of the empire, benefiting both the empire and its indigenous allies. The continued dominance of the upper classes and the differentiated language policy is evident in Wheeler's account of the educational scenario:

> During the last thirty years education in India has made an extraordinary advance under the national system introduced by the British government. Every school of any pretensions receives a grant-in-aid according to the yearly results of its teaching, and is brought under government revision; and furore for English education has been setting in, which promises to convert the wealthier classes into English-speaking people. At the same time the Native languages are by no means neglected, but Sanskrit is taught to the better classes, whilst much is being done to promote a better knowledge of the vernaculars amongst the masses.[115]

In his recent work *Cultural Politics* of *English as an International Language*, Alstair Pennycook has gone beyond the traditional dichotomies and stereotypes that characterize the historiography of English and the vernacular and has argued that English was promoted and its role strengthened in the dual discourses of

Orientalism and Anglicism. Pennycook has explored the complex ways in which both the policies existed side-by-side to serve the agenda of the colonial rule and Orientalism and Anglicism were actually complementary to each other. According to him:

> Orientalism was as much a part of colonialism as was Anglicism; . . . English was withheld as much as it was promoted; . . . colonised people demanded access to English; and finally, the power of English was not so much in its widespread imposition but in its operating as the eye of the colonial panopticon.[116]

Though the Orientalists and Vernacularists had lost their ground to the Anglicists, Sanskrit had continued to retain its importance and its existence was perpetuated and legitimized through its institutionalization. The government had continued its grant to the schools in which Sanskrit was taught. Sumathy Ramaswamy has shown that Sanskrit became increasingly available to all those who were interested in studying it as it was introduced into the curricula of numerous high schools, colleges and universities, sometimes even as a compulsory requirement.[117] M.G. Ranade supported government grants to rural schools in which traditional Sanskrit curriculum was taught, on the grounds that rigorous study of Sanskrit would elevate the moral character of the students.[118] Sanskrit also continued to be one of the major subjects to be studied in the Mumbai University.[119] It was made a mandatory second language in the guise of classical language; and in other institutions, it was allowed to be studied in lieu of the mother tongue.

The colonial rule, which provides constant historical backdrop to the post-colonial development, produced 'dependent and servile attitude' which post-independent India found difficult to shake off. The study of Sanskrit College and Elphinstone College, which reflect a conglomeration of interests and differentiated language policy, continues to be relevant today as reverberations of this policy can be heard and seen in the contemporary times. Continued prevalence of Sanskrit in India and the renewed interest in English in globalized India symbolically suggest the simultaneous existence of Brahminization and Anglicization of the masses in general and Indian intelligentsia in particular.

NOTES

1. Veena Naregal, *Language Politics, Elites and the Public Sphere: Western India under Colonialism*, New Delhi: Permanent Black, 2001, p. 57.
2. Gauri Viswanathan, *Masks of Conquest: Literary Study and British Rule in India*, 1989, New Delhi: Oxford University Press, 2000; Svati Joshi, *Rethinking English: Essays in Literature, Language, History*, New Delhi: Trianka, 1991; B.R. Bapuji, *Society, State and Education: Essays in the Political Sociology of Language Education*, Madras: T.R. Publications, 1993; Tejaswini Niranjana, *Siting Translation*, New Delhi: Oxford University Press, 1995; Alstair Pennycook, *English and the Discourse of Colonialism*, London: Routledge, 1998.
3. Jones came to India in the late eighteenth century with an ambitious aim to know India better than any other European ever knew it. His forceful presentation of the common origin of Sanskrit and European languages fired the imagination of the European scholars who popularized the notion of common origin of the European and Eastern races and biologised linguistic theory. For the critical analysis of Jones's contribution to linguistics and its repercussion on the linguistic thought in India, refer to O.P. Kejariwal, *The Asiatic Society of Bengal and the Discovery of India's Past 1784-1838*, New Delhi: Oxford University Press, 1988; Viswanathan, *Masks of Conquest*; Niranjana, *Siting Translation*; Thomas R. Trautmann, *Aryans and British India*, New Delhi: Yoda Press, 2004, pp. 28-61; Braj Ranjan Mani, *Debrahmanising History: Dominance and Resistance in Indian Society*, New Delhi: Manohar, 2005, pp. 191-2.
4. Max Müller was a German Philologist and Orientalist, who virtually created the discipline – Comparative Indology. A pioneering and painstaking edition of the *Rigveda* and the *Sacred Books of the East*, a massive 50-volume set of English translations prepared under his direction, earned great reputation for him in India as well as in Europe. Müller was greatly impressed by Ramkrishna Paramhansa, his contemporary and proponent of Vedantic philosophy, and authored several essays and books on him and in turn influenced the revivalists like B.G. Tilak. For the critical analysis of his contribution to Comparative Philology, refer to Vasudha Dalmiya-Luderitz, 'Fredrich Max Müller: Appropriation of the Vedic Past', *Journal of Arts & Ideas*, 17-18 June 1889, pp. 43-58; Trautmann, *Aryans and British India*, 2004.
5. Bernard Cohn, 'The Command of Language and the Language of Command', *Subaltern Studies IV: Writing on South Asian History and Society*, ed. Ranajit Guha, New Delhi: Oxford University Press, 1985; Henry Schwarz, 'Laissez-Faire Linguistics: Grammar and the Codes of Empire', *Critical Inquiry*, vol. 23, no. 3 (Spring, 1997): 509-35.

6. Kumkum Sangari, *Politics of the Possible: Essays on Gender, History, Narratives, Colonial English*, 1999, New Delhi: Tulika, 2001, p. 107.
7. Ibid.
8. Ibid., p. 109.
9. 'The dissemination of knowledge is in all cultivated societies the worthy occupation of talent and power. Even where the knowledge may not be of generally practical application, its possession may be endowed with specific value, and much that is little essential to the necessities of life, is of high value to intellectual ambition.'
   Hastings quoted in Sangari, p. 107.
10. Narain, p. 170.
11. H. Sharp, *Selections from Educational Records*, pt. I: *1781-1839*, Calcutta: Superintendent Government Printing India, 1920, p. 10.
12. Lynn Zastoupil and Martin Moir, *The Great Indian Education Debate: Documents Relating to the Orientalist-Anglicist Controversy, 1781-1843*, Surrey: Curzon, 1999, p. 90; Sangari, p. 110 (emphasis added).
13. Zastoupil et al., p. 7.
14. Anil Seal, *The Emergence of Indian Nationalism: Competition and Collaboration in the Later Nineteenth Century*, Cambridge: Cambridge University Press, 1968, p. 78.
15. Seal, 75.
16. Shravana is the fifth month of lunar calendar. For the details of the practice of *dakshina*, refer to *Peshwe Daptaratun Niwadlele Kagad*, vols. 42 (1942) and 43 (1943), Mumbai: Government Central Press; Ravinder Kumar, *Western India in the Nineteenth Century: A Study in the Social History of Maharashtra*, London: Routledge & Kegan Paul, 1968; Sudha Desai, *Social Life in Maharashtra under the Peshwas*, Mumbai: Popular Prakashan, 1980, pp. 90-4; A.R. Kulkarni, 'The Shastri Tradition of Pune in the Nineteenth Century', in *Maharashtra: Society and Culture*, New Delhi: Books and Books, 2000.
17. Kumar, p. 44.
18. Ibid., p. 45.
19. Ibid., p. 47.
20. Maharashtra State Archives (henceforth MSA), Political Department Diary, p. 482.
21. Kumar, p. 49.
22. H.V. Hampton, *Biographical Studies in Modern Indian Education*, Madras: Oxford University Press, 1947, p. 172.
23. Ibid.
24. George W. Forrest, ed., *Selections from the Minutes and Other Official Writings of the Honourable Mountstuart Elphinstone*, London: Richard Bentley and Son, 1884, p. 83.
25. Kumar, p. 39.

26. A.M. Sutar, 'Christianity in Western Maharashtra in the Nineteenth Century', Diss., Shivaji University, Kolhapur, 1980, p. 300.
27. *Tuladan* refers to weighing one person against various articles such as gold, silver, coconuts, etc., and distributing them to Brahmins.
28. *Bhumidaan* refers to gift of land to Brahmins, which was regarded as a highly meritorious act, etc. Sudha V. Desai, *Social Life in Maharashtra under the Peshwas*, Bombay: Popular Prakashan, 1980, p. 92.
29. Tariq Rahman, *Language and Politics in Pakistan*, Karachi: Oxford University Press, 1996, pp. 26-7.
30. McCully, p. 104.
31. Ibid.
32. Boman-Behram, pp. 498-9.
33. MSA, General Department (GD), vol. 9/10, 1821-2, p. 1.
34. Quoted in Kenneth Ballhatchet, *Social Policy and Social Change in Western India 1817-1830* (1957); London: Oxford University Press, 1961, p. 252. Also see G.T. Bapat, *Vishrambagwadyacha Itihas*, Pune: N.V. Sirdeshpande, 1950, p. 12.
35. MSA, GD, vol. 9/10, 1821-2, p. 1.
36. Ballahatchet, p. 256.
37. Quoted in K. Paddayya, 'On some Aspects of the Early History of the Deccan College', *Bulletin of the Deccan College* (2000-1), p. 54.
38. Quoted in Ballahatchet, p. 256.
39. R.V. Parulekar, Selections from Educational Records (Bombay), pp. 107-8.
40. Ballhatchet, p. 264.
41. Kumar, p. 266.
42. MSA, GD, vol. 17/349, 1836, p. 8.
43. Kumar, p. 266.
44. Ibid., p. 268.
45. Ibid.
46. MSA, GD, vol. 17/349, 1836, p. 8.
47. MSA, GD, vol. 15/385, 1837, pp. 139-50.
48. Ibid., p. 151.
49. MSA, GD, 9/526, 1840, p. 132.
50. Many early English educated natives like Bal Shastri Jambhekar, Dadoba Pandurang, Dadabhai Naoroji were employed in the Education Department. One of the three Native Inspectors of the district school was Mahadeo Govind Shastri.
51. MSA, GD, vol. 26, 1850, p. 17.
52. *Report of the Board of Education for the Year 1849*, vol. VIII, Bombay: Bombay Education Society's Press, 1851, p. 36.
53. *Report of the Board of Education for the Years 1847 and 1948* (*RBE*), Bombay: American Marathi Mission, 1850, pp. 36-7.

54. MSA, GD, vol. 26, 1850, p. 225.
55. Director of Education Archives, Pune (DEAP), *Poona Sanskrit College*, vol. 17, 1847-8.
56. DEAP, *Poona Sanskrit College*, vol. 17, 1847-8.
57. DEAP, *Poona College Report 1866-67*, vol. XII, p. 426.
58. Modhumita Roy, 'The Englishing of India: Class Formation and Social Privilege' *Social Scientist*, 21, 5-6 (1993): 37.
59. Kumar, p. 283.
60. Sangari, p. 105.
61. Thapar quoted in Sangari, p. 428.
62. C.A. Bayly, *Empire and Information: Intelligence Gathering and Social Communication in India, 1780-1870*, New Delhi: Foundation Books, 1999.
63. Maya Narkar, 'A Linguistic Study of the Nineteenth Century Marathi Translations', Diss. Shivaji University, Kolhapur, 1990; Niranjana, *Siting Translation*; Simon Sherry and Paul St-Pierre, *Changing the Terms: Translating in the Postcolonial Era*, Hyderabad: Orient Longman, 2000.
64. Sangari, p. 107.
65. Ibdi., p. 108.
66. Ibid., p. 109.
67. Ibid., p. 110.
68. Director of Education Archives, Pune. 'RBE for the Year 1845', *Board of Education 1846*, vol. I, p. 351; Sangari, p. 110.
69. MSA, GD, vol. 24-A/749-A, 1843, p. 77.
70. Sanskrit I conceive to be the grand storehouse, from which strength and beauty may be drawn for the Vernacular languages and it is therefore highly deserving of cultivation; but it cannot furnish from its stores the matter of instruction, nor can it ever be the medium of instruction to more than a few. Major Candy, *Report of Board of Education for the years 1847 and 1848*, no. VII, Bombay: American Mission Press, 1850, p. 180.
71. MSA, GD, vol. 39/409, 1837, p. 3.
72. His Lordship approves of the Board's proceedings in connection with the English school at Tanna. The inhabitants of that town, I am desired to state, should be distinctly made to understand in the event of any future application, that no English School will again be reestablished there, until they have given satisfactory evidence that they are prepared to support it, both by contributing towards the Master's salary, and by providing for the regular attendance of their children.
    RBE for the Year 1849, vol. VIII, Bombay: Bombay Education Society's Press, 1851, p. 105.
73. Ibid., p. 37 (emphasis added).

74. Warden put his argument: 'a good deal of knowledge to a few can only be promoted by a better system of education; and the surest mode of diffusing a better system is by making the study of the English language the primary and not merely secondary object of attention in the education of the natives'. A.N. Basu, *Indian Education in Parliamentary Papers*, pt. I, Bombay: Asia Publishing House, 1952, p. 221.
75. *RBE for the Year 1845*. Bombay: Government Printing Office, 1846, p. 10.
76. Ibid., p. 26.
77. Ibid., p. 24.
78. Ibid., p. 7.
79. MSA, GD, vol. 10/255, 1832, p. 58.
80. K. Paddayya, 'On Some Aspects of the Early History of the Deccan College', p. 52.
81. Surendra Prasad Sinha writes: 'At the instance of Mr. Warden, a reference was made to this college in 1825, desiring education added to this institution, and holding out the prospect of supplied with a library of the most useful works – elementary and practical – in all departments of literature, art and sciences. The proposal was acceded to with readiness.' Surendra Prasad Sinha, *English in India: A Historical Study with Particular Reference to English Education in India*, Patna: Janaki Prakashan, 1978, p. 45.
82. MSA, GD, vol. 10/255, 1832, pp. 58-9.
83. Ibid., p. 71.
84. *Report of Board of Education for the Years 1847 and 1848*, no. VII, Bombay: American Mission Press, 1850, p. 3.
85. MSA, GD, vol. 6/183, 1829, pp. 14-15.
86. *Report of Board of Education for the Years 1847 and 1848*, no. VII, p. 28.
87. *RBE for the Years 1840, 1841*, Bombay: American Mission Press, 1842, p. 24.
88. *Report 1842*, p. 27.
89. Ballhatchet, p. 293.
90. Elphinstone quoted in Forrest, p. 101.
91. Elphinstone wrote: 'While I was in Deckan I was led by an erroneous impression of the flourishing state of native schools to think that Colleges at Poona and Nassuck, with the printing of the number of books translated under the superintendence of the Persian Secretary, would be sufficient to every purpose. Further information and experience of the ill success of that plan led me to look to the School Society [i.e. the Bombay Education Society] for assistance and to suggest the formation of a new branch for Native School and School Books.' Covernton, 'The Educational Policy of Mountstuart

Elphinstone', *Journal of the Bombay Branch of the Royal Asiatic Society* (New Series), vol. II (1826), p. 57.

92. MSA, GD, vol. 9/10, 1821-22, p. 104.
93. Hampton, p. 174.
94. Naheed F. Ahmed, 'The Elphinstone College, Bombay, 1827-1890: A Case Study in 19th Century English Education', *Knowledge, Power and Politics: Educational Institutions in India*, pp. 392-3.
95. Ahmed, p. 393.
96. Ibid., p. 394.
97. Umesh Bagade, *Maharashtratil Prabodhan ani Vargjatiprabhutva*, Pune: Sugawa Prakashan, 2006, pp. 113-16.
98. MSA, GD, 10/163, 1828, pp. 41-2; Basu, p. 224.
99. MSA, GD, 10/163, 1828, pp. 46-7.
100. Sharp, p. 144.
101. R.D. Choksey, *Mountstuart Elphinstone: The Indian Years 1796-1827*, Bombay: Popular Prakashan, 1971, p. 383.
102. Hampton, pp. 167-8.
103. Ibid., p. 168.
104. Basu, p. 217.
105. Hampton, p. 68.
106. Ahmad, p. 395.
107. Ibid.
108. *RBE for the Year 1845*, p. 20.
109. Ahmad, p. 397.
110. Ibid., p. 400.
111. MSA, GD, vol. 12, 1851, p. 72.
112. Boman-Behram, p. 544.
113. Seal, p. 78.
114. J. Talboys Wheeler, *Tales From Indian History*, 1881; Calcutta: Thacker, Spink & Co., 1890, p. 198.
115. Pennycook quoted in A. Suresh Canagrajah, *Resisting Linguistic Imperialism in English Teaching* (1999), Oxford: Oxford University Press, 2000, p. 58.
116. Sumathy Ramaswamy, 'Sanskrit for the Nation', *Modern Asian Studies* 33: 2 (1999): 351.
117. Richard P. Tucker, *Ranade and the Roots of Indian Nationalism* (1972); Bombay: Popular Prakashan, 1977, p. 76.
118. Maya Narkar, 'A Linguistic Study of the Nineteenth Century Marathi Translations' Diss., Kolhapur: Shivaji University, 1990, p. 119.
119. Ramaswamy, p. 351.

CHAPTER 7

Popular Aspirations in the Periphery
The Genesis of University Education in Assam

NANDITA KHADRIA

Introduction

Aspiration for higher education, expected to be fulfilled through the establishment of a regional university, necessarily includes an element of promotion of regional language and culture within its fold.[1] In the colonial context the articulation of such an aspiration by the people of Assam, or of the Brahmaputra Valley districts of erstwhile Assam which now forms the present state of Assam, however, was a result of a more complex situation. The complexity arose from Bengali having been imposed as the official language and medium of instruction for almost 40 years in the nineteenth century[2] in Assam, as well as its being administratively linked to areas like the Sylhet district of Surma Valley (1874) and the Cachar district in the Barak Valley, both of which were predominantly Bengali-speaking areas. A study of the problematic within a given framework, that is, the situation being seen as a manifestation either of Assamese or Bengali chauvinism, or of the divide and rule policy orchestrated by the colonial rulers[3] that have been adopted by scholars to understand the complexity of the issue, would perhaps be a simpler course to follow here. However, though government policies may be linked to colonial interests of carrying out smooth and convenient administration without much burden on the treasury, a careful examination of sources also reveals contradictions in official as well as non-official views on important matters over a period of time. Biographical sketches of some pioneer administrators bring into light the fact that even within broad colonial objectives individual opinions were at times formed and decisions made on the merits of the cases locally, ignoring the broad goals of colonial administration.[4]

The necessity of establishing a university in India, with faculties of arts, law and civil engineering was officially brought to the notice of the Government of India by the Council of Education as early as 1844-5. But it was a full century before the first university in the north-east of India, viz., the Gauhati University came into being. Since the time it was constituted as a province in British India in 1874, Assam had been put under the University of Calcutta for educational purposes.[5] The demand for a university by the people of Assam in the Brahmaputra Valley was based on more than an educational need, one that reflected their regional and cultural aspirations as well as an aspiration for educational autonomy.[6] The establishment of the Gauhati University in 1948 was therefore seen by them equally as fulfilment of a cultural need as educational and economic.[7]

This paper traces briefly the course of developments and the gaps existing in the sphere of education in the early phase of British occupation of Assam, which contributed to the articulation of popular demand for higher educational institutions and a university at the regional level in the last quarter of the nineteenth century and the first half of the twentieth century. The sense of despair and insecurity of the Assamese speaking population in the late nineteenth century, their demand for restoration of Assamese language and subsequent demand for increase in higher educational institutions – culminating in the demand for a regional university located in Gauhati – the anxiety expressed by the Bengali-speaking population and the reservations of the Hills population of the province on the issue, may all be looked at either as predesigned actions or merely as dynamics of a multi-ethnic, multi-linguistic society. Through an examination of some colonial official sources, a few select biographies and contemporary writings in Assamese literature and newspapers, this paper tries to discern the various angles to the issue of demand for higher education in Assam. The larger issue of linguistic and ethno-cultural identity conflict of the communities is complex and demands an exhaustive study and analysis of existing available sources on all the aspects, which is beyond the scope of the present exercise.[8] The language aspect is therefore referred to here only for the purpose of providing a wider context to the demand for higher educational institutions in Assam.

The Background and Popular Base

Captain Jenkins, the Commissioner of Assam from 1834 to 1861, was a follower of the 'Filtration Theory' of education and firmly believed that in Assam too education should spread gradually from higher to the lower strata of society. However, school education in Assam spread fast due to very high demand for the English system of education. In fact, the demand continued to far exceed supply as with the introduction of the new revenue system people felt the need for at least a rudimentary knowledge of the three Rs.[9] Bengali was made the medium of instruction and official language of Assam in 1837 and it remained so till Assam was made a province under a Chief Commissioner in 1874. Since its annexation to British India in 1826, some 'vernacular' schools as part of the new system of education were opened in the region where teachers whose mother tongue was Assamese imparted instructions in Bengali. It was therefore an acquired language for the teachers, through which impartation of knowledge was not expected to be perfect at any rate.[10] In fact, even when Assamese was restored officially as the medium of instruction in schools Bengali had to be continued with as textbooks were not available in Assamese language till 1905, when the University of Calcutta recognized it as the second language.[11]

Assam came into contact with Western ideas through Bengal renaissance, and Raja Rammohun Roy's critique of both Indian and Western traditions and his social philosophy had in fact deeply impacted Assam's own cultural resurgence in the nineteenth and early twentieth centuries.[12] The national awareness among the Assamese therefore resulted from its contact with Bengal, which was the only channel for higher education for the Assamese and the aspirations of the middle class of Assam for greater share of jobs under the British administration. The contributions of the American Baptist Missionaries in the nineteenth century are worth mentioning in this context. Their efforts helped in the spread of education among common people and their establishment of a vernacular press paved the way for growth of Assamese literature and language. They strongly advocated for introduction of Assamese in the elementary schools, with emphasis on 'vernacular' as the medium. The mission-run schools adopted Assamese as their medium of instruction even when Bengali was the medium of instruction officially in the government schools. The first Assamese journal, *Orunodoi*, with voices from Assam was published from the Sibsagar Mission Press in 1846.[13] Subsequently, however, the missionaries shifted their focus to the hills region which was more receptive to their agenda of spreading Christian influence.[14] Last but not the least, the contribution of Anandaram Dhekial Phukan, as the first spokesperson of the Assamese people at the official level, needs a special mention in this context. In the memorandum submitted by him on behalf of the Assamese people as early as 1853, Dhekial Phukan strongly argued in favour of including Assamese along with Bengali in the new education system – with Assamese as the medium of instruction.

External Reach: Education under the University of Calcutta

Assam was included in the territorial limits within which the University of Calcutta exercised the rights conferred on it by statute. The colleges in Assam were accordingly affiliated to, and the high schools recognized by the University of Calcutta, which set the courses for colleges and higher school classes and examined candidates for matriculation from the schools and for diplomas and degrees from colleges. It was officially explained that this arrangement of bringing Assam's schools and colleges under the authority of University of Calcutta was 'a consequence of the remoteness of Assam and of its backwardness in education for long' at the time of the establishment of University of Calcutta.[15] Despite this, the province had no representation on the syndicate or governing body of the University of Calcutta and had no say in the management of its affairs, though the indirect relationship between Assam and the University of Calcutta continued. Students from Assam could train themselves in general and technical subjects in Bengal or the university colleges in Calcutta, in institutions such as the Medical College, Calcutta, and the Civil Engineering College, Shibpur, against a proportionate contribution paid by the Government of Assam to the Government of Bengal.

Earlier, during the greater part of the nineteenth century, higher education of Assam was absolutely dependent on the University of Calcutta as there were no colleges in Assam. By 1862 the schools of Assam were also affiliated to University of Calcutta for sending candidates for the entrance examination, and a collegiate section was opened in the Gauhati School in 1866. The college was, however, abolished in 1876 due to poor performance and the school reduced to a *zilla* school.[16] The demand for secondary education meanwhile continued and district schools were opened in Dibrugarh (1864), Nowgong and Tezpur (1865) and Silchar (1868).[17] There was also notable increase in private English schools by the last quarter of the nineteenth century and, consequently, an articulation of demand for higher education at the college level. Popular demand for higher education had in fact started being expressed through representations from the 1860s onwards. The initial response of the government by increasing scholarships to college students studying in Calcutta had silenced the popular voices for some time but when, in 1887, the number of fellowships was reduced to channellize resources towards medical and engineering branches of education in Calcutta, a fresh demand for a college – mostly in favour of its location in Gauhati – ensued. The Murari Chand College, established in 1891 in Sylhet, did not enhance educational opportunities for the people of Brahmaputra Valley due its locational disadvantage. In 1899, Manik Chandra Barooah made a strong case for a college in Gauhati which was supported by the Chief Commissioner, Sir Henry Cotton. A circular was thereafter issued seeking public opinion, to which overwhelming response was received. On 27 May 1901, the Cotton College was formally opened in Gauhati, with F.W. Sudmerson as its principal; it was to become the premier educational institution of Assam within a decade and a University College by its Golden Jubilee year (1951-2).[18]

With the establishment of Murari Chand College and Cotton College facilities were locally available for classes up to the first Arts standard of the university.[19] Both were however second-grade colleges to start with and made no serious change in the situation. Students had to proceed from there to Bengal to complete their education. The enrolment in the two colleges at the beginning of 1905 together was only 97. As such they did not draw any attention of the framers of the Indian Universities Act of 1904 to make special provisions for Assam and its interests in the body of the statute. However, as the first principal of the Cotton College, F.W. Sudmersen wrote in his special message sent on the occasion of the Silver Jubilee of the college, 'Gradually but inevitably Assamese students secured increasing successes and distinction . . . and Sir Ashutosh Mukherjee . . . gave the college marked approval even in its early days as a Second Grade College.'[20] Soon afterwards, under Principal Sudmersen's leadership, and with Sir Henry Sharp as the Director of Public Instructions, Cotton College began its course as a first-grade college.[21]

Of the many changes brought about by the Act of 1904, what concerned Assam most was that the territorial limits of the University of Calcutta now comprised the provinces of Bengal, Burma and Assam. Further, it changed the character of the university from a mere affiliating and examining body to a direct agent in the work of teaching and research. It removed secondary education from the control of the local Government of Assam and placed it under the university. This meant that the government retained the responsibility without the authority. The relationship between Assam and Bengal in respect to the free participation in the university was of course not affected by this, according to official observations. The amending Act passed in 1921, Calcutta University Act No.VII, however, converted the university from an imperial into a provincial institution, despite Assamese representation in the Legislative Assembly against the move. The higher institutions of Assam were to be controlled from Bengal and subject to legislation in the Bengal Council. By this time both of Assam's colleges had not only become first-grade colleges, but were ranked among the best in the university. Cotton College was the only college outside Calcutta that offered instructions beyond the honours degree standard. But Assam still did not have any representation on the governing body of the University of Calcutta, including the Senate of the Faculties.[22] The Government of India Act of 1935 took away the 'last safeguard' by including education in the list of provincial subjects which passed the control of secondary and university education of Assam into the hands of Bengal Legislature. Though it was not to the interest of the University of Calcutta to exclude students from its postgraduate classes, the Act of 1935 certainly made Assam's position more vulnerable.[23]

It is generally agreed by scholars that it was a pre-designed action on the part of the British imperialists to impose the strategy of divide and rule for trouble-free administration – which in case of Assam was by segregating the two linguistic communities. Be that as it may, there cannot be any doubt that the situation arising out of the language policies adopted by the British in Assam at various points was one of mutual suspicion and hostility. Assam's aspirations for higher education and its accompanying opportunities also cannot be separated from the larger question of Assamese identity formation, which, by the 1930s, had converged with the national identity at least in the political arena – though the regional identity continued to retain its own separate space.[24] In the sphere of regional identity the imposition of an alien language had affected the different social classes differently – but public opinion expressed through the press and other medium shared the same aspirations of restoring Assamese as the language of the province. This has also been seen as a precondition to collective linguistic patriotism in Assam.[25]

Voice through Associations and Students' Movements

As mentioned earlier, the impact of Bengal on the cultural life of Assam had continued, and in fact contributed towards fuelling Assam's aspirations for regeneration of its own language, literature and culture and to have more and higher institutions of learning of its own. Right from the memorandum of Anandaram Dhekial Phukan (1854) appended in Mills' Report on Assam, the issue of revival of Assamese language and culture had been continuously highlighted by the educated Assamese, as evident from the subsequent memorandums presented by the indigenous associations to this effect from time to time. The Jorhat Sarbajanik Sabha (1892) was moderate in its articulation of a fear of Bengali domination over Assamese, than the candid articulation of the radical Asamiya Sangrakshini Sabha. A memorandum/letter addressed to the Chief Commissioner of Assam by the Jorhat Sarbajanik Sabha in 1892 brings out their sense of insecurity as it drew a comparative picture of the situation between the two linguistic groups in the field of education and opportunity. The memorandum made the observation that in the Assam Valley there were only two graduates in 1874 – one of them a member of the ICS – which rose to 32, as compared to 50 in the Surma Valley in 1892: 'The Committee of the Sabha would earnestly hope that the graduates of this province may receive due recognition and encouragement in the hands of the local government. Such recognition and encouragement being calculated to stimulate the cause of high education in the Province.'[26] Further,

As regards the employment of the natives of the soil in the service of their own province the proportion in which they have been employed is much discouraging. . . . The country (Assam) is making a great deal of progress in all departments of national prosperity . . . while all this improvement is taking place, the number of Assamese officers is being less.[27]

While reiterating that the Jorhat Sabha did not want to belittle the services of the non-Assamese, it put forward, 'Time has, however, arrived when the main body of the service should be recruited from the natives of the province (as done in Bengal, Bihar and Orissa)'.[28] Also,

The Committee of the *Jorhat Sarbajanik Sabha* would fail in their duty if they would not inform the Government of the feeling of disappointment and regret occasioned by the recommendation of the Chief Commissioner that no scheduled posts should be reserved for Assam on the ground that the state of education in the province does not warrant such reservation within a measurable distance of time.[29]

The Jorhat Sabha continued actively till 1921, in which year the Sabha also welcomed Mahatma Gandhi on his visit to Assam. As opposed to the moderate voice of the Jorhat Sabha, the Asamiya Sabha was more forceful. In a memorandum which was presented to Jawaharlal Nehru as president of the Indian National Congress in 1937, having cited the various circumstances which contributed to the overshadowing of Assamese language and culture by Bengali, the Asamiya Sabha had concluded:

It is perhaps difficult for an outsider to realize the true feelings of the outraged manhood of Assam. Desperation has taken possession of the minds of the people. And as a means of saving the Assamese race from immediate extinction, a considerable section of the Assamese intelligentsia has even expressed their minds in favour of the secession of Assam from India. This is how the present situation appears to the average Assamese, and they look to you, the National Congress, to help the Assamese to get out of this danger.[30]

The point was qualified further,

This time the whole of the Assamese people have wholeheartedly supported the Congress candidates on the assurance that the Congress would take up provincial matters seriously. If the National Congress takes up seriously the cause for separating Sylhet and South Cachar where Bengalee predominates and stopping mass immigration from Bengal, the Assamese people will be the staunchest supporter of the Congress as a whole. A hundred years of

British rule has not been able to crush our spirit for liberty. *We want Swaraj by all means. But it is also true that we do not want it at the cost of extinction of our race* (emphasis added).[31]

The Assam Association was organized by Manik Chandra Barooah on the basis of the Indian Association founded in Calcutta earlier. The association's central office was at Gauhati till 1915, and its president P.C. Baruah used to function from both Gauripur and Calcutta.[32] Most of its leading members were also legislators, and could draw attention to issues through their speeches and debates. But it was only in the Gauhati session in 1916 that the rural and urban population came together on a national forum without any social distinction. This association merged with the All Assam Provincial Congress Committee subsequently.[33] The Assam Association was a more moderate and mature organization. It focused on appealing to the government for education and employment of the Assamese people without antagonizing it. In fact, the association – to begin with – was a proponent of British rule as opposed to the students' association. The waves of nationalism in the 1920s, however, changed the attitude of the educated middle class in Assam towards colonial rule.[34] The more radical students could also successfully demolish the arguments of the moderate associationists through debates, exhibitions, and so on,[35] and soon their efforts to create a strong public opinion for the establishment of a separate university in Assam started gaining greater public support as compared to the other political organizations in the province.

Student forums of Assam have historically voiced demands and aspirations of the people of the region. The tradition was inherited from the *Raijmel*, a public forum involved in community welfare issues, which continues to influence the public mind considerably in Assam. This is apparent from the various public debates over issues ranging, in the field of education for example, from the establishment of an educational institution to its administrative and quality aspects that engage the educated Assamese relentlessly and opens public debates through the forum of newspapers and journals.[36] Following this tradition, Assamese students continued to take active interest in the socio-political and economic development of the region in this period of great historical significance. As early as in 1907, a group of resident Assamese students of Calcutta led by P.C. Baruah submitted a memorandum to the Secretary of State, pleading for separation of Assam from East Bengal. It was pointed out by them that Cotton College could in no way compete with the standard of Dacca College since a proposal to upgrade the former was turned down by the government. As a result of this, it was stated, the educational prospects of Assamese youth were very bleak as compared to their advanced counterparts in the Bengal districts.[37]

The formation of a students' organization at the provincial level took place in 1916 in the form of Asom Chhattra Sanmilan (modelled after the Bihar Chhattra Sammelan of 1906 and the Bangiya Sahitya Sammelan) at the initiative of K.K. Handiqui. The Sanmilan at this point aimed to serve the nation through promotion of language and literature of the land. Through a collection of rare manuscripts in Assamese on various cultural aspects and their publication, Assamese literature was expected to be enriched and be the medium of Assamese national pride. Initially the Sanmilan focused on regional issues like upliftment of Assamese literature and cultural activity, but gradually moved on to larger national issues like Non-Cooperation and Civil Disobedience movements.[38] The Civil Disobedience in particular assumed a local character, turning into anti-Cunningham Circular agitation which concerned the students,[39] and the anti-opium agitation where the students played an important role, at the same time not associating the Sanmilan with the political nationalist programme.[40]

The Sanmilan, known initially as Asomiya Chhattra Sahitya Sanmilan, met for the first time in 1916 in Gauhati with Lakshminath Bezbarua, the pioneer of modern Assamese literature, as its president. It was in this very first session that its name was changed to Asom Chhattra Sanmilan so that the focus did not remain strictly literary. The presidential address of Bezbarua focused on character formation of students, though Bezbarua also reminded the students about the need for an arts college and a law college in Assam.[41] The second session had K.K. Handiqui as the organizer, and in his speech he remarked on the need to improve the standard of school education, to close the gap between school and higher education, and to make education all inclusive. In his presidential address in 1918 at Dibrugarh, Padmanath Gohain Barua defined its objectives by observing that, the Sanmilan ought to help individual efforts for the general benefit of the student community; help the student community in literary development; and encourage the students intellectually, mentally and physically.[42]

The 1919 session of the Sanmilan was presided over by Acharya Prafulla Chandra Ray, the well-known chemist and founder of Bengal Chemicals & Pharmaceuticals, India's first pharmaceutical company. A *swadeshi* proponent and author of *A History of Hindu Chemistry from the Earliest Times to the Sixteenth Century* (1902), Ray's presence inspired many students to boycott foreign goods. The 1920 session of the Sanmilan was presided over by historian D.R. Bhandarkar, who impressed the students with his explanation of *swadeshi* in relation to development of trade and commerce in India. The issue of the need for a regional university loomed large in the vision of the Sanmilan through the decade of the 1920s and early 1930s. The Assam Students' Literary Club of Calcutta and the Assam Students' Welfare League of Calcutta too joined in this demand for a university in Assam.[43]

Concern of the Educated Assamese

The middle-class Assamese of nineteenth century were mostly educated in Calcutta. Among the early Assamese educated under the new system was Jagannath Barua, a tea planter, known as B.A. Jagannath by virtue of his being the first graduate in Upper Assam, which comprises the tea districts of erstwhile Sibsagar and Lakhimpur. He graduated from the Presidency College, Calcutta, in 1872.[44] Other than Dhekial Phukan and Jagannath Barua, in the first generation of the Assamese who studied in Presidency College, Calcutta was Anandaram Barua, and the later students included Surya Kumar Bhuyan, Banikanta Kakati and Gunabhiram Barua – all distinguished scholars and personalities in different walks of life in the region. As has been observed, the educated elite of that period derived their social consciousness from the egalitarian structure of Assamese society with their roots in the rural agrarian society, which made them in no way comparable to their Western-educated counterparts in Bengal.[45] Most meritorious students from Assam used to enroll for higher education in Presidency College at the time. Krishna Kanta Handiqui, a Sanskrit scholar, however, enrolled in the Sanskrit College of Calcutta in 1915. He had secured first-class first position in Sanskrit in the M.A. examination, and later got a first-class honours degree in Modern History from Oxford, apart from studying European classical languages in Germany and France for several years. The high level of scholarship in Calcutta and the personality of the vice-chancellor, Sir Ashutosh Mukherjee, who did not allow any interference even from the imperial government in the administration of the University of Calcutta, had lasting impact on the great visionary, Krishna Kanta, who was to be the first vice-chancellor of the Gauhati University later.

The Assamese students of Calcutta in the early twentieth century were a very progressive group and much influenced by Lakshminath Bezbarua who used to publish the journal *Banhi*, and celebrate the Assamese festivals with the student community in Calcutta. They also volunteered help for the resident Assamese of Calcutta in their times of need. The first private college of Assam and the north-east came up in 1930 in Jorhat – named Jagannath Barua College – with Krishna Kanta Handiqui as its founder-principal. Despite lack of initial support from local people and opposition from the Government of India, the college got recognition from University of Calcutta under support from Syama Prasad Mookerjee. The only two other colleges of Assam at the time were Cotton College, Gauhati, and M.C. College, Sylhet, and people with inadequate means from Upper Assam had to end their education after school due to the distance to both. The J.B. College got permission to start the B.Com. course from University of Calcutta only in 1944, before which the students from Assam had to go to Dacca to get a commerce degree. There was also no women's college in Assam at the time, the first women's college being Handique Girls' College, established in 1937 in Gauhati. The J.B. College had opened a morning section exclusively for girls in 1946, and the science branch was opened later in 1950 through public contribution, putting the college in the second position with science courses.[46]

Krishna Kanta presided over the 17th session of the Assam Sahitya Sabha in 1937, where in his presidential address he emphasized the need for spreading Assamese language to the neighbouring hills so as to include the people of the Hill Districts of Assam in its cultural-social affairs. He also remarked that a separate university was needed in Gauhati for facilitating research in classical Assamese language, literature and culture, and that the purpose of this will be defeated if the proposed university were to be established in Shillong. This was reiterated in 1944 by the Assamese newspaper, *Asamiya*. The *Asamiya* was published from 1918 onwards by Chandrakumar Agarwala, and it had soon become the voice of many educated Assamese. The paper published a special university issue in August 1944, the print order for which was reportedly double the usual number. Although the movement for a regional university had started much earlier, the year 1944 was significant from the point of view of the fact that in that year a group of youths had launched a fresh wave of agitation under the leadership of Madhab Chandra Bezbaurah. Jyotiprasad Agarwala, a doyen of Assamese art, culture and music, and also the editor of the paper, wrote in his editorial note that although a reactionary government did not acknowledge the need for a local university at the time, the people of Assam were very much aware of such a need, and that this awareness encompassed all sections of the rural and the urban population equally. Agarwala's emphatic assertion that whether public or private, the university in Assam was a must, was subsequently followed by other newspapers like *Banhi* and *Assam Tribune* and gave the final push to this popular movement.[47]

Public Voice on the University Question

The Assam University Enquiry

The Assamese-Bengali question had came to occupy a crucial place in more than one sense and the scope of the proposed university was also seen in the official circles as dependent upon the settlement of the issue.[48] Even other than speaking different languages the two valleys had different historical experiences. Sylhet was a densely populated area occupied by a homogeneous population in so far as they all spoke the Bengali language, due to it being an integral part of British India prior to its inclusion in Assam, but otherwise diverse in terms of class, caste or religion. The Brahmaputra Valley, on the other hand, was historically a sparsely peopled area under the independent kingdom of Ahoms, but had gained in population since its inclusion in the British territory mostly through migration – which made it a multi-lingual, -religious, -ethnic and, -cultural entity.

With the development of education in the province it was felt by the government that, in her own interest, Assam should take part of the work on her own shoulders, such part as might be fitted to assume, and it was observed that this feeling was growing stronger with the passing of the Government of India Act of 1935 and the immediate prospect of provincial autonomy. In fact, there was a complete reversal of the official opinion which at one time had accepted the Assamese language as a dialect of Assam. The new mood was reflected in the observations of noted linguists and scholars like G.F. Nicholl, who mentioned: 'Assamese is not, as many suppose, a corrupt dialect of Bengali, but a distinct and co-ordinate tongue, having with Bengali a common source of current vocabulary. Its Sanskrit did not come to it from Bengal, but from the upper provinces of India – this all who carefully examine the matter will readily admit.'[49]

It was further observed by Sir Grierson, a noted authority on the subject:

> Assamese literature is as old, if not older, than that of Bengali and down to the commencement of the present century (nineteenth) was as copious. . . . Assamese literature is essentially a national product. It always has been national, and it is so still. The genius of its people has led it along lines of its own, and its chief glory – history – is a branch of study almost unknown to the indigenous literature of Bengal. Whether the nation has made the literature or the literature the nation, I know not, but as a matter of fact, both have been for centurics and are in vigorous existence. Between them, they have created a standard literary language which, whether its grammar resembled that of Bengali or it has won for itself the right to a separate independent existence.[50]

While appreciating that the Assamese were in the process of regaining their cultural identity, it was noted that:

> The Assamese have nevertheless reclaimed their language and are in a fair way to reclaining their authority and proceeding to a national development. . . . With a university under their own control they now feel that they would have a fair wind in the shoulder of their sail, and might at last, if they were left free from interference, set their own course in confidence of the future. Nor do they consider that this assertion of their integrity and independence conflict with the ideal of Indian nationality. Assam also, they believe, has something individual and valuable to contribute to the national effort and it is in the larger interest as well as her own that she should come in with a good heart as a respected and self-respecting partner in the commonwealth.[51]

A 'movement' was accordingly started for the establishment of a provincial university – 'taken up very enthusiastically' by the Assamese people of the Brahmaputra Valley. It, however, received 'a more doubtful, even hostile, reception' in the Surma Valley. The first official move came from Maulavi Munawwar Ali who sought permission to present a bill at the May-June Legislative Council session of 1935 for the constitution of a provincial university. Although this permission was not granted, Sir Michael Keane, the Governor, in his opening address informed the council that the Minister for Education proposed to appoint an experienced officer to enquire into the matter and report. At the same session a resolution was moved by Rev. J.J. Nichols Roy, recommending to the Government of Assam that a scheme for a university in Assam be immediately prepared and placed before the Council.[52]

In the ensuing debate, clear indications were given by the Assam Valley members in favour of a regional university and the reverse by Surma Valley members, whose voice was represented by Babu Gopendralal Das Chaudhury on the following manner: '. . . if the people of Assam Valley wish to have a university they can have it and we will help them to have it, but the people of Surma Valley do not want it and I do not see why it should be thrust on us against our will.'[53]

The draft bill proposed by Maulavi Munawwar Ali, for the constitution of a provincial university was not allowed to be presented at the Legislative Council meeting of May-June 1935, but it was further expanded by the Assam Association. However, certain decisions had to be arrived at before anything concrete could be thought of – the most important of which being the settlement of the outstanding issue between the Brahmaputra Valley and Sylhet, availability of funds *vis-à-vis* the urgency of the need, and the scope and aim of the university – with particular reference to the prevailing connection between education and unemployment. In view of the proposed introduction of the 'Assam University Bill' in 1935, J.R. Cunningham, retired D.P.I. of Assam, and better known for his infamous circular of 1930, was appointed as in-charge of an expert committee to look into various issues relating to the proposed university.[54] The committee was expected to consider public opinion regarding the issue and give its advice, but the final decision was to rest with the government. The committee made a thorough investigation into the matter and submitted its report. The government thus set out on the task of framing a definite scheme after discussing the questions raised and the responses received. There was an overwhelming response from the public in the form of individuals, groups, associations and public meetings to the questionnaire circulated – of which the Assam Association was particularly elaborate, with a carefully prepared plan.[55] The local press too was very eloquent as observed earlier – representing different points of view. No difference of opinion amongst the castes or between the Hindus and Muslims was observed by the Enquiry Committee from these responses, although regional differences pertaining to the language issue were noticed. The main difference was found between the Hindu populations of the two valleys, being very sharp and strongly expressed, thus putting the university question in an unfriendly situation.

The educated Assamese from all classes voiced their opinion – in a clear, confident and unanimous manner – that the people of Assam Valley eagerly desired to escape from the control of University of Calcutta and to have a university of their own. They reportedly wanted it immediately and majority voiced in favour of Gauhati (as opposed to Jorhat). It was observed that this university may not cover the entire province in its scope, but essentially it aimed to promote the study and stimulation of Assamese literature and culture and the 'advancement of interests of the Assamese people'. But popular voice was not limited to the cultural aspect alone. It also pointed out that the university must be more selective than the University of Calcutta, more practical, and should combine the unitary and affiliating systems. The intermediate work was to be carried out at the school level – so the university was free for higher level of training. Most importantly, '. . . the courses should aim at covering not only the requirements of the services and the professions but the full range of the cultural and economic needs and opportunities of the people of the Valley.'[56]

Apparently, by this time the popular perception was clear that a single university was not going to be acceptable to the people of both the valleys and hence the people of Assam put forward their own needs. Even had there been a meeting point between the aspirations of the people of the two valleys over the economic needs, there could have been no same thoughts on the cultural point, as the perceived need for 'enhancement' of the Assamese language and culture at that point in the history of Assam was very much in relation to the earlier imposition of Bengali language there, and its continued influence. Neither were the people of Surma Valley disposed favourably towards accepting a regional university where the Assamese language and culture predominated. The majority of the educated Bengali Hindus of Sylhet opposed the proposal of a provincial university altogether because they did not want their lot to be ultimately cast with either the Assamese or the Muslims of Sylhet, and felt secure to continue under the umbrella of the University of Calcutta despite its being overburdened. In case of a necessary separation from Calcutta, the Hindus of Surma Valley wanted the regional university to be located either in Sylhet or in Shillong. Another group voiced in favour of a single smaller university for each valley. There was also strong opposition to the proposal from the legal professionals, doctors, journalists, educationists as well as some landed aristocracy of Sylhet – comprising the elite section – on the ground that the move was premature since the province lacked the necessary infrastructure to start a university. But above all, protests were made on the ground that having been already separated from Bengal, the cutting off of Sylhet's only existing link with Bengali culture through University of Calcutta will 'complete the cultural ruin of the Bengalis in Assam'. Interestingly enough, the Muslim communities of Sylhet neither showed any particular partiality towards Calcutta, nor were they opposed to the establishment of a university in the province. Opinions varied, however, as to the nature of the proposed university, its scope of authority and location – with definite preference being shown for basing it in Sylhet.[57]

In so far as the Cachar and Goalpara districts were concerned, the former a predominantly Bengali-speaking district and the latter a border district between Assam and North Bengal, Goalpara showed indifference to the proposal, whereas Cachar followed the lead of the Sylhet Hindu community and lodged a protest. The domicile Bengali community of the Brahmaputra Valley reportedly kept out of the 'imbroglio', and the Hills population did not show much interest in the proposal, since the indigenous communities there were on the whole sceptical about the relevance of the course structure of the existing university system to the educational requirements of the Hills people. They however voiced their need for a Hills college, with reference to the educational systems of the various Hill areas.[58]

Interestingly, although there were differences of opinion regarding the proposal of a separate university in Assam as well as its location in the event of the province being granted a separate university, there was a general agreement among the divergent interest groups on the following points: first, it was voiced that any university scheme to be framed must face and deal with the question of educated unemployment; second, the university must be relieved of part or all of the intermediate work – the school system was to be reorganized and given such responsibilities; and third, the university should set higher standards than that prevailing and maintain it. In the face of covert and overt hostility of the communities towards each other, it is interesting to note that their perception of the regional educational and economic needs matched naturally with one another.

In this atmosphere of rising expectations, the Assam University Enquiry Report came as a severe blow for the Assamese as it suggested a compromise to satisfy the people of both the valleys. The plan was unacceptable to the people. Neither did the University Bill, presented by the Saadulla Ministry in the Legislative Council on 4 March 1941 satisfy the people of either valley. It evoked widespread protests from both the valleys. When invited to give his expert opinion on the bill by the Select Committee, S.P. Mookerjee too noted that it would not be good for Assam to let the bill pass as it is since he found many loopholes in it and suggested fundamental alterations to it. The discussions and debates failed to be conclusive and the movement lay dormant till 1944.[59] D.E. Roberts, principal, Cotton College, too gave very strong opinions regarding the unsuitability of the suggestions made in the Enquiry Report. As he observed:

> University Headquartes should be in close proximity to one of the major colleges, and there is a strong case for Gauhati (with its senior college) as a centre, that for Shillong, to my mind, resting mainly on the apparent necessity of placating the Surma Valley . . . Shillong . . . is remote in a very real sense from the life – and its connected problems – of the plains people of Assam – its main body. University developments in Shillong would gain nothing from, and be of no advantage to any of the existing colleges.[60]

Establishment of Gauhati University

The Dream Coming True

Despite the prolonged considerations and background research conducted by the government, the decision to establish the university was kept pending, due perhaps also to the more pressing matters at hand for the imperial government. The issue was revived when a Trust Board for the University was formed in 1944, with Gopinath Bordoloi, the first chief minister of Assam, as its president,[61] and Fakhruddin Ali Ahmad, later president of India, as the secretary. It is imperative here to make more than a passing reference to the unstinted support of Bordoloi towards this final shape given to the university project from late 1930s onwards, without which the outcome could at least have been delayed substantially.[62] He had given considerable thought to the aims and the academic and administrative aspects of the university. While confined in Jorhat Jail in 1944, the preparation of a bill for the proposed university by the League-Coalition Ministry of Assam prompted Bordoloi to compose his ideas on these aspects of the university in an (unpublished) article.[63] From this and the entries in his diary one learns of the Gandhian influence Bordoloi had over the desired education system in the lines of people's university for the region. He lamented the fact that though the villages were our economic pillars, the modern education system provided nothing towards their development, and expressed strong faith that the newly-established university in Assam should be able to fill such a vital gap in the system.[64] He was also in favour of academic and administrative autonomy of the proposed university, and as such against any control by the government in its internal affairs.[65]

The Trust Board under Bordoloi's leadership could collect Rs. 5 lakh within three months as a result of the wholehearted support of the people of Assam. The land was acquired in Jalukbari in Gauhati, and the first meeting of the University Court was held on 26 January 1948 where the chief minister handed over the land and Rs. 6 lakh to the authorities. The meeting also paid homage to the early leaders of the movement for a university, like N.C. Bordoloi, M.C. Bezbaruah, S.C. Goswami and Bhimbar Deuri. Gandhi sent his opinion that an Assamese must be chosen as the first vice-chancellor of the university. The Court chose Krishna Kanta Handiqui as the vice-chancellor, who continued in the position for nine years comprising three consecutive terms.[66]

From the beginning the Gauhati University looked up to the University of Calcutta as its role model of a national university and tried to shape it up as such under the able guidance of Handiqui. In 1949 a team under S. Radhakrishnan, chairman, University Education Commission, visited the university and was satisfied with its initial progress. To start with, it was decided to follow the model of University of Calcutta to open departments in History, Philosophy, Economics, Assamese, Mathematics, Statistics, Botany, Education and Commerce. A teachers' training course was organized with the Department of Education. In addition to B.T. classes the university provided a Teachers' Training Certificate Course in Geography.

Under the Gauhati University came all the colleges and the Law College. The Dibrugarh Medical College, the Veterinary College, Jorhat Agricultural College and the Art College of Manipur were affiliated to it. What helped the vice-chancellor in building the university most was the reassurance of non-interference from the government in the initial years, which made the university functional within a short time. As a result it soon earned acceptance from the other established institutions. The university was lucky to have a scholar and dedicated institution-builder of the stature of Handiqui in the most crucial period of its foundation. In fact, it has been observed that Handiqui was himself an institution and a subject matter for research during his lifetime itself.[67] His scholarship and administrative capabilities have been widely acknowledged in Assam as well as other parts of the country. Handiqui was also appointed the president of Inter-University Committee in 1952.[68] The nine years under his leadership saw rapid progress in the field of higher education in Assam. He paid extensive visits to different parts of the province to check the examination centres and their maintenance of discipline and decorum, which was a task conducted by the University of Calcutta till then. At the first convocation of the university in 1951, Handiqui addressed the students with hope and caution:

> Examinations as system are decried from time to time but they provide a vital link between the University and the public; and the University as the guardian of its own reputation must be able to inspire confidence. . . . The University seems to have been able to evoke enthusiasm among our students, to judge from the numbers attending the University classes (more than 800 in 1949-50). But numbers do not count, and enthusiasm and hopes are not enough; our young men must strive and work as the University itself must work and serve in dust and heat, regardless of the difficulties and discomforts inevitable at the initial stage of our common venture.[69]

The university also had to face tremendous financial strain as the second convocation address of the vice-chancellor points out, particularly in view of its enhancement of the library and other infrastructure. A visionary from his early youth, Handiqui was also sensitive to the needs of the non-ethnic population of Assam and their educational needs:

> Assam is the meeting ground of diverse racial and linguistic groups. The policy of the University is to harmonize and give due recognition to the legitimate interests of all such groups who, in their turn, are expected to regard the University as their own. It was primarily on this ground that the University of Gauhati opposed the proposal to give extra-territorial jurisdiction to the Indian Universities to help in the solution of educational problems of linguistic minorities.... The University of Gauhati supports the opinion of the Standing Committee that no University should be invested with extra-territorial jurisdiction, nor is it necessary for the solution of the language problem as there should be no difficulty in special provision being made for the study of different languages in the Universities. *A regional University should, in fact, be able to solve the educational problems of the area under its control without any outside interference affecting its autonomy or jurisdiction* (emphasis added).[70]

Krishna Kanta Handiqui's sensitivity to the existing linguistic and ethnic diversities, and future vision for the youth of the region was further evident from his second convocation address on 31 January 1955:

> Assam is a multi-lingual area, and English is likely to continue as the medium of instruction at the University for a longer period than anywhere else in the Indian Union. It is time that the younger generation should realize the importance of the English language as a great international medium of science and knowledge. . . . Since its inception the University has paid some attention to academic standards and tried to attract well-qualified men as teachers from all parts of India. Assam like other states is on the eve of large-scale development and reconstruction, and the task of providing the requisite personnel for the new departments of activities has devolved upon the State University. It is therefore all the more necessary that the University should be able to maintain its standards and provide facilities for better teaching, better learning and more effective training in methodical habits of works. . . . *It is our firm belief that given the necessary scope and facilities this University will be in a position to achieve its mission of enlightenment in this remote corner of India and act as a great cohesive force in an area inhabited by diverse linguistic groups* (emphasis added).[71]

Conclusion

The establishment of the first Open University in Assam recently in the year 2005 – named Krishna Kanta Sandikoi State Open University after the first vice-chancellor of Gauhati University – and the first of its kind to be established in the north-east more than 50 years after the first university was opened in the region, is a landmark development in the education system of the region in more ways than one. Although started as a state university, the scope of this Open University is not limited to its geographical boundary, with plans to include the entire north-east region under its umbrella by offering vocational courses in conjunction with the needs of the region.[72] Traditionally valuing higher education, the Open University signifies another step towards the fulfilment of popular aspirations for higher education, and reminds one of the visions of the founder vice-chancellor of Gauhati University of seeing it act as a great cohesive force in an undivided Assam with diverse ethnic and linguistic groups.

The main objective of this paper has been to attempt a diversion from the stereotypes of linguistic chauvinism and divide-and-rule biases for studying the popular demand for higher education in Assam and highlighting the dynamics of popular aspirations in the context of a highly divergent ethno-linguistic society. Analysing the development of higher education in this context from a long-term perspective the paper has attempted to show that the aspirations, anxieties and demands of the various interest groups were based on historical circumstances and an instinct of self-preservation in the prevailing socio-political set-up. The colonial government, on the other hand, being primarily guided by imperial dictates, rarely rose above narrow interests and factional politics, and despite sound understanding of the situation by some of its senior administrators offered solutions that were acceptable to the government but clearly unacceptable to the people concerned. The successful establishment of the Gauhati University at people's initiatives – particularly the youth of Assam who for generations dedicated their energy and efforts relentlessly to the cause – and its growth and expansion in the following decades point to the fact that the university was a legitimate demand of the people of a distant and isolated region towards the fulfilment of their aspiration for economic and intellectual development.

NOTES

1. The Department of Assamese in the Gauhati University is known to have contributed significantly to the development of Assamese language, literature and culture through research and teaching, and has had renowned scholars like Banikanta Kakati, Birinchi Kumar Barua, Maheshwar Neog, Satyendranath Sharma, Nirmalprabha Bordoloi and others as its faculty over the years. '*Guwahati Bishwabidyalyar Asamiya bibhagat MIL Samil Prasangat*', a short article by Saurabhjyoti Kashyap and Mriganka Rajbangshi, *Amaar Asam*, 29 July 2009. See also, Dhrubajyoti Barua, 'Dr. Maheshwar Neog's Contribution to Gauhati University', in the *Assam Tribune*, Guwahati, 13 September 2009.

   The Department of Major Indian Languages (MIL) of the university supplemented the Department of Assamese by producing scholarship in various languages of the region other than Assamese. In recent times, however, the proposal of a merger of the two departments evoked considerable public criticism on grounds that the Department of MIL was a necessity in terms of offering research and teaching of other Indian languages for the greater interest of regional and national unity. Letter to the Editor, *Amaar Asam*, 27 July 2009.
2. A.J. Moffat Mill, *Report on the Province of Assam, 1854*, Appendix J; Also cited in Lakshahira Das, *Development of Secondary Education in Assam*, New Delhi: Omsons Publications, 1990.
3. Amalendu Guha, in his seminal work, *Planter Raj to Swaraj: Freedom Struggle and Electoral Politics in Assam 1826-1947*, Delhi: People's Publishing House, 1977, introduced the concept of 'great nationalism vis a vis little nationalism' in the context of colonial politics in modern Assam, wherein he equates the regional middle-class nationalism with 'little nationalism'. He observes: 'This two-track nationalism is nowhere so prominently traceable as in the case of Assam. In the long run, language there proved to be the stronger binding element than caste, religion or isolated localities.' However, he adds, '. . . The incipient regional middle class did clash with its counterparts from other regions, but only up to a point. Beyond that they had generally coalesced to put forward a common front against imperialism. Despite strains and stresses in their relationship, they had moved in unison towards a fusion . . .', p. 334.
4. Particular mention may be made of individuals like Sir Henry Cotton who followed popular opinion and, despite limited resources, determined that Assam should have the nucleus of higher education. Cotton was instrumental in establishing the first college, named after him as the Cotton College in Gauhati. An unstinting service towards the growth of this institution was provided by F.W. Sudmersen, its first principal, and it was popularly noted that: 'Mr. Sudmersen was the Cotton College and

the Cotton College was Mr. Sudmersen'. David Thomson (ex-principal, Cotton College), 'A Reminiscence', in *The Golden Jubilee Volume 1951-52*, Gauhati: Cotton College, 1952, p. 81.

A.C. Hazarika in his essay on reminiscences in the Jubilee Volume wrote: 'If one recounts the name of persons who with English blood in their veins dedicated their services for the good of this country, one cannot afford to forget the name of Henry Cotton.' Prof. A.C. Hazarika, 'The Founders of the Cotton College: I. – Sir Henry Cotton', in ibid., pp. 98-9. S.K. Bhuyan, a renowned scholar and director of Historical and Antiquarian Studies, observed in his reminiscences of the College as an ex-Cottonian: 'The most outstanding landmark of the College in our days was the dynamic personality of its Principal Mr. Sudmersen', whose dedication to the job and strict adherence to discipline of the institution resulted in the visiting Calcutta University Commission's declaration of the College as the best institution under the University in 1918. S.K. Bhuyan, 'A Cottonian's Reminiscences, 1909-11', in ibid., p. 88.

5. J.R. Cunningham, *Report on Assam University Enquiry*, Shillong: Assam Government Press, 1936, p. 1.
6. Ibid., p. 11.
7. The University of Gauhati came into existence on 1 January 1948, by the Gauhati University Act of 1947 (Assam Act XVI of 1947). It was to be an affiliating, teaching and residential university with jurisdiction over all the schools and colleges in the province of Assam which were formerly affiliated to the University of Calcutta. Inter-University Board, Government of India, *Handbook of the Universities*, 1951.

   On its inaugural, Bhupen Hazarika, later a Dadasaheb Phalke awardee for his lifetime contribution in the field of music and arts, sang the song '*Jilikabo Luitore Paar*', which describes the university as the bearer of the torch that would light up the banks of the Brahmaputra and break all narrow barriers to carry the light of knowledge to far and beyond.
8. This aspect has been dealt with at length in a recent publication by L.K. Barua, *Education and Culture in North-East India 1826-2000*, Shimla: IIAS, 2006. See particularly Chapters VII, IX and X.
9. H.K. Barpujari, 'A Short History of Higher Education in Assam (1826-1900)', in the *Jubilee Volume*, 1952, op. cit., p. 9.
10. In the Anglo-vernacular schools emphasis was given from the very beginning to the study of English, and the students were eager to learn English as this paved the way for jobs in the government. But it proved to be a very difficult proposition particularly when the medium of instruction was also English. It was in a situation like this that the

Government of Bengal in 1844 decided that English be made optional in these schools and converted English schools at Gauhati and Sibsagar to Anglo-Bengali schools. As observed by historian H.K. Barpujari, the remedy proved no better than the disease, as it was not the vernacular of the mass of the students in Assam. Ibid., pp. 8-11.

11. Ibid., pp. 17-18.
12. Barua, op. cit., pp. 219-20.
13. Chandana Goswami, *Nationalism in Assam*, Delhi: Mittal Publications, 2008, p. 74.
14. Rev. E.G. Phillips, 'Mission Work in Assam by other Societies', in The Assam Mission of the American Baptist Union, Paper and Discussions of the Jubilee Conference, rpt., Spectrum, 1992, p. 215; also cited in Barua, op. cit., p. 226.
15. Cunningham, op. cit., p. 8.
16. The collegiate section was opened to fulfil the high hopes and aspirations of the people. But its university results were so disappointing, particularly between 1872 and 1874 that the government decided to revert it to its former status. Barpujari, 1952, op. cit., pp. 15-16.
17. *Report on Public Instructions in Assam*, 1881-82, pp. 4, 29; also cited in Goswami, op. cit., p. 71.
18. 'A Message from Frederick Williamson Sudmersen, the First Principal, Cotton College, Gauhati', in the *Jubilee Volume*, 1952, op. cit.
19. Facilities available to students of Assam at the University of Calcutta were not adequate. Those with scholarships or self-finance led an isolated life in Calcutta. Most of them sought admission in private colleges in Calcutta or *mofussils* which had lower standards of teaching, management and discipline than was to be expected from a local college at home. As a result only a small number of Assamese students could complete their courses successfully. Karunananda Dutta, 'A History of the Cotton College Gauhati (1901-1951)', in ibid., pp. 29-30.
20. 'A Message from Frederick William Sudmersen', op. cit.
21. Ibid. It is a matter of considerable regret that in contemporary times the college has not been able to maintain the position it had carved out for itself a century ago. Whereas some premier institutions of the country have been able to maintain their academic and infrastructural supremacy, the Cotton College, Guwahati, has reportedly been reeling under too much of government interference and nepotism and lack of accountability on the part of its teaching faculty, which has affected its quality adversely. Public awareness being very high in the province, it may only be hoped that as the people were instrumental in setting up these heritage institutions, so would it be able to play a positive role in helping the institution to recover its past glory. Amal Kumar

Das, '*Cotton College: Nakshatrar Pohar Bisari*', *Amar Asom*, 28 July 2009; and 'Cotton College: Hopes and Reality', the *Assam Tribune*, 30 August 2009.

22. Cunningham, op. cit., pp. 9-10.
23. Ibid., p. 11.
24. Barua, op. cit., p. 173.
25. Sajal Nag, 'Language, Class and Superstructure: A Study in Aspects of Nationality Formation in 19th Century Assam', in Proceedings of the North East History Association, Seventh Session, pp. 454-5; also cited in Goswami, op. cit., pp. 66-7.

    Amalendu Guha observes that in their attempt to focus on important and legitimate issues and articulate them – like the Valley's unsettled quest for a linguistic-regional identity, concern over the opium evil and their desire to be administered by sons of the soil, at least at the lower level – the prominent organizations like the Assam Association (1903-20), the Assam Chhatra Sanmilan (estd. 1916), and the Assam Sahitya Sabha (estd. 1917) side-tracked attention from their root cause, which was the colonial rule. He remarked: 'Imperialism encouraged ethnicity to play a divisive role and thus hinder the growth of nationalism.' Guha, op. cit., p. 335.
26. Assam Secretariat Proceedings No. 186, 'Public Servicc Employment for Natives of Assam', Jorhat, 14 December 1892, p. 4.
27. Ibid., p. 6.
28. Ibid.
29. Ibid.
30. Rangia, Kamarup, 30 November 1937, Memo presented by Asamiya Sangrakshini Sabha to Pt. Jawaharlal Nehru, President, Indian National Congress, 'Political History of Assam', File No. 2, 1937.
31. Ibid.
32. S.K. Barpujari, 'History of the Assam Association (1903-1921)', paper presented at the XVI Annual Conference of the Institute of Historical studies, held at Dibrugarh University, 25-8 October 1978; cited in Goswami, op. cit., p. 149.
33. Goswami, ibid., pp. 149-51.
34. Ashok Bhagawati, ed., *Bijoy Chandra Bhagawati: Nirbachita Rhachana*, Guwahati: Anwesha, 2006, p. 36. Bijoy Chandra Bhagawati was an active member of the Indian National Congress, who was influenced by Gandhian philosophies deeply, and was a dedicated worker in the Assam Pradesh Congress Committee in her struggle for freedom from colonial rule. During the 1942 movement he was arrested and put in the Jorhat Jail along with other senior leaders like Gopinath Bordoloi, Bhubaneshwar Barua, Omio Kumar Das, Siddhi Sharma and others for more than three years.

35. *Krishnakanta Sharmar Diary*, Gauhati: Asam Prakashan Parishad, 1972, p. 77.
36. To cite only a few of the numerous issues debated upon by the Assamese through letters to the editor, articles or open forums: '*Cotton Collegor Chhatrabash*' on the debate over demolition and reconstruction of historic hostel buildings of Cotton College (*Amaar Asam, Mukali Mancha*, 11 August 2009); 'Cotton College as a Deemed University' (the *Assam Tribune*, Guwahati, 11 July 2009); '*Guwahati Bishwabidyalay aru prastabita bankor rrin*', on proposed bank loans for the Gauhati University (*Amaar Asam*, 26 September 2009); merger of the Department of MIL with the Department of Assamese, Assam Science and Technology University Bill, 2009, etc.
37. Goswami, 2008, pp. 71-2, 86 and 117.
38. The first organized strike of the Sanmilan took place in 1920 in the wake of Gandhi's call for non-cooperation in the small town of Mangaldoi. National schools were being set-up as a follow-up to the movement. The students of Cotton College too joined the strike in 1921. A.C. Bhuyan, ed., *Political History of Assam*, vol. 2, Gauhati: 1978, pp. 18-19.
39. The arrest of Gandhiji on 5 May 1930 had provoked widespread *hartal* in schools and colleges of Assam, and on 14 May a procession of 500 people, who were out to protest the arrest of Abbas Tyabji, was broken up by police *lathi* charge. This was followed by the circular of 19 May brought out by J.R. Cunningham, the Director of Public Instructions, which demanded an undertaking from the strikers and their guardians to the effect that the students will follow good conduct for re-admission. This had provoked widespread resentment of the students against the circular and drew out thousands of students in protest. Under this kind of protest the circular was modified substantially by 20 June 1930. Guha, 1977, op. cit., p. 173.
40. Meeta Deka, *Student Movements in Assam*, Delhi: Vikas Publishing House, 1996, p. 62.
41. S. Bora, *Student Revolution in Assam 1917-1947: A Historical Survey*, Delhi: Mittal Publications, 1992, p. 181.
42. Ahalya Gogoi, *Prachyavidarnav Krisna Kanta Handiqui*, Guwahati: Anandaram Barua Bhasha-Kala Sanskriti Sanstha, 2003, pp. 64-5.
43. Bora, op. cit., pp. 182-3.
44. Gogoi, op. cit., p. 8.
45. Barua, op. cit., pp. 77-8.
46. Gogoi, op. cit., p. 56.
47. Geetali Tamuli and Akhil Gogoi, *Uribo Pora Hole Akou Jujiloheten: Jyotiprasad Agarwalar Pranamya Jivan*, Guwahati: Banalata, 2003, pp. 140-1.

48. The University Enquiry Report has devoted a whole chapter on this issue; Cunningham, op. cit., chapter IV, pp. 13-19.
49. G.F. Nicholl, *Manual of the Bengali Language*, London, 1894, quoted in ibid., p. 17.
50. Ibid.
51. Ibid., p. 15.
52. Ibid., p. 1.

    Rev. James Joy Mohan Nichols Roy was the grandnephew of U. Tirot Singh of Nongkhlaw Syiemship. He was one of the founding leaders of the Church of God Movement in Meghalaya and Assam which provides ministerial training in order to promote the Gospel message and prepare leaders for churches and the Christian community. He stood against the British policy in the Khasi Hills and is known for his integrated autonomous council plan and his contribution to the political solidarity of the Khasi Jaiñtia community.

    H.K. Barpujari, *North-East India: Problems, Policies and Prospects*, Guwahati: Spectrum Publications, 1998, pp. 14-15; Rev. Dr. O.L. Snaitang, 'J.J.M. Nichols Roy, Biographical Sketch', in the official website of the Khasi Hills Autonomous District Council, Shillong.
53. Cunningham, op. cit., p. 1.
54. Guha, 1977, op. cit., p. 173; Deka, op. cit., p. 62.
55. Cunningham, op. cit., p. 3.
56. Ibid.
57. Ibid., pp. 5-6.
58. Ibid., p. 6.
59. Bora, 1992, op. cit., pp. 185-208.
60. Cunningham, op. cit., Appendix II, pp. 76-7.
61. Despite ill-health, he had dedicated himself to the cause as soon as he was released from prison in 1945. N.K. Barooah, *Bordoloi Dinalekha*, (The Diary of Lokapriya Gopinath Bordoloi), vol. II, Guwahati: Asam Prakashan Parishad, 2001, pp. 0.60-0.61.
62. Bordoloi is acknowledged as a pioneer of modern education in Assam and a visionary; the quality uniquely attributed to him is his ability to strike a balance between national and regional interests. It was largely due to his efforts that within a short time after Independence Assam established its first medical, engineering and agricultural colleges as well as many technical and non-technical institutions, apart from the Gauhati University. S.D. Goswami, 'Gopinath Bordoloi: Architect of Modern Assam', the *Assam Tribune*, Guwahati, 17 August 2009.
63. G.N. Bordoloi, 'A Case for a University in Assam', typed mss., pp. 1-11; cited in N.K. Barooah, ed., op. cit., p. 0.60.
64. Ibid., p. 0.62.

65. Though not expolicit from his personal entries in the diary, unfortunately later relations between the university authorities and Bordoloi, both in the capacity as chief minister and education minister of Assam, are known to have been embittered over disputes relating to the land earmarked for university buildings. Whereas Bordoloi wanted departments like cooperative training centre, rural development training centre, Ayurvedic college, engineering college, etc., to be built on parts of the land, the university authorities refused to allow this. The popular sentiments of sympathy towards the newly set-up university had in fact prompted them to be critical of the government in this dispute, and leading dailies like the *Assam Tribune* brought the story out from the point of view of the university authorities which tarnished the government's image considerably over the issue. Ibid., pp. 0.63-0.68.
66. The initial salary of the vice-chancellor was fixed at Rs. 1,400 per month along with a rent-free accommodation. The Executive Council of the University was formed with Kakasaheb Kalelkar, Dr. S.K. Bhuyan and Amalprabha Das as its members. Ibid., p. 0.63.
67. Ashwini Kumar Sharma, *Amar Manisha: Krishnakanta Sandikoi*, Guwahati: Alok Prakashan, 2006, p. 31.
68. Abdul Majid Khan, *Amaar Krishnakanta Sandikoi*, Guwahati: Banalata, 2001, p. 18.
69. Gogoi, op. cit., p. 125.
70. Ibid., p. 127.
71. Ibid., p. 131.
72. The stated goal of the university is to overcome the barriers of age, educational qualification and geographical boundaries towards expansion of education reaching out to remote areas, farmers, housewives and those willing but neglected in the field of general education and to offer vocational courses in conjunction with the needs of the region. It was reported that around 30 prisoners in Guwahati Prison had enrolled in courses under the university's programme. The first batch was to take their examinations in June 2009 and the enrolment was to be kept open throughout the year. Hiren Saikia, '*Krishakanta Sandikoi Rajyik Mukta Vishwavidayalay: Paraparheen Siksha*', in *Amaar Asom: Deobaria Alochani*, the Sunday edition of an Assamese daily, Guwahati, 27 July 2007.

CHAPTER 8

The Artisan and Technical Education in Late Nineteenth- and Early Twentieth-century India

BIDISHA DHAR

In the latter half of the nineteenth century, in the aftermath of the 1857 rebellion, the British state sought to place its Indian empire on a sounder financial footing, leading to a tighter control of the finances of the empire. This was considered a prudent move in the event of a future challenge akin to that of 1857. It was also the time when the official policy was being increasingly determined by the rising powerful industrial bourgeoisie of England. This was enabled, to a large extent, by improved means of communication, beginning with the Indian telegraph system in 1854, the overland cable connection to Europe in 1868, the opening of the Suez route in 1869 and the submarine cable in 1870. Within India, the imperative was to connect cotton-producing districts through feeder roads to dockyards, leading to increased investments in public works, roads, harbours, and so on, to facilitate the export of raw cotton to England.[1]

The North-Western Provinces and Oudh (NWPO) too witnessed a spate of investments in the provincial railways, and other kinds of construction works throughout the 1860s and 1870s, and along with it an increase in the demand for mechanics, foremen, and workmen of the forge and the workshop.[2] In Lucknow, the railways arrived in 1862[3] and the Oudh and Rohilkhand Railway connected Lucknow to Benares, Kanpur and Shahjahanpur in a length of 52 miles.[4] Improved communication transformed Lucknow into a central trade depot but doomed a number of artisanal manufactures of the city.[5] Amongst these, weaving was particularly hit by the import of cheap, finer, machine-made European cotton cloths which had rapidly established a market. The weavers, generally belonging to the Hindu Kori and the Muslim Julaha castes, were being forced to abandon their traditional occupation and work as reapers during the harvest time or migrate in search of new means of livelihood.[6]

In other parts of India too, the condition of the Indian artisan was deteriorating.[7] The colonial state, on the one hand, considered the process as inevitable.[8] They at the same time were wary of opposition by an increasingly assertive nationalist opinion as well as others from all over the country to the declining lot of the artisan in India.[9] This was sought to be quelled by the promotion and prioritization of technical over literary education as is evident from the following quote, '. . . an education confined to literary education, leads to the creation of a discontented class. . . .'[10]

This paper explores the dynamics behind the colonial endeavour to impart technical education to boys from the traditional artisan class of the United Provinces and more specifically in the Lucknow Industrial School in the decades between 1880 and 1920. The paper looks at the specific training programme designed for the sons of artisans in the school and the kind of problems which crept up in its implementation. It focuses fundamentally on the technical curriculum followed in the schools and seeks to answer some broader questions through a micro study of the history of the Lucknow Industrial School.

Technical Education: Aims and Objectives

The colonial aversion to literary education for the artisans led to an increased emphasis on practical education from the 1860s. This was reflected in the official pronouncements on education. Charles Wood's educational dispatch of 1854, for example, commented about this 'much neglected aspect of public education in India' while W.W. Hunter's *Report of the Education Commission* of 1882 declared:

> . . . the needs of a complex state of society in India . . . was . . . some corresponding course which shall fit boys for commercial and industrial pursuits . . . a bifurcation in the upper classes of high schools – one leading to the Entrance Examination of the Universities and the other of a more

practical character, intended to fit youths for commercial or non-literary pursuits.

The 'Memorandum on Technical Education in India prior to 1886' by A.P. MacDonnell, the Officiating Secretary to the Government of India, Home Department, was more specific in its intentions – to rectify the glut in the employment sector, to find new avenues for employing the increasing number of the unemployed youth to prevent the rise of nationalist feelings, and to meet the increased demand for technically trained men in the areas of mining, railways, manufacturing and other industrial enterprises brought forth by the expansion of foreign trade and interaction with the foreign markets.[11]

It was proposed in the memorandum that in the NWPO, the Department of Education would impart instruction in free-hand drawing and in physical science in the central normal schools and the high schools. An alternative final examination for candidates interested in commercial and industrial pursuits would be conducted under the auspices of the Allahabad University. Through a re-arranged system of examinations at the matriculation level, an increased number of students could seek admission to the Roorkee College of Engineering where a course in mechanical engineering and that of workshop instruction was to be introduced. Further, Roorkee College was to be linked to the provincial education system and to include in its curriculum preparatory training courses in telegraphy, instruction for the mechanical apprentices, in addition to the already existing courses in building and road engineering, irrigation or road construction.[12] And lastly, an Industrial School would be set up at Lucknow to serve as a feeder institution to the Roorkee Civil Engineering College.[13]

In 1886 when MacDonnell prepared his memorandum there were 45 industrial schools in the country with an attendance of 1,379 students. There were mainly three types of industrial schools – missionary institutions, those associated with the PWD, especially the railways, and those which were reformatory institutions.[14] Initially, there were plans to affiliate the Lucknow Industrial School to the Mayo School of Arts, Lahore, but finally the school was associated to the Technical School, Lahore which also trained traditional artisans for apprenticeships in the railways and other large workshops.[15]

Lucknow Industrial School: Teething Troubles

The Lucknow Industrial School started functioning from 1 November 1892 in the vicinity of the Oudh and Rohilkhand Railway Workshop and near the neighbourhoods of the railway artisans colony. The area was called the Wingfield Manzil. The railway artisans, who were also the bonafide or resident artisans, resided in the areas to the east and the north-east of the Wingfield Manzil.[16] The avowed aim of the institution, Sir Auckland Colvin, the Lieutenant Governor of the United Provinces, in his Opening Day speech declared, was to impart elementary instruction in carpentry and drawing initially, and at a later stage introduce training in iron and other metal works subject to the success of the school. The elementary training, Sir Colvin emphasized, would help them to qualify as working apprentices in railway and other large workshops. Several railway authorities or 'practical men' from throughout the province were to be represented on the Committee of Management of the school to attend to the 'practical' supervision of the trainees.[17]

The Industrial School was specifically set up for the sons of the bonafide artisans. The bonafide artisans in this case were the railway artisans and attendance to the school was made compulsory for them. Along with them, poor children from the Eurasian and the Anglo-Indian backgrounds could also be admitted to the school; 20 per cent of the seats in the school were reserved for these children. Lastly, but significantly, the school was also to train the 'industrial classes' of the city.[18]

Europeans and Eurasians

A major influx of working-class Europeans into India began in the early-1850s and increased considerably in the 1870s. The immigration was related to the building of communication networks which the British undertook on a large scale from the 1850s onwards. They mainly worked as plate-layers, fitters, firemen or as semi-skilled workers in the railways.[19] They also worked as intermediaries in government departments and private European enterprises and as domestic servants, nurses, mid-wives, clerks, teachers and shop assistants for European employers. The members of this class formed a link between the European officers and their

Indian subordinates in the police service, the railways, the public works, jails, factories and engineering works. Below them was the class which comprised the orphans, vagrants, prostitutes, convicts and lunatics.[20]

By the end of the nineteenth century, these classes formed nearly half of the European population in India. These poor Europeans and Eurasians, as C.A. Bayly explains, formed a very depressed and volatile element, unsure of employment but deeply committed to the ideas of European dominance.[21] From the 1870s, with the government attempts to promote technical education amongst the Indians who could be employed on lower rates, especially for the subordinate posts in the railways, the competition amongst Indians and the poor Eurasians and Europeans for such jobs increased and this often led to racial conflicts.[22]

Contraction in the employment opportunities for unskilled and semi-skilled Europeans reduced their chances of upward social mobility and their deteriorating condition led many individuals like Lord Canning and private organizations like that of the Friend-in-Need Society to advocate free training in technical instruction for them. The fear was that in the absence of such opportunities they too would start exhibiting the worst traits of their Indian counterparts and become unmanageable as well as profitless. The plan was to employ them as local mechanics or skilled labour in railway workshops to save them from becoming vagrants, beggars or dependents on charity.[23] This concern about the lower rungs of the English society was a reflection on the colonial anxieties for maintaining an image in the colony which made it imperative to remove any degenerate European from the native gaze.

This did not imply that such degenerate Europeans could be considered equivalent to their Indian counterparts. Strong racist vibes clearly dominated the thinking of the secretary of the Friend-in-Need Society when he declared that, for the poor Eurasian children, the Lucknow Industrial School provided an opportunity to be trained 'not under a scorching sun or under the unfavourable circumstances of an Indian street but under the double shelter of the workshop's roof and supervision by professionals who are of the same race as themselves'.[24] In the 1870s, there were 4,222 Europeans and 760 Eurasians in Lucknow city.[25]

Industrial Classes

Another section of the society which the school planned to draw upon was the vague category of the industrial classes of Lucknow. In the 1870s and the 1880s, these classes in the city mainly comprised the carpenters or the *barhais*, blacksmiths, potters, the leather workmen or the *chamars*, weavers, dyers, bangle-makers, metal workers, perfume manufacturers, makers of gold and silver lace and the practitioners of *chikan* work. Majority of these workers were very poor and belonged to the Muslim community and resided in Hasanganj and Chauk areas of Lucknow.[26] The Lucknow Industrial School was not concerned about them initially. Amongst the working classes, the school tried to attract the carpenters.

The Course Structure

In order to draw such disparate sections to the school the colonial authorities sought to evolve a broad course structure which could cater to the various classes. Colonial policy documents contain elaborate discussions on the appropriate course structure. Colonel A.M. Brandreth, principal of Thomason Engineering College, Roorkee, for instance, stressed the importance of three things for the artisan – technical drawing, patient application of manual labour and strong observation power to enable him to construct figures from the drawings of an engineer. The artisan was only required to construct the product as per the engineer's direction and imagination.[27]

The curriculum, formulated by the Department of Public Instruction, comprised primarily of practical instruction in carpentry and drawing which formed part of the technical training although reading, writing, arithmetic, elementary mechanics and physics were also included in the syllabus.[28] Elementary drawing formed the basis of technical education for the artisan[29] for it was important to convert him to a skilled artificer.[30] 'Drawing with a rule and a compass', as the memorandum explained, trained the 'hand and the eye' of the workman or the artisan to cultivate greater delicacy and penmanship which was a necessary preparation for hand training for the mechanical arts.[31] This technical drawing which was envisaged for the artisan was different from the usual artistic drawing courses prescribed for art schools.[32] In fact, one finds a considerable debate even within the official circles on the issue as to whether an industrial or an art school should have been established in Lucknow. Most of them favoured an industrial school in the city which would successfully tap the hereditary skills of Lucknow's artisan population and turn them into skilled workmen so that they could qualify the entrance test for the mechanical apprentice class of the Roorkee College.[33]

This programme was supported amongst others by Lieutenant-Governor Colvin who justified his reasons for keeping the curriculum to its basics by suggesting that the industrial classes and local Europeans and Eurasians of the province had a tendency to generalize, exaggerate, to be inaccurate, and to imitate – thus rendering them incapable of any independent thinking. 'To expect any such proclivities to the contrary from them, for instance, to be proportionate, accurate, to think or to analyse or in other words to have a propensity to comprehend physical science would be without any benefit.'[34] Such perceptions about the local Europeans, Eurasians and the local artisan class seemed to enjoy a certain broad consensus in the higher echelons of colonial decision-making. M.J. White, principal of the Canning College, spoke of the need for industrial school training for the sons of the artisans since 'the artisan's son, naturally unfit for higher mathematics and philosophy, should be . . . allowed to earn an honest livelihood in a goods shed . . . or a shop'.[35]

These preconceived notions about the Indian artisan influenced the technical education programme of the colonial state which imparted only certain basic technical attributes to the colonial subjects. The colonial state had its own agenda to cater to. It was solely interested in administering a colony and increasing its production of export commodities for which new technologies and new forms of labour were required. Alongside this the colonial rulers also wanted to preserve the *status quo* in the colonial society which they thought was threatened by Western contact. This apprehension led them to restrict technical training to the teaching of craft and agrarian skills over academic education.

However, the indigenous artisan classes demanded an academic education rather than training in crafts and agrarian skills. They probably were looking for alternative livelihoods which would entail a jump in social status and certain independence. There was thus a conflict of interest between the aims and objectives of the colonial authorities and the desires and aspirations of the indigenous artisan classes. This led to the artisan class being accused of having an aversion towards manual education.[36] The conflict was acute in the Lucknow Industrial School also, where the entire actualization programme of technical education turned out to be a clash between the artisan's aspirations to improve his social status and the officials' designs of trying to contain him from doing that.

Persisting Problems

Soon after the school started functioning, the officials realized that the implementation of their plan would not be so easy. Owing to their poverty and the limited resources, most of the artisans' children came to the school for free general education or learn English or drawing to become a draughtsman or possibly a drawing master in one of the primary schools of the city which would enable him to earn Rs. 30 a month. So perturbed was the state by this tendency of the artisan that in one of his visits to the school the Lieutenant-Governor, Mr. Crosthwaite strongly recommended that the school be named 'School of Manual Training' to indicate it very clearly to the students that the objective of the school was not to offer general education. He also suggested that the English courses be revised to be only a basic language course and that the students above the age of fourteen years should be restricted to manual training alone.[37]

The management committee, however, refused to implement his recommendations of withdrawing general education and revising the English course in the industrial school curriculum fearing an exodus of students. In actuality, the English course prescribed was already a very elementary one, barely enough to make the students comprehend the working drawings and the written orders in railway workshops and to understand the instructions of the supervisors who were mostly Englishmen. A further withdrawal of it would hamper such plans. In any case the school had had a very unsettled beginning. Out of the 85 students on the roll in 1892, 38 had left the school by 1894.[38]

One of the reasons for this persistent problem of falling attendance was the poverty of the students which allowed them to receive only a minimum training, enough for subsistence. Thus scholarships were offered along with an employment guarantee in the Lucknow Iron Works[39] which had an encouraging result, with the enrolment picking up from 106 to 160 in 1895.[40] But the main contentious issue remained the lower priority accorded to general education in the curriculum and the other was the refusal on the part of the artisans to be restricted to the boundaries of the industrial school. Within a year the resultant problem was visible again when the Lucknow Industrial School was affiliated to the Roorkee Engineering College after a committee headed by Lieutenant Colonel John Clibborn,[41] the principal of the college, recommended affiliation of all the technical and industrial schools of the provinces to the Roorkee College of Engineering with the principal of the Roorkee College as the ex-officio visitor to these schools. The government plan was to standardize engineering and mechanical training in the province so that the increased demand for skilled mechanics could be met. The students from the affiliated schools were to be provided with opportunities to study in Roorkee and technical equipments and teachers from the college were to be sent to these schools.[42]

At the Lucknow Industrial School the curriculum was restructured to meet the entry qualifications of the mechanical apprentice class in the Roorkee College of Engineering. This meant a renewed emphasis on manual instruction in carpentry, blacksmith's work, glass blowing and clay modelling over general education, comprising elementary English, vernacular, mathematics and elementary mechanics, which was relegated to the night classes. The standard of the general education was so low that Lieutenant Colonel Clibborn was himself dissatisfied. So the school management arranged for night classes for the students to achieve at least a minimum standard in the instruction of English language. But the artisans, unable to take the pressure of night classes, began to desert the school.[43] After the new rules came into force in July 1897, the number on the rolls fell from 170 to 117, the average daily attendance from 138 to 105 and the percentage of attendance from 80 to 73.[44]

From 1897 to 1903 the administration tried to bring the school back on track by trying to widen the employment bases. An arrangement was worked out with the Kanpur Woollen Mills to offer internships to provide the students with a practical training in the course of dyeing, and with a few government railway companies like the East Indian, Oudh and Rohilkhand, Indian Midland, Bombay, Baroda and Central Indian Railway companies.[45] The turn of the century proved to be significant for the school. Grants were being offered to all the technical schools which were to be affiliated to the Roorkee College. And as the Lucknow Industrial School was also affiliated to the Roorkee College, it was being envisioned as a premier technical or industrial school of the region. Such plans necessitated some drastic policy changes. One of them was the appointment of a specialist instructor as the head of the school and the then headmaster, Tara Prossano Banerjee, did not fit into the new scheme of things.[46]

Tara Prossano was the first headmaster of the Lucknow Industrial School. His family lived in Lucknow, which is why he gave up a better paid job as the superintendent of the Bayley Technical School at Rangpur in the Lower Provinces of Bengal. The other reasons were ill-health and the prospects of pension from the Lucknow Industrial School.[47] He had passed out from the Sibpur Engineering College of Bengal where his supervisor had been Mr. Fouracres, a reputed teacher and more importantly an 'European expert' who would encourage him to read modern textbooks on workshop practices such as Shelley's *Workshop Appliances*, Mitchell's *Carpentry and Engineering Workshop Practice* and Weatan's *Modern Workshop Practice* among others.[48] Tara Prossano's working experience was impressive. After passing out from the Sibpur College he became the head of the Williamson School at Sibsagar, the only technical school of Assam at the time, and thereafter was the head of the Bayley Technical School at Rangpur, a principal technical school of Bengal. For some time he was also the second master of the Engineering School at Dacca. Apart from all this he was posted in some of the technical schools in Bengal, the Oudh and Rohilkhand Railway Workshops at Lucknow, the Railway Technical School, the Mayo School of Art at Lahore, the Municipal Technical School at Amritsar and the Canal Foundry and Workshops at Roorkee. And at most of these places he had worked with the Europeans.[49]

Tara Prossano's removal as the principal of the school was a hotly debated issue in the official circles of the province. Important officers such as T.C. Lewis, the Director of Public Instruction solidly backed Tara Prossano. There were others like the Inspector of Schools who was impressed with his versatility as evinced by his ability to take care of a variety of tasks such as accounts, store, and teaching mechanics apart from a certain predilection for 'man management'. The basic grounding for his multitasking capabilities happened at Sibpur, where he got lessons in mathematics, surveying, drawing and engineering. He also received some practical training in the Calcutta workshops as a foreman mechanic in practical carpentry, fitting and forge work. Thus, Tara Prossano was fit to teach general subjects and intelligent enough to supervise drawing, carpentry and smith's work.[50]

The Inspector of Schools, 2nd Circle, Mr. Cardew also agreed with Lewis that it would be difficult to replace Tara Prossano. A skilled, specialist workman would be capable of teaching one particular trade but there were doubts if he would be able to look after all the faculties that make up an institution. The headmaster ought to be proficient in all respects and Tara Prossano satisfied this requirement.[51] Other important officials too had been impressed by Tara Prossano and quite vocally supported the Principal. However, it was the Lieutenant-Governor who first demanded the appointment of a skilled workman and/or an industrial artisan who could be a specialist in one particular trade for the post of principal of the Lucknow Industrial School. He was supported by the Chief Engineer, Buildings and Roads Branch and Lieutenant Colonel Clibborn.[52] The latter and Mr. Lewis also developed some differences regarding the particular matter about the removal of the school principal.[53]

The committee which passed the final orders for the removal of Tara Prossano comprised the Chief Engineer, Public Works Department, Buildings and Roads branch, NWPO and Lieutenant Colonel Clibborn, principal of the Thomason Roorkee College and the ex-officio visitor of the Industrial School. It declared:

> . . . neither in respect to education or mechanical training was he a suitable person to put the Lucknow Industrial School on a sound footing as a pioneer school in which students will be trained to enter the mechanical classes at Roorkee. . . . In the present initiatory stage of industrial training in the North Western Provinces and Oudh, it is essential to have a man who has had that technical education and training which can only at present be obtained in England or Scotland. A man who has been educated on a proper system in a high class technical school is required.

Tara Prossano's case was discussed in the Educational Conference at Shimla (1901) where a broader programme of encouraging and expanding the role of industrial schools was discussed. But most importantly, resolutions were passed regarding the need to import technical instructors for these industrial schools from England.[54] However, by 1903, the school was again in the doldrums.[55] One important reason was the implementation of Sir E.C. Buck's *Report on Practical and Technical Education* in 1901.

Towards an Engineering College

Edward Charles Buck of the Bengal Civil Service was deputed by the Government of India to inquire into the prospects of technical and practical education in the country.[56] Significantly, the report recommended a market oriented, mass production of the artisan products. For this the government's assistance was to come in the form of initial advances, expert instructors and the provision of raw material. The aim was to utilize the dexterity of the Indian artisan and improve his production process by introducing him to better tools and hand machines.[57] And for this, the report suggested, the industrial schools premises be utilized. This required some sort of standardization in the functioning of industrial schools all over India. The recommendations were accepted by the Government of India in the 1901 Educational Conference at Shimla. The industrial schools were to develop as educational institutions where master-artisans from the markets would be called and trained to improve their working style and technique. This required a survey of the local industries. In the North-Western Provinces, Lieutenant Colonel Clibborn headed a committee to survey the local industries and implement the recommendations of the conference. The recommendations of the committee had a big impact on the functioning of the Lucknow Industrial School.[58]

The new headmaster of the school, P.H. Swinchatt, surveyed the principal artisanal workshops in Lucknow: embroidery or the manufacture of *chikan* (art muslin), calico printing, manufacture of silverware, *bidari* (inlaid work) including *zarbaland* (relief work), clay modelling, brass work, *tarkashi* (metal work). A copper-ware manufactory was also visited.[59] But even while collecting information about the industries it became clear that the artisans were against the new recommendations in the industrial school. The reasons perhaps lay, as Swinchatt described, in the working style of the artisans.[60] The artisans, for instance, the calico printers, worked along with their family members in the summer and sold their products in the winter. These were too comfortable a situation, Swinchatt considered, to abandon and get attracted to the offers of the industrial school – rent-free accommodation, advertisement of their products and instruction for the improvement of their techniques. The artisans themselves were unwilling to leave their home even for a few hours, or to be enforced within the discipline of a school curriculum.[61] Thus, even at an offer of Rs. 20 per month only three artisans came to the school – a calico printer, a coppersmith and a *tarkashi* worker. The entire mechanization programme of the industrial school was a failure because any improved method increased the cost of production. The artisans resented any suggestions to improve their techniques. What they perhaps needed was someone to tell them the means to enhance production at cheaper rates. But their expectations were belied. The number of students in this section was therefore gradually nearing zero because the industrial education it offered was not something the artisans wanted. On the other hand, due to a strict distinction between the general and technical education the students in the Roorkee preparatory class of the school were failing to qualify for the mechanical apprentice class.[62] Interestingly, in one of the petitions to the school management, the students expressed their strong intention of being trained as skilled workmen to be employed as foremen, mechanics and fitters in the railways or be able to qualify for the mechanical apprentice class in Roorkee. They were unable to do this due to the inadequate standard of general education in the school which did not match up to the standards of the Roorkee entrance examination.[63]

Meanwhile, the locomotive superintendent of the Oudh and Rohilkhand Railway, P.A. Hyde offered to employ the pass-outs from the school. The school was required to turn out a class of men who could cater to the lower grades of the mechanical section of the railways as fitters, charge men, *mistris*, carpenters, turners, smiths and foundry workers. Thus, the school committee decided to modify the curriculum according to the requirements of the railway companies. As for Roorkee, an arrangement was worked out that the headmaster of the school would nominate suitable students for the mechanical apprentice class and the entrance test would be done away with.[64]

After 1907, the school was transformed into a purely technical school and by 1912 it was renamed as Government Technical

School. Sources about the history of the school become less descriptive after this period and one does not find mention of it in the Public Instruction Reports after 1918. The overall sense that one gets is that the school stabilized after 1907. The artisans were now being attracted to the school. This could not have been abrupt. Were they attracted by the employment offers in the railways? The facts as to whether the Europeans and Eurasians continued to be given a reservation in the school become blurred. By 1918, the school was transformed to become a mechanical engineering college. Interestingly, in the *Inspection Notes* of *the Indian Industrial Commission, 1916-18*, the history of the school is recorded from 1899, that is, after Swinchatt took over as the principal. The history of the school from 1892 to 1899 was completely omitted and along with it the contributions of the first principal of the School, Tara Prossano.[65]

Conclusion

The artisan class and the colonial policy makers were at odds throughout the period of investigation in this paper. The artisans signified a resistance to the colonial designs of total domination and hegemony. What is most interesting in this whole debate is the problematic of the policy implementation of teaching the artisans English and making general education free of cost. While the emphasis of the authorities was on advancing the colonial project by solely imparting manual training to the artisans, the artisans had other plans. Most of them wanted to learn drawing to become draughtsmen and also pick up English even though the language taught at the industrial schools was of an elementary level and was barely enough to make the students comprehend the working drawings and the written orders in the railway workshops or to understand the instructions of the supervisors who were mostly Englishmen.

The clash of interests between the state and the artisans is visible throughout the period. The artisan was looking to use the industrial school as a springboard in his endeavour to achieve a certain amount of social mobility and status. This might explain the propensity of the artisans towards becoming draughtsmen as this was an independent profession and was a respite from joining the industrial labour force which was demeaning, alienating and signified a loss of independence. This was something the artisan neither was nor prepared to accept so easily. The constant refusal on the part of the artisan was perhaps indicative of the fact that he did not so easily give up his traditional occupation to get incorporated as industrial labour or as plantation worker. The artisan was, however, forced at times to adapt to the changing conditions which involved loss of his traditional skills and a certain sense of alienation. Yet he would try to manoeuvre to the best of his ability under the situation and pick up professions which afforded him a certain leeway and a certain jump in status as perceived by him. Sadly the artisan could only on occasions get his way.

NOTES

1. Sabyasachi Bhattacharya, 'Introduction', in *Financial Foundations of the British Raj*, Shimla: Indian Institute of Advanced Study, 1995.
2. Deepak Kumar, *Science and the Raj, 1857-1905,* New Delhi: Oxford University Press, 1995, pp. 136-7.
3. For details see, Veena Talwar Oldenburg, *The Making of Colonial Lucknow, 1856-1877*, New Delhi: Oxford University Press, 1989, pp. 42-8.
4. *The Gazetteer of Oudh*, 1877-8, p. 43. Also see, William Hoey, *A Monograph on Trade and Manufactures in Northern India,* Lucknow: American Methodist Mission Press, 1880, p. 2. For racial discrimination in the Railways, see, Amiya Bagchi, *Private Investment in India,* Cambridge: Cambridge University Press, 1972, p. 150.

   Racial prejudice blocked the recruitment of Indians to supervisory posts and to the posts of engineers, etc. Here a distinction was made not only between Europeans and Indians but also between Anglo-Indians and Indians.
5. For a detailed discussion of the affected trades, see part I of Hoey's, *A Monograph on Trade and Manufacture in Northern India.*
6. Gyanendra Pandey, 'Economic Dislocation in Nineteenth Century Eastern Uttar Pradesh: Some Implications of the Decline of Artisanal Industry in Colonial India', in Peter Robb, ed., *Rural South Asia: Linkages, Change and Development*, London: Curzon Press, 1983, pp. 89-129. Also see, Gyanendra Pandey, 'The Bigoted Julaha', in *Economic and Political Weekly* 18, no. 5, 1983, pp. 19-28. The Muslim *Julahas* were always singled out by the colonial state as unwilling to learn new techniques to improve their deteriorating economic condition and represented them as social bigots.
7. R.C. Dutt, *Economic History of India*, 2 vols., London: Kegan Paul, Trench Trubner, 1902-4.

8. Britain's imperialist agendas had been strengthened by the application of scientific knowledge to industry and by large accumulations of capital and mergers of banking capital with industrial capital within Britain, with new means of international transport, by securing exclusive markets, sources of agricultural and mineral raw materials, foodstuffs in the colonies, and by the implementation of reactionary imperialist ideologies to hegemonize colonial societies.
9. The decades between the 1860 and 1890 witnessed numerous peasant uprisings, tribal, anti-caste and labour movements in the face of repeated famines in the 1870s and the 1890s. There was also the rise of an articulate discourse espousing Indian economic nationalism, the formation of local associations like the Bombay Association, Poona Sarvajanik Sabha and Madras Native Association and most importantly the founding of the Indian National Congress in 1885. On the international scene, there were protests at Morant Bay on the West Indian island of Jamaica in 1865, by a group of freed slaves whose condition remained desperate despite their turning into peasant cultivators. Within Britain, the British working class protests at Hyde Park in July 1866 led the British government to characterize the labouring classes as inherently lazy, undisciplined and potentially violent in their challenge to established property relations. They had to be therefore dealt with strong hands. For details, see, Thomas Metcalf, *Ideologies of the Raj*, Cambridge: Cambridge University Press, 1995, pp. 52-9; Sabyasachi Bhattacharya, Introduction to *Financial Foundations of the British Raj*.
10. For details, see, E.C. Buck, *Report on Practical and Technical Education*, 1901.
11. Ibid., 'Papers Relating to Technical Education in India, 1886-1904', *Memorandum on Technical Education in India Prior to 1886,* pp. 1-4.
12. For details, see, *The Pioneer,* 5 April and 6 November 1892.
13. MacDonnell's *Memorandum* suggested the inclusion of the industrial schools within the Provincial Education system and affiliate them to central institutions in the various provinces to improves their condition by making them commercially viable. For a state-wise division of the number of industrial schools in the country, see *Memorandum*, p. 5.
14. For a detailed discussion of the various types of industrial schools, see, *Report of Indian Industrial Commission, Inspection Notes*, p. 97 and Alfred Croft, *Review of Education in India in 1886*, Calcutta, 1886, pp. 85-6.

    Also see, Mary Carpenter, *Six Months in India,* London: Longmans, Green and Co., 1868 and *Parliamentary Papers, 1877.* Mary Carpenter had taken an active part in the Reformatory Movement in post-Industrial Revolution England which was based on the principle of reforming the young criminals, urban poor, destitute by a moral and industrial training. There was an implicit idea that the reformation of these classes could take place only by instilling the habits of industry which would discipline them and make them capable of earning their own livelihood. Having carefully studied the principles of prison discipline, she had published *Our Convicts*. In India, she had visited a number of prisons and institutions in the Bombay Presidency and worked on prison discipline, reformatories, lunatic asylums, government schools, and female education.

Also see, Government of India (henceforth GOI), Home, Education, August 1874. Sir Auckland Colvin's Minute on Technical Education in *Papers Relating to Technical Education in India, 1886-1904*, pp. 123-31, Calcutta, 1906. For details regarding the separate training systems in the Madras and the Bombay Presidencies, see, *Memorandum*, pp. 28-40. The Lahore School supplied tools and a drawing teacher for the Industrial School, Lucknow and also set the syllabus for the latter.

15. Art schools were different from industrial schools. For details regarding art schools, see, Tapati Guha-Thakurta, *The Making of a New Indian Art*, Cambridge: Cambridge University Press, 1992 and Partha Mitter, *Art and Nationalism in Colonial India, 1850-1922*, Cambridge: Cambridge University Press, 1994.
16. Nesfield, Director of Public Instruction, NWPO to Secretary to Government, NWPO, 11 August 1892, PED, NWPO, vol. 1, January-July 1893.
17. *The Pioneer*, 6 November 1892.
18. Proceedings of the Education Department of the NWPO (henceforth, PED), 26 October 1892, vol. 1, January-June 1893, Programmes, no. 256.
19. C.A. Bayly, *The Local Roots of Indian Politics, Allahabad, 1880 1920*, Oxford: Clarendon Press, 1975, pp. 52-7.
20. David Arnold, 'European Orphans and Vagrants in India in the Nineteenth Century', in *Journal of Imperial and Commonwealth History*, 7, 1979, pp. 106-14. Some other literature on the subject is David Arnold, 'White Colonization and Labor in Nineteenth Century India', *Journal of Imperial and Commonwealth History*, 11, no. 2, January 1983, pp. 133-58.
21. Bayly, *The Local Roots of Indian Politics, Allahabad, 1880-1920*, pp. 52-7.
22. Ibid.
23. 'Proceedings of the Education Department of the NWPO', 11 August 1884, vol. 1, January-June 1893.
24. Ibid.
25. *Gazetteer of Oudh*, 1877-8.

Also see, Veena Talwar Oldenburg, *The Making of Colonial Lucknow 1856-1877,* pp. 242-6, has described the lifestyle of the European elite in Lucknow. One can also get a glimpse of the interaction between the Indians and the Anglo-Indians in the Lucknow of 1930s in Attia Hossain, *Sunlight on a Broken Column*, London: Virago/Penguin, 1988.

26. Hoey, *A Monograph on Trade and Manufactures in Northern India,* 1888.
27. This is the opinion of Colonel A.M. Brandreth, principal of Thomason Engineering College, Roorkee which he in his letter dated 21 December 1887, wrote to Sir Auckland Colvin, the Secretary to Government, NWPO. The training of an artisan and an engineer also had to be very clearly distinguished. It would be the engineer's job to make the design of a drawing marketable.
28. E. White, the Director of Public Instruction in the North Western Provinces, PED, NWPO, vol. 1, January-June 1893.
29. 'Memorandum' in *Papers Relating to Technical Education in India, 1886-1904*, pp. 36-7; Home, Education, B, Proceedings, January 1891, nos. 14-15.
30. Alfred Croft, *Review of Education in India in 1886,* Calcutta: Government Printing, 1886.
31. Mr. Tawny, the Officiating Director of the Public Instruction in Bengal, expressing his views in the 'Memorandum'.
32. For the contradictions between art school and industrial school training, see, Partha Mitter, *Art and Nationalism in Colonial India,* p. 17.
33. E. White, Director of Public Instruction, NWPO to Secretary to Government, NWPO, PED, NWPO, 19 March 1888, vol. 1, January-June 1893, Progs. no. 18.

    Ian Derbyshire, 'Economic Change and the Railways in North India, 1860-1914', in Ian J. Kerr, ed., *Railways in Modern India*, New Delhi: Oxford University Press, 2001.
34. *The Pioneer*, 5 April 1892.
35. The Canning College was established in 1864 and was supported by the landlords or the *talukdars* of the province. *The Gazetteer of Oudh,* 1877-8 recorded that 1 per cent of the students in the college were the sons of artisans and manufacturers. However, when the industrial school was established the 'respectable native gentlemen' of the province agreed to send their sons to the school so that they acquired some industrial training which was otherwise only provided in a dirty bazaar shop. Nesfield, Director of the Public Instruction to Secretary to Government, NWPO, 11 July 1893, vol. 2, July-December 1893; M.J. White, Principal, Canning College, Lucknow to the Under Secretary to Government, NWPO, PED, NWPO, 25 September 1891, vol. 1, January-June 1893, Progs. no. 54.

36. Daniel Headricks, *Tentacles of Progress Technology Transfer in the Age of Imperialism, 1850-1940*, New York: Oxford University Press, 1988, chapter 9.
37. In the beginning, the age bar was fixed at 8 years as the lower limit and 12 years as the upper limit.

    For details regarding the changes in the qualifying age, Crosthwaite, Lt. Governor, NWPO in his Minute on the Lucknow Industrial School, PED, NWPO, 7 March 1893, vol. 1, January-June 1893, Progs. no. 270.
38. T.C Lewis, Director of Public Instruction, NWPO, to Secretary to Government, NWPO, PED, NWPO, 8 May 1895, vol. 5, June-January 1897.
39. Inspector of Schools, 2nd Circle, NWPO, to Director of Public Instruction, NWPO, 30 August 1895; Locomotive and Carriage Superintendent, Oudh and Rohilkhand Railway, to Inspector of Schools, 2nd Circle, NWPO, 16 August 1895; Superintending Engineer, 2nd Circle, Provincial Works, NWPO, to Inspector of Schools, 2nd Circle, NWPO, 28 August 1895, PED, NWPO, vol. 5, January-June 1897.
40. W.N. Boutflower, Director of Public Instruction, NWPO, to the Secretary to the Government, NWPO, 2 May 1896, PED, NWPO, vol. 5, January-June 1897.
41. John Clibborn was the principal of the Roorkee College from 1892 to 1902. Before this he had served the Public Works Department (PWD) and worked in numcrous canal projects in the Terai region and also in the Sarda Canal Project. For details, see, K.V. Mital, *History of Thomason College of Engineering,* Roorkee, University of Roorkee, 1986.
42. *Proceedings of the Committee appointed by His Honor the Lt. Governor to consider the expediency of bringing the Lucknow Industrial School and other similar schools in to connection with the Thomason College, Roorkee.* Nainital, Saturday, 6 June 1896, vol. 5, January-June 1897.

    The idea was to make it the apex body of engineering training in the province. The principal of the Roorkee College became the ex-officio visitor to these schools the students from these industrial schools could come to study at Roorkee, teachers and tools from Roorkee were sent to these schools. There was considerable expansion in the Roorkee College after Clibborn became the principal in 1892. In 1896, the mechanical and the industrial apprentice classes and a few lower level courses to train foremen, technicians and skilled workers were started. Before that in 1894, to systematize the functioning of the college, the Committee of Management was constituted and the college was affiliated to the Allahabad University. For details, see, Mital, *History of Thomason College of Engineering,* pp. 148-51.
43. T.C. Lewis, Director of Public Instruction, NWPO to Secretary to Government, NWPO, 24 September 1897, PED, NWPO, vol. 10, July-

December 1899. Headmaster, Industrial School, Lucknow, to Inspector of Schools, 2nd Circle, NWPO, 2 November 1897, PED, NWPO, vol. 10, July-December 1899.

44. Ibid. The new rules implied that the duration of the total course structure of the school was shortened from nine years to six years and an increase in the per hour working of the school day. The students felt overworked and withdrew from the school.
45. T.C. Lewis, Director of Public Instruction, NWPO to Secretary to Government, NWPO, 12 July 1897, PED, NWPO, vol. 6, July-December 1897.
46. L.M. Thornton, Secretary to Government, NWPO to Director of Public Instruction, NWPO, 10 June 1899, PED, NWPO, vol. 10.
47. T.C. Lewis, Director of Public Instruction, NWPO to Chief Engineer, PWD, NWPO, 27 June 1899, PED, NWPO, vol. 10.
48. From Tara Prossano Banerjee to Director of Public Instruction, NWPO, 31 July 1899, PED, NWPO, vol. 10.
49. Ibid.
50. Report of Meeting of the Committee of Management, Roorkee Engineering College held at Nainital on the 3 August 1899, PED, NWPO, vol. 10.
51. Ibid.
52. From Secretary, NWPO to Secretary, Home Department, 14 September 1899, PED, NWPO, vol. 10.
53. From T.C. Lewis, Director of Public Instruction, NWPO, to Secretary, NWPO, 17 August 1899, PED, NWPO, vol. 10.
54. From Secretary, NWPO to Secretary, Home Department, 14 September 1899, PED, NWPO, vol. 10.
55. Atkinson, Principal, Thomason College, Roorkee, to Secretary to Government, United Provinces, 13 February 1903, vol. 16.
56. S.N. Sen, *Scientific and Technical Education, 1781-1900*, New Delhi: Indian National Science Academy, 1991, pp. 432-40.
57. The technological officer of each province along with the local associations was to identify the industries which could be developed indigenously so that the import of such articles could be stopped and for this a detailed survey would be undertaken. Weaving was identified as a viable export industry. For details, see, E.C. Buck, *Report, 1900-01*.
58. These officials who conducted the surveys would be able to instruct the teachers of the industrial schools about the industries surveyed. If such teachers were not available in India then the officials would be called from England who would first study the industry and then they would train the teachers in it. E.C. Buck, *Report*, *1900-01*. For a detailed description of E.C. Buck's Report, see, S.N. Sen, *Scientific and Technical Education in India, 1781-1900,* pp. 432-40. Sen gives a detailed account of Buck's Report but misses the discussion as to

why these policy discussions were taking place. Secretary to the GOI, Home, Education, to Secretary to Government, NWPO, 20 November 1901, PED, NWPO, vol. 13, January-June 1902.

59. Secretary, NWPO to Director of Public Instruction, NWPO, 7 December 1901, PED, NWPO, vol. 14.
60. G.N. Chakravarti, Inspector of Schools , 2nd Circle, NWPO to Director of Public Instruction, NWPO, 22 March 1901, PED, NWPO, vol. 13. Clay-modelling was already taught in the industrial school by that time.
61. Ibid.
62. Secretary to Government, NWPO to Director of Public Instruction, NWPO, 22 June 1901, PED, NWPO, vol. 13.
63. Proceedings of a meeting of the Committee of Management of the Industrial School, Lucknow, held on 16 April 1903, vol. 16.
64. Hyde, Locomotive Superintendent, Oudh and Rohilkhand Railway to Inspector of Schools, 3rd circle, Lucknow, 14 July 1906, vol. 23.
65. Indian Industrial Commission, *Inspection Notes, 1916-18,* p. 8.

REFERENCES

1. National Archives of India, New Delhi
Files and Proceedings of the following departments of the Government of India: Home Dept. (Education) files
Papers Relating to Technical Education in India (1886-1904), Calcutta, 1906.
2. Uttar Pradesh State Archives, Lucknow
Files and Proceedings of the following departments: Education Department
3. Official and Semi-Official Publications
Buck, E.C., *Report on Practical and Technical Education,* 1900-1.
Gazetteer of Oudh, 1877-8.
Indian Industrial Commission, Inspection Notes, 1916-18.
Report of the Education Commission, 1882.
Report of the Indian Famine Commission, 1880.
Report of the Indian Industrial Commission, 1916-18, vols. I-IV, *Evidence* (Calcutta 18).
Report of Public Instruction (RPI), 1907, 1911-15.
Papers Relating to Nainital Industrial Conference, 1907.

Books and Articles

Arnold, David, 'European Orphans and Vagrants in India in the Nineteenth Century', in *Journal of Imperial and Commonwealth History* (*JICH*), vol. 7, 1979, pp. 106-14.

Arnold, David, 'White Colonisation and Labour in Nineteenth Century India', in *JICH*, vol. 11, no. 2, January 1983, pp. 133-58.

Baber, Zaheer, *The Science of Empire, Scientific Knowledge, Civilisation, and Colonial Rule in India*, New York: State University of New York Press, 1996.

Carpenter, Mary, *Six Months in India,* London: Longmans, Green and Co., 1868.

Chatarji, A.C., *Notes on the Industries of the United Provinces,* Allahabad: Government Press, 1908.

Hoey, W., *A Monograph on Trade and Manufacturers of Northern India,* Lucknow: American Methodist Mission Press, 1880.

Keene, H.G., *A Handbook for Visitors to Lucknow*, Calcutta: Thacker, Spink and Co., 1875.

Mital, K.V., *History of Thomason College of Engineering*, Roorkee: University of Roorkee, 1986.

Nevill, H.R., ed., *Lucknow: A Gazetteer,* vol. 37, *District Gazetteers of the United Provinces of Agra and Oudh*, Allahabad: Government Press, 1904 and 1907.

Oldenburg, Veena Talwar, *The Making of Colonial Lucknow,* New Delhi: Oxford University Press, 1989.

Sen, S.N., *Scientific and Technical Education in India, 1781-1900,* New Delhi: Indian National Science Academy, 1991.

CHAPTER 9

Vernacular Medical Education and the *Indian Medical Gazette*

SAVITRI DAS SINHA

More than sixty years after India became independent, English remains by far the most favoured medium for higher education, and not just professional medical education. It is worth looking at a short-lived experiment of imparting medical education in Indian languages and identify the causes that led to its demise.[1] Having its genesis after Lord Macaulay's minute, Vernacular Medical Education (VME) occupied a special niche, and had specific objectives. 'Macaulay's minutes had dismissed "the whole native literature in India and Arabia" as less valuable than "a single shelf of a good European library".'[2] The economic, the expedient, the scientific, and the idealist aspects came together to create a favourable ground for medical education to be imparted in the vernacular languages in several medical schools and colleges. However, this was primarily a nineteenth-century phenomenon and did not survive very long.

Nineteenth-century India had two types of institutions for imparting medical education in Indian languages – Native Medical Institutions (NMIs) and VME. Initially, the NMIs taught indigenous systems of medicine with a small component of Western medicine. Subsequently, there was a growth of institutions teaching Western medicine through Indian languages, a process known as VME. This article deals only with VME in institutionalized settings.

The NMI was established in June 1822, when Calcutta (now Kolkata) was very much the seat of the empire. Anil Kumar agrees that Orientalism had a lot to do with the conception of the NMI.[3] In

1822, a proposal was placed before the government for establishing a native medical institution for teaching both Western and indigenous systems of medicine. All systems of medicine were to be given equal status. The Medical Board had based this recommendation on the excellence of the available treatises in the Ayurveda.[4] However, the compulsions of economics and politics – the need for inexpensive local recruits for the army, as well as the need for showcasing British science – were equally, if not more, important. So, the institution continued for only 10 years (1824-34). This was because many did not feel that Oriental learning would be of any use because of the inherent and intrinsic superiority of Western science. It was also found that Indians were quite unenthusiastic about the three-year course for reasons that had more to do with the prospects of subsequent employment.[5] It is interesting that the Calcutta Medical College (CMC) was founded in 1835 by closing the NMI, Sanskrit College and Madrasa. Right from its inception in 1835, a military class in 'Hindoostani' was started for training Indians for subordinate doctors for the army. A Bengali vernacular class for similar civilian appointments in district and *mofussil* hospitals and jails was opened in 1853. The military and vernacular classes differed from those of the NMI as they taught Western medicine in Indian languages and their curriculum did not contain any major components of indigenous medical systems. Vernacular medical classes were conducted at many places including Agra, Madras and Nagpur. Punjab had a system for training *hakeems* and *vaids* in Western medicine.VME does not exist in the country today. However, some of its basic philosophy is coming back in the recent proposal for a three-and-a-half-year Bachelor of Rural Medicine (BRM) course.

This article looks at VME primarily through the eyes of the *Indian Medical Gazette (IMG)*. The *IMG* started its publication in 1866 and was mostly edited by Indian medical service personnel. It has been in continuous publication since its inception till today. It had a wide contributorship and readership, thus diverse views on the subject had been expressed. Being a general medical journal, it was a broad reflector of social and medical conditions and events. Therefore, the views expressed in the *IMG* regarding VME assume special significance. To impart Western medicine to the Indian population engaged the minds of the academics and British administrators. Thus, from the very first year of publication of the

IMG, there were articles dealing with the medium of instruction for teaching Western medicine that had contemporary relevance. While studying VME in the context of the *IMG*, the following questions have been raised: What were the reasons for establishing the vernacular medical course? What were the reasons for its popularity and what were the difficulties of running a vernacular medical science programme? What does the *IMG* have to say about the professional status of the vernacular class? What were the *IMG's* views on the decline of the vernacular programme? Can the reasons for VME's decline be compared to the ones for the decline of higher education in the vernacular today and did those reasons exist, even in a modified form, in the early years of the last century? Also, did vernacularization help in giving a better Indian perspective to medical training?

Christian Hochmuth felt that strong indigenous influences moved into Western medicine, but whether vernacularization added to the process has not been discussed.[6] One can also study the *IMG* to get clues for the reasons for the demise of VME.

Articles in the *IMG* essentially relate to the following:

(a) the suitability of the vernacular medium for imparting medical education and the organization of such classes;
(b) the difficulties and limitations of translating medical works;
(c) the class composition and employment prospects of students with vernacular education; and
(d) perception of such doctors, especially their professional abilities by the lay public as well as by the medical establishment.

Need for Vernacular Medical Education

What were the reasons for medical education through the Indian languages? The reasons were to propagate knowledge of medicine, to address the needs of the people in the villages and *mofussils*, and to supplant practitioners of indigenous systems of medicine, like *hakeems* and *kobirajs*. As early as 1866, we have the example of Joseph Ewart (surgeon, Bengal Medical Service; professor of physiology, and curator of the Pathological Museum), who advocated that the future propagation of medical knowledge 'by engrafting it upon the vernacular languages, and making it in this manner accessible to every native who can read the language of his ancestors'.[7] There is also an editorial entitled 'Vernacular Medical Education' which opens with a perceptive remark on the ephemeral nature of British rule and its legacy: 'Medicine is no longer an educational experiment; it is an accomplished fact and we really believe that if the social science and equalizing tendencies of the present day should find their legitimate issue in our withdrawal from the country, empty beer bottles should not be the only vestige of our short rule.'[8]

The native doctor was supposed to supplant the practitioners of indigenous systems of medicine.[9] As the main enabler of this medical mission in the vast hinterland just outside the main cities – 'the so-called "Native Doctor" of the medical college is actively at work, and doing good service; service that is so well appreciated that even remote from any European influence, he rapidly supersedes the antiquated *kobiraaj* and *hakeem*.'[10] The *IMG* was in favour of supplanting *kobiraj* and quacks who 'infested' towns and villages in Bengal. This was expressed again in 1873.[11] The *IMG* realized the potential of university graduates, who though ignorant in English, were felt to be sufficiently grounded in the principles and practice of medicine and surgery to replace the *kobiraj*. However, the medical and educational departments had not taken any steps for extending this useful branch of the profession.[12] It was also observed by the *IMG* that the native doctors who gave up government service were highly successful in their community.

At that time formal VME was imparted in Agra and Calcutta and the *IMG* editorial commented on the demand-supply gap, the supply not being sufficient for hospitals and jails.[13] The journal even drew up a budget for funding vernacular schools in large health stations (as medical colleges might not be sufficient to meet the demand).[14] The probable cost per month was estimated to be as follows:

Civil Surgeon's allowance as Superintendent and Teacher of

one branch	Rs.	200
3 Sub-Assistant Surgeons at Rs 200	Rs.	600
Stipends and contingencies	Rs.	200
Total	Rs.	1,000

Source: 'Vernacular Medical Education', *IMG,* February 1867, p. 47.

The order in which the subjects were to be studied were first, anatomy, physiology and surgery; second, medicine and midwifery; and third, elementary chemistry and materia medica. The organization would have a civil Surgeon with additional duties of superintendent and principal, and three sub-assistant surgeons as teachers. It also mooted the idea of a vernacular licentiate. Again, the emphasis was on reaching out, through the scientific, civilizing, philanthropic and unifying mission of medical relief to the suffering 'socially, politically and philanthropically' which would be expedient. It was hoped not only to bring comfort and welfare of the people, but 'would cement attachment to the Government and tend to allay mutual prejudices of race'.[15] It would do good both to the recipient and the donor.

Another form of vernacular education, though less formal, was to be imparted to the youth from the hereditary healing castes. The *IMG* extracted a long letter by Dr Shaw, Inspector-General of the Medical Department, Madras, which urged on the government to utilize the hereditary physicians of the country, 'the "*hakeems*" and "vytians" by inducing young of those castes to study at the Charitable Dispensaries throughout the country'.[16] It was doubtful about the financing of such a scheme. Like the scheme in Punjab, it proposed to attract potential students by starting a scholarship scheme, offering a monthly stipend and to guarantee employment. However, the Madras government wished to try out a voluntary cess which made the writer doubt its success. This idea had been propounded in Madras as early as 1862, but could not succeed due to the opposition by the Principal Inspector General, Dr Cole. Two very interesting things stand out: (1) VME for traditional healers and midwives (*dai* or *dhye*) was often not a centrally organized effort but relied on the individual initiatives of civil surgeons, and (2) several small towns in Madras like Cuddalore, Manargoody and Cuddapah trained Indian women in the practice of midwifery (as again was the practice in Punjab). This article, 'Vernacular Medical Education in Madras', also commented on the caste system. While the emphasis was on training youth belonging to the hereditary healer castes, the article had a very contemporary viewpoint on the hereditary professions.[17] It also called for the scientific investigation of some of the empirical treatments of traditional medicine in an atmosphere where all knowledge of healing was to be considered equal.[18]

Administering VME

A report of a meeting of the Bengal Branch of the British Medical Association (BBBMA) very strongly advocated the improvement of VME, as it felt that it was preposterous to suppose that the medical wants of 200 million human beings would be adequately met through the medium of a foreign language.[19] As vernacular practitioners were to constitute the major bulk of the profession, they were to be given education equal in quality to the English-speaking classes. The *IMG* probably shared the same feelings as had been expressed by Sir Frederick Halliday before the Select Committee of the House of Commons on Indian territories on 25 July 1853 that English education ultimately swallowed up everything else.[20] The BBBMA particularly called for deficiencies in surgery and midwifery to be corrected, as *kobirajs* and *hakeems* were deficient in these areas and public were disappointed with the native doctors in times of difficult labour.[21] The association said that there were very few doctors in India and with 'seasons of war, famine and epidemics', there was definitely a greater need for such vernacular practitioners.[22] But one finds an emphasis on the class distinction between the university and the vernacular practitioners. It was said that the pass-outs of the vernacular medical schools were to function in areas where the university graduates were unwilling to operate. It is interesting that the *IMG* described them as 'working men' who would fulfil medical necessities.[23] However, the universities were meant to regulate the quality of VME practitioners who would always remain subordinate to the university graduates.

Articles published in the *IMG* on VME related to its spread, to the inevitable increase in the cost of such an education and the sharing of facilities with the English class.[24] The article 'Vernacular Medical Education' praised the work on VME.[25] There were not only several collegiate institutions in the capitals of several presidencies and important schools at Agra and Lahore, but several 'minor governments' were continuing this work. However, taking the students of the Nagpur schools into account, it pleaded that medical education must be made, 'not a local, but an imperial consideration'.[26] The immediate catalyst for this article was that there was substantial budgetary provision for the salaries of principals and native teachers. However, the provision for contingent expenditure and stipend for students was considered to be insufficient, more so when the number of students was on the rise. While the extra expenditure required was being met from the contributions from the municipal funds, the *IMG* feared that 'as a rule, Municipalities become afflicted early in life with a tight-press in the chest and have a constitutional tendency towards bankruptcy'.[27]

Hospitals for Clinical Instruction

With reference to VME, the *IMG* also lamented the lack of infrastructure and grants for running the hospitals attached to VME institutions, without which clinical instruction was incomplete. It was thought that local philanthrophy and government assistance would bring in improvement. Thus an appeal to the Chief Commissioner, J.H. Morris appeared in the *IMG*:

> Without an hospital, a medical school is but a lecture-hall, a medical student but a paper man and a book-worm. Now, what is the condition of Nagpore in this respect? There is certainly a city hospital for in-patients, and there are three out-door dispensaries. But the city hospital consists of two wretched, ill-constructed sheds, mean and unattractive in appearance, unventilated and incapable of ventilation; badly situated with reference to the wants both of the sick poor and of the students, and, in consequence, crowded only with the miserable and wretched who come but to obtain shelter and to die.[28]

Concept of Barefoot Doctors

The *IMG* in the article 'Vernacular Medical Education', in the early 1870s, suggested the extension of the medical schools to the districts (*sudder* stations) in association with a reasonably sized hospital to train village doctors.[29] The Nagpur Medical School was built on that principle. The main basis of the extension was the need for a village doctor.

The editorial 'Subordinate Medical Education in India' believed that there was sufficient number of people who wished to learn modern medicine for their own livelihood and to cater to their own community.[30] A similar view was also expressed by Surgeon-Major Edward Lawrie, principal of the Hyderabad Medical School, speaking at the annual prize distribution on 12 December 1887.[31] A detailed costing had been done in the editorial of 1872 to justify that the savings from dispensaries would to a large extent offset the cost of medical education.[32] However, it was explicitly clear that the village doctor was not intended to go in for higher education and a university degree, for which the Medical College of Bengal was founded in 1835.[33] Perhaps, an idea of Indian interest in such an education can be had from the numbers enrolled in the Vernacular Licentiate Class (training private practitioners) and the Native Apothecary Class (training for government service) which had 333 and 145 new entrants, respectively. The 478 new entrants of the vernacular classes were choking the facilities of the medical college and the 350-bedded medical hospital.[34]

Women and VME

VME also impacted women's medical education in India. The transition of nurses and *dais* to trained midwives and eventually doctors can be seen as a gradual process. Trained midwives were required to teach *dais* because 'one of the greatest difficulties is the natural unwillingness of women to receive instruction upon this subject from teachers of the opposite sex'.[35] The *IMG* agreed that there were opportunities to instruct *dais* in Calcutta and Jeypore (present Jaipur). So a School of Midwifery was established in Amritsar in 1867 (with a small attached lying-in hospital). This was managed by a lady who 'studied in, and holds the diploma of, one of the most celebrated hospitals in the British Isles for imparting professional education to those who would be "the only obstetric practitioners employed by the majority of persons in India"'.[36] However, the *IMG* was clear that they were not advocates for an extensive class of 'lady doctors, nor for the practice of medicine in its full extent by women' – a task for which few women were fitted 'either by physical constitution or by previous education'.[37] However, during this period medical schools for women were firmly established in North America.[38]

What Went Wrong with VME

If all was so fine with VME, then what went wrong? An anonymous letter to the editor by a native teacher pointed this out.[39] The letter was in response to an article published in the *IMG* on

2 September 1872 which advocated the spread of VME.[40] The letter was perceptive, full of insight and not a little pained at the basic assumptions, philosophy and practice of this educational effort. What is also so striking about this letter is the quality of English prose from this 'native teacher' of a vernacular school, a voice which comes straight from the heart. The teacher said that the mode of selection emphasized tests for barely elementary knowledge skills.[41] The students selected with rudimentary requirements were taught functional medicine 'within the shortest possible time and with the most economical eyes as regards the number of subjects constituted modified science'.[42] There were problems with the subjects taught, 'the meagerness of which will strike any, even the most superficial adviser, and will not, of course, bear comparison with what one obtains in any of the higher schools of medicine'.[43] The subjects taught in the VMEs were anatomy (descriptive and surgical), materia medica (with only a little of chemistry), medicine and surgery. This course was thus an empirical one for physiology and chemistry had no place in it. Modern medical science, which today pride on the era for 'scientific medicine', will find an echo of their thoughts in the nineteenth-century native teacher who remarked on its 'totally unscientific character': 'To what advantage can one learn medicine without a competent knowledge of pathology and therapeutics (a knowledge which presupposes a knowledge of physiology and chemistry), or what is the use of practising medicine if we cannot diagnose and treat disease in its multifarious forms.'[44]

The reforms advocated by the writer included the teaching of physiology and chemistry, addition of 'midwifery', the diseases of women and children, medical jurisprudence and 'good clinical instruction' which would result in 'safe and useful' doctors.[45]

Overcrowding and Inadequate Facilities

VME institutions soon became so crowded with students that the number threatened to choke CMC. The huge increase in load had resulted in inadequate facilities – the students could not listen to the lectures, the library was ill-equipped and bureaucratic rules prevented the purchase of new books. The dissecting rooms were a series of sheds and the practical rooms cellars. The vernacular classes were discriminated against, yet there was an eagle eye looking at the accounts. The increase of fees from Rs. 1,410 in

1,830 to Rs. 30,568 in 1872 with 62 per cent paying for their own education was approvingly commented upon. The total number of students on the rolls at the beginning of the session in 1873 were 1,394 of which there were 445 in primary or English classes; 41 in the apothecary class; 136 in military or hindustani classes; and 772 in bengali classes.[46]

Soon it was felt that the hospital and other facilities including dissection were insufficient. In order to relieve congestion, the vernacular classes (the Native Apothecary Class and the Vernacular Licentiate Class [VLC]) with their 823 students of the Bengalee classes of the CMC were shifted in 1873. The Bengalee classes were established by taking over a municipal hospital at Sealdah, called the Campbell Hospital, named after Sir George Campbell, the Lieutenant-Governor of the province; and the Urdu section was shifted to the Temple Medical School at Patna.[47]

The pass-outs were designated as graduates of the college and were also awarded Vernacular Licentiate in Medical Sciences (VLMS). They were appointed as sub-assistant surgeons – later re-designated as hospital assistants. The criticism of the vernacular course (based on the opinion acquired from several senior professors and civil surgeons) was that it emphasized 'parrot'-like rote learning without much practical or clinical instructions.[48] The *British Medical Journal* also considered this important enough to carry the report of the *IMG* in some detail and almost verbatim.[49] However, the *IMG* was very hopeful that the graduates in vernacular medicine would supplant the '*kobirajs* and quacks' in towns and villages of Bengal.[50] In spite of such enthusiastic support, VME could not continue and as per the *Report of the Calcutta University Commission*, 1919 (vol. III, p. 53), Bengali was the medium of instruction in Campbell School only till 1904. After a transition phase from 1904 to 1908, when both Bengali and English were used, classes were held only in English. In fact, the epithet 'vernacular' was discontinued in 1911.[51]

Nomenclature and Hierarchy

It was in 1868 at the meeting of the BBBMA that a call for great increase in the number of vernacular medical practitioners (native doctors), who should form the bulk of the profession, was given to provide efficient medical aid to all classes of population.[52] It was felt that the need to be connected with the universities was immaterial. Even at the hey-day of VME, there was an emphasis on sound and comprehensive professional education as in English-speaking classes. The *IMG* in its article 'English Training for Native Doctors' felt that some knowledge of English was required to bring the students out of isolation.[53] The *IMG* suggested that the students should be taught some amount of English, especially at Agra and Lahore. The *IMG* found that in Calcutta many students in the military class of the medical college could attend an English school during their spare time, but the majority of them learn on their own. In Agra and Lahore, on the other hand, it was more difficult to acquire the required degree of competence in English on their own. The journal also advised the professors of medical colleges and schools to institute an English class for the teaching of native doctors who would eventually become hospital assistants, so that they pass into the service of the government. To quote the *IMG*, 'they will not only reap advantages themselves in the increased pay for the accomplishment, but they will be much more useful servants to the state and to their immediate masters'.[54] This emphasis on turning them into 'useful servants to the state' was a change in thought from the feelings expressed in the *IMG* in 1869. The then Lieutenant-Governor had said: 'To impart knowledge, generally, in a foreign tongue, must of necessity greatly increase the difficulties of education.' 'In England', he added, 'where the Latin and Greek languages are considered an essential part of a polite education, all general instruction is conveyed, not in those languages but in the vernacular of the country.'[55]

The change in the nomenclature of the pass-outs of the VME from 'native doctor' to 'hospital assistant' evoked several opposing reactions. The *IMG* establishment was by and large supportive of the change in the nomenclature from 'native doctor' (a term they felt was 'obnoxious') to 'hospital assistant'. At the first instance, to a modern reader, 'the obnoxiousness seems to lie in "Native"' with all its racial and imperial connotations.[56] But very soon one realizes that this was hardly an issue. The problem was in classifying the pass-outs of such a system as a 'doctor' – native or otherwise.[57]As the 'Native Teacher of Medicine' writes in a letter: 'It may be the original intention of the originators and supporters of the system of VME had been to make these men simple assistants, but somehow or the other, these intentions had not been fulfilled.'[58] Perhaps, by renaming them 'hospital assistants', the government got rid of the burden of expectations that arose from the use of the term 'doctor'. By not dignifying him/her with the title of a healer, all deficiencies in selection, curriculum, employment prospects and social status were at one stroke of the pen, irrelevant. For the 'Native Teacher of Medicine' the name was everything. He was sure that whatever be the intentions of the founders of the vernacular medicine course, the Native Doctor had a valued place in society, which some found to be objectionable. 'Need we then tell them that the really objectionable thing in a native doctor is not his name, but the assumption by him of the true functions of a doctor.'[59] However, even with the term 'hospital assistant', the Native Doctor was 'busily and successfully' plying his craft as did ever his confrere the native doctor of old. In this context the *IMG's* view is interesting: 'No more in our time is it possible for a native doctor to cease to be doctor because you have chosen to change his name, than it was in Juliet's time for a rose to lose its fragrance by being called something else.'[60]

Vernacular Medical Textbooks

In the *Centenary of the Medical College Bengal (1835-1934)* there is a reference to the massive effort of translating books into the vernacular languages and the difficulties in doing so.[61] To name a few, these included *A Treatise on Materia Medica* (in Bengali) by Baboo Durga Das Kar; *Midwifery* (in Bengali) by Baboo Ananda Charan Khastgir; and *Anatomy* (Urdu) by S.P. Johns. It also mentions vernacular monthly periodicals, edited by Baboo Jadunath Mukherji (LMS) and Eman-Uddin, published at Chinsurah and Agra, respectively. The need for textbooks was expressed by the *IMG* from time to time. It was felt that the VME had been introduced but no attempt had been made to help the students in studying the vast science. It was also suggested to form a society in the model of the Sydenham Society which would be of help in publishing original works as well as translations.[62] The problem of writing in vernacular which discourages the Indian doctor from writing another book had been highlighted:

> A poor sub-assistant surgeon writes a book in Bengalee, and when it goes to the press a heavy estimate of costs is given to him; he feels his pocket and gets frightened; after some consideration, he borrows money with the hope of repaying from the proceeds of the sale of his book. As a matter of

course, to give facilities to the poor students and native doctors in buying his book, he makes the price low and finds the sale of the book has not half covered his costs.[63]

In 1869, the *IMG* urged that good vernacular textbooks be generated, as none were available and the class notes (even at their best, which was rarely so) were inadequate. Emphasizing the need for vernacular textbooks it praised the efforts of the Governor of the North West Frontier Province who offered to pay for the same and expected the same stimulus from the Medical Department, otherwise it would result in a deficiency in textbooks for native doctors. Emphasis was also placed on the need for borrowing from ancient literature, both in Sanskrit and vernacular.[64] The idea was that such borrowings would enrich the practices of medicine itself. The *IMG* argued:

> We have been too much in the habit of keeping hakeems and baids at arm's length, and of sneering at their antiquated systems. But a new school is forcing itself into notice. The Anglicists of Macaulay must be content with the results which they are obtaining with the aid of the education grant, now swelled into something more than half a million sterling, and leave some of the field open to the Orientalists, whose pecuniary help has not hitherto been more than at the rate of fourteen and a half d. for every thousand souls.[65]

In April 1869, the *IMG* commented that rather than direct translation of medicine books in the vernacular (as suggested by Dr Ewart, officiating principal of the medical college), adaptation might be better but the best would be an original composition.[66] Original works were suggested on medicine, midwifery, medical jurisprudence and surgery. This was more so because rapid changes had rendered portions of books like Hooper's *Physicians Vade Mecum* obsolete. Also, the tropical climate changed the natural history of disease, and the management of diseases almost unknown in Britain was required. This viewpoint is also an indicator of the perceived importance of the discipline of what was to be known as 'tropical medicine'. Adaptations were also suggested for Drutt's *Surgeon's Vade Mecum*, with supplements from Fayrer's *Clinical Surgery*. Again, in view of the extensive adaptation, a new work was thought to be better. Similarly, Tyler Smith's work on obstetrics in translation may not be so good as an original Gray's *Anatomy*,

Fowler's *Chemistry* and interestingly for, Baboo Durga Dass Kar's book *Materia Medica* along with Waring's *Indian Materia Medica* were suggested for translation. Financial arrangements for the translation were suggested and qualifications of an editor were specified as follows: an eminent person in the field, skilled in teaching and a good linguist to translate either books or original compositions in English. The actual translation would be done by native teachers, who would be paid per page, for which they would also get the assistance of a *pandit*. There is an interesting insight as to why medical officers in India did not write much: 'Here men make no more in writing than if they simply lived out their period of service, and avoided getting into trouble!' those who did (unlike their counterparts in England), did so only for their reputation. How true even today! [67]

Dr S. Goodeve Chuckerbutty in his introductory lecture to the Medical College, Calcutta, session of 1870-1, urged the passing-out students to translate works into the vernacular. He said that while he was a strong advocate of English education, he could not overlook the vast advantage of vernacular classes, especially 'cheapness and facility of comprehension'.[68] However, the absence of sufficient number of vernacular textbooks was indeed a disadvantage. Translation of texts was done even within the European languages, each of which had a strong medical tradition of its own. Hence it was very important for Indians to translate the English texts. He mentioned:

> The work is simple enough, being merely to translate from English into the vernaculars. This is a kind of work which is carried on in all civilized countries, and thus all valuable books are being constantly rendered from one language into another among all European nations. And if this is done by those who have a rich medical literature of their own, how much more must it be required by a people whose medical literature is scarcely yet in its infancy!I would advise you, therefore, to translate from English into the vernaculars, every medical work you can manage to get.[69]

The CMC authorities informed that the Bengali classes had not been trained so thoroughly in medicine. They received a good deal of theoretical instruction but not had enough practical and clinical instruction as was necessary. The Lieutnant-Governor realized the need to 'provide the vernacular classes with a good set of Bengali manuals or translations', and 'the necessity for providing vernacular classes with textbooks framed in accordance with a rational and uniform system of scientific nomenclature'.[70] Some vernacular works on medicine were translated into Bengali in 1883.[71] These were Chakrapanidatta's work *Drabyagunagrantha* (Book Describing the Properties of Objects), published by Kabiraj Kailash Chandra Sen. Kabiraj Rasik Lal Gupta undertook the reprinting work of a very large and authoritative work on Hindu medicine by Bhaba Misra titled *Bhaba Prakash*. A similar reprint of one of Bagbhat's most celebrated works titled *Astangahridaya*, was undertaken by Kabiraj Bijayaratna Sen Gupta. An interesting pamphlet on the history and uses of tobacco was written by Babu Jogesh Chandra Ghosh.[72]

The need to translate an increasing number of English books to vernacular was an inescapable component of vernacular education in India, including medical education. Lionel Bently has shown that the British administrators and educationists argued in favour of limiting the translation rights of authors in the interest of diffusion of education in India.[73] He writes that the Imperial Copyright Act of 1842 or the Indian Law of 1847 were ambiguous with regard to translated works and when there was a proposal to adopt translation rights in 1876 and 1885, several authorities, including W.C. Capper, Commissioner, Fyzabad Division; R.S. Risley, Assistant Secretary to the Government of Bengal, and Courtenay Ilbert, the legal member of the Viceroy's Council argued that it 'might stand in the way of translations being made [from English into vernacular], and might thus interfere in the diffusion of knowledge'.[74]

The voicing of the specific need to diffuse medical education in the vernacular language has already been discussed. Education, in general, was a part of 'white man's burden' – a logic accepted not only by the British, but also by prominent Indian reformers like Raja Rammohun Roy. Lord Macaulay (1835) in his minute on education was clear that there should be 'a class of persons Indian in blood and colour, but English in taste, in opinions, words, and intellect'.[75] While many British administrators agreed to this view at the time and believed that English education provided a means of creating such a class of people, some like Hodgson Pratt (Inspector of Schools in Bengal and founder of the Vernacular Literature Society), felt:

> To make the acquisition of the English language the sole condition upon which twenty-five millions of people shall obtain access to stores of valuable information . . . is a gross injustice: that such a system must deprive the great

mass of the native population of all means of improvement or progress; and perpetuate the great evils which have ever been present in the East – that of making learning a class distinction.[76]

Conclusion

Articles in the *IMG* tell us about the difficulties that can arise in teaching advanced courses in a language different from the one used for creating the body of knowledge. Hence all developments necessarily have to be available in translation which becomes unviable both because of its delay and poor economics. There was a historical overview of VME on some of its aspects in Koilas Chandra Bose's address to the students of the Medical College, Calcutta in 1919.[77] Bose mentioned that only the rich in India had the privilege to get treated by English doctors and the rest of the population were left at the mercy of the quacks.[78] There had been attempts made by India as also other developing countries to make health care accessible to all and take it to areas that are otherwise not served by the generally urban-centred degree holders. These efforts have essentially envisaged a stratification of medical care based on the skills of the service providers. There had also been an issue (paralleling) the name change from 'native doctor' to 'hospital assistant' – whether people with lesser training at all deserved to be called doctors or not. This issue surfaced in developed countries like the USA too. Due to increased health care costs, for example, army paramedics dispensed a fairly comprehensive and sophisticated range of medical first-aid.

The concept of nurse practitioners who can also prescribe medicines arose in the 1960s in response to a shortage of doctors in underserved areas.[79] China's barefoot doctors were prominent in the 1960s and 1970s. The *IMG* had discussed this idea of barefoot doctors much earlier. In 1938 a National Planning Committee was constituted with Pandit Jawaharlal Nehru as its chairman, who appointed a Sub-Committee on National Health under the chairmanship of Col. S.S. Sokhey. Col. Sokhey called 'the cornerstone of the scheme of their recommendations (was) a Community Health Worker for every 1,000 of village population'.[80] It was negated by the Bhore Committee in 1946. About 30 years ago, West Bengal started a 'barefoot doctor' programme but had to abandon it after about four years since these doctors agitated for parity with MBBS doctors and demanded a condensed degree to come back to the cities and practice.[81] In its recent *avatar*, the three-and-a-half-year course of Bachelor of Rural Medicine and Surgery (BRMS), renamed the Bachelor of Rural Medicine (BRM) is being debated and has got support even though medical bodies like the Indian Medical Association (IMA), the largest non-government organization of allopathic doctors in the country, opposed the same in district hospitals.[82]

Medicine is subjected to two conflicting forces. One relates to reaching equity and universal health care which manifests itself in a shorter duration of training and use of local languages; the other end of the spectrum is represented by super-specialization, long spells of expensive training and preparation, representing the forefront of discovery and advances. The experiment with VME in colonial India represents an attempt towards the first goal and an analysis of its success and failure has a bearing on current medical education as well as higher education. Interestingly, as recent as 2010, the National Translation Mission, Central Institute of Indian Languages, had undertaken a project for translating knowledge texts spread over 69 disciplines including medicine, such as *Ganong's Review of Medical Physiology*. Some of the suggested texts include textbooks for undergraduate studies.[83]

However, VME died a natural death by the early twentieth century. There is not much discussion on the decline of the VME in the *IMG*. Anil Kumar has discussed the causes for the decline of the VME.[84] One of the reasons could be the requirement of a basic knowledge of English for admission to the VM course. These students were thus similar to those eligible for a Licentiate of Medicine and Surgery (LMS). Also there was a spread of English education, accompanied by a realization that translations (ultimately of a limited set of books), could not be sufficient to impart the rapidly advancing complexities of medical science – even at the level lower than the university medical degree. Today, there is an increasing demand for English education, and the class divide between those who are fluent and those who are not is evident to the poor as well. All medical education is in English and in spite of efforts to promote Hindi and other languages, at least there is no sign of any progress in imparting medical education in the Indian languages. The factors acting today are globalization, which has resulted in English becoming an international language in a world without frontiers. The desire of all sections of the population to escape from the underclass, which is characterized by its lack of knowledge of the English language, and very importantly the significantly poorer employment opportunities for those who are not fluent in English combine to promote the growth of English education. In Uttar Pradesh, Chief Minister Mayawati has re-introduced English education in primary government schools because it offers an opportunity for the Dalits to break out of their abysmally low social position.[85] Similar efforts are being made in Tamil Nadu by introducing English medium in corporation schools after its efforts to offer quality education in Tamil language, free of cost, did not succeed.[86] The same social aspirations which relate to English language today were operative then and were responsible for the decline and demise of VME.

Even today English is seen as a passport to higher education in India. It is clear from the *IMG* and other related journals that similar factors - poor status and pay and intellectual isolation - were, to a great extent, responsible for the failure of the experiment in VME in the late nineteenth and early twentieth centuries. Also as the students acquired a knowledge of medicine, they also acquired a desire to know English, for they discovered, what we know to be a fact, that no textbook worthy of the name are written in Hindustani, that all improvements in medicines are recorded in English, and that the sources of their teachers' knowledge are to be found in English publications.[87] The University of Calcutta, founded in 1857, shut its doors to Bengali for nearly 80 years with its resolution of 1859 that students would no longer be permitted to answer in any indigenous language. They must write all papers in English, except language papers. It was only after the Matriculation Resolution was passed in 1935 that vernacular was accepted as a medium of instruction.[88]

Recent data collected by the National University for Education Planning and Administration (NUEPA), on the monitoring system developed for the Sarva Shiksha Abhiyan programme, shows that the number of students opting for English medium from Class I-VIII has grown by 150 per cent between 2003 and 2008, while the number of those opting for Hindi has grown by just 32 per cent.[89] English was and is the passport to a bright future. It was also important that the 'native doctor' understood some English, as lack of knowledge kept him or her away from advancement and also hampered communication. However, an in-depth knowledge of English could not be expected from doctors whose pay was much less than the sub-assistant surgeon.[90]

NOTES

1. In 1860, as per the regulations of the University of Calcutta, the students were divided into the following classes: (1) Primary or Ceylon, (2) Apprentice, (3) Hindoostanee and (4) Bengalee class. The Primary or Ceylon class was of five years duration and students were eligible to sit for the Licence in Medicine and Surgery, and Bachelor of Medicine and Doctorate of Medicine tests. The course curriculum of the other three were of three years duration. The students of Apprentice classes were recruited from the European, Anglo-Indian and Christian communities and were required to pass an entrance examination in English, history, geography, arithmatic and colloquial vernacular.

Classes	Course Curriculum	Duration
Apprentice	1st year: Anatomy, Chemistry, Physiology, Dissection & Attendance at the Dispensary for twelve months 2nd year: Anatomy, Physiology, Materia Medica, Surgery, Dissection and Hospital Attendance for twelve months 3rd year: Medicine, Surgery, Midwifery and Hospital Attendance for twelve months	3 years
Hindoostanee	1st year: Anatomy, Dissections, Materia Medica and Practical Pharmacy 2nd year: Anatomy, Dissections, Materia Medica, Medicine Surgery, Practical Pharmacy and Hospital Attendance for twelve months 3rd year: Clinical Medicine, Clinical Surgery, Dissection of Surgical Regions and Hospital Attendance for twelve months	3 years
Bengalee	The curriculum was the same as that of the Hindoostanee class, only the medium was instruction was Bengalee. In 1864, the Bengalee class was rearranged. It was divided into two: a lower one, the 'Native Apothecary' class and a higher one 'Vernacular Licentiate Class'. This was done to supply efficient subordinate medical assistants to government hospitals and dispensaries and also to train a superior class of students through vernacular languages for independent practice.	

See *The Centenary of the Medical College Bengal, 1835-1934,* Calcutta, 1935, p. 43.

2. Lionel Bently, 'Copyright, Translations and Relations Between Britain and India in the Nineteenth and Early Twentieth Century', *Chicago-Kent Review,* 2007; 82: 3, pp. 1181-1240.
3. Anil Kumar, *Medicine and the Raj: British Medical Policy in India, 1835-1911,* New Delhi: Sage, 1998, p. 19.
4. Ibid.
5. NMI was to follow a three-year course conducted in vernacular languages.
6. Christian Hochmuth believes so and quotes: 'The clinical instruction of the London and Paris schools is scarcely more applicable to the exigencies of the [indigenous student's] practice, than would the knowledge of a Deal Pilot be in avoiding the dangers which beset the navigation of the river Hooghly. . . . The greatest danger which appears to beset the Native Medical Student is that of becoming too exclusively *English* in his lore and in his practice.' Quoted from 'Medical Education: Bibliographical Record', *Indian Annals of Medical Science, 1855*, pp. 722-3, in Christian Hochmuth, 'Patterns of Medical Culture in Colonial Bengal, 1835-1880', *Bulletin of the History of Medicine*, vol. 80, 2006, p. 39.
7. Joseph Ewart, 'Introductory Address Delivered at the Commencement of the 32nd Session of the Calcutta Medical College, on Friday, 15th June, 1866', *IMG,* September 1866, p. 271.
8. 'Vernacular Medical Education', *IMG,* February 1867, p. 47.
9. The nomenclature 'native doctor' was used by the British for those Indians who were trained by the British surgeons, in-charge of hospitals, on the general aspect of diseases and on European modes of treatment. However, they received no systematic education. They were appointed by the government two to each regiment and one or more to each Civil Station. The native doctors started their careers as compounders and dressers and had to appear for examinations before going in for higher rank and pay, see *The Centenary of the Medical College, Bengal 1835-1934*, op. cit., p. 2.
10. 'Vernacular Medical Education', *IMG*, February 1867, p. 47.
11. Ibid., October 1873, p. 268.
12. Ibid., February 1867, p. 47.
13. Ibid.
14. Ibid.
15. Ibid.
16. 'Vernacular Medical Education in Madras', *IMG,* August 1867, p. 205.
17. Ibid.
18. 'It is needless to point out how much more easily this could be done, were the Hakeems, the Baids, and the Physicians and Surgeons of the

modern European School brought to consider themselves as equals and colleagues, members of the one profession, and workers for the one great end – the relief of suffering mankind.' Ibid.

19. 'Meeting of the Bengal Branch of the British Medical Association', *IMG,* May 1868, pp. 113-15.
20. It was felt that the vernaculars were being neglected by the Indian authorities. Sir Frederick Halliday said: 'The Government professes in all its schools and colleges to teach English and the vernacular, but it does it imperfectly. Wherever English is taught it swallows up everything else; the natives are so anxious to obtain it and there is so much greater interest and excitement with respect to it on the part of those who are at the head of educational affairs, that there is more attention and more exertion bestowed upon education in English than upon education in the vernacular; and the whole of the means of education at their command being insufficient, the vernacular is likely to be the more pinched of the two, so that this is not done which might be wished.' See Baman Das Basu, 'Vernacular Education in the Days of the East India Company', *History of Education in India Under the Rule of the East India Company,* Calcutta: The Modern Review Office, 1922, pp. 98-9.
21. 'Meeting of the Bengal Branch of the British Medical Association', *IMG,* May 1868, pp. 113-15. This would also perhaps demonstrate the superiority of the Western medicine over the ancient system of medicine.
22. Ibid.

    Even in England in times of medical emergencies, whether military or civil, the services of apothecaries, assistants or medical students were gladly utilized.
23. Ibid.
24. 'Vernacular Medical Education', *IMG,* October 1868, p. 237; ibid., September 1872, p. 210; ibid., February 1873, p. 52.
25. Ibid., October 1868, p. 237.
26. Ibid., p. 238.
27. Ibid.
28. Ibid.
29. Ibid., September 1872, p. 210; and February 1873, p. 52.
30. 'Subordinate Medical Education in India', *IMG,* January 1869, p. 19.
31. Dr Lawrie, addressing the annual prize distribution on 12 December 1887, said, 'As the students acquired a knowledge of medicine, they also acquired a desire to know English for they discovered, what we know to be the fact, that no textbook worthy of the name are written in Hindusthani, that all improvements in medicines are recorded in English, and that the sources of their teacher's knowledge are to be found in English publications.' 'The Hyderabad Medical School', *IMG,* January 1888, p. 21.

32. 'Vernacular Medical Education', *IMG*, September 1872, p. 210.
33. In 1946 the Bhore Committee had overruled the previous committee of 1940 headed by Lt. Col. S.S. Sokhey which had advocated 'barefoot doctors'. The rational for 'barefoot' doctors, in a broad sense, is very similar to that for vernacular medical class. Finally, the university system expanded and in spite of its limitations, continues till today as the dominant medical training model.
34. 'Vernacular Medical Education', *IMG*, September 1872, p. 210.
35. Ibid., March 1868, p. 64.
36. Ibid.
37. Ibid.
38. Steven J. Peitzman, 'Why Support a Women's Medical College/Philadelphia's Early Male Medical Pro-Feminists', '*Buletin of the History of Medicine,* vol. 77, 2003, pp. 576-99.
39. 'Vernacular Medical Education', *IMG,* February 1873, p. 52.
40. Ibid., September 1872, p. 210.
41. The examination consisted of:

    '1st – Reading with fluency a passage of some well-known work in Urdoo and Hindee.

    2nd – Explaining the meaning of words and phrases.

    3rd – Reading with fluency a passage written in a fairly legible hand in Urdoo and Hindee.

    4th – Writing from dictation, &c, &c.

    5th – Arithmatic as far as the rule of three, &c, &c.'

    'Vernacular Medical Education', *IMG*, February 1873, p. 52.
42. Ibid.
43. Ibid.
44. Ibid.

    A proposal for the teaching of midwifery and the diseases of women and children to the Vernacular and Hindoostanee classes was sanctioned in 1868 vide Financial Resolution No. 371, dated 21 January 1868. Dr Meer Ashruff Ali was transferred from the Agra Medical School to teach these subjects and Dr Kanai Lall Dey, LMS, was appointed to teach Chemistry and Medical Jurisprudence. These latter two subjects were added to the curriculum of the Vernacular Class in 1869 to improve the practical medico-legal knowledge of native doctors in- charge of sub-divisions stationed in distant places, see *The Centenary of the Medical College Bengal, 1835-1934*, op. cit.
45. Ibid.
46. 'Vernacular Medical Education in Bengal', *IMG,* October 1873, p. 268. It is interesting to note that the number of students enrolled in the Apothecary, Military or Hindustani and Bengali classes were a total of 949 against 445 in English or Primary classes. The English or Primary

classes were taking the full university curriculum of five years; and Apprentice, Hindoostanee and Bengalee had only three year courses. What is interesting, though not highlighted, in the editorial 'Vernacular Medical Education in Bengal', ibid., but mentioned in the article 'The Calcutta Medical College', *IMG,* June 1873, p. 158, is the extremely poor pass percentages: only 106 students passed the final examination in 1873. This was out of a total enrolment of about 750 of which 69 were declared as independent medical practitioners and 37 as hospital assistants. The article entitled 'The Calcutta Medical College', ibid., has presented a statistics of enrolment in different classes as follows:

Enrolment in different classes

Years	Primary class	Bengali class	Military class	Total
1860	160	144	131	435
1861	180	134	95	409
1862	200	146	64	410
1863	186	156	70	412
1864	189	193	91	473
1865	177	226	123	526
1866	196	242	156	594
1867	233	304	188	725
1868	243	327	163	753
1869	273	353	104	730
1870	341	443	135	919
1871	388	508	150	1,046
1872	445	635	146	1,226

47. *The Centenary of the Medical College Bengal, 1835-1934,* op. cit., pp. 54-5; O.P. Jaggi, *Medical Education and Research*, New Delhi: Atma Ram & Sons, 1979, p. 46.
48. 'Vernacular Medical Education in Bengal', *IMG*, October 1873, p. 268.
49. Ibid., *BMJ*, November 1873, p. 579.
50. Ibid., *IMG*, October 1873, p. 268.
51. *The Centenary of the Medical College, Bengal (1835-1934),* op. cit., p. 44.
52. 'Meeting of the Bengal Branch of the British Medical Association', *IMG*, May 1868, pp. 113-15.
53. 'English Training for Native Doctors', *IMG*, August 1869, pp. 167-8.
54. Ibid.
55. 'Subordinate Medical Education', *IMG,* March 1869, p. 59.
56. 'Vernacular Medical Education', *IMG*, February 1873, p. 52.
57. As early as 1867 the editorial on 'Vernacular Medical Education' said, 'we would especially recommend the disuse of the ridiculous

title of "Native Doctor", which is as unmeaning as incorrect', *IMG*, September 1867, p. 226.

58. 'Vernacular Medical Education', *IMG*, February 1873, p. 52.
59. Ibid.
60. Ibid.
61. *The Centenary of the Medical College Bengal, 1835-1934*, op. cit., pp. 54-5.
62. 'An Indian Publishing Medical Society' by Kristodhun Ghose, Sub-Assistant Surgeon, in-charge of the Bhaugulpore Charitable Dispensary, *IMG,* November 1868, p. 252.

    In an article, 'A Survey of Bengali Writings in Science and Technology, 1800-1950', published in the *Indian Journal of History of Science,* 1989, vol. 24, pp. 8-66, Durgaprasad Bhattacharya, Ranjit Chakravarty and Rama Deb Roy have mentioned about the appointment of a committee by the Medical College Council in 1867 to examine textbooks and to suggest good approved English textbooks for translation into the vernacular. *Materia Medica* in Bengali by Baboo Durgadas Kar was the only vernacular textbook that could be approved. The publications in Urdu on anatomy, medicine, midwifery, chemistry and materia medica by Meer Ashruff Ali of the Agra School were considered too elementary. The committee recommended the translation of a standard English textbook on each subject. The authors have also shown that in 1875, Calcutta School Book Society published a catalogue of Bengali titles available in different libraries. It had listed a total of 1,544 titles of which 333 were on science and technology (including 99 books on medicine).
63. Kristodhun Ghose, 'An Indian Publishing Medical Society', op. cit.
64. 'Subordinate Medical Education', *IMG,* March 1869, pp. 59-60.
65. Ibid., p. 60.

    It is to be noted that with modernization and globalization, Macaulay's children are more firmly entrenched in the modern medical establishment than ever were in colonial times. For right or wrong, the applications of experimental science have progressively denied the Orientalists any opportunity to take over Western medicine.
66. 'Subordinate Medical Education', *IMG,* April 1869, p. 84.
67. Ibid., p. 85.
68. Dr S. Goodeve Chuckerbutty, Medical College, Calcutta, session 1870-71, 'Introductory Lecture', *Indian Annals of Medical Science,* 1871, vol. XXVII, p. 58.
69. Ibid., p. 70.
70. 'Vernacular Medical Education', *IMG*, October 1873, p. 268.
71. Ibid., May 1885, p. 156.
72. Ibid.

73. Bently, op. cit., p. 1186.
74. Ibid., p. 1188.
75. B.D. Basu, op. cit., p. 90.
76. See Bently, op. cit., n. 29, p. 1190.
77. 'An Address to the Students of the Medical College, Calcutta: Koilas Chandra Bose, Delivered at the Distributions of Prizes, 1919', *IMG*, December 1919, pp. 441-6.
78. Ibid.
79. Subrata Sinha, 'Nurse Practitioners Worth Considering in India?', *National Medical Journal of India*, vol. 23, 2010, p. 122.
80. Debabar Banerjee, 'The Politics of Rural Health in India', *International Journal of Health Service*, January 2005, pp. 783-96.
81. Kinjalka Ghosh and K. Ghosh, 'Bachelor of Rural Health Care: Cutting the Root and Watering the Stem', *National Medical Journal of India*, July-August 2010, p. 250.
82. 'MCI Proposal to Start New Short-term Medical Course to Train Rural Doctors Faces IMA Opposition', *National Medical Journal of India*, March-April 2010, p. 125.
83. Available at www.ntm.org.in (accessed on December 2010).
84. Anil Kumar, op. cit.
85. *Dalit Voice: The Voice of the Persecuted Nationalities Denied Human Rights*, 16-28 February 2010, vol. 29, no. 4. Available at www.dalitvoice.org/Templates/march 2010/articles.html (accessed on 14 August 2010).
86. 'Letter from Chennai', *National Medical Journal of India*, November-December 2010, p. 364.
87. 'Bengal Medical Act', *IMG*, April 1933, pp. 218-19.
88. 'Indian Medical Council', *IMG*, April 1935, p. 219; 'The Punjab Medical Council', *IMG*, April 1935, p. 219.
89. *The Times of India*, 5 December 2009.
90. 'Subordinate Medical Education', *IMG*, March 1869, pp. 58-60.

CHAPTER 10

Advising Indian Education

Central Advisory Board of Education 1920-1947

SUSHIL PRASAD

> With whatever depth of vision and sympathetic imagination the Board might have tackled the educational problems in the past; it could not escape the fact that there was no free national government to support it. In spite of its desire to have the fullest scope it had to keep itself somewhat in restraints. Now things have changed. The nation about the educational problems of which you are going to deliberate has its own government at your disposal. The government in its turn expects that you, too, offer your deliberations with the same tenacity of purpose and breadth of vision as are guiding the administration today. . . . Its lengthy reports covering thousands of pages are a record of the zeal and ability with which the task was handled in the past thirteen years and the present day educational activities of the country bear testimony to it.
>
> Maulana Abul Kalam Azad, in his speech delivered at the sixteenth meeting of the CABE held in Delhi on 12 January 1948.

Abul Kalam Azad, the first education minister of free India adequately describes the role played by the Central Advisory Board of Education (CABE) in giving advice for developing educational policy under the colonial regime. Due to obvious political reasons, its recommendations could not be implemented in letter and spirit which he regretted, as is evident in the above statement. But in the changed political set-up he reposes faith in the ability of the board and wished that it will be allowed to work freely and its experience in the field will be given due importance. In other words, he was of the opinion that the board should be made a real power in the field of Indian education to overcome its backwardness. With this hope he attended almost every meeting of the board till his death.

The CABE is a body in the Department of Education, Ministry of Human Resources, Government of India. A prestigious forum of scholars, thinking leaders and administrators since 1920, it has been providing a place for widespread consultation and examination of issues of educational development. Several important decisions have been taken by the government on the basis of the advice of the CABE. Lately in August 2004 the government reconstituted the CABE after a gap of 10 years. Few people are aware that the CABE came into being in the inter-war years. The Government of India Act of 1919 (popularly known as Montague-Chelmsford Reform) under its provision of diarchy transferred the subject of education from the jurisdiction of the imperial government to the provincial governments. This changed the educational role of the Government of India from that of an executive to an advisor. Thus the need of a think-tank as a central body for idea and advice to the provinces on education arose. The need for such a body was also felt for ensuring coordination among various provincial education departments with the objective of getting better results.[1] Ever since it was set-up with these broad objectives, the functioning of the CABE has faced several hurdles. The biggest one came in 1923 in the form of financial constraint which led to its suspension for the next 12 years. During the short period of its first phase, however, it promised a lot for the betterment of Indian education and gave it a definite direction. The revival of it in 1935 provided an impetus for more spirited action in the second phase, between 1935 and 1947. The CABE attempted to reconstruct Indian education and give it a distinct nationalistic orientation.

This paper attempts to understand the embedded discourse that was carried forward by the CABE between 1920 and 1947. It deals with events, processes and personalities under CABE involved in Indian education. The period 1920-47 was a great period of transition in the history of Indian education. The paper therefore proposes to use the CABE as a prism to unfold the different strands of educational discourse. The paper is divided into three broad parts. The first part deals with the background to the formation of the CABE. The second part, by the way of highlighting its functioning between 1920 and 1923, attempts to find out the circumstances that led to the abolition of the CABE in 1923. The story of reconstitution of the CABE in 1935 after a gap of 12 years and the details of its functioning up to the Independence is dealt in the third part of the paper.

The Embryo and the Birth

The Government of India Act of 1919 divided the government's subjects into two parts: reserved and transferred. Departments of strategic importance like finance, defence, and communication were reserved for the central government, while departments of health and education and agriculture were transferred to the provincial governments under the charge of Indian ministers. This constitutional change deprived the Government of India of power, which it held for over 60 years, of framing an educational policy applicable to the whole of India.[2] This also meant end of the executive power to implement the policies. The process of provincialization of education provided a new opportunity for the Indians to develop the kind of educational structure they were in search of. Whether it did really happen is a point to explore. Another important aspect is to understand the impact of provincialization of education. W.S. Meston provides some clue in this respect: 'Nothing so noticeable happened as the emphasis was placed upon provincial autonomy in educational matters on the one hand, and the desire for a somewhat closer degree of interprovincial unification on the other.' What was the impact of the Act of 1919 on Indian education might not be simple to explain, but the need for a central body was felt as a result of it.

On 24 January 1920, H. Sharp, Secretary of Department of Education, submitted a follow-up to the Act of 1919 before the Viceroy General-in-Council. He elaborated why there should be a permanent board of education under the imperial government. The ground, he stated, was, 'with the transfer of education the need for expert advice will be greatly increased. A minister in a local government is likely to be strongly influenced by extra-educational motives.'[3] Even before Sharp's idea there had been suggestions for such an advisory body.[4] The Calcutta University Commission Report (1919) was of the opinion that the Government of India could perform an invaluable function by defining the general aims of educational policy by giving advice and assistance to local governments and to universities; it could act as an impartial arbiter in cases of dispute and help to obtain the service of scholars; it could also guard against needless duplication of works by assembling and supplying information. The Government of India Secretariat Procedure Committee in its report went a step further by suggesting two boards for the proposed departments of Education and Public Health. The proposed boards would publish annual reports of their proceedings and would have the right of submitting their recommendations to the viceroy through the chairman.[5] The Joint Select Committee on the Government of India Bill also endorsed the proposal to form a central body to look after the educational theme. Sharp, the main architect of the move, strongly presented his viewpoint in his proposal to Muhmmad Shafi, the member of Governor-General-in-Council. Muhmmad Shafi agreed with Sharp's points and suggested that the Educational Commissioner of the Government of India should be the chairman of the board. On the composition, it was proposed that board should be largely a non-official body consisting of the following:[6]

- The Educational Commissioner with the Government of India as chairman.
- An expert member from Great Britain.
- Two vice-chancellors of universities in India, one of the whom should be a whole-time officer.
- Two principals of privately-managed colleges.
- Four directors of public instruction; and
- four persons (non-official Indians) who might not be immediately engaged in education but should have interest in the subject.

The Governor-General-in-Council accepted the proposal of Sharp with minor changes. The member-in-charge Muhammad Shafi emphasized that the function of the board should be advisory. He stated:

> Whenever the agenda of a meeting included any matter concerning technical issues, it was to be sent to the department concerned and the department would be invited to send a representative to take part in the deliberations regarding that matter. The members of the Board were to be

appointed by the member-in-charge of Education with the approval of the Governor-General.

It was also decided that meetings of the board would be held quarterly. An agenda of each meeting would be prepared sufficiently in advance of the date thereof to enable the members to come prepared with their opinions.[7] The Governor-General finally appointed J.A. Richey, Educational Commissioner with Government of India (Chairperson); Srinivas Sastri, Member of the Council of Bombay; R. Littlehailes, Director, Public Instructions, Madras; Sir Chimanlal Harilal Setalvad, Member of the Executive Council, Bombay; Raghunath Purushottam Paranjpe, Principal, Fergusson College, Poona; P.J. Hartog, Vice-Chancellor, Dacca University; J.C.R. Ewing, former Vice-Chancellor of Panjab University; Sir S.N. Banerjea, Minister for Local Self-Government, Bengal; C.F. de la Fosse, Director of Public Instruction, United Provinces; Dr. Zia-ud din Ahmed, Principal Mohammedan Anglo-Oriental College, Aligarh; G. Anderson, Director Public Instruction Punjab; Nawab Muhammad Abdul Majid, Member, United Provinces Assembly; and A.I. Mayhew, Director, Public Instruction, Central Provinces as the first members of the CABE.[8]

Even as the CABE was formed certain doubts and criticisms came from the Indians regarding its position and utility. The first controversy arose over the omission of a few names. J.A. Richey, the Chairman of the board insisted that Fazl-i-Hussain, who was a member of the Panjab University Provincial Legislative Council should be in the board in the place of Muhammad Abdul Majeed.[9] He also suggested replacement of the physically ill, J.C.R. Ewing with Garfield-Williams.[10] Muhmmad Shafi too was not happy with the composition. Richey on his part pointed out the absence of Pandit Madan Mohan Malaviya, the Vice-Chancellor of Banaras Hindu University and of Sir Ashutosh Mukherjee, the Vice-Chancellor of Calcutta University. 'Pandit M.M. Malaviya', he said, 'was not only a leading Hindu authority on education but is also the Vice-Chancellor of the Banaras Hindu University. He can hardly be ignored without running the risk of bitter public criticism.'[11] But Sharp did not buy his argument and stated, 'I cannot regard him as a leading authority on education.' In case of selection of M.M. Malaviya, he feared, it would be necessary to induct the Vice-Chancellor of Aligarh Muslim University.[12]

Some questions also rose regarding the utility of such a body. Sir Sankaran Nair was of the view that board was unnecessary. It would cause intervention with local governments, frustrate the objectives of provincialization and whittle away the minister's sense of responsibility.[13] Richey attempted to pacify these concerns by arguing that though the board had no administrative authority, its advice as a body composed of well-known educationists must carry weight.[14] He was joined by Sir Setalvad, who stated that local bodies would not be reluctant to accept the CABE's advice if it directly consulted them. But if suggestions came from the centre on behalf of the CABE then it might be taken as intervention.

Concerns and Actions of the First Phase

The first meeting of the CABE was held between 17 and 19 February 1921 in Delhi.[15] Honourable Khan Bahadur Mian Muhammad Shafi, Member for Education of Governor-General-in-Council welcomed the members and explained the aims and functions of the board. J.A. Richey put forward the agenda for discussion and outlined the role of the CABE in future.[16] There was considerable discussion on the Government of India's advice to invite suggestions from the general public with the view of making the system of education more national in character. Further, issues like control of degrees in India, equivalence of university examinations, the extension of primary education and national education were dealt with in detail.[17]

The second meeting of the CABE was held on 2 and 3 June 1921. It passed 16 different resolutions and sent it to the Government of India. The first two resolutions dealt with the introduction of mental intelligence tests in schools and colleges. The board suggested that experiments should be made in order to prepare a set of mental intelligence tests suitable for Indian students.[18] The subject of vocational education was discussed next. Milligan, Agricultural Adviser to the Government of India, and R.P. Hadow, Deputy Secretary to the Public Works Department, were special invitees to participate in the proceedings.[19] The board suggested that a vocational course in agriculture of four years duration leading to the intermediate examination should be introduced. The board was unanimous in thinking that agricultural education after intermediate stage could only be taught satisfactorily in an agricultural college. The issue of technical education, handicraft education, commercial education, medical education and engineering education also figured in the discussions.[20]

In the next meeting, the board carried over the ongoing debates and took up several new topics as well.[21] Education of the Anglo-Indian community, utilization of Ludlow Fund, grants for European schools, establishment of an all-India examination for European Scholar, recruitment of university professionals and staffs were other issues discussed in the third meeting. As part of the concern for the education of the 'defected', the education of the blind, deaf and mute were deliberated upon. In the fourth meeting, the issues of Montessori system of education, education of depressed classes, education at home and sex education were before the board. But due to several constraints these could not be pursued.

The board functioned well for over two years. By the end of 1922, it started facing financial constraints. While the constraints were common to all the departments due to the recommendations of the Retrenchment Committee, CABE was one of the severely affected. The Retrenchment Committee went to the extent of suggesting the dissolution of the CABE and the post of Educational Commissioner.[22] As a result, CABE was abolished in 1923. In its short span of three years CABE attempted to understand the complex interplay of nationalism and imperialism on Indian education in seven meetings.[23]

The result may be termed positive from several angles. The board constituted several committees comprising famous experts on the required theme and deliberated upon issues before making recommendations to the Government of India and the provincial governments. In this sense it held great promises for the betterment of Indian education, which, however, was soon shattered. William Meston commented, 'It is not too much to say that the country has had to pay for more during the past ten years for what the abolition of this Board has involved than its maintenance would have cost.'[24]

It was a surprise that the Indian political leaders, who were also the founding members of the board, did not take interest in the CABE affairs. Sir S.N. Banerjea and Sir Chimanlal Setalvad had constantly been absent and later both resigned their membership. M.M. Malaviya declined to continue to be a member on the ground of ill health. Resignations, however, did not necessarily reflect the Indian leader's indifference. Some of the leaders got accommodated in the provincial governments. The ministerial posts were too significant for these leaders than working as CABE members. The indifference also probably resulted from the general sidelining of the subject of education in spurt of national movement. CABE remained in suspension till 1935. Although a lot took place in Indian education during the late 1920s and early 1930s, the void of a central body to witness, direct and coordinate these developments was very much felt.

Revival of the CABE

According to the recommendations of the Retrenchment Committee, the Government of India amalgamated the Department of Education and Health with the Department of Revenue and Agriculture. The combined department was placed under charge of a single member of the Viceroy's Executive Council.[25] The strength of the new department had reduced considerably, though the workload intensified. The new department had to deal, besides education, with other matters such as archaeology and museum, municipalities, sanitation and public health, agriculture and veterinary science, cooperation, famine, land revenue, emigration, zoological and botanical surveys, forestry, drugs manufacture, and records.[26]

Education naturally received little attention, much to the disappointment of those concerned with it. As early as in 1925, the very first demand for CABE's revival was made in the Government of India.[27] In the First Conference of Educational Administrators from the provinces held in January 1927, the issue was further raised. The demand was reiterated in the next Conference of the Administrators in January 1928. Closely following this, the Auxiliary Committee of the Indian Statutory Commission (popularly known as the Hartog Committee) expressed regret that the board which promised usefulness was sacrificed in pursuance of a policy of retrenchment. The advice of such an institution on a subject in which fresh advances were being constantly made in India was vital if the country were to remain at par with other countries in educational progress. The committee underlined the need that each province be kept constantly in touch with the experiences and progress of other provinces. The committee strongly recommended the reconstitution of the CABE under chairmanship of the Educational

Commissioner with the Government of India. Despite such concerns, the revival of CABE could not be possible for many years due to several hurdles.

The major obstacle was created by the Department of Finance, Government of India. It outrightly rejected the proposal on the ground of financial constraints and called it 'extra burden'. The Department of Finance stated that, 'Owing to the present financial stringency, it is unlikely that it will be possible to set-up the proposed organization in the near future.'[28] These were the days of the world financial depression which the government aptly cited as the reason. The member-in-charge of the Department of Education, Health and Lands rejected the refusal of the Department of Finance. It suggested a way: 'If we would establish it in November 1931 we need only the expenditure for next four months and that won't be unbearable for the Department.'[29] Nevertheless, the Department of Finance rejected the proposal. The clash of opinion between these two departments eventually led to the intervention of Governor-General-in-Council. The Governor-General approved this proposal of reviving the CABE by arguing that 'establishment of advisory board would be sympathetically considered if the finance situation permits.'[30] Meanwhile, it was decided to ask the opinion of the provinces on the matter. The Department of Education, Health and Lands, therefore, addressed a letter to the various provinces of British India for their responses.[31] The letter quoted at length the suggestions made by the Statutory Committee for the revival of the CABE and also highlighted its expected structure and functions.

However, the responses from different provincial governments were lukewarm. The Government of the United Provinces and the Punjab strongly supported the scheme, whereas the three Presidency governments (Bombay, Calcutta and Madras) hesitated to support the move though later on the governments of Bengal and Bombay agreed to accept it in principle. The governments of Madras and Bihar and Orissa also accepted the move but raised certain concerns. The Government of Madras reacted in the following manner: 'Apart from the fact that the deliberations of the Board in the past have been of little benefit to this presidency this government considers that in view of financial stringency, the present is an inappropriate time for the consideration of the scheme.'[32] Meanwhile, the All India Educational Conference which was held at Delhi in December 1934 passed a resolution in support of the revival of the CABE.[33]

Amidst the pressure for revival, the Department of Education, Health and Lands proposed for initiative and the issue was raised in Governor-General's Council in 1935. The move took a favourable twist when Sir Girija Shanker Vajpayee, the Member-in-Charge of education in the Governor-General-in-Council personally took over the responsibility. His strong advocacy with some modification to the original proposal resulted in a positive response. The modification asked only for the revival of CABE and postponed the idea of revival of the Bureau of Education.[34] This modification reduced the cost of the proposal from about Rs. 43,000 to about Rs. 30,000 which prompted the Finance Department to accept it.[35] The Governor-General-in-Council approved the move on 18 January 1935. Thus CABE was reconstituted on 8 August 1935 by a notification of the Government of India, which stated the objectives of reconstituted CABE as: 'to advise on any educational question referred to it by the Government of India or by any local governments; to call for information and advice regarding educational developments of special interest or value to India; and to examine this information and circulate it with recommendations to the Government of India and to local governments.'[36] Though various forces worked behind the revival of the CABE, the main credit went to Sir G.S. Vajpayee, who was keen to bring about change in the education system. In the very first meeting of the CABE after revival, he as the Education Secretary and chairman of the meeting, sketched its importance, and defined the day as 'the proudest event of his tenure'.[37]

The vital importance to India of educational reconstruction, which is the subject first, has aroused such widespread interest, evoked such wealth of comment in recent years that no words of mine are needed to give it added significance. The main function of the Board is to test and shift and cohere the current educational thoughts of the day and to import to what may result from such creative effort the lasting impulse of a progressive policy.[38]

Synthesizing the National Upsurge (1935-1944)

The period from the rebirth of the CABE in 1935 to the adoption of the plan of post-War Educational Development in India in 1944 may be described as a period of preliminary planning on how to reconstruct the national education system. The concept of educational reconstruction was the basic idea in working out a system of national education based on coordination among the provinces and the centre. The enthusiasm required to take on this mammoth task was very much present during the period which is evident in the proceedings of the CABE. The board took up several issues related to reconstruction of Indian education by appointing a number of committees on different aspects of education.

The agenda of the very first meeting marked one such step in the desired direction. The issues relating to unemployment of the educated surfaced as a dominant subject. The board felt the need for a radical readjustment of the present system of education in schools not only to prepare pupils for professional and university courses, but also to enable them, at the completion of appropriate stages, to choose diverse occupations. It sought to separate vocational instructions from the literary stream.[39] It argued that the prevailing system put stress unreasonably on purely literary form of instruction which became worse when it was examination-centric. The curriculum at the school level or higher level did not take care of the need of rural students, which hampered the possibility of growth of rural India.[40] The board was of the opinion that there was a need for change in the educational system to make the society vibrant. With this in view the board came out with the following recommendations:[41]

- Primary education should aim at providing at least a minimum of general education and training and ensure permanent literacy.
- The lower secondary stage should contain a self-contained course of general education and constitute suitable foundation either for higher education or for specialized practical courses.
- In rural areas the course at this stage should be attempted to match rural requirements.
- The higher secondary stage of education should include institutions with varying lengths of courses; and
- each province should organize employment bureaus for the purpose of counselling.

The problem of unemployment loomed so large that it continued to figure in the next few meetings of the board. The board reiterated the need for a radical reform in the system of Indian education to address this challenge.[42] A. Abbott, former Chief Inspector of

Technical Schools, Board of Education, England and S.H. Wood, Director of Intelligence, Board of Education and Ministry of Health, England, were invited by the board to look into the grave situation of Indian unemployment and to suggest ways to vocationalize Indian education. They visited the United Provinces, Punjab and Delhi to get first-hand information on conditions of unemployment.[43] The committee thoroughly discussed the duration, scope and content of most of the courses that should be followed by Indian technical institutions in its widely acknowledged report.

In the meantime, the Wardha Educational Scheme also appeared in educational discourses. The scheme, a brain-child of Mahatma Gandhi, stressed on imparting education through some craft or productive work.[44] CABE wanted to amalgamate the elements of the Wardha scheme and the Abbot-Wood reports. It set up a sub-committee under the chairmanship of B.K. Kher, Premier and Education Minister, Bombay, for this purpose.[45] The Kher Committee analysed the features of the Wardha scheme and the Wood-Abbott committee and recommended vocationalization of Indian education alongside the scheme of basic education. It suggested the introduction of basic education in rural areas, the age range for compulsion to be six to fourteen years, the medium of instruction to be the vernacular of people, and English not to be introduced as an optional subject in basic schools. It also recommended some other measures like a common language for India, which should be Hindustani with both the Urdu and Hindi scripts. The Kher Committee further emphasized on the training of teachers and recruitment of more women teachers with a view to promoting girls' education and stood for raising the status of teachers.[46]

Some controversy arose over the recommendations of the Kher Committee. On the point that basic education should first be introduced in rural areas, some members were of the opinion that it would be easier to control and watch its implementation in municipalities rather than in the countryside. Ultimately the rural thrust was decided.[47] The age of entry for basic education was another point of contention, but again the recommendation of the sub-committee was accepted. The question of the medium of instruction was another subject that generated debate, but the board stood for the medium of vernacular language. The board thus generally approved all the recommendations of the Kher

Committee. CABE worked on these lines and constituted several committees for special attention on the areas of adult education, social service and public administration, school-building, health of school-going children, recruitment of education officers and technical education.[48]

Restructuring under the Sargent Scheme 1944

The plan of Post-war Educational Development in India was an attempt to prepare a comprehensive national policy on education and perhaps this is one of the most important contributions which the board made for solving the educational problems. It may also be said that the modern movement for educational planning in India began with the Sargent plan of 1944. Despite several limitations, including absence of projection of population growth, the impact of inflation and such other weaknesses, its recommendations were noteworthy in many ways. The board believed that any form of social or political community would never prosper unless the needs of the rising generation are taken care of including physical fitness, intelligence and integrity of character.[49] The committees of the board visited different parts of the country, to investigate the conditions and to familiarize itself with the problems. The outcome of the detailed study appeared in the board's comprehensive report prepared by John Sargent. The report, divided into 12 chapters, consisted of a wide range of topics including basic education, primary education, high school education, university education, adult education, the training of teachers and the education of the handicapped, employment bureau and administration, and so on.[50]

The Sargent Scheme met with severe criticism over different issues. The most important among them was related to its cost and the time frame suggested for the universalization of primary education which was declared as prohibitive for a country like India. The Sargent Scheme estimated that as many as 18 lakh teachers will be required at the rate of 1:30 teacher-pupil ratio for the basic primary school alone. Further, the scheme also came up with the idea that minimum qualification for the teacher should be matriculation and training of two-three years. In this way only 35 per cent of the matriculates could become teachers and that at this rate the full quota will be reached in about 40 years.[51]

K.G. Saiyidain, a contemporary educationist, termed this time frame too long to meet the urgency of Indian education. He explored the possibility of attaining this target within a shorter period of time. 'I am entirely in favour of exploring all possible ways of shortening this interval, in so far as this can be done without lowering the standard of teacher's qualification and training unduly and sacrificing the quality of education at the altar of quantity', he argued.[52] S. Nurullah also disapproved the very basic tenets of its recommendations.[53] On the question of teacher's qualification he proposed that for such a massive literacy programme it is not advisable to stick with fixed qualification for the teacher. 'I am not aware of any country in the world which has organised a scheme of mass education on the assumption that no one who does not have the main ideal qualification should be appointed as a teacher. We should be prepared to make the best of what is available and leave the ideal at every teacher in service being fully qualified and trained to be achieved, if necessary, by next generation', he suggested.[54] Saiyadain endorsed Nurullah's idea that matriculation need not at this stage be regarded as an absolutely necessary qualification for teachers. He provided the examples of England and USA to show how they developed their education without the availability of adequate number of trained teachers.[55]

Next criticism pertained to the issue of teacher-pupil ratio which was determined to be 1:30 by the commission. This was declared utopian by Saiyadain. 'Let us adopt the more modest average of 40 or 45 which is better than that in many western countries level today', he commented.[56] Many were not comfortable with the Sargent Scheme's suggestions based on the US or UK experiences. They preferred to follow the Russian example, as it had revolutionized its educational system within a short span of time, outside the Western model. Nurrullah commented, 'Russia has not attained the ideals of the Sargent Plan. Why should India, then be tied down to these ideals and not attend to what is immediately practicable?'[57]

The protagonists of the Sargent Scheme, however, were not convinced. In the opening speech, Sir Jogendra Singh, Chairman, CABE, in the meeting of 1945, stated that the time period of 40 years was based on the calculation of availability of trained teachers. The full scheme envisaged employment of 2.25 million teachers at the final stage and at present India had only 20,000 trained teachers.[58]

He was of opinion that no educational plan in any country would succeed unless steps were taken to secure efficient teachers. The recommendations of the Sargent Scheme with regard to training, recruitment and conditions of service of teachers, in his opinion, represented the minimum compatible with the success of a national system of education.[59] The debate demonstrates how keen India was to overcome India's educational and economic backwardness.

The CABE in Independent India

Post-Independence India placed more challenging tasks before the board. Prime Minister Pandit Jawaharlal Nehru identified the role of education in his inaugural speech in the January 1948 session of the CABE:

> In the plans for rebuilding the nation, education had an important place, because that was the basis for all other activities. India's misfortunes were not completely over but still they could not be allowed to put the question of education in the background. Practical steps must be taken immediately to implement their plans for improving the country's education.[60]

Similarly, the prime minister showed confidence in the ability of the board and asked it to advise the government on the implementation of various reports, which was not done. Maulana Abul Kalam Azad, Minister for Education, in the same meeting drew the plan for future action that was to be taken with the help of the board. He praised the work of the board and assured that the new government would implement its recommendation.

In the changed political situation, the board's jurisdiction widened. Several plans for educational reconstruction were brought out from time to time, but hardly any were operationalized.

Conclusion

The survey of the ideas and initiatives of the CABE during 1920-47 does not indicate any major breakthrough. Lack of will of the colonial state and dearth of adequate financing prevented the board from having any significant effect. However, the CABE attempted to define the future of Indian education, which might be described as an important contribution. The failure to achieve the set goals may be seen as a case of indifference of nationalists and the constantly changing imperialist designs of the colonial state. Political priorities of Indians in the phase of mass mobilization for the Indian National Movement was a factor behind the Indian inaction. Unfortunately education was not an important agenda in the struggle for independence. This was the reason why some big names of Indian nationalism did not join the CABE. The Indian nationalists hardly voiced a protest while the Board was disbanded in 1923.

The colonial government on its part did not provincialize the subject education in real sense under the provision of diarchy. The autonomy of the provinces was severely curtailed. The government tried to regulate the functioning of the board according to its own wishes. Various topics which were important for national education were ignored on the plea of their being politically delicate. The board had the advantage of continuity after its revival in 1935. Unlike earlier colonial policies, the policy on education was guided by a group of provincial education ministers, Indianized civil servants and colonial administrators. Although their political masters came and went, the board tried to remain committed to its primary objectives. It could not overcome all the problems but some advances were made. One thing, however, is certain – that the participants in the educational discourse under its aegis wanted change.

NOTES

1. Notes of H. Sharp, Constitution of a Central Advisory Education Board, Education, 'A', nos. 15-16, August 1920.
2. William Meston; *Indian Educational Policy: Its Principles and Problems*, Madras: The Christian Literature Society for India, 1936, pp. 36-7.
3. Notes of H. Sharp, 1920, op. cit.
4. The Calcutta University Commission was appointed in 1917 under the chairmanship of Michael Sadler, the Vice-Chancellor of Leeds University. The commission was asked to inquire into the condition and prospects of the University of Calcutta.
5. Notes of H. Sharp, 1920, op. cit.
6. Ibid.
7. Ibid.
8. Ibid.
9. Ibid.
10. Ibid.

11. Ibid.
12. Ibid.
13. Ibid.
14. Ibid.
15. Minutes of the First Meeting of the CABE, Education, 'B', nos. 88-92, September 1921.
16. Proceedings of the Department of Education, nos. 15-16, August 1921.
17. Ibid.
18. Minutes of the Second Meeting of the CABE, Education, 'B', nos. 173-80, March 1921.
19. Ibid.
20. Ibid.
21. Minutes of the Third Meeting of the CABE, Education, 'B', nos. 87-98, June 1922.
22. Ibid.
23. Sequence of seven meetings conducted by the Board are as follows:.

First Meeting	February 1921	Delhi
Second Meeting	June 1921	Simla
Third Meeting	October 1921	Lucknow
Fourth Meeting	January 1922	Delhi
Fifth Meeting	May 1922	Simla
Sixth Meeting	October 1922	Poona
Seventh Meeting	February 1923	Lahore

24. William Meston, op. cit., p. 196.
25. *Ninth Quinquennial Review*, vol. I, GOI, 1921, pp. 18-19.
26. Ibid.
27. Department of Education, Health and Lands, Branch Education, 'B', December 1927, nos. 210-38.
28. *Central Advisory Board of Education, Silver Jubilee Souvenir (1935-60)*, (*CABE Jubilee Volume*), Ministry of Education, Government of India, 1960, pp. 3-4.
29. Ibid.
30. Proposed Revival of the CABE, Ministry of Health, Education and Land, Education Branch, File No. 86-3/32-E, serial nos. 1-17, 1932.
31. Proceedings of the Ministry of Health, Education and Land, Education Branch, 'A', Letter No. 48 dated 8th, nos. 79-82, January 1931.
32. *CABE Jubilee Volume*, op. cit., pp. 5-8.
33. Ibid.
34. The Bureau of Education was established at the headquarters of the central government under the Educational Commissioner in 1915. Its main objectives were to collect and collate educational information in India and abroad and to arrange quinquennial review on the progress

of education in India. However, it was abolished in 1923 after the recommendation of the Retrenchment Committee.

35. Proceedings of the Department of Health, Education and Land, Education Branch, File No. 2-1/35-E, 1935.
36. Ibid.
37. Proceedings of the meetings of the CABE, First Meeting, December 1935, *CABE Jubilee Volume*, op. cit., pp. 14-18.
38. Ibid.
39. Ibid.
40. Ibid.
41. Ibid.
42. Ibid.
43. Proceedings of the CABE, 3rd Meeting, January 1937, *CABE Jubilee Volume*, op. cit., pp. 28-36.
44. Genesis of the Wardha Scheme goes back to 1937 when Gandhiji first conceived the idea to provide a practical solution to the Indian educational problem.
45. Proceedings of the Fourth Meeting of CABE, December 1938, *CABE Jubilee Volume*, op. cit., pp. 37-45.
46. 'Post-War Educational Development in India, Report by the CABE', Bureau of Education, Delhi, 1944, pp. 9-10 (henceforth, CABE Report 1944).
47. Proceedings of the meetings of the CABE, Fourth Meetings, December 1938, *CABE Jubilee Volume*, op. cit., pp. 37-45.
48. Reports of the committees appointed by the CABE in India (1938-43), Bureau of Education, Delhi, 1946, p. 2.
49. CABE Report 1944, op. cit, p. 2.
50. Ibid.
51. Ibid.
52. K.G. Saiyidain, 'Introduction', in T.K. Menon, ed., *A Symposium on Post-War Education in India*, Baroda: Padmaja Publication, 1945, pp. i-xiv.
53. Syed Nurullah, 'The Time Factor in the Sargent Scheme', ibid., pp. 77-83.
54. Ibid.
55. Ibid.
56. Ibid.
57. Ibid.
58. Proceedings of the 11th meeting of the CABE, *CABE Jubilee Volume*, op. cit., pp. 127-41.
59. Ibid.
60. Proceedings of the 14th meeting of the CABE, 1948, ibid., pp. 185-200.

PART III

WOMEN AND EDUCATION

CHAPTER 11

Colonial Anxieties

The State Embodiment of the Female Teacher-'Trainer', 1808-1931

TIM ALLENDER

Tracing the story of female education in colonial India means operating at many levels. Even at the most basic level divergent priorities emerge. The nebulous pursuit of counting enrolments, favoured by the British unable to breach local language barriers, and not cognizant either of indigenous pedagogic traditions, produced seemingly irreconcilable realities in the latter half of the nineteenth century. For example, provincial government reportage towards the end of the nineteenth century put female literacy at between 1 and 2 per cent of the female school-age population.[1] The Hunter Commission of 1882 put the figure of girls attending primary schools – the vast bulk of its nominal enrolments – at 23,850 with another 58,570 girls in private institutions.[2] Yet key players such as Mary Carpenter, and indeed the Viceroy's government itself, were willing to ignore school girl education almost entirely, content, instead, to focus on the Western-imposed 'interim' step of establishing female normal (teacher training) schools first in just 14 centres scattered thinly across the vast subcontinent.

This level of superficiality regarding female education warrants a closer look at Krishna Kumar's clever location of education within the political setting of the Raj. A new education was certainly introduced by the British to a very small minority of girls. But the lack of a broader engagement makes it difficult to argue even a reshaping of existing indigenous traditions before global imperatives intervened in the mid-twentieth century.[3] And this even though 'female education' created anxieties amongst the British more than any other topic concerning their education project in the seven decades between 1854 and 1924.

Official Intervention

Charles Wood's Education Despatch of 1854 identified for the first time an official space for 'female education' in state deliberations by bringing it into the bureaucratic ambit. He also imposed a formal Western moral imperative, claiming 'native' elites wanted a 'good' education for their daughters because by this means a far greater proportional impulse is imparted to the educational and moral tone of the people than by the education of men.[4]

This development did much to cut-off the earlier symbiotic Western and Eastern collaborations that were based on the rich Orientalist thinking of the previous two generations, as well as those female education traditions that were wholly indigenous in origin.[5] Chris Bayly has already written about the withering away, by the mid-nineteenth century, of sympathetic Orientalist connections in the transference of information between Eastern elites and relatively weak early British colonial governance that was mostly carried out by males.[6] State schooling from the revolt of 1857 onwards, with its attendant provincial curriculums, textbooks and administrative fiat, played a large part in shutting down this earlier felicitous intellectual interchange. However, for females the premature imposition of Western professionalism, inappropriately transmogrified for the subcontinent, resulted in a much starker form of disengagement and Wood's 1854 schooling mission for females, as a consequence, remained hopelessly embryonic until the early twentieth century.

Early Engagement

In elite circles in pre-British India there were strong precedents of female intellectual participation. In the mid-seventeenth century, Mughal ruler Jahangir flaunted the dominant position that his most favoured wife, Nur Jahan took in the public affairs of his vast empire,[7] and Emperor Aurangzeb's daughter Zinat al-Nisa was celebrated and credentialed for her *naskh* script calligraphy of the sacred words of the Koran.[8] On another level, the Rajputs of central India allowed women to directly participate in their government and British records in the early colonial period showed occasions when the Delhi Sultanate deferred to an elite cohort of highly educated women decision makers.[9]

Broader engagement was not possible in all parts of India. In more remote parts of Ranjit Singh's fiefdom, in the more *purdah*-bound north-west of the subcontinent, there were probably only a few indigenous girls schools that could be said to constitute any kind of formal indigenous institutionalized tradition. The rare indigenous accounts that survive at Anarkali's Tomb in Lahore show only 12 small, fee-charging schools in 1858 across its vast plains, mostly attended by low-caste girls, the daughters of barbers and shoemakers.[10] And in Madras any reliable records seem to have been blotted out by the early colonial missionary presence.

However, in two key provinces, Bombay and the North-Western Provinces (NWP), there was considerable engagement with the indigenous base largely as a result of earlier European-Orientalist collaborations. In Bombay, in the south-west, a strong tradition of native societies had served female education well. Begun in the 1820s, and set-up by collaborations between European and indigenous intellectuals, they had built dictionaries and pursued lively exchanges in many educational forums as a means to 'engraft' Western knowledge upon Eastern language. Foremost amongst these, as far as female education was concerned, was the Students' Literary and Scientific Association where 'native' patrons, along with wealthy Parsee benefactors, built upon this collaborative tradition to fund schools that educated a total of 1,200 girls in 1858.[11] Many more girls attended boys' schools in this period. And Parsee benefactors were also savvy enough to establish schools for girls taught by male teachers; teachers conveniently trained in some Western secular knowledge at fledgling government normal schools, but then rejected by the state for their refusal to give up their Zoroastrian beliefs. These female schools had a three-stage curriculum where Sanskrit was taught alongside algebra and village accounts, with their patrons confident enough to seek official recognition by inviting government inspection.[12]

In the NWP the sympathetic response which clever European intervention had elicited amongst locals was even more impressive. Here the long-standing Director of Public Instruction (DPI) Henry Reid – serving under the reforming Lieutenant-Governor James Thomason – had drawn upon the ideas of one of the leading Orientalists of the age, Lancelot Wilkinson. This was to build a sophisticated system of *halkabandi* (village circle) schools designed to engage poor boys with basic education in their own language, in preference to government funds being siphoned off by wealthier subscribers to build large urban schools and colleges.[13] Once established, Reid also used these village schools to 'quietly' educate girls: the two-step approach to prevent 'premature attention and interference', as he put it, by the state. As in Bombay, this encouraged subscriptions by wealthy elites as well as a rare activism in the NWP by influential *pandits* (Hindu teachers), giving rise to some 288 girls schools with 4,927 students, mostly from middle-class backgrounds.[14] Many of these girls also subsequently taught their sisters, mothers and daughters in the household.

Reid, and his counterpart Edward Howard in Bombay, knew that their work of educating females required delicate handling. In the Punjab in the early 1860s, a politically inspired and sudden experiment to educate girls, mostly to stamp out female infanticide, had nearly sent the provincial education department bankrupt.[15] But both Reid's and Howard's patient work had already clearly demonstrated what was possible without strong intervention from the centre.

Teaching 'Character' and 'Respectability'

However, what ultimately proved to be a more powerful tradition for the state was that which had already emerged in Bengal. Here a strong pretext had emerged for viewing female indigenous education through the prism of Victorian moral norms of family, 'character' and respectability, and also using Western educational instructional models. In the 1820s the Calcutta School Society and the British Foreign School Society began educating 'heathen' daughters from elite indigenous families and those belonging to poorer families.[16] The first calls were also heard for more female teachers so as to produce 'respectable native ladies' as moral exemplars of the Raj. Miss Cooke, 'eminently qualified', was recruited from London to lead these endeavours and in contrast to Andrew Bell's Monitorial School in Madras a generation earlier, the Lancaster model was introduced for the girls of Bengal with 25 young monitors, abandoned wives and widows, at its core.[17] Developments in Bengal encouraged the building of stereotypes in London, communicated by the missionary lobby and later articulated publicly by the Secretary of State, Lord Ellensborough in 1858. Most enduring amongst these was that female education was necessarily severely restricted because of a 'strong prejudice against female schools' by the 'native' communities of the subcontinent.[18]

In the early 1860s, both Reid and Howard, sensing that their rationale for engaging with the indigenous female base was now being critically undermined, were prepared to stridently argue their respective cases based on far greater experience of what was to be found on the spot. Howard saw Ellenborough's assertion as traceable to Europeans and Hindus, 'degenerate from their Aryan ancestors', rather than the broader indigenous population of his province. His years of delicate negotiation and engagement in Bombay had taught him that matters concerning 'female honour' did not prevent girls from going to school, or being taught by older males. For him it was 'usual' to see Muslim girls attending indigenous schools, and Parsee patrons dissecting secular knowledge for their daughters from curriculums embedded in other belief systems and philologies.[19]

Reid, in the NWP, seeing most of the educational institutions in his province destroyed by the revolt, also witnessed most girls' schools quickly re-establish. He had an unusually active Indian Civil Service (ICS) made up of ex-Army men, some of whom had developed a strong interest in female schooling and were conscious of international developments concerning the education of girls from poor families.[20] He viewed the female indigenous base as remarkably resilient, particularly when Jat elders at Agra College, such as Kalyan Singh, or the widowed daughters of Brahmins at Aligarh, used their traditional influence to recruit indigenous female teachers, often the daughters of wealthy zamindars, who were able to teach Urdu, some Sanskrit as well as basic literacy and numeracy.[21] For Reid, Howard and others, these were the results of patient intellectual interactions between worthy educationists on both sides of the colonial divide in the previous two generations. However, their protests were scarcely heard when it became clear that London's approach had been fundamentally changed by the key intervention of the Unitarian, Mary Carpenter, building on the more conscious and restricted colonial education mentality emanating out of Bengal.

New Colonial Mentalities and the Carpenter Shibboleth

Mary Carpenter's intervention was highly significant. It sponsored energetic debates on female education, particularly within the ranks of the ICS, if not so much within the education service itself, in the late 1860s. This level of individual influence had not been seen before, even in the mid-1850s. What made it possible was that Carpenter had direct access to the Secretary of State for India, Sir Stafford Northcote, amongst others, at Westminster, and because her ideas chimed, at least superficially, with the recently determined Raj strategy.[22]

Carpenter arrived in India in 1866, the first of four visits, determined to impose Western female teacher-training on India – now a key feature of new government thinking. 'Training' for her could only be through the aegis of 'European or other Christian teachers' from England even though she saw its final object being to provide teachers for indigenous schools.[23] Ramusack's 'maternal imperialist' tag could be easily applied but her approach was more complex than just this.[24] Carpenter's views were imbued with the subtlety of a very sophisticated Orientalist thinking begun with her father's close friendship with Rammohun Roy, who contributed the *Unitarian Repository*, and her own friendship with the next generation of Indian educational luminaries, most notably Keshub Chunder Sen and Satyendranath Tagore.[25]

Another imperative had emerged by this time that was soon linked to female education, but now was responsible for it being organized much more deliberately along racial lines. This was the issue of Eurasians. Concern about Eurasians was one of the few issues that had long compelled the state to consider girls as well as boys in its policy declarations simply because anxieties about the miscegenation of European blood (often the result of alliances between Indian women and long-departed European soldiers) was an issue that had forced it to embrace both genders. By the late 1850s anxieties arose in the Raj that, uncontrolled, this child population threatened to undermine presumptions of the 'superiority' of the Europeans, which it projected to powerful indigenous elites, especially if these children later became vagrants. And in 1860 the Viceroy, Lord Canning, issued a key despatch responding to these growing fears about '. . . a class dangerous to the state'.[26] The central government in Calcutta had kept a careful tally of its Eurasian population and it did its best to offer stipends for the schooling of these girls and boys. But by the late 1850s, with the arrival of a second generation and exploding numbers, this was no longer possible. Finding them jobs was the new focus and for Canning the future for Eurasian girls was to be as teachers of 'good character and training', badly needed '. . . [to] bring their talents to so uncertain and . . . so discouraging a field of labour.'[27]

With these imperatives in place, Carpenter's lobbying unleashed a conservative narrative in India that was to be perpetuated by the state for the rest of the century. And more than this her theoretics were to be appropriated to justify an even more restricted female rationale that melded the state's official ethic of 'moral' female education and its ongoing worries about the Eurasian population.

Imposing Western Professionalism

It is beyond the scope of this paper to fully explore the ethic of Western female professionalism and its development in the West. There were distinctive brands carried forward by women graduates of the relatively new Girton and Newnham colleges at Cambridge and by other places of professional learning such as the Maria Grey College in London and like institutions in Europe. One approach was to educate women professionals to imitate that of the men whilst others favoured a distinctly feminized profession for women. More immediate to the emergence of feminized professional ethics was the schooling experience in England, although the creation of formal education positions for women sometimes lagged behind what was happening in India. Women from working class and lower-middle-class families working in Pupil-Teacher Centres were able to demonstrate their ability for academic work, long hours and extra-curricular activities.[28] But it was the middle-class women who gave female teacher professionalism a greater form through their long struggles in England to gain adequate representation on the governing boards for girls' high schools as well as access to the School Inspectorate – with the first Chief Woman Inspector, Maude Lawrence (daughter of retired Viceroy John Lawrence as it happens) yet to be appointed in 1905.[29] As Alison Oram has argued, women developed a gendered language of professionalism, appropriating the male ethic of liberalism, individualism and merit to include equal rights.[30] Copelman elaborates on this new ethic, including the right to a public role even though class sensibilities remained in place as it did for most male professions of the period.[31] These battles, begun much earlier than this in England and fought by a more connected and communicating group of women there, served to solidify a female professional rationale, which was then imported to India.

Although Carpenter admitted that '. . . female education is now generally accepted by the enlightened part of the Native community as very desirable', the state now permitted the importation of her Western template. This template required that the Training Mistress in each school could only be an 'English certified teacher' who was also a European or 'other Christian' teacher and where there were to be separate quarters for Christian and non-Christian boarders. This last provision was based on Carpenter's genuine cultural sensitivities given the fear of many indigenous families that their daughters would be converted. Carpenter also made provision for the transporation of day-pupils to school and for the servants of the daughters of wealthy parents. But her calculations contained two key flaws. She envisaged that the European teacher ethic would eventually filter down and cross race and class divides even though a similar theory of 'filtration' for boy schooling had been abandoned by the state a generation earlier.[32] She also encouraged the thorough learning of local language by her agents in the field but the ethic and skills associated with the English professional teacher training was her only model.

Partly as a result of the influence of Indian intellectuals she had met in England and the Brahmo Samaj message they conveyed, Carpenter was genuinely interested in the next step of dissemination of her brand of education to the broader population.[33] But she underestimated the more immediate barriers between Eurasians and Indians. There was also the ongoing problem of the state refusing to spend money on subsequent female education, which left her schools unintegrated educational islands, easily discredited in the eyes of local intellectuals because they diverted most available money for the expensive salaries needed for her 'trained' European superintendents. This money might have otherwise been made available for employing many more indigenous teachers. (At the time the salary of one European headmistress approximated to the salary of 300 indigenous female teachers). Reid, Howard and other experienced educators, who understood much better the complexities of the Indo-Western intellectual landscape, might well have employed these indigenous teachers to greater purpose. A more radical approach (already favoured by the Orientalist Radhakant Deb in 1851 for colonial education generally) was that state-funded indigenous teachers could have been used in the vast sea of indigenous schools if the state had chosen to circumvent its own obstructionist departmental and ICS personnel.[34]

Colonial 'Malignancies': 1872-1877

Instead, a more damaging and racially exclusive narrative emerged. Most of the teacher-training schools founded in Carpenter's name did not last very long, though here were exceptions. In Madras, a very dynamic import, Elizabeth Brander (nee Bain) spent almost her entire career specializing in teaching the kindergarten pedagogy of Froebel's Gifts. At Hyderabad and Poona, Carpenter's schools continued to operate. But in key centres such as Calcutta and Bombay, Carpenter, on the last of her four visits, admitted 'most had been given up'.[35]

There was also the problem of location of several such which were away from concentrated European centres, or adjacent to military cantonments that used local women for prostitution purposes.[36] Neither location was likely to project the rigid moral custodian ethic that was supposed to come with good female teacher 'training'. In Nagpur, one such normal school was established and personally visited by Carpenter in 1869, resulting in the introduction of a differentiated 'accomplishments' curriculum of needlework and music, although the determination of these women to learn Urdu (the language of elite Indian men) created some early disquiet. The school had been made possible by the influence of Mahadeo Rao, the local *tahsildar* (revenue officer) who had promoted female education in the district.[37] And its enrolment was mostly of young Hindu widows whose progress as students had received favourable government inspection.

However, the uncertain intersection of East and West soon brought problems that would reverberate throughout India. In 1872 its competent headmistress, Mrs Young, suddenly died after a visit from the infectious diseases police investigating one girl student who had been diagnosed with syphilis and some unofficial correspondence to the Lieutenant-Governor suspecting other students of being equally 'vicious' with the disease. A frenzy of official outrage then erupted to discredit the school. Accusations were also made that even the school's needlework classes were strongly associated by the indigenous community with local courtesans, who likewise sewed their clothes.[38] The unwanted symbolism that Nagpur's prurience represented to the state, prompted it to quickly close the school and to abandon its young women to their fate – no longer accepted by the European but equally rejected by their own community because of their incurable disease.

More significantly, the Nagpur scandal reflected a broader malaise in the 1870s. For indigenous elites, whose consciousness was deepening because of a rising colonial print culture and some elevation in literacy, the early tentative connections of female education with the colonial state were breaking down. The diffuse and the informal systems of knowledge amongst women had traditionally reflected the weakness of its custodians and the intense social competition between them. But the Raj assumed, what Foucault later stereotyped, that the influence of thought in education circles reflected the power of its authors.[39] Such authors in India were almost exclusively male. The different colonial embodiment of these unfortunate Indian women of Nagpur Normal School, and other similar government schools meant that they could have no such voice. And for the subaltern the rejection of these females just as powerfully ended any pretence of a holistic British system that was ready to elevate women of whatever caste or race according to acquired classroom knowledge.

As a result of the Nagpur scandal, the newer female teacher-training schools recently set-up by government, in addition to those Carpenter had sponsored, were suddenly closed down in 1875 and their work handed over to the missions. A stronger meta-narrative now emerged linking into the earlier state fears regarding the Eurasian population but responsive also to its changing demographics. Middle-class Eurasian parents who had done well under Raj commerce and who wished their daughters to follow English habits now infiltrated many of the remaining normal schools, even in Madras, causing considerable dislocation because many existing Indian parents refused to allow their daughters to be taught alongside them. As well, the mission normal schools, like Mrs Winter's Society for the Propagation of the Gospel (SPG) School at Delhi, had been successful in turning out Indian Christian graduates; a frightening development for most indigenous parents.

Ironically, many of these educated converts were to later move into impoverished indigenous communities shedding in the process the proprieties of Western form, 'discipline', 'tidiness' and 'hygiene' associated so strongly by the state with its model female teacher.[40] And the modest female normal schools set up by the Church Missionary Society (CMS) were already particularly suspect. There were frequent frustrations heard amongst European educators that schooling for girls all too often ended in child marriage. But this mission was responsible for recruiting girls singly in remote communities via its network of catechists, usually aged between 10 and 12 years. It then 'educated' them as teachers for less than a year before recruiting them to marry other converts within the broader mission ambit at the age of just 13 or 14 years.[41]

Organizing Eurasians: 1880-1904

State insecurities about female education strategy were also driven by definitional problems. The term 'Eurasian' itself – now central to the strategy – was unstable and dependent on changing government regulations in the nineteenth century. For females it was the most worked and re-worked racial categorization of the period largely because relevant state exigencies were so changeable. In the early days of the Raj, Eurasian could mean, 'Anglo-Indian' – Europeans who had lived in the Raj for 30 years or more. As a phrase that guaranteed one's ethnic purity, it was then adopted by people of part-Indian descent as proof of their European ancestry until the 1850s when it denoted mixed-race people who followed a European lifestyle. Schools also had their own hidden racially-based entrance rules, whilst school photographs of elite finishing schools demonstrate that some of these also chose to recruit students from wealthy Indian families using the term 'Eurasian' to credential them for social mobility via advantageous marriages or professional employment. As such, enrolment in the Western classroom, by the wealthy of partly Indian descent, had a part to play in this racial transference.

However, race, no matter how defined, remained a critical factor.

The colour and class bars of female institutions were not openly publicized but they were consciously observed and controlled by women themselves. There were no applied formulas for the category of Anglo-Indian or Eurasian, even by the early twentieth century, although the terms became largely interchangeable. Exclusionary categorizations could be determined by place of birth or inability to conceal skin colour, as well as the give-away railway employment of parents. Irene Edwards – herself of Scottish, Portuguese and Hindu descent – described something of how race and class was organized within a heavily stratified, male-dominated British social ambit:

> I knew a girl in Peshawar – an Anglo-Indian. She was white with blue eyes, but because her parents lived in Peshawar she was known to be Anglo-Indian. She knew I used to go to the club because I used to talk about parties there, the tennis, the dances and she wanted to join. . . . I asked a lady doctor who had influence, I asked her to try and get Celia in . . . she told me I don't think we'll succeed because everybody round here knows Celia is an Anglo-Indian. I told this lady doctor: 'well so am I' she said yes, but people don't know it here.

And there were the exclusionary spaces that Indians and Eurasians organized themselves:

> We were not bitter about this – the Anglo-Indians. We accepted it because this bar, not only the colour bar, but the class bar, cut right across India. We as Anglo-Indians did not allow Indians into our Institutes. We were allowed as members of the corporals clubs . . . even some sergeants messes allowed Anglo-Indians – others did not – we knew the club for officers was absolutely out of the question, not only for Anglo-Indians, but for all white people who were not officers. . . . The higher you went the greater the prejudice against Anglo-Indians. . . . The Indians, on the other hand, looked down on the Anglo-Indians because they were neither one thing nor the other . . . they used to call us 'kutcha-butcha', that is half baked bread or 'teen pao' (three quarters), it depended on the shade of your colour.[42]

In some ways these personal accounts distract from the broader story of the development of colonial female education on the subcontinent. But they point to the very strong racial divide so rarely acknowledged by the state in its official reports and how significant it then was when the Bengal government decided to introduce a new European Code in 1884 that heavily favoured female training schools only for Eurasians.[43]

Teaching Eurasian Women

In 1876, in the last year of her life, Carpenter reluctantly accepted that it would be Eurasians who would carry her banner for the foreseeable future. Hindu women were not part of the approach because 'none appear to be available, except widows, as all Hindu girls are married very young . . . [and] the mental condition of adult widows . . . render it impossible that in a few years' tuition should fit them to be teachers.'[44]

A limited tradition of teaching Eurasians had already been established in the 1850s. Lawrence Military Asylums, set-up mostly for Eurasian 'orphans' as early as 1849, had become harbingers for some modern European teaching practices that absent soldier fathers liberally funded. Using this model, and that offered by a Martiniére school at Calcutta,[45] private-venture schools began to emerge taking advantage of the favourable grant-in-aid provisions for this class of schools and with them an influx of European women and American teacher-trainers. Elite government schools for girls were transformed in the lush and comfortable hill stations of Kurseong, Darjeeling and Simla, whilst the Catholic Loreto order cleverly used its schools in these last two centres to subsidize its mission of educating poorer Eurasian girls – mostly of darker Portuguese skin – in the hot and dusty suburbs of Calcutta and Asansol in Bengal.[46]

It is beyond the scope of this paper to examine the machinations of Eurasian teacher training up to 1920. But it is clear that state preoccupation with this cohort, Carpenter's influence that prematurely imported Western professional ethics, as well as state reluctance to spend any real money on schooling of Indian girls had eschewed any real chance of the colonial state building more spontaneous and lasting connections with the indigenous community that concentrated on lower order schooling first.

For the broader Indian schoolgirl population, government custodianship claims in the 1870s continued to rely on inflated and optimistic primary school enrolments. This was even though its decentralization policies after 1871 made these schools reliant on municipal and district councils whose preference was for spending local taxes on roads and sanitation rather than neglected European-sponsored schools. A more revealing product of the Raj's funding neglect was that very few Indian school girls made it to higher levels of schooling and it was enrolment in training colleges that mostly outnumbered even these. For example, in Bengal the number of Indian female scholars in high schools outnumbered those in female normal (teacher training) schools, 612 to 36, but in all other provinces the ratio was reversed: Madras 38 female high school scholars to 119 female normal school scholars; Bombay 25 to 66; NWP nil to 85; Punjab nil to 208; and Central Provinces nil to 20.[47]

Remnant Female Professionalism

Professional contact between European and Eurasian educators remained sporadic throughout the nineteenth and early twentieth centuries, inhibited by their thin dispersal across the vast sub-continent. As early as the 1860s, the CMS, organized in England the Indian Female Normal School and Instructional Society, with patrons based in Europe. Its work in India saw little professional cooperation because its agents were chiefly concerned with conversion rather than academic matters.[48] Later in the century, conferences of the so-called Domiciled (European and Eurasian) Community often excluded women educators despite girls making up over half of the children in these schools.[49] There were also sporadic provincial conferences for women educators and an all-India conference in 1916: the impetus for this last conference came from women in England pressuring the Secretary of State, Austen Chamberlain.

Unlike the impressive deliberations of the Lady Dufferin Fund for nursing, these conferences struggled to change the official female education policy or extract the much needed funding. The organization with most official backing in India was the National Association in Aid of Social Progress and Female Education in India. Its sponsors were the governors of the major provinces and chief ministers of the princely states. But reflecting the very low priority that the state gave to girl schooling, this association soon turned its attention to the more productive business of coordinating nursing training and deployment for midwifery as well as vaccination campaigns.[50] For Eurasian education the sectarian divide between Catholic Loreto communities and Protestant missions, and the market competition for students among competing institutions, lessened even further possibilities for professional collaboration.

And, remarkably, in 1912 the longstanding inspectress for Bengal, Lilian Brock, obtained the Secretary of State's permission to travel to Norway and Denmark to study kindergarten pedagogy for four months. But she did this without any reference to the world-class work of Elizabeth Brander in neighbouring Madras.

What was happening in England was more coordinated at the committee level. Antoinette Burton has argued that feminist writers living in England at this time created images of 'needy' Indian women merely to encourage British women to think of themselves as committed to a 'racial motherhood' and as part of an imperial civilizing mission.[51] This *modus operandi* drove much more effective organization at the metropolis. The Missionary Settlement for University Women was an essentially missionary organization funded by women graduates from an extensive network of alumni of English and Scottish universities, living in England and Scotland. However, two sisters, Ellen and Marian Storres, were the first representatives of this organization to travel to India. Despite many polite afternoon teas and visits to schools, including Bethune College in Calcutta, they were skilfully discouraged by established women teachers from founding any educational enterprise of their own and had to be eventually content with building a boarding house in Bombay instead.[52] In 1913 a powerful memorial signed by Beatrice Webb, the Aga Khan, Masters of three Oxford colleges, the vice-chancellor of Manchester University, Duleep Singh's (the exiled son of Ranjit Singh) daughter and senior retired members of the ICS was sent to the Secretary of State. It criticized state policy that had seen most funding for female schooling go to Eurasian children at the expense of Indians, unlike the Americans in the Philippines and the Japanese in Korea.[53] Limited possibilities also opened up for Eurasian girls of relatively wealthy families to complete their education in England at places like Maria Gray College in London.

There were European women who taught Indian girls in this period above primary school level but they were mostly disconnected from the state. Their work was more defined by the separate but imponderable dynamics of India's many regions: Travancore in the south with its prosperous Izhava middle class connecting with Western commerce but still strongly referenced by the arcane rule of its Maharajah; the heavy missionary education bearing of Madras counterpoised by the *vidyalayas* (indigenous girls' schools) in the coastal Andhra region; the vast central plateau of the Deccan and its major princely states; the fertile plains of the Punjab in the north awkwardly embracing the old Delhi Sultanate and a tribal west; the Calcutta periphery, negotiating a separate east and west Bengal and its strong migration waves; the rising Hindu nationalist ideologues of Maharashtra; and the exotic of Mandalay in British Burma. Though still strongly Western education oriented, two such women in the latter colonial period were Eleanor McDougall and Louise Ouwerkerk.

The senior European staff of the Women's College in Madras, led from 1914 for 23 years by Eleanor McDougall (a graduate from Edinburgh University in English Literature and History), developed a college degree course and then a one-year teachers' diploma at the attached St Christopher's Teacher Training College, which McDougall established in 1923. This knowledge confluence, melded with an ethic of service to surrounding poverty-bound villages, was to prepare teachers to serve the growing number of high schools for girls in southern India.[54]

McDougall's own teaching subjects were unusually broad, including Greek and Roman history, Western philosophy and Scripture. And her strategy was to employ younger European teachers, more flexible to adapt to India, even if they had not yet attained the academic qualifications of other applicants. One junior teacher saw her as 'homely' in appearance despite her academic reputation, her 'gait halting' and a blend of sadness with humour.[55] But she was confident enough to allow her diverse common room to speak freely on academic matters. Margaret Hunt, a professor in the college at aged 24, because of her European MA, recalled in the early 1930s: 'I cannot remember talking politics at our senior table but [I] had more conversations with my younger Indian colleagues and have shared their devotion to Gandhi and their concern about his imprisonment.'[56]

Louise Ouwerkerk (holding a degree in economics from Cambridge University) was a rarity of the age, teaching female students at the Women's College at Trivandrum, in Travancore, from 1929 to 1939. She was distracted by niggling concerns from the Dewan (chief revenue officer) – a reforming Hindu – about corrosive Western intellectualism that threatened the strong Eastern traditions of the elite girls in the college. Ouwerkerk viewed India as '. . . simply not fit for home rule' but she also saw

Western universities in India as 'nurseries of Western Imperialism and exploitation'. A supporter of Ramsay MacDonald, and teaching his brand of internationalism, her approach was to teach political science by finding ways of 'applying Western methods' in culturally sensitive terms to her college girls.[57]

Negotiating a New India

This paper has not dealt with creative enterprises such as the Bethune School in Bengal, or other impressive institutions that more latterly catered for indigenous female learning such as the SNDT Women's University in Bombay, or what was happening in Kerala in the south where education always charted a more advanced course. But state preoccupations with a mostly Eurasian cohort had an important part to play in the rejection of its emerging Western professional ethic, partly because this limited cohort did not have carriage of the rising national movement's configuration of the role of women for an independent India. The Eurasian pre-occupation had also appropriated the colonial female education project at the expense of Indian girls.

However, more substantially, a new female ethic emerged, particularly within the Hindu polity, that was predicated on strong cultural traditions and which sought to negotiate a nexus between responsible 'mother' in the household and in public action/social service as a more efficient means of combating illiteracy, child marriage, imperialism and grinding economic deprivation.[58] The controversy that erupted over the publication of Katherine Mayo's *Mother India* in 1927, and ably portrayed in Mrinalini Sinha's most recent book, demonstrated just how potent the new symbolism was by this time.[59]

Indian women activists were developing their own sense of *bhaginivarg* (sisterhood); cutting across caste and religion to improve their lives, even enlisting the Raj to enact laws to protect them against the medieval interventions of child marriage, *sati* and widowhood: customs that violated Vedic purity.[60] However, key women's organizations such as the Seva Sadan (founded in Bombay in 1908 with the aim of improving women's welfare by developing social service networks) banned their members from participating in nationalist activities in public, which it saw as a male domain.

There were some Western cross-overs in this latter period. For example, provincially based women's education groupings, such as the Vanita Samaj in central India, chose a platform that was to encourage female professional education and the earning of degrees before marriage.[61] And women belonging to the Parsee community of Maharashra and elite Bengali women used their college education to further social reform.[62] However, the European embodiment of a professional female teacher had been rendered in terms that were too simplistic and rigid. In contrast, Indian feminism was played out on a broader canvas of complex European, Eurasian and indigenous female aspirations that intersected in unanticipated ways, and also against a backdrop of rising communal and nationalist consciousness, where the treatment of women was always a common denominator in renovating Hinduism.

After the First World War, the influential All India Women's Conference (AIWC) carried this further by stressing the importance of physical and moral education: though the latter was now expressed in Indo-specific terms. At its most radical the national movement threatened to push women further back into socio-religious and household spaces separate from the pan-national political agendas of their fathers, husbands and brothers. This was when Brahmin and Hindu revivalism threatened to produce strong communal and class refuges, inaccessible to broad sections of the population, both male and female, whilst Gandhi's Wardha scheme moved the agenda to kitchen and village-based crafts as a financial means of extending education to all.

For the Hindu polity, the unwillingness of the men to accept an equal role for women forced Hindu feminists, who for the most part did not reject Hinduism, to pursue a separate social agenda that restricted their capacity to lobby for broader political reform concerning women's rights.[63] And indigenous women converts, many of whom had spent a lifetime working to improve the lot of their underprivileged and disempowered counterparts, were rejected by the broader women's reform movement in the early twentieth century because their liberal social reform agendas were sullied by foreign ideas and beliefs that had little place in the radical *Swadeshi* movement. Furthermore, leading activists with an eye on developments in Britain, including Cornelia Sorabji who had tried to open up the legal profession to women, lost their earlier influence when they later opposed the nationalist campaign of boycotts.[64] Whilst the schooling of Indian girls, so long neglected under the Raj and still based on the household, became a public issue for social reformers with the slogan 'educating a girl means educating a family'.[65]

In 1917 just over 1.2 million Indian girls – 58 per cent Hindu and only 24 per cent Muslim – were listed as being enrolled in mostly elementary schools of some description, with government recording increases of between 20 and 58 per cent compared to five years earlier (except for Bengal that recorded a decline of 5.5 per cent). However, for high schools, out of a total of 25,948 girls (including nearly 12 per cent attending boys' high schools at this time) over 59 per cent were still either European, Eurasian or Christian converts.[66]

After the Indianization of the Education Service in 1919, girls' schools and colleges underwent unprecedented expansion between 1921 and 1931 with female education institutions increasing from 23,500 to 33,900 and their enrolment going up from 1.4 million to 3.1 million; although nearly all of this increase was due to private sources funding mostly urban schools.[67] What was also noticeable was that in the decade after the First World War there was a significant blurring of racial boundaries regarding enrolments in European/Eurasian elementary schools compared to schools for Indians, partly because of government policies of school amalgamation and the removal of unpublicized racial regulations. For example, whilst enrolments of Europeans/Eurasians in so-called European schools increased by only 5.1 per cent between 1921 and 1926, the number of Indians enrolled in European schools increased by 111.9 per cent and the number of Europeans in Indian schools increased by 62.9 per cent in the same period.[68] These changes at last saw greater Indian schoolgirl participation, and without the earlier direct colonial state interventions that had mostly restricted funding to elite forms of education and professional teacher training.

With the national movement developing a different role for its women, Western stereotypical thinking remained dominant in colonial top-down policy making. The senior men who ran education in India in the late colonial phase still clung to their nineteenth-century preconceptions. In 1915 William Hornell, brought back recently from England to become Director of Public

Instruction of Bengal, conceded that in all 'progressive countries' it was now accepted that the average girl was 'probably' of equal 'intellectual capacity' compared to the average boy. But his caveat for a different curriculum was now based on physiology. '. . . the physical changes which take place before womanhood is attained are in some cases such a tax on a girl's vitality that it is frequently more stupid cruelty to force a girl to endure the same physical and mental strain to which a healthy boy can be safely exposed'.[69]

And as late as 1929, Sir Phillip Hartog (author of the last major report on education in British India before the Round Table Conference of 1931), did not view female teacher training as designed to equip female teachers to be able to facilitate higher academic thinking and theorizing in their students. Rather, it was to enhance their teaching of 'practical subjects':

> The temptation for teachers, unless they are specifically trained, is to make even practical subjects theoretical and to teach from the textbook rather than from actual experiment and demonstration. Especially in domestic science, perhaps the most important subject of all to Indian girls, is the need for some centre of training teachers in the most modern and effective methods.[70]

Ultimately it was to be Jawaharlal Nehru, in the 1950s, who brought the focus back to the issue of women's education based on full social equality with men and with new high school and tertiary opportunities for them. The state – this time fully independent from Britain – took on direct responsibility for these higher education institutions, but in a way that offered far greater access to all women and with a professional ethic much more closely linked to the needs of the new nation. Global influences and the economic modernization imperatives of India as a non-aligned state were now the primary agents of change.

NOTES

1. These figures were assembled by each province and reported in successive education quinquennials published by the Calcutta government between 1892 and 1912.
2. W.W. Hunter, *Report of the Indian Education Commission*, Calcutta: Superintendent of Government Press, 1883, p. 531.
3. Krishna Kumar, *Political Agenda of Education: A Study of Colonialist and Nationalist Ideas,* New Delhi: Sage, 1991.

4. Ibid., p. 388.
5. Orientalists were a group of intellectuals, working mostly in the 1820s and 1830s, from Europe and India who were interested in establishing a stronger confluence of knowledge between East and West, usually assuming the superiority of neither. These endeavours were designed to deepen human knowledge. Local and ancient language and the 'engraftment' of knowledge onto these from other cultural domains was of their principal interest.
6. C.A. Bayly, *Empire and Information: Intelligence Gathering and Social Communication in India, 1780-1870,* New Delhi: Oxford University Press, 1997.
7. A. Eraly, *The Mughal Throne*, London: Widenfeld and Nicolson, 2003, pp. 277-8.
8. This 1670 copy of the Koran is now part of the Nasser D. Khalili Private Collection, London.
9. Arthur Howell, *Education in British India Prior to 1854 and in 1871*, Calcutta: Government Printing, 1871, Section XI.
10. 'Abstract Statement of Female Schools Established in the Punjab in the Year 1857-8', in *Education*, 31 July 1858, nos. 131-58, Lahore: Punjab Secretariat Library, Anarkali's Tomb.
11. E.I. Howard, *Report of the Director of Public Instruction, Bombay, 1857-8*, Orient India Office Collection (OIOC), V/24/861, pp. 11-16.
12. T.B. Courtis (Acting Education Inspector, Northern Division) Appendix B in E.I. Howard, *Report of the Director of Public Instruction, 1862-1863*, OIOC V/24/864.
13. For greater detail on this scheme for boys see T. Allender, *Ruling Through Education: The Politics of Schooling in the Colonial Punjab,* New Delhi: New Dawn Press, 2006, ch. 1.
14. H.S. Reid, *Report of the Director of Public Instruction, North Western Provinces, 1858/59,* OIOC V/24/908, pp. 55-57 and H.S. Reid, *Report of the Director of Public Instruction, North Western Provinces, 1859/60*, OIOC V/24/908, pp. 46-50.
15. T. Allender, 'Surrendering a Colonial Domain: Educating North India, 1854-1890', in *History of Education* (United Kingdom) 35: 5, 2006, pp. 45-63.
16. Peary Chand Mitra, 'A Biographical Sketch of David Hare', n.d. cited in J.A. Richey, *Selections from the Education Records*, part II, 1840-59, Calcutta: Government Printing, 1922, pp. 35-7.
17. 'Central School for the Education of Native Females', founded by the Society of Ladies, 25 March 1824', in Richey, *Selections from the Education Records*, p. 38.
18. President of the Board of Control (Lord Ellensborough) to the Chairman and Deputy Chairman of the Court of Directors, 28 April

1858 in *Report of the Director of Public Instruction, Bombay 1857-8*, OIOC V/24/861, p. 11.

19. E.I. Howard, *Report of the Director of Public Instruction, Bombay, 1857/8*, OIOC V/24/861 pp. 11-24.
20. They were especially interested in developments concerning poorer girls in the Mediterranean countries as well as at the Working Women's College in London.
21. H.S. Reid, *Report of the Director of Public Instruction, NWP, 1859/60*, OIOC V/24/908, pp. 46-50.
22. Nigel C. Sargant, *Mary Carpenter in India*, Bristol: A.J. Sargant, 1987, p. 72.
23. Mary Carpenter to Secretary to the Government of India, 20 July 1867, in Mary Carpenter, *Six Months in India*, vol. 1, London: Longmans, 1868, p. 159.
24. Barbara Ramusack, 'Cultural Missionaries, Maternal Imperialists, Feminist Allies: British Women Activists in India, 1865-1945', *Women's Studies International Forum*, vol. XIII, no. 4, 1990, pp. 309-20. For fuller discussion of this literature see Ruth Watts, 'Mary Carpenter and India: Enlightened Liberalism or Condescending Imperialism?' in G. Sherington and C. Campbell (eds.), *Education and Ethnicity, Paedagogica Historica*, Suppl. Series, vol. VII, 2001, pp. 206-7.
25. Keshub Chunder Sen (1838-84), theist, dynamic leader of the Brahmo Samaj and social reformer, combined Christian doctrines and devotional practices of Hindu Vaishnava cults in his writings. In touch with other leading reformers of the age in India, such as Dayananda Saraswati, founder of the Arya Samaj, he advocated education for women and rallied against the status of 'untouchability'. Satyendranath Tagore (1842-1923), the elder brother of Rabindranath Tagore, likewise belonged to this tradition, particularly the part that focused on the rights of women. His wife gave up the veil at home and she was the first Indian woman to enter Government House at the invitation of the Viceroy.
26. 'Minute by the Governor General, 29 October 1860', no. 2, Government of India Proceedings, OIOC P/188/75.
27. Ibid.
28. W. Robinson, 'Women and Teacher Training: Women and Pupil Teacher Centres, 1880-1914', in J. Goodman and S. Harrop (eds.), *Women, Educational Policy-Making and Administration in England*, London: Routledge, 2000, ch. 6, pp. 99-115.
29. J. Goodman and S. Harrop, 'The Peculiar Preserve of the Male Kind: Women and the Education Inspectorate, 1893 to the Second World War' and J. Goodman and S. Harrop, 'Governing Ladies: Women Governors of Middle Class Girls' Schools, 1870-1925', in Goodman and

Harrop (eds.), *Women, Educational Policy-Making and Administration in England,* chs. 3 and 8, pp. 37-55, 137-55.
30. A. Oram, *Women Teachers and Feminist Politics, 1900-1939*, Manchester: Manchester University Press, 1996, pp. 103-4.
31. D. Copelman, *London's Women Teachers: Gender, Class and Feminism, 1870-1930*, London: Routledge, 1996, pp. 199-226.
32. Mary Carpenter to Sir Stafford Northcote, 8 October 1867 in Government of India Education Proceedings, 1877, OIOC P/1000, p. 94.
33. A monotheistic faith combining the Upanishads (sacred Hindu texts believed to lead to spiritual emancipation) with the ethics of Christianity. It advocated the social freedom and cultural emancipation of women from *sati* and early marriage and propogated widow remarriage.
34. J.C. Bagal, *Radha Kanta Dev, 1784-1867*, Calcutta: Government Printer, 1957, p. 47.
35. Mary Carpenter to the Marquis of Salisbury, 30 August 1876, *Education Proceedings*, Government of India, 1877, OIOC P/1000, pp. 95-9.
36. Only at the end of the century did the clever undercover work of Elizabeth Andrew and Kate Bushnell in army barracks fully expose these excesses to the British public. E. Andrew and K. Bushnell, 'Cantonment Life in India', in P. Tuson (ed.), *The Queen's Daughters,* Reading, Berkshire, UK: Ithaca Press, 1990, pp. 176-99.
37. Colin Browning MA, Offg. Inspector General of Education in the Central Provinces 'Report of Education in the Central Provinces for 1866/7', Nagpur, 1870, OIOC V/24/996, p. 12.
38. Chief Commissioner, Central Provinces, to the Government of India, *Education Proceedings*, 5 January 1873, no. 377 OIOC P/520.
39. M. Foucault, 'Two Lectures', in N. Dirks, G. Eley and S. Ortner (eds.), *Culture/Power/History: A Reader in Contemporary Social Theory,* Princeton, 1994.
40. See, for example, Padma Anagol's interesting binary of Christian convert feminism and its non-denominational application to the Indian population, as distinguished from the Western ethics of their European missionary teachers. P. Anagol, *The Emergence of Feminism in India, 1850-1920*, Aldershot: Ashgate, 2005, pp. 42-50.
41. 'Pupils of the Benares CM Normal Female School from January 1863 to January 1871', CIO 10/16, CMS Archive, Birmingham University, United Kingdom. This list includes the names and fate of some 104 girls with an average age of 15 years. The age of these trainee-teachers increased temporarily after Carpenter's first visit to India in 1866.
42. Mrs Irene Edwards, Transcript August 1973, Selections from edited

transcript with Vere, Lady Birdwood, October 1973, OIOC MSS Eur. T.7.

43. 'Draft Code of Regulations for European Schools . . . Accepted by the Government of India' October 1884, Government of India (Home Proceedings), 1884, OIOC P/2257. The code, first developed in Bengal, soon was applicable across the subcontinent. It was revised on even more favourable terms in 1905.
44. 'Mary Carpenter to the Marquis of Salisbury', 30 August 1876, *Education Proceedings*, Government of India, 1877, OIOC P/1000, p. 95.
45. The Martiniére schools at Calcutta, Lucknow and Chandernagore were established as early as 1817, funded from the generous bequest of a Frenchman, Captain Martiniére. He had collaborated with the British after the Battle of Pondicherry and made his fortune acting as Nawab of Oudh's factotum, including importing European furniture for his master, as well as coining his money, casting his cannon and grinding his indigo. The terms of Martiniére's will specified the establishment of three schools '. . . to educate a certain number of children of any sex to certain age and to have them put as apprentices to some profession when at the conclusion of their school.' These schools were for Europeans and Eurasians but the Calcutta school, in particular, with a relatively secure funding base evolved in the next 70 years to cater to the daughters of Raj civil servants and petty bureaucrats. The curriculum was one of European accomplishments taught using pupil-teachers under European teachers and with most of the school accommodated as boarders. A.J. Lawrence, 'Report of the Existing Schools for Europeans and Eurasians Throughout India', Calcutta: Government Printing, 1873, OIOC V/27/861/1 Sect. II, p. 1.
46. W.W. Hornell, 'Fifth Quinquennial Review of the Progress of Education in Bengal, 1911/12 to 1916/7', OIOC V/24/985, pp. 99, 115, 130-2.
47. 'A Note on Female Education Submitted by Dadabhai Naoroji to the Indian Education Commission, 1882', Document 46 in S. Bhattacharya, J. Bara, C.R. Yagati and B.M. Sankhdher (eds.), *The Development of Women's Education in India: A Collection of Documents, 1850-1920,* New Delhi: Jawaharlal Nehru University, 2000, pp. 88-90.
48. See 'Annual Reports of the Indian Female Normal School and Instructional Society' (1863-79), CMS Archive Section II, reels 57-8 (microfilm), OIOC.
49. H. Sharp, *Report on the Conference of the Domiciled Community*, dated 8 January 1913, no. 23, India Education Proceedings, 1913, OIOC P/9193.
50. See *Journal of the National Association in Aid of Female Education in India,* April 1882, no. 136, OICO L/PJ/6/70; September 1883, no. 153 OIOC L/PJ/6/105.

51. Antoinette Burton, *Burdens of History: British Feminists, Indian Women and Imperial Culture, 1865-1915*, Chapel Hill: University of North Carolina Press, 1994, pp. 82-3.
52. 'Missionary Settlement for University Women in Bombay Articles', OIOC MSS Eur. F. 186, vol. 140.
53. 'Memorial on the Education of Girls and Women in India to the Rt. Hon. Austin Chamberlain, Secretary of State for India' included in Secretary of State to Government of India, 5 November 1915, no. 191, Proceedings of the Government of India (Education), OIOC P/9942.
54. 'Minutes Regarding Appointment of Women's Sub-Committee', 4 July 1912, Continuation Committee of the World Missionary Conference, Edinburgh, 1910, OIOC MSS Eur. F. 220.
55. Papers of Margaret Hunt, OIOC MSS Eur. F. 241, p. 32.
56. Ibid., p. 65.
57. Louise Ouwerkerk (1904-39), Travancore 1929-39. Ouwerkerk Collection, OIOC MSS Eur. F. 232, vol. 60, entries for 28 June; 7, 14, 19 July; 3 August; 27 September; 4, 11 October; 10 November 1929.
58. Partha Chatterjee, 'The Nationalist Resolution of the Women's Question', in Kumkum Sangari and Sudesh Vaid (eds.), *Recasting Women: Essays in Colonial History*, New Delhi: Kali for Women, 1989.
59. Mrinalini Sinha, *Specters of Modern India: The Global Restructuring of an Empire,* London: Duke University Press, 2006.
60. Padma Anagol, *The Emergence of Feminism in India, 1850-1920,* Aldershot: Ashgate, p. 219.
61. Yashodabai Joshi, '*Amchi Jivanpravas*' [Our Lives Together], Poona, Venus, 1965, p. 59, cited in Padma Anagol, *The Emergence of Feminism in India, 1850-1920,* p. 65.
62. Suruchi Thapar-Bjorkert, *Women in the Indian National Movement: Unseen Faces and Unheard Voices, 1930-42,* New Delhi: Sage, 2006, p. 55.
63. Anagol, *The Emergence of Feminism in India*, pp. 22-55.
64. For a detailed analysis of Cornelia Sorabji's professional connections with England see Antoinette Burton, *At the Heart of the Empire: Indians and the Colonial Encounter in Late-Victorian Britain,* Berkeley: University of California Press, 1998, pp. 110-51.
65. Aparna Basu, 'A Century and a Half's Journey: Women's Education in India, 1850s to 2000', in Bharati Ray (ed.), 'Women of India: Colonial and Post-colonial Periods', vol. IX, pt. 3 of the *Project of History of Indian Science, Philosophy and Culture,* New Delhi: Sage, 2005, ch. 9, p. 195.
66. These figures were compiled from H. Sharp, 'Progress of Education in India, 1912-1917', Seventh Quinquennial Report, vol. 2, tables 143 and 147, pp. 169 and 173, OIOC V/24/4431.
67. Karuna Chanana, 'Social Change or Social Reform', in Carol

Mukhopadhyay and Susan Seymour (eds.), *Women, Education and Family Structure in India,* San Francisco: Westview Press, 1994, pp. 37-58 cited by Sabyasachi Bhattacharya, 'Introduction', in Sabyasachi Bhattacharya, Joseph Bara, Chinna R. Yagati and B.M. Sankhdher (eds.), *The Development of Women's Education in India,* p. x.

68. 'Memorandum of the Progress of Education in British India between 1916 and 1926', OIOC V/27/860/11, p. 70.
69. William Hornell to the Secretary of the Government of Bengal, 29 May 1915, no. 60. Bengal Education Proceedings, 1915 OIOC P/9640, p. 12.
70. Sir Philip Hartog, 'Notes and Memoranda on the Growth of Women's Education in India, August 1928-January 1929', in Hartog Collection OIOC MSS Eur. E. 221/51.

CHAPTER 12

Elite Conflict and Women's Education in Princely Mysore, 1860-1947

PARIMALA V. RAO

The Elite and Women's Education: A Historical Background

The elite is a group or social category of people in a social system that occupies a position of privilege or dominance. Traditionally, in India, the membership of elite has depended on social background rather than economic circumstances.[1] Colonialism gave space to the rise of new elites. Most of them were economically impoverished but had enormous social and cultural capital in terms of their higher caste status. Modern education gave them a tool to synthesize the European Enlightenment ideas with the liberal and egalitarian part of the Indian tradition. It was this class of elite which played a transformative role in the transition of the Indian society from a feudal mooring to a modern liberal society. The persons belonging to this class are known as 'reformers'. However, the colonial state which gave space to the emergence of this class also played a decisive role in curtailing its growth. The recognition of the economically dominant class as 'the respectable class', by the colonial states gave cultural capital and strengthened feudal ties. The feudal background coupled with modern education enabled this class to reinforce feudal hierarchies and gender and caste disabilities.[2]

The gender and caste disabilities have been the core of Hindu society and denial of education and sacred knowledge to women has been the cornerstone of patriarchy for nearly two millennia. In a society where, as Manmathnath Ghosh wrote in 1863, 'dullness in a girl was considered a virtue and smartness in conversation a crime',[3] smarter and competent women were a threat to patriarchy. This denial was effectively enforced by a clever superstition that a literate woman was certain to become a widow soon. As a result by the beginning of the nineteenth-century women throughout India were illiterate.

The Protestant missionary societies were the first to address the issue of girl's education. In the 1820s they established schools for girls in various parts of India. Due to the prejudices associated with these institutions, girls belonging to lower castes and Indian Christians benefitted. The upper-caste girls remained outside the school system. J.E. Drinkwater Bethune pioneered women's education in India in the 1850s. Later Iswarchandra Vidyasagar in Bengal, Mahadev Govind Ranade in the Bombay, K. Veeresalingam in the Madras Presidencies led powerful social movements to eradicate gender-based inequalities.

The colonial state, which supported social reform and assisted the Hindu reformers in the abolition of *sati*, female infanticide and child marriage, did little to start schools for girls. So, the onus of establishing schools and encouraging the neighbourhood to send the girls to schools was left on the Indian men. This process was often extremely contested and violent. In Mysore the contestations between the reformers who wanted to encourage girl's education, and the opponents got entwined around caste, linguistic, and regional identities.

Pre-Colonial Mysore

Mysore was a well-administered kingdom at the beginning of the nineteenth century. Diwan Purnaiya efficiently managed the affairs of the state as Maharaja Krishnaraja Wodeyar III was a mere child. The queen mother, Lakshmi Ammanni, who acted as a regent, kept the palace intrigues under control. The queen mother died in 1810 and the Maharaja who turned sixteen that year decided to take over the administration. The young and inexperienced Maharaja became a pawn in the hands of palace conspiracies; accordingly he removed Purnaiya from the post of Diwan. The administration during the next two decades went through the hands of a number of corrupt Diwans supported by various interest groups in the palace. Nepotism reigned supreme and most of the administrative posts were given to the relatives of various Diwans.[4] The local chiefs called *polegars* and powerful landlords rebelled against the authority of the Maharaja.[5] Many Indian princes were bound by caste and kinship to large and powerful groups of landed gentry in their states which lent legitimacy to their regimes from below. But the Mysore royal family of the Wodeyars was sealed off within an endogamous caste called Arasus whose number according to the 1881 census was less than 1,000.[6] Hence, the Maharaja had limited local support. In an attempt to gain popular support the Maharaja toured throughout the state to redress the grievances. In 1831, the corrupt local administrator of Nagar district, a relative of a former Diwan, was replaced by a relative of the Maharaja. This led to a powerful rebellion by the dispossessed administrator. The Maharaja's army had also been a victim of corrupt Diwans, and when the Maharaja could not effectively control the rebellion he sought British assistance. This led to a temporary takeover of Mysore by the British.

The Early Years

The British took over Mysore and in 1832 appointed Mark Cubbon to administer the province.[7] Cubbon was a patriarch of the conservative colonial school who prevented any progressive ideas from entering the province. He carefully cultivated the support of the Mysorian elite who in turn extended complete cooperation to the British. Though Cubbon undertook no developmental works and remained a mere efficient revenue collector he has been hailed as a benevolent administrator.[8] Cubbon asserted that 'the chief aim of the administration was to maintain law and order'.[9] During his 26 years of administration he neither took any initiative to start educational institutions nor did he encourage any private initiative with government aid. The people of Shimoga, a small town, managed to start an English school on their own and continued for a few years. In 1853 they approached Cubbon to make arrangements for appointing a qualified teacher. This was supported by C.K. Naidu, an official in the government, but Cubbon chose to 'reserve it for future consideration'.[10] In 1853, J. Garrett, an Englishman living in Mysore, sent a note to the government which contained an elaborate plan for establishing a teachers' training institute (then called Normal School) and a school in every district under the native management. In 1854 he once again urged the government to support private initiative in establishing schools and once again Cubbon 'reserved it for future consideration'.[11]

Another elaborate plan was submitted by the Judicial Commissioner Devereux in 1854, in this instance, for establishing village schools in every large village, along with eighty taluka and four divisional schools and a central college.[12] Though Cubbon established the department of education and appointed J. Garrett as its head, under pressure from the Government of India,[13] he refused to implement Devereux's plan.[14] Cubbon's consistent opposition to the establishment of schools in concrete terms meant that the number of English-educated Mysorians available for filling up of government posts remained negligible in this period.

The local Mysorian elites, who supported Cubbon, too opposed the development of educational infrastructure in the province in order to maintain their traditional privileges. When the colonial government demanded to know as to why no schools had been established during the 26 (1834-60) years, Cubbon explained that 'the territory of Mysore was unfavourable for the introduction of new measures amongst a population naturally suspicious and to some extent disposed to identify the progress of education with the loss of caste'.[15] He concluded the report by stating:

> There is widespread feeling of distrust and suspicion among the people. . . . I am not prepared to suggest any alterations in existing arrangements for carrying on the great duty of raising the moral, intellectual and physical conditions of Her Majesty's subjects . . . latent feeling of suspicion to which I have referred and of which I have seen many indications, has led me to exercise great caution.[16]

As the state of general education was such under Cubbon, women's education received no encouragement. The Christian missionaries made the earliest efforts in this direction. The Wesleyan and the London Missions established girls' schools in 1840. The taboo attached to these missionary schools appears to be less here in comparison to the Bombay Presidency,[17] as the statistics for Mysore suggest that there were 398 upper-caste Hindu girls as against 166 grouped under the official category of 'others' which included Indian Christians.[18] *Mysore Recorder*, a leading journal, supported the missionary efforts and criticized the opponents of women's education.[19] The upper-caste Hindus too volunteered to establish girls' schools.[20] The administrative report for the year 1862-3 mentions the existence of three girls' schools wholly managed by non-Christian natives, a fact that Cubbon never mentioned in his report to the colonial government.

A Shift in Policy

The retirement of Cubbon brought about a change that the common man was clamouring for. It ended the personalized paternal government headed by Cubbon and began a new era with the appointment of Levin Bentham Bowring (1862-70) as the Chief Commissioner of Mysore. Immediately after joining, Bowring received petitions from 'Brahmins, caste Hindus, untouchables and Muslims across the province to start schools for both boys and girls'.[21] This demolishes the theory promoted by Cubbon that setting up of schools would lead to rebellion. Bowring found it 'gratifying to observe that the desire for education continues to increase'.[22] The huge difference in public opinion regarding education within a span of two years cannot be attributed to any radical differences in the living conditions of the people. Besides, there was neither any revolutionary change in the society nor was there a social reformer vigorously advocating the cause of education. The change can thus be attributed to the mental make-up and the outlook of the two administrators.

Soon after taking over the administration, Bowring accepted Devereux's plan which consisted of not only establishing government schools but also encouraging private initiative through a grant-in-aid scheme. According to this scheme, individuals or a group of individuals were encouraged to set-up schools and run them successfully for a few years, after which the government would provide financial assistance.[23] Within a year, one high school and 16 primary schools were established by private endeavour. By the year 1864-5, the number of private institutions went up to 81. Of these, 64 received grant-in-aid from the government while 17 of them sustained entirely on private initiative. There were 5,642 students in these schools of which 365 were girls.[24]

Bowring's idea of educating the people was not confined to city dwellers. He saw that the existing rural schools were incompetent as most of them were indigenous, lacked financial grants and did not follow any government rules with regard to recruitment or syllabus. Access to these schools was also limited to a few upper-caste boys. Bowring subscribed to the idea that the farthest distance a child could walk was 4.5 miles and, accordingly, established schools called *hobli* (a group of village) schools at a distance of every 4.5 miles.[25] These schools were supported by 1 per cent cess collected in the villages. They also conducted night classes for the benefit of labourers who paid a nominal fee to defray the cost of lanterns. Bowring ordered the revenue officials to distribute textbooks in remote rural areas. The administrative report for the year 1866-7 states that a number of leading members of the Muslim community had urged the government to start girls' schools and also sought permission to start a private girls' school.[26] In the following year, Bowring ordered an assessment of the public reaction to the establishment of girls' schools. The response received by the government was favourable.[27] Eight schools were established within three years and 237 girls joined them immediately.[28] By the time Bowring left Mysore in 1870, besides the numerous *hobli* schools where rural boys and girls studied, there were 334 government schools of which 5 were girls' schools, with 10,565 boys and 1,360 girls and 412 grant-in-aid schools, of which 28 were girls' schools with 14,539 boys and 935 girls enrolled.[29]

Bowring modernized the province by expanding the administrative apparatus, set up courts and hospitals and built roads and bridges. His desire to fill up the posts with native officials in 1867 resulted in a greater demand for English-educated natives. Since their number was small, persons from Madras Presidency were brought in to fill up the posts.[30] Though Bowring initiated an era of building educational infrastructure, his administration of eight years could hardly be expected to produce a large number of English-educated elite to fill in the administrative posts.

The Elite in Conflict

The period of direct colonial rule in Mysore also witnessed intense lobbying on the part of the Maharaja and his supporters in London for the restoration of the throne to the Maharaja. The throne was restored to the Maharaja in 1881. By the time of rendition, there were 125 Indian officials drawing a salary of Rs. 100 and above consisting of 16 from Madras Presidency (called the Madras Party), 33 Tamil-speaking Hebbar Iyengar Brahmins (who identified themselves as Mysore Party), 36 local Brahmins and 40 local non-Brahmins. If we exclude the Madras Party and Tamil-speaking Hebbar Iyengars, then we can say that the local Kannada Brahmins and non-Brahmins had an almost equal share in the administration with the non-Brahmins in the lead. The Madras Party consisting of mostly Tamil Brahmins along with the Hebbar Iyengars inflated the number of Brahmins in the administration. Though the Madras Party was small in number, by virtue of their seniority, they occupied seniormost positions in the administration. This was resented by the Mysore Party and they led a movement demanding 'Mysore for Mysorians' and protested against what they called 'the Brahminocracy from the southern Presidency displacing the Mysorians'.[31] This cry was, however, devoid of any linguistic or regional cultural identity. The Mysore Party had no local Kannada-speaking persons. Most of the people in the so-called Mysore Party had roots in Madras Presidency. Some of the Madras Brahmins tried to assimilate themselves with the local population. Diwan Seshadri Iyer's daughter was married to a local Mysorian.[32] Mysore during 1870-1917 thus witnessed an intense triangular conflict among the Madras Party, the Mysore Party and the elite Mysorians. The common men and women of the province of Mysore had no say in it. Very often the Kannada Brahmins and non-Brahmins joined hands to vote against the government proposals in the Mysore Representative Assembly and many Kannada Brahmin officials opposed the policies of other Brahmins.[33] When the non-Brahmin movement began in Mysore, Kannada Brahmins came to be grouped together with other Brahmins and branded as oppressors.

The Madras Party was politically a fiercely independent group and supported the Indian National Congress. Though they owed their position to the British they did not shy away from criticizing colonial policies that adversely affected the interests of Mysore. Seshadri Iyer was a close, personal friend of Gopal Krishna Gokhale. Rangacharlu published the earliest critique of the British rule in Mysore.[34] As a young officer in the Madras Presidency whose career was altogether dependent upon the colonial system, he had the courage to criticize it. He published a pamphlet titled *Bribery and Corruption in the Revenue Department*, which exposed his senior British officers.[35] He took initiative in establishing the Mysore Representative Assembly in 1881.[36] Rangacharlu and Seshadri Iyer advocated modernization of administration, women's education and a rise in the marriageable age of girls. Diwan Seshadri Iyer's Note on women's education determined the future direction of the province.[37]

However, there were financial constraints. Mysore was the most heavily burdened of all the tributary states, as it paid one-third of its revenue every year as subsidy to the colonial government.[38] Therefore, there were no surplus resources to indulge in philanthropy and women's education always had an adverse cost-benefit ratio. The fact that the government spent an appreciable sum implied that the policy decisions were taken with a definite agenda for reform than administrative prudence. The Mysore Party and the local landed and elite Mysorians opposed reform. They were supported by conservative Europeans who had settled in the province as pensioners and coffee planters. The Mysore Party soon realized that it would no longer be a contender for the post of Diwan if it opposed reform. It thus began to compete with equal vigour for social reform and advocate women's education in its weekly paper *Karnataka Prakasika*.[39] The elite Mysorians who opposed any reform became isolated but soon got a channel to voice their opposition in the form of the newly established Mysore Representative Assembly.

The Women's Education

The Mysore Party, even before rendition, had taken individual initiatives in starting girls' schools, often in their own homes, in rented rooms and in village temple courtyards. These primary schools had an average of 30 to 40 students and the girls attending these schools were aged between five and thirteen. The medium of instruction in these schools was entirely in the local language and the textbooks printed by the government for the boys were utilized.[40] The curriculum was taught by the master himself without appointing any additional teachers.[41] By the year 1871, these single-teacher schools had 1,664 girls in Bangalore and Mysore districts alone.[42] Unlike the boys' schools where the students from the upper castes dominated, the girls' schools had students from diverse caste backgrounds. One such school at Chickmagalur had 95 girls of which 30 were Brahmin, 20 Vaishya, 8 Naidu, 20 Lingayat and 17 belonged to other castes. There are numerous letters commencing from 1895 onwards by these masters stating that since they were old they could no longer maintain the schools, and requested the government to take over these.[43] These letters categorically state that there was no objection from the local population to merge them with the existing boys' schools.[44]

Though women's education received whole-hearted support from the majority of people, yet there were reservations regarding the teaching of English and science subjects. The *Karnataka Prakasika* opposed teaching of these subjects at the Maharani's High School on the ground that 'the retired social habits seldom if ever, bring them into contact with the outer world, especially with English speaking people and proficiency in English to them, would at best be a doubtful and valueless accomplishment'.[45] However, such opposition did not acquire a keenly contested ideological battle the way it did in Maharashtra under Bal Gangadhar Tilak.[46] The criticism died down slowly as the girls began to acquire high-school education and write the matriculation examination. The same paper devoted a full column nine years later appreciating the educational accomplishments of a girl in English and science subjects.[47]

Both Diwan Rangacharlu and Diwan Seshadri Iyer, who belonged to the Madras Party, had to counter opposition to women's education within the Representative Assembly, which consisted of both local Mysorian Brahmin and non-Brahmin elite. They vehemently opposed every measure to educate women. Diwan Rangacharlu condemned the opposition to women's education by stating that

> The mother is the earliest educator of the future soldiers, statesmen or men of letters. At her knee, the embryo genius learns his alphabet and receives in fact his rudimentary grounding in useful knowledge . . . if we would rise up a generation of great learned, good, moral men we must take care that they are blessed with mothers to whom the early education of their sons and forming of their character can be safely trusted.[48]

With such forceful support by the turn of the century, women's education came to be accepted as a norm rather than a novelty. As a result, by 1897, Mysore had 136 government girls' schools, which included 69 Urdu girls' schools;[49] and some enthusiastic parents were willing to send their daughters even to boarding schools.[50]

The officials in the government belonging to the Madras Party matched this enthusiasm by giving liberal grants. They supported the establishment of girls' schools and instituted scholarships for widows. Narasimha Iyengar of the Madras Party was instrumental in establishing the Maharani's High School at Mysore in 1880. The school differed from other government schools for girls as the facilities provided were on a par with the schools meant for European children. The school was a kind of a social leveller as it was attended by women from the nobility, court officials and poor widows.[51] By 1890, the school had 500 students. The opponents of women's education, who could not digest the fact that a majority of the common people supported such a venture, began to spread the rumour that the purpose of the school was to provide girls to the Maharaja and Narasimha Iyengar. Such rumours were also encouraged by local officials. It was the iron hand of Diwan Seshadri Iyer that saved the school. He challenged the opponents of women's education by immediately making it a government institution and opening its doors to untouchable girls. The Maharani's High School started the F.A. or First in Arts classes in 1900 to facilitate the matriculate girls to join classes conducted for graduates by the Madras University.[52]

The Diwans also had to contend with hostility in the Assembly for the Infant Marriage Resolution Act in 1893. The majority of elite Mysorians opposed the Resolution and began to organize meetings against government's undue interference in the freedom of an individual, including the privacy of their domestic relations. The Mysore Party opposed the Infant Marriage Bill.[53] Diwan Seshadri Iyer argued that it was a matter of urgent concern because according to the 1891 census, 21,938 out of 90,152 Brahmin women were widows, and most of them were child widows. When the Resolution was introduced in the Assembly, only 53 members comprising 32 Brahmins and 21 non-Brahmins supported, while the rest comprising 81 Brahmins and 85 non-Brahmins opposed it.[54] Sensing that it was impossible to convince the hostile crowd, Seshadri Iyer did not invite the members to vote. He simply obtained the Maharaja's consent and, declaring that he had the support of various religious heads, passed the law. This measure was criticized by the elite Mysorians. Historians have lamented over a lack of democratic nature of the Assembly and have expressed the opinion that 'the Representative Assembly was meant to merely inform the people of the policies and programmes of the government and not to give the people the power of controlling the administration'.[55] The violation of the democratic norm actually benefited the cause of women. The effectiveness of this law can be judged by the fact that in the next decade the percentage of widows actually came down.

The closing years of the nineteenth century witnessed the gradual but large-scale passing over of private girls' schools into the hands of the government (Table 12.2). The process was aided by ageing school masters who, not being able to maintain the schools any longer, requested the government to take over the institutions.[56] The devastation caused by the plague during 1897-1900 affected women's education. The number of girls in the teacher training institute came down from 39 to 8 (Table 12.1). A number of teachers in the unaided girls' schools died during the period. In the year 1899 alone the government took over 79 of these unaided schools and began to conduct them in government boys' schools.[57] In order to effectively manage these schools, the government established committees consisting of local elites like lawyers, doctors and businessmen. These committees began to act in a highly arbitrary and unlawful manner, which resulted in the members of these committees interfering in the day-to-day functioning of the schools, much to the detriment of their progress. The girls' schools thus became centres of local caste-class politics.

Table 12.1: Teacher Training Institutions for Women

Year	Number of institutions	Strength	Number of women in men's institutions	Total number of women undertraining
1869-70	1	10	-	10
1889-90	1	39	-	39
1899-1900	1	8	-	9
1909-10	2	26	-	26
1919-20	3	63	-	63
1929-30	3	88	-	88
1939-40	3	121	14	135
1949-50	3	196	29	225

Source: Compiled from the Administrative Reports of Mysore for respective years.

Table 12.2: Number of Girls' Schools by Management, Grade and Period

Year	High			Middle			Primary*			Total		
	G	P	T	G	P	T	G	P	T	G	P	T
1869-70	–	–	–	–	–	–	–	–	–	5	28	33#
1879-80	–	2	2	2	11	13	12	38	50	14	51	65
1889-90	2	2	4	3	14	17	16	39	55	21	55	76
1899-1900	2	2	4	11	16	27	124	60	184	137	78	215
1909-10	2	2	4	39	23	62	148	66	214	189	91	280
1919-20	5	2	7	90	31	121	370	246	616	465	279	744
1929-30	5	2	7	55	14	69	480	100	580	540	116	656
1939-40	5	7	12	36	10	46	407	55	462	446	72	520
1949-50	11	23	34	84	31	115	541	44	585	636	98	734

Source: Compiled from the Administrative Reports of Mysore for respective years.

Notes: G: government, P: private, T: total

* All primary schools had middle school sections too.

Combined total of primary and middle schools. This does not include nearly 600 unaided single-teacher schools in rural areas.

This kind of parallel control with no apparent interest in the progress of women's education weakened departmental control and discipline.[58] The Inspector-General of Education, H.J. Bhaba suggested that these committees be abolished altogether.[59] However, the government decided to continue them though with a general supervisory power.[60]

Unlike the pattern in general education where the Brahmins dominated, women's education showed an egalitarian trend. By 1890-1, government schools had 8,902 Hindu and 687 Muslim girls; of the Hindu girls 39.9 per cent were Brahmin, 38.6 per cent backward castes, 13.6 per cent Lingayat and 4.5 per cent Vaishya.[61] Of the 212 girls in a government school at Bangalore, 86 were Brahmin, 31 Lingayat, 16 trading caste and 79 belonged to the backward castes.[62] Of the four girls who received scholarship, one was a Brahmin and three belonged to the backward castes. All of them were widows.[63] The trend of non-Brahmin girls maintaining a lead over the Brahmin girls was apparent throughout the province and in all categories. A large chunk of private endowments towards women's education also came from non-Brahmins and women themselves.[64]

When the administration went into the hands of P.N. Krishnamurthi of the Mysore Party in 1901, the policy of discouraging women's education began to be pursued. Though no policy decision was taken at a formal level, yet the projects were quietly shelved under the pretext that adequate funds were not available with government. In 1904, an Urdu school made a request for a grant of Rs. 350 per month to start a teacher training school. Though the Inspector General of Education forwarded the request with a favourable note, yet the Secretary rejected it on the grounds that 'it is too early and too costly to establish'.[65] Requests for take-over of schools and establishment of new schools were similarly rejected because there was no provision in the budget.[66] During this period, no schools were taken over by the government.

By 1904, girl students began to knock the doors of the college. In that year, 575 girls passed the high school and many among them sought admission in the Central College, which admitted only boys. The principal refused admission and proposed that the government should add a college section to the existing girls' schools.[67] A college section to the Maharani's High School was reluctantly added at Bangalore.[68] The opponents of women's education raised their heads again. They first opposed the starting of the college section on the pretext that there were very few female high school pass-outs. When they could not stop the process, they began to oppose the admission of Indian Christian girls into the Maharani's College. The Inspector General of Education, H. J. Bhaba, and the managing committee of the school firmly stood in favour of the Christian girls.[69] Opposition to women's education also manifested when a backward-class widow named Saraswati, of the same high school, secured a scholarship in 1903. Questions were raised about her status as a widow. The opponents also accused her of having been born to a prostitute and her blacksmith husband having left her due to her objectionable character. Yet again, both the Inspector General of Education and the managing committee firmly stood by her, which helped her to complete her education.[70]

In 1906, the administration again came under the control of the Madras Party. As many as 7,000 un-aided primary schools made requests for being converted into government institutions with proper buildings, trained teachers and a uniform curriculum. Already 2,417 government co-educational primary schools were in existence which meant that the conversion of all schools would provide an adequate number of schools to accommodate the entire population of 6 million. The memorandum proposed the conversion of 1,000 schools a year for seven years but the government found the cost of Rs. 7 lakh – that would be incurred in the conversion process over a period of seven years – prohibitive and therefore directed the conversion of only 250 schools a year out of which 100 were to be girls' schools. In that year the fee for education at the primary level was also abolished.

M. Visvesvaraya was the first Mysorian to be appointed as the Diwan in 1912. He was an engineer by profession and held progressive ideas. Though a Brahmin he exhibited scant respect for caste, regional and linguistic chauvinism. He had spent most of his time outside the province and had no local support. He regarded education as a remedy for all the socio-economic evils of India. Whenever he was on tour, he visited girls' schools, enquired about their functioning, and always assisted them with resources. In 1913, hc visited the girl's school at Sringeri, which had a strength of 68 girls and expressed dissatisfaction at the fact that a town with a population of 3,000 people could send only 68 girls to school. He also directed the local officials of the education department to ensure the admission of girls from untouchable communities.[71] He made a proposal for the establishment of a boarding school for untouchable children but this was turned down by M. Shama Rao, a senior Mysore Brahmin official in the education department.[72] By 1912, there were four girl students in the Mysore University.[73] The Mysore Economic Conference passed a resolution stating that the duty of the government went beyond giving aid to those who applied for it.[74]

Despite Visvesvaraya's progressive ideas, and the Maharaja's active support to women's education, the period between 1914 and 1920 saw the cause of women's education being adversely affected at various levels. Most of the political leaders supporting the Congress movement, except V.S. Srinivasa Sastri, were the supporters of Bal Gangadhar Tilak.[76] They adopted Tilak's opposition to women's education as an article of faith. V.S. Srinivasa Sastri faced formidable opposition when he tried to organize meetings of the Servants of India Society to support Gokhale's Compulsory Education Bill in

1911.[77] There was also a decided opposition from the elite Mysorian Brahmin officials – who by now had become senior officials – as well as the newly emerging non-Brahmin movement leaders.

Visvesvaraya's efforts to implement compulsory education for girls faced vigorous opposition.[78] The proposal was strongly opposed by some officials who insisted that the infrastructure had not been sufficiently developed to undertake the task.[79] They also insisted that girls should not be taught English and science but only Kannada, arithmetic and domestic science.[80] The Inspector General of Education, M. Shama Rao, and a senior official, Y. Narasimharao, opposed the idea of imparting compulsory education to girls. They unofficially forwarded a note to the Diwan and the Secretary to the government on what they called 'the objections raised by certain officials' along with a note stating: 'I am not in favour of making the compulsory education regulation applicable to girls; at present compulsion should be applied to boys, not girls. When the percentage of school going girls rose from 9 to 20 or 25 per cent, compulsion should be introduced to girl's education'.[81] The proposal was firmly rejected by Diwan Visvesvaraya who ordered that immediate steps be taken to build infrastructure.[82] V.S. Subramanya Iyer, Secretary to the government, too, rejected the proposal stating: 'the need for compulsion in case of girls is much greater and therefore more urgent than in case of boys.... In view of the urgency of the need for this reform, I am to request that early order.'[83] The year 1915 saw the introduction of compulsory education for girls in 27 places and a proposal was made to extend it to another 40 at a cost of Rs. 40,000 the succeeding year.[84] A note by Visvesvaraya expressed concern that the scheme of compulsory education was working well in only 238 out of 300 centres. The Inspector General of Education C.R. Reddy opposed it by stating that 'there is no need for a more rapid expansion of compulsory education to rural areas'. Reddy demanded a time frame of at least ten years.[85] Here, by opposing the efficient extension of compulsory education to rural areas, C.R. Reddy was opposing the non-elite non-Brahmins from gaining access to education.

In spite of opposition from official circles and the newly emerging elite, women's education continued to make steady progress (Table 12.3). By 1918, in Bangalore city, 2,460 girls in the age group of 7 to 10 years were attending schools, while 2,800 girls in the same age group were not attending schools. Mysore was much

Table 12.3: Number of Girls by Stages of Instruction
(Does not include girls studying in boys' schools)

Year	High	Middle	Primary	Total
1869-70	–	138	1,711	1,849
1879-80	5	165	3,394	3,564
1889-90	13	487	7,758	8,258
1899-1900	17	457	14,933	15,407
1909-10	31	831	20,030	20,892
1919-20	146	2,382	53,477	56,005
1929-30	328	**	58,798	59,126
1939-40	1,207	8,231	74,898	84,336
1949-50	7,757	34,572	2,09,531	2,51,860

Source: Compiled from the Administrative Reports for respective years. Besides this there were 1,732 girls studying in co-educational *hobli* schools.[75]

Note: ** Included under primary schools.

ahead with 3,515 girls attending schools and 912 not attending them. The government proposed the establishment of 26 schools with 68 teachers in Bangalore and 14 schools with 53 teachers in Mysore in order to effectively enforce compulsory education for girls.[86] Though there was improvement in the percentage of girls entering primary schools yet only 0.20 per cent of them entered high schools (Table 12.4).

C.R. Reddy began to oppose the teaching of English, science and mathematics for girls, which were the key subjects to enter high school. If the girls had no foundation in these subjects in the primary and middle schools, they could hardly be expected to learn higher mathematics and science in the English medium in high

Table 12.4: Percentage of Boys and Girls in the School

	High School	Middle English	Middle Vernacular	Vernacular Upper Primary	Vernacular Lower Primary
Boys	1.87	7.45	2.43	40.09	48.16
Girls	0.20	3.55	2.04	31.91	62.32

Source: Home/Education 226 of 1918.

schools. Since both the Maharaja and Visvesvaraya were strong supporters of girls' education, C.R. Reddy and his deputy B. Dasappa very intelligently undermined the official policy. During 1917-18, the strength of the Vani Vilas Girls' School rose from 215 to 370.[87] So the school management decided to start a hostel to facilitate the girls coming from distant areas to study and approached the government for funds. The Maharaja supported the scheme and personally studied the plan and suggested improvements in the elevation.[88] C.R. Reddy successfully opposed the construction of the building.[89] He also opposed the appointment of male teachers in girls' high schools.[90] He insisted that the medium of instruction for girls should be Kannada and vehemently opposed the idea of teaching English to women.[91] Proposals were placed before the Mysore Representative Assembly and Mysore University Senate to restrict women from being educated in the English medium.[92] Though the proposals got defeated, yet a strong opposition from the newly emerging elite and a section of officials within the administration definitely contributed to the slowing down of the process of building infrastructure for women's education.

The departure of Visvesvaraya and the appointment of Kantaraj Urs as the Diwan further strengthened the hands of the opponents of girl's education. Now the Maharaja stood completely isolated. Kantaraj Urs, C.R. Reddy and B. Dasappa effectively out-manoeuvred the Maharaja and the Registrar of the Mysore University, V. Subramanya Iyer in all important matters. Around this time the Maharaja had taken interest in a proposal to start bachelor courses in science in the Vani Vilas Institute at Bangalore and had strongly recommended it. An order to that effect had also been issued. In 1920, the Maharani's College in Mysore wanted to start bachelor courses in science and approached the registrar. C.R. Reddy communicated to the that similar courses had already been sanctioned to the Vani Vilas Institute in Bangalore. Reddy informed the Vani Vilas Institute that the science courses could not be taken up due to financial constraints. He informed the principal of the Maharani's College that the girls from there could pursue the science courses at the Central College in Bangalore which was a boys' college. Reddy argued that he was against male teachers teaching girls in the high schools and not in the colleges by stating that 'as the discipline and tone of a high school are not quite good or manageable as those of a college'. Reddy promised F.L. Usher, principal of the Central College, that a new building would be handed over in time for admitting girls. The building was not completed and the courses could not be started for some years.[93] All through the year the Maharaja was kept in the dark.[94] This manipulative measure not only denied the girls of the 1920s a chance to pursue higher studies in the sciences but also denied future science teachers to the girls' high schools.

During 1920-47, the dominant forces in Mysore that influenced women's education were the elite non-Brahmins and Mahatma Gandhi. The Gandhian opposition to modern education assisted elite opposition to women's education. The public contribution to girls education fluctuated drastically (Table 12.5). Though the statistics show an aggregate increase in the number of girls admitted, yet the higher education for women was successfully resisted. During this time women were denied entry into the civil service. In 1923 A. Kanakamma, a first-class graduate, was not allowed to take the Mysore Civil Services examination on the grounds that 'it is not desirable to admit women candidates'. Once again the file was not sent to the Maharaja and the senior officials took the decision.[95] The Vani Vilas Institute could establish a hostel for its students only in 1936-7.[96] The degree courses of the Maharani's College Mysore were shifted to Bangalore in 1939. This measure once again undermined women's education. Though many people did muster enthusiasm to postpone the marriage of their daughters to send them to the colleges, it was too much to expect of them to

Table 12.5: Expenditure on Girls' Schools.

Year	Government	Local funds	Municipal funds	Fees	Private contribution	Total
1879-80	18,175	–	–	10,099	10,906	39,180
1889-90	30,786	1,264	–	687	35,073	67,810
1899-1900	79,282	3,056	1200	543	35,533	1,19,614
1909-10	1,21,339	9,109	2,209	2, 709	46,857	1,82,223
1919-20	3,32,875	82,859	214	5, 887	60,733	4,82,568
1929-30	5,77,885	53,871	17, 879	7, 601	38,184	6,95,420
1939-40	5,59,032	1,06,356	38,267	23,614	83,373	8,10,642
1949-50	18,61,522	-	14,920	2,93,428	26,744	21,96,614

Source: Compiled from the Administrative Reports of Mysore for respective years.

send them 200 miles away. The government instead of facilitating women's education actually hindered its growth.

The elite conflict in the province of Mysore during 1860-1947 was much more complex and nuanced than a simple dichotomy between Kannadigas and Tamilians, Mysorians and Madrasis, and Brahmins and non-Brahmins. This study shows that these categories were not absolute in terms of their linguistic, cultural, and caste identity. Moreover the policies of the Mysorian elite were detrimental to the interests of women's education. Mysore did not witness a powerful social reform movement like those of Bengal and Bombay presidencies. In the light of continued opposition from the local Mysorian Brahmin and non-Brahmin officials and members of the Representative Assembly, women's education could hardly have made any progress without the active support the Diwans and officials from the Madras Presidency. The Mysorian and non-Mysorian conflict has been viewed as emergence of local nationalism, struggle to control the bureaucracy, class struggle and a period of stagnation in Mysore. The period of strong Diwans like K. Seshadri Iyer has been viewed as a period of autocratic rule, which undermined the democratic spirit of the Mysore Representative Assembly. Similarly, the non-Brahmin movement has been represented as non-Brahmin opposition to Brahmin domination in the field of education. This study shows that Kantaraj Urs and C.R. Reddy, while representing themselves as the leaders of the non-Brahmin movement and opposing Visvesvaraya, actually shared their concerns with Mysore Brahmins like M. Shama Rao, and Y. Narasimharao as far as women's education was concerned. So, what is true in the sphere of patriarchal real-politic need not necessarily be true in the sphere of gender equality.

NOTES

1. Edmund Leach and S.N. Mukherjee (eds.), *Elites in South Asia*, Cambridge: Cambridge University Press, 1970, pp. ix-xiv.
2. For a discussion on this see, Parimala V. Rao, *Foundations of Tilak's Nationalism: Discrimination, Education and Hindutva*, New Delhi: Orient BlackSwan, 2010.
3. Manmathnath Ghosh in the *Bengali*, dated 13 January 1863, quoted in S. Bhattacharya et al., *Development of Women's Education in India 1850-1920*, New Delhi: Kanishka, 2000, p. 29.

4. M. Shama Rao, *Modern Mysore*, Bangalore: Higginbothams, 1936, pp. 401-6.
5. Bjorn Hettne, *The Political Economy of Indirect Rule: Mysore 1881-1947*, New Delhi: Concept, 1978, pp. 30-3.
6. James Manor, *Political Change in an Indian State: Mysore 1917-1955*, New Delhi: Manohar, 1977, pp. 10-11.
7. H.V. Sreenivasa Murthy and R. Ramakrishnan, *A History of Karnataka*, New Delhi: S. Chand, 1977, pp. 316-17.
8. K.N.V. Sastri, *The Administration of Mysore under Sir Mark Cubbon*, London: G. Allen & Unwin, 1932, p. 222.
9. Letter from Cubbon to the Officiating Secretary, dated 12 January 1860. Home/Education, 1 of 1860.
10. Home/Education, 1 of 1853, nos. 1-13.
11. Ibid., Letters from J. Garrett to C.K. Naidu dated 11 October 1853, 22 March 1854.
12. Home/Education, 1 of 1856, no. 1.
13. Home/Education, 1 of 1857, nos. 1-3.
14. Cubbon to the Officiating Secretary, dated 12 January 1860. Home/Education, 1 of 1860.
15. Letter from Cubbon to the Officiating Secretary, dated 12 January 1860. Home/Education, 1 of 1860.
16. Ibid., p. 2.
17. Parimala V. Rao, 'Women in the Nationalist Discourse: A Case Study of Tilak's Approach to Women's Education and Emancipation', in S. Bhattacharya (ed.), *Development of Modern Indian Thought and the Social Sciences*, New Delhi: Oxford University Press, 2007, p. 243.
18. *The Administrative Report of Mysore for the Year 1862-63*, p. 5.
19. *Mysore Recorder*, 30 April 1863, Editorial, p. 1.
20. Home/Education, 1 of 1856, no. 1.
21. Home/Education, 5 of 1862, p. 8.
22. Ibid., p. 24.
23. Memorandum accompanying Garret's letter to the Secretary to the Commissioner, dated 24 October 1863. Home/Education, 11 of 1863.
24. *The Administrative Report of Mysore for the Year 1864-1865.*
25. A handwritten note by Bowring in the file of Home/Education, 8 of 1868.
26. *The Administrative Report of Mysore for the Year 1866-1867*, p. 16.
27. *The Administrative Report of Mysore for the Year 1867-1868*, pp. 8-9.
28. *The Administrative Report of Mysore for the Year 1871-1872*, pp. 74-5.
29. *The Administrative Report of Mysore for the Year 1870*, p. 10.
30. Donald R. Gustafson, 'Mysore—1881-1902: The Making of a Model State', unpublished Ph.D. thesis, University of Wisconsin, 1969, p. 64.
31. R. Ramakrishnan, *Press and Politics in an Indian State: Mysore 1859-1947,* New Delhi: Delta Publishing House, 1994, p. 28.

32. Bjorn Hattne, *Political Economy*, p. 74.
33. Home/Education 150 of 1914, pp. 1-2
34. *The British Administration of Mysore by a Native of Mysore*, London: Longman & Co., 1874.
35. Bjorn Hattne, *The Political Economy*, p. 121.
36. Ibid., p. 87.
37. K. Seshadri Iyer's Note in Home/Education, 8 of 1890, pp. 1-2
38. M. Shama Rao, *Modern Mysore*, Bangalore: Higginbothams, 1936, pp. 84-5.
39. *Karnataka Prakasika*, 13 April 1869, p. 2.
40. Home/Education, 10 of 1891, p. 1.
41. Home/Education, 9 of 1897, pp. 1-8.
42. Conversion of Empress Girls' School at Tumkur into a Government Institution, Home/Education, 7 of 1890, pp. 1-3
43. Conversion of a Hindu Girls' School at Chickmagalore into a Government Institution, Home/Education, 63 of 1897, pp. 1-4.
44. Conversion of Aided Kannada Girls' School at Mandya into a Government Institution, Home/Education, 3 of 1895, pp. 1-12.
45. *Karnataka Prakasika*, 3 April 1882, p. 2.
46. Parimala V. Rao, 'Women's Education and Nationalist Response in Western India: Part I Basic Education', *Indian Journal of Gender Studies*, vol. 14, no. 2 (2007), pp. 307-16.
47. *Karnataka Prakasika,* 20 April 1891, p. 2.
48. Diwan Rangacharlu's speech reported in *Karnataka Prakasika*, 3 April 1882, pp. 1-2.
49. Home/Education, 28 of 95, 1895-6, pp. 1-12.
50. *Centenary Booklet of Mitralaya School* (Bangalore, 1970), p. 8.
51. Home/Education, 9 of 1885, p. 6.
52. Letter from J.H. Bhaba to the Secretary to the Government of Mysore, dated 19 March 1900, pp. 1-3.
53. Gustafson, *Mysore 1881-1902*, p. 221.
54. Made Gowda, *Modern Mysore State 1881-1902*, Prasaranga, Mysore, 1997, p. 137.
55. Ramakrishnan, *Press and Politics*, p. 106.
56. Conversion of Empress Girls' School at Tumkur into a Government Institution, Education, 7 of 1890, pp. 1-3.
57. *Proceedings of the Government of Mysore*, July 1899, p. 19.
58. Management of Girls' Schools by Committees, Government memo dated 15 December 1898, Education, 8 of 95, pp. 1-12.
59. Ibid. H.J. Bhaba (I.G. of Education) to the Secretary to the Government of Mysore.
60. Ibid. Final Government notification, dated 10 February 1902.
61. *The Administrative Report for the Year 1890-91,* pp. 2-3.

62. Statement of Girls in Each Community, 30 June 1905, Education, 206 of 1904, p. 92.
63. Ibid., p. 97.
64. Endowments, Education, 41 of 1914, pp. 6-23; 50 of 1915, pp. 1-30; 50 of 1915, pp. 1-2.
65. Normal School for Mahomedan Mistress, Education, 27 of 1904, pp. 1-7.
66. Education, 280 of 1904, pp. 1-4.
67. The Question of Raising the Standard of the Government Girls' Schools at Bangalore, Education, 206 of 1904, p. 1.
68. Formation of F.A. Classes in Maharani's College, Education, 29 of 1899, pp. 1-7.
69. Admission of Native Christian Girls into Maharani's College, dated 20 November 1902, Education, 54 of 1902, pp. 1-6.
70. Scholarship to Out-ridden Students in the Maharani's College at Mysore, Education, 34 of 1903, pp. 1-2.
71. *Indian Patriot*, 24 March 1930.
72. Scale of Estimate of Panchama School, Home/Education, 150 of 1914, pp. 1-2.
73. Report on Public Instruction in Mysore 1913-1914, Home/Education, 67 of 1914, pp. 1-3.
74. Progress of Educational Matters, Home/Education, 148 of 1914, pp. 1-5.
75. *The Administrative Report for the Year 1869-70*, p. 103.
76. H.V. Sreenivasa Murthy and R. Ramakrishnan, *A History of Karnataka*, p. 327.
77. *The Indian Patriot*, 30 August 1911.
78. Letter from I.G. to Secretary to the Government of Mysore, dated 7 May 1915, Home/Education, 7 of 1914.
79. Compulsory Education for Girls' Home/Education, 26 of 1916, pp. 24-70.
80. Copies of Proceedings, Home/Education, 12 of 1915, p. 8.
81. Letter dated 3 January 1917, Home/Education, 26 of 1916, pp. 24-70.
82. Ibid., dated 9 February 1917.
83. Ibid., V. Subramanya Iyer's letter to I.G. of Home/Education, dated 16 November 1916.
84. Diwan M. Visvesvaraya to the Maharaja; Home/Education, 42 of 1915, pp. 66 and 75(a).
85. Visvesvaraya's note dated 10 August 1918, C.R. Reddy to the Secretary to the government dated 6 April 1918, Home/Education, 222 of 1917, nos. 10-16.
86. Government Order No. 671-4, dated 22 July 1918, Home/Education, 3-17-44, pp. 1-2.

87. Home/Education, 226 of 1918, nos. 1-7.
88. The letter from the Maharaja dated 28 December 1918, Home/ Education, 34 of 1917, nos. 12-16.
89. C.R. Reddy to the Secretary to the Government of Mysore dated 14 June 1918, Home/Education, 34 of 1917, nos. 12-16.
90. Home/Education, 27 of 1917, nos. 170-203.
91. C.R. Reddy's letter to Secretary to the Government, dated 2 December 1918. Remodelling of Women's Home/Education, 170 of 1917.
92. Registrar V.S. Iyer's letter to the Secretary to the Government, dated 5 December 1918, Home/Education, 160 of 1918, p. 23.
93. Home/Education, 72 of 1920, nos. 3-15.
94. All correspondence end at the Diwan's office and none were sent to the palace office. See Home/Education 72 of 1920, nos. 3-15.
95. Home/Confidential Branch, 116 of 1923, nos. 37-40.
96. Education, 17 of 1936, nos. 28-32.

CHAPTER 13

Muslim Female Education Movement and Shaikh Muhammad Abdullah, 1874-1965

GULFISHAN KHAN

Shaikh Muhammad Abdullah (1874-1965), founder of the Women's College of Aligarh Muslim University and an epoch-making personality, was among those conscious promoters of change who chose to become publicists and activists for the cause of women. A pioneering figure, he made the subject of women a central topic in his programme of socio-cultural reform and redefinition, expressing his concern, above all, through the newly available medium of print. The central concern of his reformist agenda was the provision of formal education for Muslim women.[1] A true product of the Aligarh movement, his aims and aspirations were those espoused and propagated by the luminaries of the movement. In his own life he sought to achieve the same high goals as were set by the pioneer reformers - including formal education of Muslim women which he thought was an unfulfilled aspect of the historic Aligarh movement.[2] Shaikh Muhammad Abdullah belonged to what the historian Lelyveld called 'Aligarh's First Generation'.[3] The present paper highlights the ideas of this great thinker in the context of the societal changes taking place at this crucial period of Indian history.

Shaikh Muhammad Abdullah was born as Thakur Das in June 1874 in a Brahmin family of zamindars in village Bhantani in the Poonch district of Jammu. He joined the newly established Mohammedan Anglo-Oriental College in May 1891. Being the descendant of an aristocratic Kashmiri Brahmin family, his proficiency in Urdu and Persian gave him full membership of Aligarh *biradari* (brotherhood).[4] Theodore Morison;[5] T.W. Arnold, professor of philosophy from 1888 to 1898 and the author of *Preaching of Islam*,[6] biographer, literary critic and professor of Arabic and Persian (1883-98); Shibli Numani (1857-1914); Babu Jadav Chandra Chakravarty, the mathematician;[7] and Maulana Abbas Husain[8]—the distinguished British and Indian scholars who served the institution in its first classical phase - were the teachers of Shaikh Abdullah.[9] But above all, Syed Ahmad Khan (1817-98), the renowned pioneer of the movement and founder of the Mohammedan Anglo-Oriental College, was the role model of Abdullah throughout his life. Abdullah's autobiography *Mushahidat wa Taasurat* (*Observations and Experiences*) begins with a reverential tribute to the achievements of this grand old man of Aligarh.[10] Under the benevolent guardianship of the great visionary Syed Ahmad Khan, then in the twilight of his long life, Abdullah obtained an F.A. and B.A. followed with a professional degree in law.[11]

Abdullah was a prolific writer and his contribution as a publicist for the cause of women is comprehensive and wide-ranging. His public career synchronized with the rise and strengthening of the forces of anti-imperialism, nationalism, separatism and communalization of Indian politics, - developments in which he was an observer as well as an active participant.[12] His concern with women's rights centred on the issue of provision of formal education but his discourses also encompassed other aspects such as the *purdah* (veiling or seclusion), polygamy, nature of relationship between the spouses and above all the legal rights of Muslim women. A protagonist of equal rights of women, Abdullah believed that formal education of women on modern lines was a cause as well as panacea for Muslim retrogression in the subcontinent. In his view female education was crucial for the socio-economic advancement and cultural reconstruction of the Indo-Muslim community.

In post-Independence India too, Abdullah sought to convince his literate readership that without the light of knowledge and reason brightening the minds of almost half of the population of the country, the nation cannot progress and emerge into the modern era of science and reason.[13] Abdullah articulated his views on ideas of an ideal/modern Islamic womanhood through his innumerable essays, pamphlets and articles, apart from his well-known biographical reminiscences.[14] Most of his writings were published in Urdu magazines and periodicals, especially in the Lahore-based women's magazine *Tahzib un Niswan* and *Risala Khatun*, two of the 'Big Three'.[15] *Risala Khatun* (*Lady/Gentlewoman's Magazine*) was founded by him in 1904 as an organ of the Women's Education Section of the All India Muslim Educational Conference, a national organization established in 1886 by Syed Ahmad Khan at Aligarh. The objective of the journal was: 'To spread education and to relish taste for knowledge among the *purdah*-observing women (*masturat*), to make available reading material for them to enlighten their thinking and taste through the dissemination of fresh ideas.'[16] It also aimed at creating awareness about the condition of Muslim women, and to convince Muslim men of the need for improvement in their lives under changed political circumstances. Shaikh Abdullah's journalistic venture proved a successful literary vehicle in changing the Urdu-speaking educated elite's attitudes towards the question of female education. Through the medium of this vernacular periodical he waged a successful war (*jihad*) against the antagonistic forces of what he termed, bigotry (*ta'assub*) and ignorance (*jahalat*).

Abdullah was also one of the co-founders and the moving spirit of *Anjuman Khawatin-i-Islam* (All India Muslim Women's Association), an organization devoted to the cause of Indian Muslim women.[17] The aim of the association was to impart the movement an all-India character and thus to foster an increased sense of community and social consciousness. Through this platform he sought to sensitize Muslim people to the cause of women's education.[18] From the same forum he raised his voice against the Punjab and UP Tenancy Act which denied Muslim women a share in agricultural property (*jaidad*), and also supported resolutions against polygamy.[19] The focus of this pioneer organization was on provisions of formal education for women. This also served as a forum of debate on issues such as the *purdah*, age of marriage, child-care, health, polygamy and other related questions. The organization entertained truly all-India aspirations. Established under the presidentship of the Begum of Bhopal, Sultan Jahan Begum (1858-1930), some of the prominent non-Muslim participants were Sarla Devi Chowdhurani, founder of Bharat Stree Mahamandal and a niece of poet Rabindranath Tagore, and the poetess and nationalist leader Sarojini Naidu.[20]

Defining Reforms

The conceptual framework presented by Kenneth Jones in his broad study of the socio-religious reform movements suggests two distinct types of movements during the colonial era, one transitional and the other acculturative. The transitional movements had their origins in the pre-colonial Indian society and made use of indigenous forms of socio-religious dissent with little or no influence from the colonial milieu. The acculturative movements originated within the colonial milieu and were led by individuals who were the products of cultural interaction with the West.[21]

Similar to this general classification, corresponding strands could be identified in the movement for Muslim women's reforms in the late nineteenth century. The first was led by the *ulama*, the upholders of the Islamic normative traditions, who devised a programme of social reform mostly independent of European influence. They were largely independent of any engagement with European critique of Indian women and did not define themselves by either emulating or opposing a European pattern. The second one incorporated social reformers, apologists and vernacular publicists who were motivated by their encounters with the colonial power, responded directly to the European critiques and took examples from the Western prototypes.[22] The models provide useful tool for analysing the process of interaction between the colonial power and the colonized. The *ulama* were affected by the Western - and the reformers preserved continuity with the pre-British society. Again it is difficult to draw a line between the religious reformers and the vernacular publicists and essayists, the products of the age of print culture. Despite the identified dichotomy between the two types of reform models, there existed certain overlapping domains. Both attempted to define and redefine acceptable or unacceptable customs as they fought within their religious community. Both the groups identified here were coming to terms with realities of political power in India and social, economic and cultural challenges of the prevailing situation. Both believed that Muslims were impoverished and lacked progress and were thus seeking development for them. But they did so in terms of their own cultural tradition of revitalization of community life through reform.

There were varied motivations behind their concern for women and they sought to revitalize family life by means of women's education. The efforts of the *ulama* as represented in the Deoband tradition sought to revalidate Islamic law and Prophetic example in Muslim daily life. Both advanced ethical arguments to defend the position of women in the *Shariat* and contended that education would enable them to perform their roles as wives, mothers, daughters and sisters in conformity with the norms of respectability in the polite society. The other group consisting of publicists was the proponent of new forms of thought and social behaviour.[23] The concern of the second group was marked by the compatibility of Islamic principles with modernity. It aimed to rescue religion from narrow interpretation, opening up Islam as a vital force in women's and men's daily lives. The aim of the protagonists belonging to both these broad categories – the reformers of Aligarh School who sought to provide formal education for the *ashraf* women as well as the *ulama* who sought to educate women in the true practices of Islam – was to secure better moral and material life for their women and their families. One of the jewels they believed was reason/intellect (*aql*). Women and men were endowed with the same faculties and both were responsible for their conduct.[24]

It is a story of upper and middle class women as disseminated through the print culture in which apparently all local and class variations were subsumed in the term 'Muslim women' geographically dispersed, linguistically diverse and culturally diffusive minority was placed under the term *qaum*. In both the discourses Muslim women were identified as the object of the male reformist programme. In the case of the proponents of Western education their focus was on the upper and middle-class women. For the women of the deprived sections the latter often came forward with the pious advice which suggested intelligent application of T.B. Macaulay's downward filtration theory of 1835. Once educated, women should be ready for social service and social work, especially among the less fortunate sisters who had been denied access to learning. This would be service to their community.[25]

Interpretation of the Legacy

Shaikh Abdullah's expose on women was heavily embedded in the contemporary socio-intellectual milieu. The re-examination of the traditionalist conception of the woman and her rights was part of the reformist agenda of the thinkers associated with the modernizing and Westernizing programme of Syed Ahmad Khan, later termed as the Aligarh Movement. The late nineteenth-century reformers had already articulated an ideology of social and educational reforms. It was left for the next generation to translate these ideas into practical reality. Shaikh Abdullah's ideas on the status of women in Islam and gender relations also echoed the views of these social and educational reformers, mostly associated with the Aligarh movement. However, in his autobiographical reminiscences compiled in the post-Independence India, Shaikh Abdullah sought to persuade his readers that providing modern education for Muslim women was uniquely his contribution.[26] He alleged that Syed Ahmad's thinking on this crucial issue was strictly traditional despite his thorough knowledge of Islam. He was overwhelmed with respect for traditions (*qadam parasti*) and adherence to customs (*riwaj parasti*). Abdullah further writes that Syed Ahmad was not in favour of modern education for women and he disapproved the very idea of opening modern Western-style colleges for them. Like a conservative, he supported traditional home education for women, and was also a firm supporter of *purdah*.[27] These are certainly Shaikh Abdullah's afterthoughts. It is also an oversimplification of Syed Ahmad's otherwise complex position.

Syed Ahmad voiced his fears that the condition of women was in need of attention. Women, he believed, were in need of reform and required improvement more than men. He pointed out that the problem with women lay in apparent lack of common sense and exercise of rational faculties. 'They indulge in frivolous customs and absurd practices in day-to-day affairs. Their respect for wrong customs and ill-informed practices spoil every occasion – be it marriage, birth, death, illness or any other social event. Gross ignorance and respect for baseless customs and traditions lay at the root of their irrational behaviour.'[28] Additionally, Syed Ahmad Khan also wrote powerful reformatory treatises in advocacy of widow remarriage reminiscent of his pre-1857 puritanical writings. He regarded the problem of widow remarriage a more serious issue than the publicized custom of child marriage. He sought to highlight the serious social implications which could and did arise from the neglect of this social problem. He took Swami Dayanand Saraswati to task that he should have taken up this perilous societal problem rather than preaching about theism.[29]

Syed Ahmad Khan also sought to highlight the legal rights of Muslim women.[30] He pointed out that Islam gave many rights and privileges to women whereas legal inequities against women existed even in a civilized nation like England. Like the British Utilitarian John Stuart Mill (1806-73), Syed Ahmad concluded that the legal position of the British women was no better than that of a slave.[31] He argued that if discrimination and injustice against women existed in the legal system of a civilized and progressive nation like Britain nothing more inequitable could be imagined.[32]

Furthermore, Syed Ahmad stressed the need to treat a woman as a companion and friend than as a servant. The reason for the existing low status of Muslim women was not the *Shariat* but the attitude of Muslim men who did not follow the teachings of Islam and denied the rights and privileges granted to women under the Islamic law.[33] Syed Ahmad Khan was acutely conscious that he had not been able to undertake any measures to provide modern education for women. The reformer confessed that the low socio-economic status of Muslims in general was a great impediment in formulation of any plan of female education. On the issue of *purdah* Syed Ahmad Khan wrote that a great amount of intellectual deliberations have gone into the question of the validity of *purdah* but all in vain. In his view the *purdah* as prescribed in the Islamic *Shariat* was the right mode of living. But the practice had become excessive in India. On the other hand, in the advanced societies of the West, it was on the other extreme.[34]

Sayyid Mumtaz Ali (1860-1935) was another prominent reformer whose radical interpretation of the status of women in Islam as espoused by him in his monograph on the rights of women titled, *Huquq un Niswan* and propagated through his weekly journal *Tahzib un Niswan*, powerfully informed the gender-perspectives of Shaikh Abdullah. The extra-exegetical and liberal interpretations of the Deoband *alim* on the status of women in Islam were the principle influences on his outlook. Abdullah considered this early champion of women's rights as 'an enlightened gentleman, a great supporter of female education'.[35]

Mumtaz Ali regarded female education as an issue of crucial importance. Whether women should be given education was no more a question of debate as there was acceptance that women should also be provided with similar formal education as their male counterparts. He underlined that knowledge was power, and women should not be deprived from it. The question which needed to be examined was what sort of knowledge should be imparted to them. In his opinion women should be provided the same education because God endowed them with the same intelligence and rational faculties as men. But the community needed to come forward with its own initiatives as otherwise it was simply impossible to subsist on government charity. He recommended the formulation of a uniform educational policy with a central organization and unitary command independent of the government. One of the essential requirements was the selection of books for the curriculum which should be recommended by a duly formed committee and availability of such books was a prerequisite before launching a programme of female education.[36] Yet, education was not always the criteria of happiness in a marriage. Willingness to adjust with the life partner was equally important. Mumtaz Ali, using his sociological acumen, cited the example of Shivnarain Agnihotri, the founder of Dev Samaj, who was no less than an ideal man in his exemplary treatment of his wife. He also recommended that the liberal and sympathetic attitude of the Arya Samaj leader towards women and a balanced approach towards gender relations was worth emulating for the Muslims too.[37]

Besides, there were other younger men at Aligarh who evinced genuine interest in the education of Muslim women. Most of them, being all members of the self-conscious Muslim intelligentsia, are described by Shaikh Abdullah also. Among these reformers and educationists he mentions the names of Sayyid Karamat Husain (1854-1917), Professor of Law at the college[38] and Khwaja Ghulam-us Saqlain (1870-1915), one of Aligarh's brightest stars in the field of Urdu journalism and founder of *Ikhwan us Safa* (Brothers of Purity). Both are described by Shaikh Abdullah as great sympathizers of the cause of women. The former was his teacher and the latter, whom he regarded as 'a true supporter of female education',[39] was a friend and hostel-mate.

Moreover, Shaikh Abdullah had enjoyed the rare privilege of close interaction with most of the great luminaries of the Aligarh movement. Abdullah had been associated with Sahibzada Aftab Ahmad Khan, secretary of the Sir Syed Memorial Fund and a leader of the Aligarh Old Boys Association, whom he considered 'a true promoter of female education'.[40] Shaikh specifically mentioned literary critic and historian Shibli Numani. Sheikh Abdullah wrote that Shibli through his moving speeches, delivered in his characteristic rhetoric eloquence, awakened his compatriots to the need for improvement in the condition of women.[41] Delhi-born historian and biographer Zaka Ullah (1832-1910)[42] and novelist and administrator Maulawi Nazir Ahmad Dehlavi (1830-1912),[43] were personal acquaintances of Shaikh Abdullah. Most of all, the ideas of the foremost poet and writer of Aligarh School, Khwaja Altaf Husain Hali (1837-1914), as propagated through his writings, exercised lasting influences on the contemporary thinking. Shaikh Abdullah recollected that his unparalleled poetry provided invaluable ideological sustenance to his mission. Most of all, the incomparable poetical composition of the poet-philosopher, *Chup ki dad*, proved as effective an instrument in bringing about a change in the attitudes and outlook of its listeners towards women as did his epic poem, the immortal *Musaddas*: *Madd-o-jazr-i-Islam* (*The Ebb and Flow of Islam*, 1879) on the entire weltanschauung of the Indo-Muslim community. Shaikh Abdullah claimed that the poignant verses of *Chup ki dad,* which almost revolutionized educated Muslims' attitude towards females and their sufferings, were composed by Hali on Shaikh Abdullah's personal request.[44]

Gender Perspective and Necessity for Reforms

British rule with its new concepts of progress and change was always in the backdrop of modernist concern with education of women. Abdullah believed that new knowledge was essential to meet the economic and political challenges of the twentieth century. He stressed the point that Western culture as manifested under the British rule represented inter-civilizational clash and therefore there was a compelling necessity for adjustment and accommodation with the new forces of social change. Modern educational institution had become essential to help adjust with the scientific and technical advances of the period.[45] The new scientific knowledge and technological inventions had redefined the very nature of cultural discourse. He felt that the Western civilization had different concepts of progress. It had also changed the pace of progress. He observed that the inventions like railways, telegraph, and the printing press had revolutionized the entire level of human action. What was earlier expected to be accomplished in hundreds of years, now with the help of modern techniques could be achieved within years.[46] In the preface of the first issue of the journal *Khatun*, Shaikh Abdullah reasoned thus:

> At present the Indian society had undergone a complete social transformation which amounts to a revolution. These changes in thought, outlook, and beliefs under the colonial regime had no parallel in the previous history of India. . . . Evidently Turkish sultans, the Khaljis, and Tughlaqs as well as their successor the Mughals professed Islamic faith. It seems, as if the present Hindustan is no more the same country. Even the earth and heavens had changed.[47]

In conformity with the reformers of the Aligarh movement, Shaikh Abdullah also maintained illiteracy and ignorance among women as a factor of backwardness of Muslims. The roots of backwardness among Muslims could be traced from the early decades of the eighteenth century, when loss of political power accompanied socio-cultural decline. The establishment of British rule hastened the decline further. Political decline was accompanied by the socio-economic deprivation of Muslims which manifested in the intellectual stagnation of the community. During the period of decay, Muslims denied their women the right to seek knowledge, an attitude contrary to the spirit of Prophetic traditions. Foreign domination further precipitated this irreversible process of the plight of the community. Like Hali, Abdullah also pointed out the relativity of decline and progress – that progress in one epoch can become decline in another. This theme of decline, in the view of Abdullah, had been poignantly depicted in the poetry of Hali. He cited the famous *Musaddas*, the poetical masterpiece of the poet: 'If anyone sees the way our downfall passes all bounds, the way that Islam, once fallen, does not rise again, he will never believe that the tide flows after every ebb, once he sees the way our sea has gone out.'[48]

But, instead of glorification of Muslim achievements, Abdullah pointed out that Muslims made no effort to reverse the decline. Lack of initiative on the part of Muslims to improve their lot was a big stumbling block in their progress. Abdullah sought to impress upon his community that Indian Muslims must realize that education was absolutely essential in the times of rapidly changing social and cultural milieu. The acquisition of knowledge on modern scientific lines was the only effective means to save the Muslims from further degeneration and socio-economic decline. Education was also a powerful antidote against all social evils born out of ignorance. For a better future, like the *ulama*, Abdullah also urged Muslims to take recourse to the path of self-help and self-determination. He reiterated that self-help was the key to individual and national progress, as in his view, individual progress and social advancement were the outcomes of individual efforts. Abdullah quoted Quranic *ayats* to support his viewpoint: 'Verily never will Allah change the condition of a people until they change what is in themselves' (Holy Quran, S. 13: 11); and the second verse, 'That man can have nothing but what he strives for' (Holy Quran S. 53: 39).[49]

Shaikh Abdullah was also aware of European critique of the status of women in Islam. One of the earliest pieces of his writing is a review article of an early English feminist writer, Lucy Garnett's book, *The Women of Turkey and Their Folk-lore* (1890). The article was published in *Mohammedan Anglo-Oriental College Magazine.* In this he commented upon Garnett's appreciation of the legal rights of women granted under the Islamic law and also her observations on *purdah* as practised in Turkey.[50] Abdullah also noted various developments in favour of women in other countries, Eastern and Western, and appreciated that women were now being educated in other Islamic countries to the benefit of their religion and country. He specifically noted developments in female education in Turkey, Egypt, Russia, China and the Central Asian *khanates* of Khiva and Bukhara. In Egypt, he noted that women had founded their own associations and a number of journals were edited by them.[51] He frequently cited the example of Turkey to awaken his fellow Muslims to the urgency of educating women. The Turks, explained Abdullah, who were looked down and denigrated as the 'sick man of Europe', had succeeded in achieving 100 per cent female literacy rate. Like the (female) companions (*sahabiyat*) of the Holy Prophet, Turkish women participated in nation building. They were equal partners in every walk of life. Compared to Turkey, the situation in India was quite disappointing, where hardly two out of 100 women were able to read and write.[52]

In an editorial of *Khatun* he noted that in Europe the question of freedom and equality of women had emerged as an important issue of debate along with the right to education. In the late eighteenth century, the French Revolution (1789) gave impetus to the notions of equality and liberty and gradually women in England and France claimed equal political right. The origins of the notions of liberty and equality could be traced to the process of waning of feudalism. However, amongst the Asian nations too, Chinese women had put forth their claims for political rights. In the case of Indian Muslim women, the issue was confined to education, as the Indian women had yet to emerge out of the prevailing state of ignorance.[53] Again in 1930, about two decades later, in an article published in *Tahzib un Niswan*, he explained the meaning of freedom of women. He pointed out that the idea should not be equated with immodesty. It meant 'that equality (*masawat*) between the two, men and women, should be maintained. Women should be granted their natural rights (*qudrati huquq*). Men should not be allowed to exercise unrestrained authority over them.'[54]

Abdullah noted with deep regret that in India not only the Muslim women but females in general suffered disproportionately from illiteracy: if comparative literacy between men and women was taken as an index of education, women lagged far behind. By quoting the official educational statistics, Abdullah observed that there were hardly two educated females out of 100 which meant only 2 per cent of the female population were able to read and write. Later in 1933, in an address to the Women's Section he wrote that out of 1,000 women there were only 12 literate women among the Muslims.[55] Among the Hindus also, Abdullah noticed, the female higher education had so far remained the preserve of a few only.[56] Nevertheless, he optimistically looked forward to a day when at least 75 per cent female literacy would be achieved in India.[57]

The traditional reformers and the Westernizing elite both viewed women as central to the family; therefore their dignity and honoured roles were seen as essential for the preservation of family and also its improvement. Both stressed that women bore the responsibility for the welfare of family and they were transmitters of values to the future generations. An illiterate mother was unable to give adequate guidance to her children. Therefore, one of the purposes of educating the women was that they would become better wives, better mothers and skilled home-makers. Shaikh Abdullah sought to persuade his readers in similar reformists refrain that the Muslim community cannot progress until the mothers of future generation were properly enlightened. An educated woman would prove to be a better mother who would raise her children healthy, disciplined, and as good citizens of the nation. He emphasized that mothers played crucial role in the character building of their children. Abdullah reiterated that mother is the first teacher of the child and what she teaches the child influenced the whole course of his/her life and thereby the cumulative life of the whole community. Consequently, her own education was of paramount importance.[58]

Shaikh Abdullah firmly held that Islam gave many rights to women but these have not been realized because Muslims have not followed the teaching of the Prophet in recognizing the need for women to be educated. Without education women would not know the rights granted to them under the Islamic law. Therefore, by educating their girls Muslims will be rendering a great service both to their community and the nation. Furthermore, Abdullah acted upon his firmly-held conviction that in Islam, acquisition of knowledge was an essential obligation (*farz*) of every believing Muslim man and woman. Therefore, by educating their children, sons as well as daughters, Muslims would be fulfilling their religious obligations.

Unlike his teacher Karamat Husain, and almost like Mumtaz Ali and Ashraf Ali Thanawi (d.1943), the Deoband *alims*, Abdullah advocated similar curriculum for boys and girls. This stemmed from his firm conviction of intellectual equality between the two sexes. It was an egalitarian assumption based upon Islamic principles and women were considered capable of entertaining higher realms of thought. He remarked:

> We hold such people in contempt who argue that there was absolutely no necessity to impart women with the knowledge of subjects like history, geography, literature, logic, philosophy, mathematics and natural sciences. Quite opposite to this view, women needed to study these subjects even more because compared to men they had little opportunity to experience and observe the world. Why to deprive them even from bookish knowledge?[59]

Abdullah firmly believed that there was no inherent difference in the intellectual capacities of the two, and scientific experiments had also proved that both possessed the same intelligence and emotional quotient. In spite of different biological functions, he contested, the intellectual superiority of men had in no way been proven. On the contrary, experience had shown that girls if given the chance were more diligent students than boys. If women lagged behind men in every field of life, that lack of achievement was not due to any inherent weakness, rather due to the obvious fact that the women so far had been denied equal opportunities to develop their potentialities. The distinctions between men and women that are justified on religious grounds was the reflection of customary attitudes. The present state of the lack of knowledge and experience among women was a product of social conditions and not an inherent defect.[60]

Shaikh Abdullah sought to emphasize that education for women was essential from the point of view of religion also. He maintained that education and religion were twins, and both were complementary to each other. He contended that those who regarded religion and knowledge as antagonistic could enjoy neither the blessings of religion nor the benefits which knowledge bestow upon its seekers. As a critic he raised the question as to how the knowledge of natural and physical sciences could be detrimental to the cause of religion.[61] On the other hand, an ignorant and uninformed woman would not be able to discover the true essence of religion. Without knowledge he/she would be groping in darkness, as the poet-moralist Shaikh Sadi so aptly said: *be ilm na twan khuda ra shanakht.*[62]

Abdullah believed that good education would promote human virtues among women. Without mentioning the Greek philosophers Socrates and Plato, he said that education would enhance self-consciousness/knowledge of self (*ahsas-i-zat khud*). 'Know Thyself' or the capacity for or habit of self-examination and self-criticism was a vital source for individual and national progress, because self-awareness and retrospection, would make every human being (male or female) conscious of her/his natural and inherent potentialities. This self-recognition of one's assets would stimulate greater level of activities, which in turn, would lead to individual progress and advancement.[63] Education would promote use of intellect (*aql*), one of the fundamental requisites for technological advancement and social development. Intellect or use of reason shows the way in every human activity in both temporal and spiritual matters. Exercise of one's mental faculties is *de rigueur* in every human affair including religion. This is a quality which distinguished human beings from the other components of nature; though composed of the same matter, it is only the human beings who are endowed with unique intellectual powers.[64]

Women and Public Sphere

Unlike the earlier reformers Shaikh Abdullah envisioned integration of women in the public sphere. Conscious of the women's suffrage and emancipatory moves in the country (such as the Government of India Act of 1935 which granted women limited franchise in provincial and federal assemblies), Shaikh Abdullah held that women should also participate in national politics. He encouraged college graduates to contest for seats in the representative councils, and called upon them to develop their speaking skills to articulate their views on issues of concern for the community in the representative assemblies, such as the Legislative Council of India.[65] On the occasion of the silver jubilee celebrations of the college, Abdullah advised educated women to carve out respectable positions for themselves in the public spheres:

> I would like to convey the message to the young ladies and girls of this nation that it is now the time that they should be ready to shoulder the enormous responsibilities of carrying forward the torch of progress and advancement. I would like to foretell them the good news that if they would be prepared for self-help, no power, no authority would be able to deprive them from their rights. They would be equal partners in the heritage of their motherland (*madar-i-Hind*). They would be entitled to their shares in the property inheritance, and they would be co-sharers in the government services. They would be able to claim their share in all those positions which had been the exclusive prerogative of men.[66]

In the view of Shaikh Abdullah, an educated woman should enter all those professions which would suit her qualifications and aptitude. In his opinion women possessed remarkable skills for what we now call the 'caring sector' and medicine and teaching could be the ideal professions for them. Educated women could also choose all those services and professions which had been the preserve of men. They could also learn arts and crafts. But above all, education would make them better human beings:

> Would it be not an aim worth achieving? Education holds its forte in creating skilled professionals but prime importance of education is to open the gateways of a civilized society composed of compassionate, rational, and humane individuals who have the ability to lend a responsible hand in the development of both religion and society.[67]

Reflections

Shaikh Abdullah's life and activities as a social reformer symbolized the emergence of an English-educated Muslim colonial elite who had to face the ideological and institutional challenges of colonialism and nationalism. In the event of confrontation with the new forces of change, this group had to redefine its cultural identity and to restructure the social position of its women. The process of intellectual influence is a complex one, but some trends are identifiable. The broad-spectrum presentation of Abdullah's writings shows the complex interplay of the contemporary socio-intellectual streams in the elite's approach to many problems of female education and other related issues. Above all, Shaikh Abdullah echoed a number of themes articulated by the nineteenth-century social reformers and religious thinkers, modernists as well as the traditional ideologues. Most of his ideas sound familiar because many of these themes were espoused by the Muslim educational and social reformers associated with the Aligarh Movement.

Unquestionably, the nature and terms of the debates are greatly enlarged and expanded with focus on education in the discourses of Shaikh Abdullah. He also seems unique in his concentration on the issue of formal education of women and in his idea of considering education as an efficacious route to the advancement of the country. He viewed education as an essential prerequisite for preparing women for their duties towards their families and nation. He saw modern (*jadid*) education as a powerful means to equip women with intellectual autonomy. He argued and rightly so, that if educated, women would be able to assert their rights and prerogatives, and it will not be easy to deprive them.

Shaikh Abdullah showed greater awareness of the outside world as compared to his predecessors. His world was much vaster as well as complex in terms of time and space. He was well informed of the burgeoning international women's movements, such as the demands for civil rights, right of suffrage and right to work as autonomous moral beings in the European nations. He was able to comprehend the developments and progress of women's issues directly from the sources such as English newspapers, magazines as well as through direct contact with the heavily anglicized atmosphere of colonial Aligarh. His discourses were well informed by the seminal ideas and concepts of nineteenth-century social evolution, progress and civilization, as shown in his emphasis on equality between the sexes and equality of opportunity. Abdullah's Western education enabled him to have access to the sources of Western social thought and provide a comparative perspective with the West. He could not devise a way to assimilate these ideas within the Islamic framework. Abdullah referred to similar movements of women's emancipation in China and Japan. But in his own case he was careful to point out that he was seeking to provide an Islamic model. He sought to underline the fact that his reformed woman was not an imitation of the West. Rather it was an Islamic view of women, with their rights and duties towards family and society that he upheld. Additionally, he also asserted that the social reforms in Turkey, Egypt and Central Asia, the models he invoked, were also not the outcome of the Western impact; rather the social reforms in these countries were based on Quranic injunctions and *ahadith*.[68]

Shaikh Abdullah imbibed the ideas of reform and modern education for women from the pioneers of the historic Aligarh movement, yet, what distinguished him from the older generation of social reformers was his successful 'appropriation' of these powerful ideas. He transformed pure intellectual debates into practical reality. In the process of 'appropriation', he disseminated these views as his own. He sought to evolve no theoretical construct. He was a practical visionary, being more of an educator than a political theorist who had pragmatic approach to the emerging problem. He argued for progressive gender relations based on extra-exegetical and liberal interpretation of Islamic law.

Shaikh Abdullah's ideas are far from being a systematic exposition of the status of women in Islam, her legal rights and obligations. In his exposition there are obvious dichotomies too. Perhaps his discourses could be identified as the writings of a public spirited person. An amalgam of various strands of contemporary thoughts and strategies reverberated in his ideas on the status of Indian Muslim women. It is not an easy task to categorize his writings under any single rubric such as the Eastern/Western, Islamic/secular. He followed 'pick and choose' from various cultural traditions, what has been termed as the acculturative and transitional models of reform. Various trends described under the abstract concepts of traditionist, modernist, secular and fundamentalist are discernible in his varied discourses on gender relations. It is a modernist discourse if Islamic modernism means re-examining Islam in terms of contemporary realities. He also represented Islamic feminism if the term is equated with progress, emancipation and empowerment of women through education.

Continuous engagement with the question of compatibility between Islam and modernity is a prominent feature of Shaikh Abdullah's reformist thought and activities. Shaikh Abdullah represented the progressive and forward-looking world of Aligarh intelligentsia in its British imperial setting. His discourses embodied new idioms of public discourse and activity reflective of the social ambience of twentieth-century Aligarh. His discourses are infused with colonial Aligarh's ideal of dutiful service to the Muslim community, the hallmark of the Aligarh Movement. Moreover, he also consciously sought to emphasize the importance of self-renewal and refashioning, which the age of modernity seems to demand for survival. He presented a male vision of ideal Islamic womanhood. His writings represent the emergence of a new trend of a publicist and activist who sought to carve out for women a public sphere without denying them their traditional place in the realm of domesticity. He sincerely sought to produce a new woman of substance who was literate and educated, and for whom education and gainful employment were respectable undertakings.

In Abdullah's view education was not meant for broad intellectual training alone, it was also aimed at raising the social and economic status of women. In his advocacy of equal employment opportunities for women as that of their male counterparts, Abdullah's thinking is clearly revolutionary. He showed radical departure from all previous Muslim reformers who believed that women should be educated because, as wives, educated women would be better companions of their husbands, and as mothers they would be able to provide proper guidance and training to their children. Empowerment of women with literacy and their integration into public life remains a unique contribution of Shaikh Abdullah to the Islamic feminist thought.

More than the Western and South-East Asian paradigm, in his advocacy of rights of women, there are parallels and contrasts with those of the Arab Muslim reformers of the liberal age, such as Qasim Amin (1865-1908), the French educated Egyptian disciple of Muhammad Abduh (1849-1905), and Muhammad Rashid Riza (1865-1935).[69] And yet his avant-garde discourses reveal deep imprints of a vibrant intellectual environment which was unique in its own right for it was in the pluralistic discursive context of India that the modern Islamic feminism emerged.[70] Direct comparison with the social reform movements in other parts of India, more specifically with the province of Bengal, and explicit references to the Arya Samaj leader Dayanand Saraswati (1824-83) and Shivnarayan Agnihotri of Lahore show that these social movements were not taking place in isolation and social reformers and thinkers were aware of each other's reformist agendas and rhetorics. Similarly, Shaikh Abdullah often referred to the positive attitude of the upper and middle class Hindus towards education and modernization under the British rule. The achievements of the other Indian communities were always present in his thoughts, not as an antithesis but as a productive element. On the other hand, his criticism of the legal status of women in Hindu society echoed the familiar British criticism of widow remarriage and the much publicized practice of *sati*.

Finally, like the traditional religious elite, Shaikh Abdullah also grounded his arguments in the Holy Quran and *ahadith*, the sayings and practices of the Prophet, the sources of Islamic law. He sought recourse to the Islamic law because it is always through the application of Islamic law that change has been effected in Islamic societies. A reinterpretation of law proved to be the most effective agent in moulding the social order and community life of Muslims. Abdullah also acted upon his firmly held notion that education was the most effective instrument for social change and economic development. His concern for *Shariat* could also be explained as an attempt to place his views in the context of religion and morality. He exhorted Muslim brothers to restore the same equal rights to women granted to them under the auspices of their faith. The reason of his appeal to the moral conscience of Muslims was due to the realization of the fact that what Islam granted to women was denied by man and society in practice. Hence his pleas that men and educated society should change their attitude towards women and recognize their right as equal human beings.

NOTES

1. Gulfishan Khan, 'Shaikh Muhammad Abdullah: The Founder Speaks', *Aligarh Muslim University Gazette*, vol. 43, no. 12, December 2006. Also see Gail Minault, 'Shaikh Abdullah, Begam Abdullah, and Sharif

Education for Girls at Aligarh', in Imtiaz Ahmad (ed.), *Modernisation and Social Change Among Muslims in India*, New Delhi: Manohar, 1983, pp. 207-36.

2. Shaikh Abdullah, *Sawanih-i-Umari-i-Abdullah Begum* (*Autobiography of Abdullah Begum*), Delhi: Koh-i-Nur Press, 1954, pp. 20-52.
3. David Lelyveld, *Aligarh's First Generation: Muslim Solidarity in British India,* Princeton: Princeton University Press, 1978.
4. Initially, under the influence of Maulawi Hakim Nuruddin, successor of Maulawi Ghulam Ahmad Qadiyan, he accepted Qadiyanism. But later in Aligarh, he embraced mainstream Sunni faith. See, Shamsur Rahman Muhsini, *Hayat-i-Abdullah*, Aligarh: Female Education Association, 1982, pp. 19-26.
5. Theodore Morison was Professor of English (1889-99) and Principal of the M.A.O. College (1899-1905) and author of one of the earliest histories of the college he served. Safi Ahmad Kakorawi (ed.), *Morison's History of Mohammadan Anglo-Oriental College*, Aligarh: Sir Syed Academy, Aligarh, 1988.
6. T.W. Arnold, *The Preaching of Islam: A History of the Propagation of the Muslim Faith*, 1913.
7. J.C. Chakravarty was Professor of Mathematics from 1883 up to his retirement in 1916. For Morison's views about his dedicated services to the college, see, Safi Ahmad Kakorawi (ed.), *Morison's History of Mohammadan Anglo-Oriental College*, p. 27.
8. For Maulana Abbas Husain, ibid., pp. 66, 81, 93.
9. For the staff and academic atmosphere of the college, see David Lelyveld, *Aligarh's First Generation: Muslim Solidarity in British India*, pp. 186-203.
10. Shaikh Muhammad Abdullah, *Mushahidat wa Taasurat* (*Observations and Experiences*), Delhi: Jamal Printing Press, 1969, pp. 2-107. Written in the post-Independence India, when the author was more than seventy years of age, it contains a rich wealth of information.
11. Ibid.
12. Gulfishan Khan, 'Shaikh Muhammad Abdullah (1874-1965): Interpreting the Indian National Movement "A Nationalist Discourse",' presented at the Indian History Congress: The Sixty-Eighth Session, Delhi, 2008.
13. For a powerful exposition of these ideas of Shaikh Abdullah, *Islam mein Aurat ka Darja* (*Status of Women in Islam*), Aligarh: Khidmat Press, n.d., Shaikh Abdullah, *Apeel banam Musalmanan i-Hind* (*An Appeal to the Muslims of India*), Aligarh: Aligarh Muslim University Press, n.d.
14. Shaikh Muhammad Abdullah, *Mushahidat wa Taasurat*. Also see, Lubna Kazim (ed.), *A Woman of Substance: The Memoirs of Begum*

Khurshid Mirza (1918-1989), Delhi: Zubaan, 2005, pp. 20-43.

15. Gail Minault, 'Women's Magazines in Urdu as Sources for Muslim Social History', *Indian Journal of Gender Studies*, 5: 2, 1998, pp. 201-13. More recently some of the rare writings of Shaikh have been published. M. Nadeem and Muhammad Qasim Siddiqui (eds.), *Intikhab-i mazamin Shaikh Muhammad Abdullah*, 2 vols., Aligarh: Female Education Association, 2004, 2007.
16. *Khatun*, vol. 8, no. 9, September 1912.
17. Gail Minault (ed.), *The Extended Family Women and Political Participation in India and Pakistan*, Delhi: Chanakya Publications, 1981, pp. 83-108.
18. Shaikh Abdullah, 'All India Muslim Ladies Conference se Khitab', in Janab Nafees Dulhan Sahiba (ed.), *Report Ijlas Yazdaham All India Muslim Ladies Conference Maqam Hyderabad Dakan,* Hyderabad: Shamsul Islam Press, 1929. The same was published in *Tahzib un-niswan*, dated 11 and 18 May 1929.
19. Shaikh Muhammad Abdullah, 'Wirasat niswan ka am riwaj suba Punjab mein' (Practice of the Female inheritance in the Punjab), *Tahzib un niswan*, 8 June 1929, pp. 537-40; Gail Minault, *Secluded Scholars: Women's Education and Social Reform in Colonial India*, New Delhi: Oxford University Press, 1998, pp. 283-307.
20. Ruler of the princely state of Bhopal was an ardent supporter of the cause of female education and a patroness of the institution. For a biography of Sultan Jahan Begum see Siobhan Lambert-Hurley, *Muslim Women Reform and Princely Patronage: Nawab Sultan Jahan Begum of Bhopal*, London: Routledge, 2007.
21. For the conceptual framework for socio-religious movements, Kenneth W. Jones, *The New Cambridge History of India III. 1 Socio-Religious Reform Movements in British India,* Cambridge: Cambridge University Press, 1989, pp. 1-14.
22. Barbara D. Metcalf, 'Reading and Writing about Muslim Women in British India', in Barbara D. Metcalf (ed.), *Islamic Contestations: Essays on Muslims in India and Pakistan*, New Delhi: Oxford University Press, 2004, pp. 99-119.
23. Shaikh Muhammad Abdullah, 'Muslim Girls' Kalej Aligarh ke Mukhtasar Tarikhi Halat' (A Brief History of Aligarh Women's College), *Tahzib un niswan*, 28 November, pp. 1142-7, and 12 December 1936, pp. 1199-1203.
24. Barbara D. Metcalf, 'The Making of a Muslim Lady: Maulana Thanawi's Bihishti Zewar', in Milton Israel and N.K. Wagle (eds.), *Islamic Culture and Society: Essays in Honour of Professor Aziz Ahmad*, New Delhi: Manohar, 1983, pp. 17-38.
25. Shaikh Abdullah, 'Muslim Girls Kalej', op. cit., p. 48.

26. Shaikh Abdullah, *Mushahidat*, section entitled '*Tahrik talim niswan*', pp. 198-210.
27. *Sawanih*, p. 16. To prove his assertion Shaikh Abdullah quoted Syed Ahmad's speech delivered at Lahore in 1884 in response to an address presented to him by the women of Punjab. For the text of the speech see, Mohammad Sirajuddin (ed.), *Honourable Sir Sayyid Ahmad Khan Bahadur ke Lekcharon ka Majmua*, Lahore: Islamiya Press, 1890, pp. 178-81. This address is reproduced in his autobiography. See, *Mushahidat,* pp. 199, 205-8.
28. He sought to illustrate his point by citing example of various age-old practices generally associated with child birth. See, Sir Syed Ahmad Khan, 'Hindustan Mein Auraton ke Halat,' in Maulana Ismail Panipati (ed.), *Maqalat-i-Sir Sayyid, Nayab Rasail wa Mazamin*, Lahore: Majlis i-taraqqi-i-adab, 1962, vol. V, pp. 188-93.
29. Syed Ahmad Khan, 'Bewa auraton ka nikah na karne mein kya fasad hai', 'Bewa auraton ka nikah na karne ka natija', in ibid., vol. V, pp. 200-8.
30. Syed Ahmad Khan, 'Auraton ke Huquq', in ibid., vol. V, pp. 198-9.
31. Ibid., pp. 194-6. For Syed Ahmad Khan's close interaction with the Delhi College refer to Gulfishan Khan, 'Sayyid Ahmad Khan: Some Early Influences', in Abdul Ali and S. Ahsan (eds.), *Contribution of Sir Syed Ahmad Khan to Islamic Studies*, Aligarh: Institute of Islamic Studies, Aligarh Muslim University, 2005, pp. 43-61.
32. Syed Ahmad Khan, 'Auraton ke Huquq', in Maulana Ismail Panipati (ed.), *Maqalat-i-Sir Sayyid, Nayab rasail wa mazamin*, vol. V, pp. 198-9.
33. Ibid., pp. 194-9.
34. See, Syed Ahmad Khan, 'Purdha', in Maulana Ismail Panipati (ed.), *Maqalat-i-Sir Sayyid, Nayab rasail wa mazamin*, vol. V, pp. 186-7.
35. 'Muslim Girls Kalej', p. 24; *Mushahidat*, p. 205; Gail Minault, 'Sayyid Mumtaz Ali, and "*Huquq un-Niswan*": An Advocate of Women's Rights in Islam in the Late Nineteenth Century', *Modern Asian Studies*, 24, I (February 1990), pp. 147-72.
36. The books read by women and listed by Mumtaz Ali were: 'For prose: Rah-i-najat, Bad hamd, Subh ka sitara, Miftah al-Jannat, qayamat nama, Hazari masala, Tuhfat al-zaujain, Khair al-najat, Maulud sharif, Dah makhzan, Taqrir-shahdatain, Tarjuma mishkat. For poetry: Kanz al-musalla, Risala benamazan, Wafatnama, Nasihatnama, Bist masail mushtamal bar Miraj nama, Lorinama, Qissa dai Halima, Qissa Bilal, Nur nama, etc. Besides Qissa Shah Rum, Qissa Shah Yaman, Qissa Ahl-i-Bayt, Diwan-i-Lutf, Tafsir Sura Yusuf, Masnawi Gulzar-i-nasim. Other books of Urdu read by women were Gul-i-bakawali, Badr-i-Munir and Qissa Chahar Darwesh.'

37. *Huquq un niswan*, pp. 143-4.
38. See section Yad-i-raftgan, in 'Muslim Girls Kalej', pp. 19-30. Karamat Husain served as Professor of Law in the Aligarh College from 1891 to 1895. See David Lelyveld, *Aligarh's First Generation: Muslim Solidarity in British India,* pp. 192-3; *Sawanih* p. 16; Hamid Ali Khan, *Hayat-i Maulana Karamat Husain*, Lucknow: Al-Nazir Press, n.d.; Gail Minault, 'Sayyid Karamat Husain, and Education for Women', in V. Graff (ed.), *Lucknow Through the Ages*, New Delhi: Oxford University Press, 1997, pp. 155-64.
39. 'Muslim Girls Kalej', p. 22; also see, *Mushahidat*, p. 205. Two other prominent figures mentioned by name as supporters of female education by Shaikh are Sayyid Amir Ali, judge High Court, and Badruddin Tayyibji, judge, Bombay High Court. See, *Sawanih*, p. 16.
40. 'Muslim Girls Kalej', p. 23; *Mushahidat*, p. 205. On his career, see, David Lelyveld, 'Three Aligarh Students: Aftab Ahmad Khan, Ziauddin Ahmad, and Muhammad Ali', *Modern Asian Studies*, 9, 2, April 1975, pp. 103-16.
41. 'Muslim Girls Kalej', pp. 21-2.
42. Shaikh Abdullah, 'Zakaullah Obituary', *Khatun*, December 1910; Mushirul Hasan, *A Moral Reckoning: Muslim Intellectuals in Nineteenth Century Delhi*, New Delhi: Oxford University Press, 2005, pp. 185-235.
43. Shaikh Abdullah, 'Nazir Ahmad', *Khatun*, August 1912, Also see, *Moral Reckoning*, op. cit., pp. 132 84. For a latest appreciation of Nazir Ahmad as one of the great Muslim thinkers of the nineteenth century see Christina Oesterheld, 'Deputy Nazir Ahmad and the Delhi College', in Margrit Pernau (ed.), *The Delhi College, Traditional Elites, the Colonial State, and Education before 1857*, New Delhi: Oxford University Press, 2006, pp. 298-324.
44. 'Muslim Girls Kalej', pp. 5, 20-21. In his verse such as the *Chup ki dad* (1905) Hali tried to awaken the conscience of his patriots to the pathos and tragedy of womankind in India. Hali's *Majalis un nisa* and his poem *Chup ki dad* has been translated into English by Gail Minault and published as *Voices of Silence,* Delhi: Chanakya Publishers, 1986. For reception of Musaddas in the contemporary educated elite see, Christopher Shackle and Javed Majeed, *Hali's Musaddas: The Flow and Ebb of Islam*, New Delhi: Oxford University Press, 1997, pp. 37-8.
45. *Apeel*, p. 5.
46 *Mushahidat*, p. 217.
47. Ibid., p. 216.
48. *Apeel*, p. 2. For the text and translation see, Shackle and Majeed, *Hali's Musaddas: The Flow and Ebb of Islam*, pp. 13, 102-3.
49. *Apeel*, pp. 11-12; Also see, Shaikh Abdullah, '*Usul wa tanzeem jamiat al-ahbab*', Aligarh: Muslim University Press, 1941, pp. 14-15, and

Shaikh Abdullah, 'Progress Dependent Upon Hard Work', *Raz-i-taraqqui*, September 1946. .

50. Shaikh Abdullah, 'Turkey ki auratein' (Women of Turkey), *Mohammedan Anglo-Oriental College Magazine*, vol. 3, no. 3, 1 March 1896, Aligarh: Aligarh Institute Press, pp. 137-45. Lucy Mary Jane Garnett (1849-1934), was an English folklorist, writer and traveller and author of *The Women of Turkey and Their Folklore* (1890).
51. Shaikh Abdullah, 'Dusre mamalik mein talim-i niswan', *Khatun* January 1908.
52. *Apeel*, pp. 5-6.
53. Shaikh Abdullah, Azadi-i niswan, Editorial, *Khatun*, vol. 8, no. 3, March 1912, pp. 45-7.
54. Shaikh Abdullah, 'Auraton ki azadi', *Tahzeeb un niswan*, 24 July 1930.
55. *Intikhab-i-mazamin*, vol. 2, p. 25.
56. *Talim-i-niswan wa huquq-i-niswan*, op. cit., and also see, *Islam mein aurat ka darja*, p. 8.
57. *Apeel*, p. 6.
58. For a clear exposition of role of women in family life see, *Islam mein aurat ka darja*, pp. 18-19, Also see his remarks in *Mushahidat*, p. 48.
59. Shaikh Abdullah, *Khatun*, vol. 6, no. 8, August 1909.
60. Shaikh Abdullah, 'Talim i-niswan wa huquq i-niswan' (Education of Women and Rights of Women), An address delivered to the Provincial Educational Conference held at Badaun in March 1924, The same was published in *Tahzib un niswan*, dated 12-19 April 1924; 'Muslim Girls Kalej', pp. 35-6.
61. 'Muslim Girls Kalej', pp. 33-4.
62. *Islam mein aurat ka darja,* p. 17.
63. 'Muslim Girls Kalej', p. 31.
64. Ibid., p. 32, *Islam mein aurat ka darja*, p. 18.
65. 'Muslim Girls Kalej', pp. 17-18. Talim-i-niswan wa huquq-i-niswan, *Tahzib un niswan*, 12, 19, April 1924.
66. 'Muslim Girls Kalej', p. 3.
67. Ibid., pp. 36-8.
68. *Talim i niswan wa huquq-i-niswan*, op. cit.
69. Albert Habib Hourani, *Arabic Thought in the Liberal Age, 1789-1931*, Cambridge: Cambridge University Press, 1988, pp. 164-9, 239, 350.
70. Mansoor Moaddel, 'Religion and Women: Islamic Modernism versus Fundamentalism', *Journal for the Scientific Study of Religion*, vol. 37, no. 1 March 1998, pp. 108-30.

CHAPTER 14

Training Maternity and Child Welfare Professionals

Demands and Constraints in the Early Twentieth-century India

CH. RADHA GAYATHRI

Every society expects women to go through the process of child birth and society considers it a duty to find ways and means to minimize the risk entailed in such a process. The risks involved in child birth were so high that a woman surviving the process was considered to be blessed with a 'second life'. Every possible endeavour was made to lessen the mortality of the mother during child birth. India has even today the dubious distinction of having one of the highest maternal mortality rates in the world, estimated to be as high as 407 maternal deaths per 1,00,000 live births, about four times higher than the National Population Policy (NPP) 2010 goal of 100 per 1,00,000 live births. Even a century ago the scenario was almost the same. The present paper is an attempt at understanding the medical education opportunities available in India (focusing on north India) for women who were involved in running the Maternity and Child Welfare (MCW) centres, which were established with the specific goal of reducing maternal and infant mortality.

This paper probes into how the training institutes of the MCW professionals, i.e. health visitors, had to struggle at every stage right from inception for their survival. The process of establishment of the MCW section at the All India Institute of Hygiene and Public Health (AIIHPH) at Calcutta and Lady Reading Health School at Delhi stand testimony to this fact. Besides these two institutional histories, postgraduate training opportunities and research done on women-specific diseases are also briefly gauged. Before studying these institutes, it becomes imperative to briefly understand the gravity of the problem of maternal mortality and the MCW movement in India for understanding the significant role of these great institutes.

Losing Mothers

There were no reliable statistics yet it was estimated that while the births in India in 1921 were 77,74,776, maternal mortality was 1,08,852, i.e. 14 deaths per 1,000 births.

> A country which has met with signal success in combating the general and the infant death rate, which has spent money freely and has passed several enactments for the greater protection of women in child birth, has yet done little to reduce the maternal mortality. What hope then can there be for India, where every distressing condition endured by mothers in England is magnified a hundred fold?[1]

Often the detailed figures of the maternal death rates collected from the provinces were not accurate, and those of the rural areas were quite incomplete. It was noted by the Public Health Commissioner in his report that,

> They are incomplete as they stand, but serve to indicate the volume of work which is now being done in this department, the increase of its ramifications and the enormous field yet to be overtaken. The movement is in its infancy in India, but the conditions crying for amelioration are only too potent to all; and the tedious reiterations of statistics many of which are inaccurate serves all the more to focus on these urgent problems the attention of all who think.[2]

Very slow progress was made in reducing the maternal mortality rate and the status continued unaltered year after year. By 1936 the number of women dying during child birth every year was nearly 1.5 lakh and this figure further inflated with the inclusion of the deaths due to abortion. While an epidemic disease assuming these proportions demanded and received attention from local authorities, health departments and the public too, the deaths of women from preventable causes did not receive the same attention. The explanation may be partly that the facts were not known sufficiently, partly because mortality from child-bearing does not occur in epidemic form, but it must also be due to the too commonly held view that it is inevitable that some women must die during child birth. 'Some women' in each area naturally become thousands when applied to the whole of India.[3]

MCW Movement in India

By the turn of the century there was a paradigm shift in the understanding of maternal and child health.[4] Post-First World War phase saw maternity and child welfare care gaining great attention so much so that it became a movement. 'In the 1920s, the discourse on child birth and health took place against a changed political background. Motherhood and fertility were no longer condescendingly regarded as predominantly moral issues but as social problems linked with women's health and living conditions.'[5] Antenatal supervision of the expectant mothers, skilled assistance at child birth, institutionalized medical facilities wherever necessary and post-natal care of the mothers were the aspects addressed in the MCW movement to curtail the high maternal mortality rate.

A two-pronged approach of preventive and curative care was undertaken to tackle maternal mortality. While curative care included providing medical infrastructure like the opening up of exclusive women's wards in hospitals and dispensaries, establishing women's hospitals, training and recruiting women medical professionals, and so on, preventive care was far more comprehensive. It included long-term plans like ways and means of pushing back the age of motherhood to a suitable period when a woman is more capable of easily bearing a child, providing adequate nourishment for the expectant mother, extending adequate medical aid for the expectant mother, limiting the number of children, opening MCW centres and so on. Of these, emphasis was on the antenatal work as it was considered the single best measure that would produce the maximum benefit to the expectant mother and MCW centres became the most successful maternal health care units.

Dufferin Fund Committee was established in 1885 to supply medical aid to Indian women through women doctors. In 1918 this fund, with a small assistance from Government of India, opened the Lady Reading Health School at Delhi to train health visitors. This was followed by the establishment of the Lady Chelmsford All India League for Maternity and Child Welfare in 1919, which focused on running health schools, training of *dais* (indigenous midwives) at different MCW centres and propaganda. MCW movement in India received great impetus due to the assiduous efforts of the Countess of Reading. In 1930 the Maternity and Child Welfare Bureau was established by the Indian Red Cross Society.

The MCW movement gradually spread all over India and the provincial governments of the Punjab, Bengal and of other provinces made contributions which rendered many health schools nearly self-supporting. There was slow but definite progress and MCW work did penetrate into the public consciousness also. 'The movement has come to stay. It must develop before great progress in reducing the infantile mortality can be expected and it is for Indians themselves to promote and carry forward this development process if they wish to participate in the results on a scale commensurate with the impact of the subject.'[6] In 1934 the number of welfare centres in England and Wales was 2,884, while the number in India was 684, of which North-West Frontier Province had 2, the Punjab 96, Delhi 26, United Provinces 166 excluding 13 sub-centres, Bihar and Orissa 23, Bengal 41, Central Provinces 57, Bombay 81, Madras 153, Coorg 1, Assam 3 and Burma 22.[7]

Structure of MCW Centres

The organization of the MCW centres varied according to the size and locality. In all the municipality areas MCW work was carried out under the supervision of the respective health officers and the expenditure in the large municipalities was entirely met by the local authorities themselves. Delhi was the only province, besides Madras, where women doctors were recruited for organizing the MCW centres both in urban and rural areas.[8] MCW work was mostly undertaken by philanthropic organizations and the expenses were usually met from publicity funds, public donations and municipal contributions. Depending on the flow of funds, the staff at MCW centres varied.[9]

The MCW centres were run by qualified health visitors and medical facilities were provided for women before, during and after confinement. The health visitors' duties were to visit mothers after confinement; to supervise as many confinement cases of *dais* as possible; to train *dais* for the indigenous *dais* examination and to attend the baby clinic. Home visitation was very significant for only by visiting the home of the patients could some of the worst kinds of ignorance and prejudices be successfully overcome. Moreover during such visits friendly advice on proper feeding for the mother and the child, sick nursing, clothing, ventilation, drainage and home economics were given. The other most important duty of the health visitor was the training and inspection of the midwives and *dais*. In addition to health care work regular lecture classes were held for indigenous *dais*. The training of probationer *dais* and midwives was also carried out at these centres which were recognized by the United Provinces State Medical Faculty.[10] Sometimes these trained midwives were sent for health visitors' training to the Lady Reading School in Delhi. Refresher courses were also held for *dais* in at most centres order to prevent any deterioration in knowledge or standard of work. In turn the public health inspectors carried out the inspection of the work of health visitors in the MCW centres.

There was a growing demand from the middle classes for maternity homes but there were very few hospitals available with this facility. Invariably most of these hospitals and clinics were situated in the district or the *tehsil* headquarters and the rural areas hardly had any access to these medical institutions. Most of the women were thus dependent on the traditional *dais*. MCW centres became a viable and cheaper alternative to the women's hospitals. Hospitals and dispensaries mostly helped women in child birth and other immediate medical needs. On the other hand, MCW centres providing prenatal care became preventive centres as well as training centres for the *dais*. While maternity hospitals and homes were more expensive to equip, to staff and to run, MCW centres were much cheaper. For example, the UP branch of the Lady Chelmsford League, in cooperation with the provincial branch of the Indian Red Cross Society controlled child welfare work and opened many centres in cities and some small towns. These centres played an important part in the propagation of antenatal and post-natal knowledge to expectant mothers.[11]

Medical Education and Women

Curative health care consists of treatment of patients by medical professionals, and for a long time women were kept apart from this profession. Although women's entry into the medical profession was not welcomed, the social conditions and the peculiar situation in India where women went only to women doctors, necessitated the training of women doctors. Despite many social discriminations and discouragements, medical education for women grew slowly in India under the tutelage of missionaries, philanthropic organizations and the state. By 1920 there were some institutes in India providing medical education for women.

The educational opportunities available for women and the importance given to midwifery in medical training increased after the 1920s. There was no single local coordinating agency in India and it was the General Medical Council of Great Britain which recognized the Indian medical degrees from 1892, and acted as a coordinating and inspecting body. Periodically the General Medical Council appointed three inspectors (one each for medicine, surgery and midwifery) whose duty was to be present at the final examinations of each of the 23 licensing bodies and to report to the General Medical Council (for transmission to the Privy Council) on the sufficiency of the examination. Sir Norman Walker from the General Medical Council, in his report of 1927, clearly noted that except at the Madras Maternity Hospital the opportunities for the study of Practical Midwifery were scanty in India. At medical colleges in Lahore and Lucknow the opportunities for training students in midwifery was almost negligible due the strict practise of *purdah* system and the social customs in these provinces. It almost led to the non-recognition of Indian medical degrees and to overcome this shortcoming, the students of these colleges for many years were sent to other provinces to get training in practical midwifery. These developments clearly reflect the priority given to midwifery training, yet it remained a neglected area.

Looking into Maternal Mortality

Maternal and infant mortality occurred due to a large number of obscure diseases which attacked the mother and through her affected the child. Some of these diseases were unique to India yet there was hardly any attempt at investigating or researching them. The pressing need for research in this area was also discussed at the All India Maternity Child Welfare Conference at Delhi in 1927 and a resolution was passed asking the Government of India to appoint a female medical professional as a full-time research officer for a period of at least three years to work with a research institution in one of the large towns of India.[12] In March 1929, a memorandum was presented by the Association of Medical Women in India to Her Excellency Lady Irwin asking for the extension of medical aid to women in India and one of the suggested needs for medical relief was the 'provision for at least two research posts in order that women may undertake research into the conditions of diseases in pregnancy, childbirth and infancy'.[13]

The investigations carried out by the Indian Research Fund Association was the first organized effort in this direction, though it was of a temporary nature. This preliminary research has shown the need for long and patient enquiry to find the causes and remedies of these diseases.[14] Sometimes research was left totally to the occasional services of honorary workers. Dr. Margaret Balfour was closely associated with maternal care in India and worked at various levels in the Women's Medical Services (WMS). She undertook important research to identify the causes of maternal mortality in the country. In her application to the Indian Research Fund Association, Dr. Balfour wrote: 'Little is known of the causes of the high maternal death rate. It was known that contracted pelvis, the toxaemias of pregnancy puerperal sepsis and other diseases and accidents of labour are common, but no enquiry has been made as to their relative frequency or the causes which may lead to them.'[15] Her research was funded partially by Indian Research Fund Association. Dr. Balfour worked in an honorary capacity and Dr. Lucy Wills, one of the WMS doctors and assistant to Dr. Balfour in this study was paid Rs. 125 per month by the Indian Research Fund Association. Another study of significance was conducted by Dr. Cujrel Wilson and this was also partially funded by the Indian Research Fund Association.

A research department for maternal care and specifically for diseases related to pregnancy was never established in any university or in any of the research organizations in India before 1930s. When the AIIHPH was established in 1933 it was proposed that the institute would carry on research in maternal care besides offering a postgraduate course in it. It was hoped that the two WMS doctors, who were to be the faculty (one professor and one assistant professor) for the MCW section, would also engage in research. But teaching, administrative and routine executive duties and with various consultation at clinics under the MCW scheme left hardly any time for the teachers to take up systematic research even though they had vital information readily available to them. In this connection it was pointed out:

> The present day defect of medical education in India is quite apparent in the fact that hardly there is any place of international repute and fame in the researchers concerned in art of healing held by a body of practitioners which can boast of no less than 30,000 members. . . . Rarely they come out to find out something new in art of healing and capable of pursuing it with patience and faithfulness.[16]

Public Health Institute, Calcutta

All over the country maternal welfare schemes were coming up in response to the stirring of social conscience by the continued high infantile and maternal death rates. These welfare schemes were under the charge of medical women who had training in preventive care. However, the whole teaching process in medical colleges and schools was focused on curative medicine and they hardly got any training in preventive care. It was observed that due to lack of training in preventive care a fresh graduate doctor 'continues hospital methods in the welfare clinics, makes her cards simply a record of prescriptions given and very little better than a compounder's sheet. In the rare instances where she does continue to study after qualification she does not know to which textbooks to turn or where to see working, a model scheme.'[17] A strong need was felt for organizing a regular course to train the graduates of MBBS and sub-assistant surgeon grade to take up the administration and executive posts in the new maternity and child welfare schemes. Another problem was with the nature of MCW work in India itself, as a report indicates:

> This work all over India has grown up sporadically without much fore thought, planning or co-ordination, and mostly by voluntary agencies that deserve great credit for initiating the work. The need for trained women graduate who could take charge of the work and direct and develop it on proper lines has been felt and hitherto the only means of obtaining such training was to proceed to London or else where.[18]

The AIIHPH was the only Indian institute which offered a postgraduate diploma in MCW for a very long time. There were very few facilities for postgraduate instruction in different medical colleges in India. While practically each of the medical colleges offered degrees of Doctor of Medicine, Master of Surgery, and so on, the facilities were not such as those in the British postgraduate medical colleges or other international centres of graduate study. Only in Madras was a Council of Postgraduate Medical Education formed to coordinate postgraduate medical education.[19] Of all the universities and institutions offering medical education only (AIIHPH) and Madras University offered a Diploma in Obstetrics and Gynaecology and Diploma in Maternity and Child Welfare respectively. The specially organized nine-month Diploma in Public Health course at AIIHPH and the six-months Diploma in Tropical Medicine course at the School of Tropical Medicine, both at Calcutta, were exceptions. Besides this there was no organization to coordinate and foster postgraduation education in any of the universities till 1947.

The genesis and growth of the AIIHPH throw light on the importance given to this course. Public health was gaining prominence in public consciousness by the 1920s. Major General Sir J.D Graham, the then Public Health Commissioner with the Government of India, in his annual report for 1925, said: public health 'presents a grand and unlimited field for public health workers, but it is well to recognize that the improvement cannot be achieved without a careful system of specialized training in institutes or schools devoted to public health teaching and research and that cannot be done without adequate financial support'.[20] Major General Sir John Megaw, head of the Calcutta School of Tropical Medicine and Hygiene, held similar views which were expressed from time to time in the annual reports of the school.[21] W.S. Carter, Associate Director of the Rockefeller Foundation, met General Megaw and General Graham on various occasions and became deeply impressed with the necessity for establishing an All India Institute of Hygiene where purely public health subjects, especially related to Indian requirements, could be dealt with. He on behalf of the Rockefeller Foundation addressed the Government of India in terms of embodying these proposals and the Foundation offered to provide the cost of acquiring the site selected, build and equip the AIIHPH. The recurring cost of staff and maintenance of this institute was to be borne by the government.[22] The Government of India gratefully accepted this munificent offer and the institute was formally started on 30 December 1932. The general administrative control was vested in the Director General, Indian Medical Service, subject to the ultimate control of the Government of India through the Department of Education, Health and Lands.

The AIIHPH provided three courses of instruction:[23]

1. Diploma in Public Health of the Calcutta University and Diploma in Public Health and Hygiene of the Faculty of Tropical Medicine, Bengal. It was a postgraduate course for university medical graduates or holders of Licentiate Medical Certificate of a university
2. Doctorate of Science (Public Health)
3. Special courses in which MCW was a section with 10 lectures and four hours of practical work.

Travails of the MCW Section

The AIIHPH was to have six sections of Public Health Administration, Malariology and Rural Hygiene, Epidemiology and Vital Statistics, Nutrition and Bio-chemistry, Sanitary Engineering and Maternity and Child Welfare. In 1933 the Faculty of Tropical Medicine and Hygiene of Bengal decided to create a Diploma in MCW to be given to women graduates after training and examination at the institute. The course was designed for producing medical personnel sufficiently trained to take on administrative posts in connection with the organization and control of MCW work in India. The standard of teaching in different subjects was kept high and it was also considered necessary that the initial requirement of the candidates taking up the course should be that of university graduates and not that of licentiates.

Initially in 1928, the Government of India undertook to meet the annual recurring cost of the AIIHPH, subject to a limit of Rs. 3 lakh. There was a sudden financial crisis at the end of 1931 and the General Purposes Sub-Committee of the Retrenchment Committee recommended that the initial annual cost to government on account of the institute should not be allowed to exceed Rs. 2 lakh until the financial stringency lasted. This recommendation was accepted by the government and it was decided to open only four sections with the allotted sum of Rs. 2 lakh per annum. The two sections of Sanitary Engineering and MCW were to remain in abeyance pending the improvement of financial conditions.[24] This closure of the MCW section came as a major setback to the MCW movement in India. The poignancy was reflected in the report of the AIIHPH:

> The delay in the opening of a MCW section is very regrettable. It may not be expedient, however desirable, immediately to deflect large sums of money from curative to preventive medicine but it is surely a duty as well as wisdom to help voluntary or official bodies to initiate and develop effective local schemes by making it possible for them to secure the services of trained personnel. . . . It seems neither fitting nor just that a section potentially so beneficial should have to struggle along under the handicap imposed by an uncertain and limited income.[25]

The Countess of Dufferin Fund was very keen and anxious about the opening of the MCW section and considered its establishment as an urgent need. They agreed to lend the services of a suitably qualified officer of the WMS for the purpose of teaching and research in maternity and child welfare and also to meet the pay of the officer.[26] The proposal regarding the opening of the section was at first only for the year 1932-3, but was extended to the next two years. Jean M. Orkney of WMS was sent to the institute to initiate the section and the Countess of Dufferin Fund granted the necessary funds to finance the section. The Red Cross Association of India, realizing the importance of the section of MCW and especially the necessity for providing post-graduate instruction in the work for women graduates agreed to finance the section partially.[27] At the instance of these two voluntary organizations the section was kept open on a temporary basis[28] and it was only in 1937 that the Government of India took it over.

The year 1932 was spent in drawing up the syllabus for a diploma course for medical graduates in MCW and in making practical arrangements for the work of the diploma students. The existing facilities could not be used for teaching and demonstration purposes and financial considerations made it impossible to establish a model centre attached to the MCW department of the institute. Her Excellency Lady Willingdon was approached and she graciously promised to help in securing a suitable building. In 1933 the course was commenced with three students of which two were awarded the diploma in July 1934. This first batch was more or less experimental and a few alterations were made in the course to be effected from the next session, which started on 24 October 1934, in which two more students were admitted.[29] There were many problems in the accommodation of the students. It was also felt that the arrangements made for training in midwifery, venereal diseases and hospital antenatal work were far from satisfactory for a postgraduate course.[30]

From its inception the MCW section faced problems due to lack of funds. The Secretary, Governing Body and Scientific Advisory Board, Indian Research Fund Association, wrote to the Chief Medical Officer; WMS, Countess of Dufferin Fund on 9 January 1934:

> With regret that I have to inform your council that the Government of India have expressed their inability to increase their grant for 1934-35 to AIIHPH. The continuance of the MCW section at the institute will, therefore depend on the attitude which your council take in regard to the value of this work to the institute and to India as a whole. It would be very regrettable if this work, so well begun with your committee's generous assistance, were brought to an untimely end.[31]

On 18 January 1934, the Countess of Dufferin Fund sanctioned the grant for 1934-5 and was unable to grant the request for a further grant of Rs. 3,000 to complete the scheme by establishing a midwifery section. It also expressed that the Countess of Dufferin Fund will not incur any further expenditures on the institute and by then it should be incumbent upon the government to resume the liability. The Indian Red Cross Society also agreed to grant funds to reopen the MCW section for 1934-5. These grants were to support the department only till 31 March 1935, which meant withdrawing the services of the WMS officer lent by the Countess of Dufferin Fund, who was the only teaching staff at the MCW section and thus the closure of the section itself. Lt. Col. A.D. Stewart, Director of AIIHPH, wrote to Director General of the Indian Medical Services on 12 April 1934 on the subject of opening the two sections:

> Dr. Orkney, who has had large experience on the subjects of MCW section, has been instructing students of Diploma in Public health class and the class of DMCW, the special subject of the section. If the funds of Countess of Dufferin Fund are discontinued then the services of Dr. Orkney, specialized instruction in MCW for D.P.H. students will cease down and MCW will shut down. The valuable ground it has gained will be lost and MCW clinic would be closed.[32]

The same problem had arisen in the next financial year also. The Countess of Dufferin Fund authorities were not willing to finance the MCW section after the year 1934-5 either in the form of

Dr. Orkney's salary or otherwise. It considered that the government should undertake the responsibility for the continuance of the section as it was primarily the liability of the government under their agreement with the Rockefeller Foundation. The Countess of Dufferin Fund decided to withdraw the services of Dr. Orkney from the AIIHPH as she was required to relieve Ruth Young as Director of the Maternity and Child Welfare bureau of the Indian Red Cross Society.[33] Dr. Orkney relinquished duty on 13 December 1935 and was replaced by M.N. Edwards of the WMS in a temporary post. On 27 December 1935, the Public Health Commissioner of India noted: 'The D.G. and I would regard the closing down of this section at the institute as a tragedy and we are afraid it might have serious repercussions in the attitude of the Rockefeller Foundation towards future proposals for financial aid to public health schemes in India.'[34] The government grant to the Countess of Dufferin Fund was restored to its original figure of 3.70 lakh on the condition that it will continue to finance the institute for another year.[35] Thus the Countess of Dufferin's Fund agreed to finance the MCW again during the financial year 1936-7 and refused to do the same from the following year. And finally government took over the full responsibility of the section in 1937.

From 1934, a refresher course of one month duration was conducted for health visitors every year at the AIIHPH.[36] Similarly, a short course of four weeks on the organization of the MCW and school medical services suitable for public health officers responsible for the administration and supervision of such schemes, and a refresher course for medical women holding the diploma in MCW was held every November.[37] The admission was restricted to persons holding certificates of having passed the health visitor's examination from any of the recognized health schools giving training in English.

Over the years the importance of a diploma was recognized by the medical professionals and there was a great demand for it. Yet the licentiates were denied the same at the AIIHPH. The requirement of the candidates taking up the course for a diploma in MCW at the AIIHPH was that of university graduate degree and not licentiate. It was felt that standards of subjects and training should be high for the personnel involved in the organizing and controlling of MCW work in India. Accordingly the requirements were kept high and thus, the diploma was denied to medical licentiates though they were numerically more than medical graduates and the same was true for women doctors who were very few compared to the licentiates. The other major issue of concern for the female licentiates was that at the provincial and local level most of the hospitals were run by the licentiates and there were rarely any doctors available to run MCW centres even in the urban areas. At the 29th Conference of All India Medical Licentiates Association held on 24-6 December 1938 it was resolved that:

> The Government of India be requested to give facilities to medical licentiates to go in for MCW diploma course opened in the AIIHPH of Calcutta; that in the opinion of this house the government have done a great injustice to the largest medical group in depriving the medical licentiates of the benefits of this course who cater to the needs of the largest number of people in India.[38]

This resolution was considered by the department in consultation with the Director General, Indian Medical Services, who opined that the standard of teaching the different subjects at the AIIHPH were too high for licentiates. Yet the lowering of the standards of the course was not agreed upon. He also advised that the legitimate demand of the licentiates must be met by providing a separate and more suitable course for them for there was definitely a great need for a class of workers with lower medical qualifications and with the necessary training in MCW. It was hoped that such persons, though they may not be capable of taking up responsible administrative posts, would be able to take charge of welfare centres and run them. As the MCW section was already in financial crisis this short-term course was never taken up at the institute. A similar kind of course in MCW was introduced at Lady Reading Health School from 1940 but it was only for sub-assistant women surgeons.

The MCW section, thus from its inception, was in a crisis and always received a secondary treatment from the government. The director of AIIHPH wrote to Director General, Indian Medical Service on 16 February 1935 stating that 'the government was apparently not desirous of treating the section as an integral part of this institute inasmuch as the rules for diploma in Maternity and Child Welfare were not incorporated in the prospectus of this institute but were issued in a separate prospectus'.[39] Secondly, the section was established for the twofold purpose of postgraduate teaching and research. While the former purpose was fulfilled, the latter never took off as there were never adequate staff and resources. Teaching, administrative and routine executive duties and various consultation at clinics under the MCW scheme left hardly any time for the teachers to take up research. Valuable information about conditions which influenced maternal health was accumulating and readily available on the record cards of the welfare centres. But no one was there to classify this data and do research. There was great demand for health visitors who were appointed by the municipalities and charitable bodies for running MCW centres. But by 1938, only 350 of the 828 welfare centres were provided with health visitors in India. As the opportunities available were very few, there were very few trained health visitors available.

Lady Reading Health School, Delhi

Health visitor was the most important medical person involved in MCW services. The success or failure of MCW services was dependent on her personality, knowledge and skill and thus her training was considered as a matter of utmost importance. One important aspect of the work of health visitors was to supervise the indigenous *dais*, as Lady Hartog emphasized:

> A number of highly trained mid wives are being turned out by the large hospital but one of the chief branches of maternity work is the endeavour to train indigenous dais in modern hygiene methods. This is being carried out to some extent in all the provinces by doctors, by voluntary societies or by health visitors. The best results are found when the training is in the hands of the health visitors; who can continue to supervise the dais and look after they are not to drop back again into their old ways.[40]

The foundation of the training of the health visitors in India was laid by two English ladies: Miss Graham and Miss Griffin, who came from England in 1914. They were instrumental in the establishment of the Delhi Health School and they also laid down the broad lines for the requirements of health visitors and these were followed by other Indian health schools as they came into existence.[41] The health visitors' training was based upon a midwifery course with an additional 12-18 months training in both theory and practicals in MCW care. Field training was given in both rural and urban health centres. The preliminary educational qualification for health visitors was matriculation and its equivalent. The final examination was held by the Provincial Nursing Council or by authorities appointed by the provincial governments. The Health Visitors' League was established in 1922. By 1947 there were training schools for health visitors at Delhi (1918), Lahore (1921) and Lucknow (1923) in north India.

The first institute which trained health visitors in India was Lady Reading Health School in Delhi. The Countess of Dufferin Fund, assisted by a small grant from the Government of India, opened it in November 1918. In 1931 the school came under the administrative control of Indian Red Cross Society (Maternity and Child Welfare Bureau) and in 1952 the government took over. The school was opened with ten pupils of European, Anglo-Indian and Indian origin. These women received practical training in sanitation and infant welfare work under the health officer and the lady health visitors. They also attended lectures given by medical men and women on physiology, infant welfare, tropical diseases, sanitation, first aid and home nursing. After six months of training, six students passed the final qualifying examination.[42] Those who were not already qualified midwives were required to complete their midwifery training in recognized hospitals. These women later on took up posts under municipalities and charitable bodies for the supervision of *dais* and general health works. The role of Lady Reading School for Health Visitors in training girls from all over India as health visitors was greatly appreciated and in no time there was a great demand for lady health visitors as well as the school.[43]

Although the Lady Reading School was a prestigious institute giving training to health visitors for about a decade, its diploma was not recognized in many provinces of India. The school was managed by a committee of which the chairman was the Public Health Commissioner with the Government of India and the members included the Assistant Director of Public Health, Delhi Province, the Medical Officer of Health, Delhi and the Director of the Maternity and Child Welfare Bureau, Indian Red Cross Society. It was further strengthened by the inclusion of the Educational Commissioner in 1937.[44] In addition the LRHS was granted annually Rs. 6,000 from the government and it was under the control of the Director of Public Health. Examination work was conducted by examiners who were to see that students attain a proper standard of knowledge, both theoretical and practical, and in fact two of the examiners were members of the WMS. The school had, therefore, a considerable degree of official recognition and status. Yet the diplomas issued by the school were not recognized in many provinces for a very long time as they were signed by the Public Health Commissioner as 'Chairman of the School' and not as the Public Health Commissioner.[45]

The registration of the Lady Reading Health School Diploma under the Nurses, Midwives and Health Visitors Registration Acts in the various provinces was possible only if the diploma was granted by a government department instead of by a voluntary committee. The secretary of the school therefore suggested in 1937 that the diploma be signed by the Public Health Commissioner as such to give it the required government recognition. After an official inquiry and a lot of deliberations the proposal was accepted in the same year. For many years Lady Reading Health School was the only institution training health visitors in India. By 1938 there were six schools at Delhi, which had two, Lahore, Madras, Nagpur, Poona and two more were proposed at Calcutta and Lucknow. [46]

Sub-Assistant Surgeons: Hesitant Recognitions

Besides the training of the health visitors a short-term course in MCW for licentiates was also conducted at Lady Reading Health School. The greater part of MCW work was carried on with the help and often under the direction of women doctors. Most of them had no training for it and the provision of a course for graduates at the AIIHPH was the first step taken in this direction. This had actually done very little to meet the problem as only women graduates with MBBS degrees were trained. After training, even if available, these doctors were too expensive for most local authorities or voluntary organizations to employ and most of the MCW work was left to a large extent in the hands of sub-assistant surgeons.

One of the resolutions passed at the 29th Conference of the All-India Medical Licentiates Association held at Guwahati from 24 to 26 December 1938 was that the licentiates be considered for the diploma course at AIIHPH.[47] For many reasons the suggestion to lower the standard of admission to the Institution of Hygiene course was not accepted and a very short course in that institution for sub-assistant surgeons was not possible due to the shortage of funds. However, Lady Reading Health School recognized the need and came forward to provide the same with some help from other institutions in Delhi. There was always some accommodation and teaching material readily available at the school from 15 April to 31 July every year, when no classes were held.

There was a proposal for a course of four months for sub-assistant surgeons in MCW work at the Lady Reading Health School, Delhi and on 26 May 1937 the Additional Deputy Secretary readily accepted it.[48] The course constituted both lectures and practical work in MCW for women doctors at the school and at the welfare centre attached to the institute. This course was held on alternate years depending on the demand for it. A certain number of scholarships for the course were also available from the MCW Bureau funds, which was given to the students at the rate of Rs. 50 per month for four months. On completion of the course an examination was held and a certificate was awarded to successful candidates.[49] In the first year 14 applications for 12 vacancies were received (UP 5, NWFP 2, Mysore state 1, Holker state 1, Orissa 1, Delhi 1, Bombay 2, and Punjab 1). The selection of candidates was made on 29 February 1940 and the course in MCW for sub-assistant surgeons was conducted for the first-time in Lady Reading Health School from 15 April to 15 July 1940.

Conclusion

Social customs like *purdah*, early marriage and social segregation denied Indian women, education and access to medical interventions, except the services of the indigenous *dai*. With great perseverance and time and patience, many of these barriers were broken down and by the early decades of twentieth century both Western education and health care system for women gained some footing and was spreading throughout the country. Though modern health care system was considered as an indicator of imperial benevolence, the poor status of health care for women reflected the imperial government's reluctance to fulfil the task.

The public health policy itself was hardly developed, which was further marred by the financial shortage of the provincial governments after the decentralization of 1920. Maternal health care occupied but a small place in the general public health policy of the colonial government as they considered it desirable but at the same time a luxury they were not willing to indulge in.

Though WMS was the only state intervention, it was handed over to the Countess of Dufferin Fund, a voluntary organization, for a payment of fixed grant-in-aid. WMS was like 'no one's child' and treatment meted out to it was that of an illegitimate child. Like most of the colonial utilitarian experiments, the Indian women's medical education and health care systems were largely left to philanthropy and local governments. This meant financial constraints causing a vast gap between supply and demand and sub-standard services. Thus ill-equipped civil hospitals catered to the urban population, while large masses in rural areas had to fall back on MCW centres and indigenous *dais*.

Medical education institutes were very few in India and even among these a very small number of institutes were open for women. Despite many social taboos associated with the medical profession for girls, a few women came forward for training. As regards research in diseases specific to women, like oestomalacia, there was almost no work in any of the medical institutes during that period. Even though there were many diseases of women unique to India there was hardly any research on them as it was an expensive venture. Whatever research was conducted was the occasional service of honorary workers, who were burdened with teaching, and administrative work to undertake any research. In tropical medicinal research the subject of maternal care hardly received any attention. It has often been stated and with considerable degree of truth that scientific research work and knowledge of disease in India has far outstripped its practical application throughout the country. Whatever scanty research was done by voluntary doctors could never get a chance of practical implementation and findings were often left as mere research papers.

The opening and running of the MCW section at the AIIHPH shows the secondary treatment meted out to women's health. The MCW section of the AIIHPH was in crisis from inception and the paper showed clearly that it was only due to the initiatives of Countess of Dufferin Fund and the Indian Red Cross society that this section was able to survive. Though the importance of the Diploma in MCW was greatly recognized and was in demand, it was not opened to the licentiates who catered to the medical needs of large populations at the provincial and local levels. The case study of Lady Reading Health School only proves that it was philanthropy of a few people and independent organizations which held training for the much-in-demand health visitors. The irony is also that even though it was the only school training health visitors, its diploma was not recognized for a long time.

The reluctance of the state to take direct responsibility for women's health care or the training of medical professionals left Indian women to largely depend on the traditional *dais* for their medical needs. The study reflects the long struggles that went in the educational institutions training women medical professionals and the constant sense of insecurity they felt at every step over the survival of the institutions. Despite these setbacks and disappointments the MCW professionals were the only hope for a large number of women in India during the first half of the twentieth century.

NOTES

1. M.I. Balfour, 'Maternal Mortality: A Comment on the Report on Maternal Mortality During Childbirth in England by Dr. Janet Campbell of the Ministry of Health, with a Reference to Maternal Mortality in India', *Indian Medical Gazette*, December 1927, p. 621.
2. Annual Report of Public Health Commissioner with Government of India, 1924, p. 26.
3. Abstract from Annual Report of Public Health Commissioner with Government of India, 1933, *Indian Medical Gazette*, March 1936, p. 170.
4. Though MCW movement focused on both mother and infant health care, the present paper probes only into the earlier aspect.
5. Dagmar Engles, 'The Politics of Child Birth: British and Bengali Women in Contest, 1890-1930', in Peter Robb et al. (eds.), *Society and Ideology: Essays in South Asia*, New Delhi: Oxford University Press, 1993, p. 228.
6. Annual Report of Public Health Commissioner with GOI, 1927, p. 106.
7. Abstract from Annual Report of Public Health Commissioner with GOI, 1934, *Indian Medical Gazette*, July 1937, p. 449.
8. Bhore Committee Report, 1946, p. 65.
9. For example, in rich municipality areas like Delhi the MCW staff usually consisted of two European health visitors under whom were two Indian lady health visitors and two trained *dais*. The poorly funded MCW centres could only afford a nurse *dai*.
10. Abstract from the Annual Report of the Director of Public Health of United Provinces and Oudh, 1927, p. 84.

11. Dr. Prakash Chandra, 'Public Health Conditions in UP', *Indian Medical Gazette*, December 1933, p. 727.
12. National Archives of India (henceforth NAI), File no. 114-15-Health 'B', October 1927 Education, Health and Lands (henceforth EHL) Department.
13. NAI File no. 24-Health 'Deposits', September 1927, EHL Department.
14. Ibid.
15. NAI File no. 155-6-Health 'B', February 1925, EHL Department.
16. *Indian Medical Journal*, June 1934, p. 321.
17. Annual Report of the Countess of Dufferin Fund for the year 1932, p. 38.
18. Annual Report of the AIIHPH for the year 1934, p. 16.
19. Bhore Committee Report, vol. 1, 1946, p. 166.
20. Annual Report of the AIIHPH for the year 1934, p. 10.
21. Sir Leonard Rogers conceived the idea in 1914 of establishing an institute in India for postgraduate study in tropical medicine and hygiene. In 1920 the Calcutta School of Tropical Medicine and hygiene was started due to his perseverance and enthusiasm and to the generosity of the Governments of India and Bengal and some private benefactors. This institute combined teaching and research in both tropical medicine and hygiene. A professorship in hygiene was established and a course of instruction arranged in the school for the diploma of the public health of the Calcutta University. However, there were many limitations to the course. Aspects of public health were rapidly, developing, requiring the full attention of a single worker and teacher for each aspect. Public health was no more a single entity and it was impossible for a single person to cover these diverse aspects. Thus maternity care hardly received any attention in this course.
22. Sirish N. Kavadi, *The Rockefeller Foundation and Public Health in Colonial India 1916-1945: A Narrative History*, Mumbai: Foundation for Research in Community Health, 1999, pp. 98-100.
23. NAI File no. 55-5/32-Health, EHL Department.
24. Ibid.
25. Annual Report of AIIHPH for the year 1934, p. 42.
26. NAI File no. 55-20/32 Health, EHL Department.
27. NAI File no. 32-7/35 Health, EHL Department.
28. Maternity and Child Welfare section received further grants in 1934 from the Calcutta Health Week Committee, Indian Football Association, Calcutta Corporation and individual donations from B.M. Birla, Khaitan and other generous individuals.
29. There were no students for the diploma of MCW in the session 1935-6. The Course began in October 1936 with only one student.
30. Indian Medical Gazette, November 1937, p. 709.
31. NAI File no. 32-2/34-Health, EHL Department.

32. NAI File no. 32-9/34-Health, EHL Department.
33. NAI File no. 32-21/35-Health, EHL Department.
34. Ibid.
35. The government gave an annual grant-in-aid of Rs. 3,70,000 to the Countess of Dufferin Fund for the maintenance of WMS. In 1932 as a retrenchment measure the government reduced the grant to the Countess of Dufferin Fund from Rs. 3,70,000 to Rs. 3,44,300. The original amount was restored in 1936 and one of the conditions for restoration was continuation of the Maternity and Child Welfare section at the AIIHPH in 1936-7.
36. NAI File no. 32-12/37-Health, EHL Department.
37. NAI File no. 32-18/35-Health, EHL Department.
38. NAI File no. 18-4/39-Health, EHL Department.
39. NAI File no. 32-7/35-Health, EHL Department.
40. Lady Hartog, *Living India*, London, 1935, p. 154.
41. Robert. J. Blackham, 'The Heath Visitor in India', *The Journal of the Royal Society for the Promotion of Public Health*, 1925, 46, p. 451.
42. Abstract from the Annual Report, Countess of Dufferin Fund 1919, *Indian Medical Gazette,* February 1921, p. 72.
43. Public Health Report on Delhi Province for the year 1931, p. 29.
44. NAI File no. 59-1/37-Health, EHL Department.
45. Ibid.
46. Abstract from Annual Report PHC with GOI 1935, *Indian Medical Gazette*, April 1938, p. 250.
47. NAI File no. 18-4/39-Health, EHL Department.
48. Ibid.
49 The short-term course at LRHS included the following lectures and practicals:

Lectures

Organisation of MCW	8
Ante-natal and Post-natal care	10
Infant and child care	8
Diseases of children	8
Hygiene and public health	16
	50 hours

Practical work

Clinic attendance twice weekly at the Ramchand Lohiya Welfare Centre (Dr's. consultation clinics).

Home visiting, *dai* training and supervision (as health visitor's course).

Hospital antenatal clinic, postnatal clinic and V.D. clinic (Lady Hardinge College Hospital or other women's hospital in Delhi).

Children's ward, Lady Hardinge Hospital (one day a week), Other practical work, attendance at Tuberculosis clinic, Delhi, New Delhi Municipal Maternity and Child Welfare Centre, deaf and dumb school, school medical inspection.

Contributors

TIM ALLENDER is an Associate Professor at the University of Sydney. He has worked extensively on colonial education, with particular reference to India, and is the author of *Ruling through Education: The Politics of Schooling in Colonial Punjab* (2006). His other research area is teaching and learning of history curriculum in global context.

JOSEPH BARA coordinates the research programme of the Educational Records Research Unit, Jawaharlal Nehru University. He has been a Fellow at Indian institute of Advanced Study, Shimla. Besides editing three books, he has published a number of articles on social and educational history of modern India in reputed journals in India and abroad. Presently his interest is Gandhi's educational idea.

I.K. CHAUDHARY is Professor and Head of the Department of History, Ranchi University. He has done wide research on the regional history of Mithila and Jharkhand. His publications include *Some Aspects of Social Life in Medieval Mithila* (1988). His other research area has been the revolt of 1857 in Jharkhand.

DILIP CHAVAN is Associate Professor of English and coordinator of Dr. Ambedkar Chair Centre at Swami Ramanand Teerth Marathwada University, Nanded. His research and publications have been on social history of Maharashtra and educational politics in contemporary India.

BIDISHA DHAR completed her Ph.D. at Centre for Historical Studies, Jawaharlal Nehru University. Apart from her research interests she has taught at the University of Jadavpur, Kolkata as a Guest Lecturer.

CH. RADHA GAYATHRI works at Educational Records Research Unit, Jawaharlal Nehru University, New Delhi. She has published *Female Medical Education in Colonial India* (2008). Her research interest and publications are in history of education, medicine and gender studies.

S. IRFAN HABIB holds the Maulana Abdul Kalam Azad Chair at National University of Educational Planning and Administration, New Delhi. He has published extensively on social history of science in the context of nineteenth-century India in international journals and has edited three books in this area. In addition, he has authored *To Make the Deaf Hear: Ideology and Programme of Bhagat Singh and his Comrades* (2007).

NANDITA KHADRIA works at the Educational Records Research Unit, Jawaharlal Nehru University. She has taught in University of Delhi, Jawaharlal Nehru University, and worked as Lecturer in Omeo Kumar Das Institute of Social Change and Development in Guwahati. Her research interests and publications also include agrarian and economic history with particular reference to Assam.

GULFISHAN KHAN is Associate Professor in Medieval Indian History, at the Department of History, Aligarh Muslim University. Her research interests span the intellectual history of Muslims of South Asia and other contiguous areas. She is the author of *Indian Muslim Perceptions of the West during the Eighteenth Century* (1998), Currently Dr. Khan is working on historiography, architecture, Sufism and interfaith.

DEEPAK KUMAR is Professor of History of Education and Science at Zakir Husain Centre for Educational Studies, Jawaharlal Nehru University. He is known for his book *Science and the Raj* (2nd edn., 2006). He convened and presided over the International Association of Historians of Asia Conference in 2008.

SUSHIL PRASAD is presently working as an Indian Foreign Service officer, posted at the Embassy of India in Mexico. He has completed his M.Phil at the Zakir Husain Centre for Educational Studies, Jawaharlal Nehru University and his research interest includes curriculum studies.

PARIMALA V. RAO is Assistant Professor of History of Education at Zakir Husain Centre for Educational Studies, Jawaharlal Nehru University. She has written extensively on gender, caste and class in the history of Indian education. She is the author of *Foundations of Tilak's Nationalism: Discrimination, Education and Hindutva* (2010).

SUVOBRATA SARKAR is a Research Scholar at the Zakir Husain Centre for Educational Studies, Jawaharlal Nehru University. His research interest and publications are in the social history of technology in colonial Bengal. Recently he has published, *The Quest for Technical Knowledge: Bengal in the Nineteenth* (2012).

SAVITRI DAS SINHA is presently working as Senior Technical Editor, *The National Medical Journal of India,* All India Institute of Medical Sciences, New Delhi. She has also worked on the Selected Works of Jawaharlal Nehru, Teen Murti Bhawan and worked as Assistant Editor with Indian Council of Historical Research. Her research interest is on early medical journals in India.

Bibliography

Abbott, A. and S.H. Wood (1937), *Report on the Vocational Education in India*, Delhi: Manager of Publication.

Abrol, Dinesh (2006), 'Democratising Indian Higher Education', *Social Change,* vol. 36, no. 3, September, pp. 121-60.

Adam, William (1941), *Reports on the State of Education in Bengal (1835 and 1883)*, ed. Anathnath Basu, Calcutta: University of Calcutta.

Agarwal, S.N. (1944), *The Gandhian Plan for Economic Development for India,* Bombay: Padma Publishers.

Aggarwal, J.C. (1976), *Indian Women: Education and Status Including Major Recommendations of the Report of the National Committee on the Status of Women in India, 1971-74*, Delhi: Arya Book Depot.

Aggarwal, J.C. (1984), *Landmarks in the History of Modern Indian Education*, New Delhi: Vikas.

Ahmad, Leila (1993), *Women and Gender in Islam*, New Haven & London: Yale University Press.

Ahmad, M.M. Zuhurrudin (1935), *Present Day Problems of Indian Education (With Special Reference to Muslim Education)*, Bombay: The Ismail College.

Airan, J.W. (ed.) (1967), *College Education in India,* Foreword by Asoka Mehta, Bombay: Manaktalas.

Allender, Tim (2006), 'Surrendering a Colonial Domain: Educating North India, 1854-1890', in *History of Education*, 35: 5, pp. 45-63.

——— (2006), *Ruling through Education: The Politics of Schooling in the Colonial Punjab,* New Delhi: New Dawn Press.

Anagol, P. (2005), *The Emergence of Feminism in India, 1850-1920*, Aldershot: Ashgate.

Andrew, E. and K. Bushnell (1990), 'Cantonment Life in India', in P. Tuson (ed.), *The Queen's Daughters*, Reading: Ithaca Press, pp. 176-99.

Andrews, C.F. (1930), *Mahatma Gandhi's Ideas: Including Selections from his Writings,* London: George Allen & Unwin Ltd.

Apple, Michael W. (1982), *Education and Power*, Boston: Ark Paperbacks.

Arnold, T.W. (1913), *The Preaching of Islam: A History of the Propagation of the Muslim Faith*, 2nd edn., London: Constable and Co. Ltd.

Badheka, Gijubhai (2004), *Divaswapna: An Educator's Reverie,* New Delhi: National Book Trust.

Bagal, J.C. (1956), *Women's Education in Eastern India: The First Phase*, Calcutta: World Press Pvt. Ltd.

——— (1957), *Radhakanta Deb 1784-1867,* Calcutta: Government Printer.

Bagchi, Amiya Kumar (1972), *Private Investment in India 1900-1930,* Cambridge: Cambridge University Press.

Banerji, Nripendra Chandra (1921), *The Ideal of Swaraj in Education and Government,* Madras: Ganesh.

Bara, Joseph (2000), 'Christian Missionaries and Popular Education in India 1910-40', *Indian Social Science Review*, 2, 2, pp. 301-30.

Basu, Aparna (1974), *The Growth of Education and Political Developments in India 1989-1920*, New Delhi: Oxford University Press.

——— (1982), *Essays on the History of Indian Education*, New Delhi: Concept.

Basu, B.D. (1867), *The History of Education in India Under the Rule of the East India Company*, Calcutta: Modern Review Office.

——— (1923), *Rise of the Christian Power in India*, Calcutta: Brahmo Press.

Bayly, C.A. (1975), *The Local Roots of Indian Politics: Allahabad, 1880-1920*, Oxford: Clarendon Press.

——— (1997), *Empire and Information: Intelligence Gathering and Social Communication in India, 1780-1870*, New Delhi: Oxford University Press.

Bhagavan, Manu (2003), *Sovereign Spheres: Princes, Education and Empire in Colonial India,* New Delhi: Oxford University Press.

Bhargava, M.L. (1987), *Hundred Years of Allahabad University*, New Delhi: Asish Publishing House.

Bhatnagar, Shyam Krishna (1969), *History of M.A.O. College Aligarh*, Aligarh: Asia Publishing House.

Bhattacharya, Sabyasachi (1971), *Financial Foundations of the British Raj*, Simla: Indian Institute of Advanced Study.

——— (1997), *The Mahatma and the Poet: Letters and Debates Between Gandhi and Tagore, 1915-1941*, New Delhi: National Book Trust.

——— (ed.) (1998), *The Contested Terrain: Perspectives on Education in India*, New Delhi: Orient Longman.

Biswas, Arun Kumar (ed.) (2001), *History, Science and Society in the Indian Context*, Kolkata: The Asiatic Society.

Bjorkert, Suruchi Thapar (2006), *Women in the Indian National Movement: Unseen Faces and Unheard Voices, 1930-42,* London and New Delhi: Sage.

Bose, D.M., S.N. Sen and B.V. Subbarayappa (eds.) (1971), *A Concise History of Science in India*, New Delhi: Indian National Science Academy.

Bose, P.N. (1906), *Essays and Lectures on the Industrial Development of India*, Calcutta: Newman & Co.

—— (1921), *National Education and Modern Progress*, Calcutta: Kar, Majumdar Publications.

Bourdieu, Pierre and Jean-Claude Passeron (1977), *Reproduction in Education, Society and Culture*, tr. Richard Nice, rev. edn., London: Sage.

Bruce, J.F. (1933), *A History of the University of the Punjab,* Islamabad: Modern Book Depot.

Buck, E.C. (1901), *Report on Practical and Technical Education, 1901*, Simla: Government Press.

Burton, Antoinette (1998), *At The Heart of the Empire: Indians and the Colonial Encounter in Late-Victorian Britain,* Berkeley: University of California Press.

Carnoy, Martin (1974), *Education as Cultural Imperialism*, New York: Longman.

Carpenter, Mary (1868), *Six Months in India*, London: Longmans, Green, and Co.

Chakraborty, Bidyut (1992), 'Jawaharlal Nehru and Planning, 1938-41: India at Crossroads', *Modern Asian Studies*, 16, 2, pp. 275-87.

Chanana, Karuna (2001), *Interrogating Women's Education: Bonded Visions, Expanding Horizons*, Delhi: Rawat.

—— (2004), *Transformative Links Between Higher and Basic Education: Mapping the Field*, New Delhi: Sage.

—— (ed.) (1988), *Socialisation, Education and Women: Explorations in Gender Identity*, New Delhi: Orient Longman.

Chapman, P. (1839), *Hindoo Female Education*, London: Seeley and Burnside.

Chaturvedi, S.N. (1930), *The History of Rural Education in the United Provinces of Agra and Oudh 1840-1926*, Allahabad: Indian Press.

Coomaraswamy, Ananda (1910), *Art and Swadeshi*, Madras: Ganesh.

Copelman, D. (1996), *London's Women Teachers: Gender, Class and Feminism, 1870-1930*, New York: Routledge.

Copland, Ian (2006), 'Christianity as an Arm of Empire: The Ambiguous Case of India Under the Company: 1813-1858', *The Historical Journal,* 49, 4, pp. 1025-54.

Cox, Jeffrey (2002), *Imperial Fault Lines: Christianity and Colonial Power in India, 1818-1940*, Stanford, California: Stanford University Press.

Crook, Nigel (1996), *The Transmission of Knowledge in South Asia*, New Delhi: Oxford University Press.

Dahiya, Bhim S. (1996), *Higher Education in India: Some Reflections,* New Delhi: Khama Publishers.

Dalmia, Vasudha (1997), *The Nationalization of Hindu Traditions: Bharatendu Harishchandra and Nineteenth Century Banaras*, New Delhi: Oxford University Press.

Das, Santosh Kumar (1930), *The Educational System of the Ancient Hindu*, Calcutta: Mitra.

Davenport, T., D. De Long and M. Beers (1988), 'Successful Knowledge Management Projects', *Sloan Management Review*, vol. 39, no. 2, pp. 43-57.

Dayal, Har (1908), *Thoughts on Education*, New Delhi: Rajdhani Granthagar.

Dharampal (1983), *The Beautiful Tree: The Indigenous Indian Education in the 18th Century*, Delhi: Biblia Impex.

Dionne, Russel and Roy Macleod (1979), 'Science and Policy in British India, 1858-1914: Perspectives on a Persisting Belief', *Proceedings of the Sixth European Conference on Modern South Asian Studies*, Paris: CNRS, pp. 55-68.

Dreze, Jean and Amartya Sen (1995), *India Economic Development and Social Opportunity*, New Delhi: Oxford University Press.

Dugvekar, H.V. (ed.) (1917), *National Education*, Benares: Bakabodha Office.

Dutt, R.C. (1902-4), *Economic History of India*, 2 vols., London: Kegan Paul, Trench & Trubner.

Forbes, Geraldine (1999), *Women in Modern India*, The New Cambridge History of India 4: 2, Cambridge: Cambridge University Press. (Originally published 1996.)

Foucault, M. (1994), 'Two Lectures', in N. Dirks, G. Eley and S. Ortner (eds.), *In Cultural Power/History: A Reader in Contemporary Social Theory,* Princeton: Princeton University Press.

Gandhi, M.K. (1936), 'Primary Education in Bombay', *Harijan*, 26 September.

——— (1937), *Educational Reconstruction*, Bombay: Navajivan Publishing House.

——— (1951), *Basic Education*, Ahmedabad: Navajivan Publishing House.

——— (1962), *The Problem of Education*, Ahmedabad: Navajivan Publishing House.

——— (1981), 'Drain Inspector's Report', *Young India, 1919-1931*, vol. 9, Ahmedabad: Navajivan Publishing House.

——— (2000), *An Autobiography or The Story of My Experiments with Truth*, Ahmedabad: Navajivan Publishing House.

——— (2008), *Hind Swaraj or Indian Home Rule,* Ahmedabad: Navajivan Publishing House.

Ghosh, Aurobindo (1981), *National Education,* Allahabad: Leader.

Ghosh, J. (1926), *Higher Education in Bengal Under British Rule*, Calcutta: Book Company.

Ghosh, J.C. (1947), 'Industrial Planning for India', *Science and Culture*, XII, pp. 345-47.

Ghosh, Suresh Chandra (1989), *Education Policy in India since Warren Hastings*, Calcutta: Noya Prokash.

——— (2009), *History of Education in Modern India* (rev edn.), New Delhi: Orient Blackswan.

Goodman, J. and S. Harrop (eds.) (2000), *Women, Educational Policy-Making and Administration in* England, London: Routledge.

Gopal, S. (ed.) (1976), *Selected Works of Jawaharlal Nehru*, vol. IX, New Delhi: Orient Longman.

Gowda, Made (1997), *Modern Mysore State 1881-1902,* Mysore: Prasaranga.

Gramsci, Antonio (1971), *Selections from the Prison Notebooks of Antonio Gramsci*, ed. Quintin Hoare and G.N. Smith, New York: International Publisher.

Guha, Ranajit (1982-8), *Subaltern Studies*, vols. I-VII, New Delhi: Oxford University Press.

Gupta, S.P. (1979), *Modern India and Progress in Science and Technology*, New Delhi: Vikas.

Habib, S. Irfan and Dhruv Raina (eds.) (2007), *Social History of Science in Colonial India*, New Delhi: Oxford University Press.

Haines, C.R. (1886), *Education and Missions in India and Elsewhere,* Cambridge: Deighton, Bell and Sons.

Hasan, Mushirul (2005), *A Moral Reckoning: Muslim Intellectuals in Nineteenth Century Delhi*, New Delhi: Oxford University Press.

——— (ed.) (1998), *Knowledge, Power and Politics: Educational Institutions in India*, New Delhi: Roli Books.

Headrick, Daniel R. (1988), *The Tentacles of Progress: Technology Transfer in the Age of Imperialism, 1850-1940*, New York: Oxford University Press.

Hettne, Bjorn (1978), *The Political Economy of Indirect Rule: Mysore 1881-1947,* London: Curzon Press.

Hoey, William (1880), *A Monograph on Trade and Manufactures in Northern India,* Lucknow: American Methodist Mission Press.

Howell, Arthur (1872), *Education in British India Prior to 1854 and in 1870-71*, Calcutta: Government Printing.

Hunter, W.W. (1883), *Report of the Indian Education Commission, 1882-83*, Calcutta: Superintendent of Government Printing.

Hurley, Siobhan Lambert (2007), *Muslim Women Reform and Princely Patronage: Nawab Sultan Jahan Begum of Bhopal*, London: Routledge.

Iyer, Raghvan N. (ed.) (1986), *The Moral and Political Writings of Mahatma Gandhi,* vol. I, Oxford: Oxford University Press.

Jayawardena, Kumari (1995), *The White Woman's Other Burden: Western Women and South Asia During British Rule*, New York: Routledge.

Jha, Amarnath (1941), *Occasional Essays and Addresses,* Allahabad: Kitab Mahal.

Jones, Kenneth W. (1976), *Arya Dharma: Hindu Consciousness in 19th Century Punjab*, Berkeley: University of California Press.

——— (1989), *The New Cambridge History of India III, 1: Socio-Religious Reform Movements in British India,* Cambridge: Cambridge University Press.

Kabir, Humayun (1956), *Education in New India,* London: Allen and Unwin.

Kakorwi, Safi Ahmad (ed.) (1988), *Morison's History of the M.A.O. College, Aligarh,* Lucknow: Markaz-e-Adab-e-Urdu.

Kamat, A.R. (1988), 'Education and Social Change: A Conceptual Framework', in Amrik Singh and G.D. Sharma (eds.), *Higher in India: The Social Context*, New Delhi: Konark, pp. 25-45.

——— (1989), *Perspectives for Educational Reform in India*, vol. 1: *Studies in Educational Reform in India,* Bombay: Himalaya Publishing House.

Karlekar, Malavika (1986), 'Kadambani and the Bhadralok: Early Debates Over Women's Education in Bengal' *Economic and Political Weekly*, vol. 21, no. 17, April, pp. WS25-WS31.

——— (1993), *Voices from Within: Early Personal Narratives of Bengali Women,* New Delhi: Oxford University Press.

Keay, F.E. (1938), *Indian Education in Ancient and Later Times,* Humphrey Milford: Oxford University Press.

Kelly, G.P. and P.G. Altbach (1986), 'Comparative Education: Challenge and Response', *Comparative Education Review*, vol. 30, no. 1, February, pp. 89-107.

Khan, Abdul Rashid (2001), *The All India Muslim Educational Conference: Its Contribution to the Cultural Development of Indian Muslims 1886-1947*, New Delhi: Oxford University Press.

Kopf, David (1969), *British Orientalism and the Bengal Renaissance: The Dynamics of Indian Modernisation 1773-1835*, Berkeley: University of California Press.

Kripalani, J.B. (1946), *The Latest Fad, Basic Education*, Wardha: Hindustan Talimi Sangh.

Kumar, Deepak (1995), *Science and the Raj: A Study of British India*, New Delhi: Oxford University Press.

——— (1996), 'The "Culture" of Science and Colonial Culture, India 1820-1920', *The British Journal for the History of Science*, vol. 29, no. 2, June, pp. 195-209.

——— (ed.) (1990), *Science and Empire: Essays in Indian Context*, New Delhi: Anamika Prakashan.

Kumar, Krishna (1988), *Education and Society in Post-Independence India: Looking Towards the Future,* Edinburgh papers in south Asian Studies no. 9, Edinburgh: Centre for South Asian Studies.

——— (1989), *Social Character of Learning,* New Delhi: Sage.

——— (1990), 'Quest for Self-Identity: Cultural Consciousness and Education in the Hindi Region, 1880-1950', *Economic and Political Weekly*, vol. 25, no. 23, 9 June, pp. 1247-9; 1251-5.

——— (1991), *Political Agenda of Education: A Study of Colonialist and Nationalist Ideas*, New Delhi: Sage.

Kumar, Nita (2000), *Lessons from Schools: The History of Education in Banaras*, New Delhi: Sage.

———(ed.) (1994), *Women as Subjects: South Asian Histories*, Charlottesville: University Press of Virginia.

Kumar, Ravi (2006), 'When Gandhi's Talisman No Longer Guides Policy Consideration: Market, Deprivation and Education in the Age of Globalisation', *Social Change*, vol. 36, no. 3, pp. 1-46.

Kumarappa, J.C. (1936), *Why the Village Movement?*, Wardha: All India Village Industries Association Publication.

Kwiek, Marek (2003), 'The State, the Market, and Higher Education: Challenges for the New Century', in Kwiek, Marek (eds.), *The University, Globalisation, Central Europe*, Frankfurt and New York: Peter Lang Scientific Publishers, pp. 71-114.

Laird, M.A. (1972), *Missionaries and Education in Bengal: 1793-1837*, Oxford: Clarendon Press.

Lelyveld, David (1978), *Aligarh's First Generation: Muslim Solidarity in British India,* Princeton: Princeton University Press.

Liddle, Joanna and Rama Joshi (1986), *Daughters of Independence: Gender, Caste and Class in India*, New Brunswick, New Jersey: Rutgers University Press.

Lourdusamy, J. (2004), *Science and National Consciousness in Bengal, 1870-1930*, New Delhi: Orient Longman.

MacLeod, Roy and Deepak Kumar (eds.) (1995), *Technology and the Raj: Western Technology and Technical Transfer to India, 1700-1947*, New Delhi: Sage.

Majumdar, B.B. (1967), *History of Indian Social and Political Ideas,* Calcutta: Firma KLM.

Majumdar, Bhagaban Prasad (1973), *First Fruits of English Education (1817-1857),* Calcutta: Bookland.

Malaviya, Madan Mohan (1905), *Prospectus of a Proposed Hindu University for the Promotion of Scientific, Technical and Artistic Education Combined with Religious Instruction and Classical Culture*, Allahabad: Belvedere Steam Printing Works.

——— (1911), *The Hindu University of Benares: Why It Is Wanted and What It Aims At*, Allahabad.

Manor, James (1977), *Political Change in an Indian State: Mysore 1917-1955,* New Delhi: Manohar.

Mayhew, Arthur (1926), *The Education in India,* London: Faber and Gwyer.

McCully, B.T. (1940), *English Education and the Origins of Indian Nationalism,* New York: Columbia University Press.

McDougall, Eleanor (1943), *Lamps in the Wind: South Indian College Women and Their Problems*, London: The Cargate Press.

Meston, William (1936), *Indian Educational Policy its Principles and Problems*, Madras: The Christian Literature Society for India.

Metcalf, Barbara. D. (1990), *Perfecting Women: Maulana Ashraf Ali Thanawi's Bihishti Zewar*, Berkeley and Los Angeles: University of California Press.

——— (2006), *Islamic Contestations Essays on Muslim in India and Pakistan*, USA: Oxford University Press.

Metcalf, Thomas (1995), *Ideologies of the Raj*, Cambridge: Cambridge University Press.

Mill, James (1969), *James Mill on Education*, ed. W.H. Burston, London: Cambridge University Press.

Minault, Gail (1986), *Voices of Silence*, Delhi: Chanakya Publishers.

——— (1998), *Secluded Scholars: Women's Education and Social Reform in Colonial India*, New Delhi: Oxford University Press.

——— (ed.) (1981), *The Extended Family Women and Political Participation in India and Pakistan*, Delhi: Chanakya Publications.

——— (ed.) (1995), *Women as Subjects: South Asian Histories*, Virginia: University Press of Virginia, Calcutta: Stree, 1995.

Misra, B.B. (1978), *The Indian Middle Class: Their Growth in Modern Times*, New Delhi: Oxford University Press

Mital, K.V. (1986), *History of Thomason College of Engineering, 1847-1949*, Roorkee: University of Roorkee.

Mitter, Partha (1994), *Art and Nationalism in Colonial India, 1850-1922*, Cambridge: Cambridge University Press.

Mohammad, Shan (ed.) (1972), *Writings and Speeches of Sir Syed Ahmed Khan*, Bombay: Nachiketa.

——— (ed.) (2003), *The All India Muslim Educational Conference: Selected Presidential Addresses 1886-1947*, Delhi: A.P.H. Publication Corporation.

——— (ed.) (1978), *The Aligarh Movement: Basic Documents, 1864-1898*, Meerut: Meenakshi Prakashan.

Mukherjee, Satish Chandra (1902), *An Examination into the Present System of University Education in India and a Scheme of Reform,* Imprint, Calcutta: Dawn Office.

Mukherjee, Haridas and Uma Mukherjee (1957), *The Origins of the National Education Movement (1905-1910),* Calcutta: Jadavpur University Press.

Mukherjee, Himangshu B. (1962), *Education for Fullness: A Study of the Educational Thought and Experiment of Rabindranath Tagore*, Bombay: Asia Publishing.

Mukherjee, S.N. (1957), *History of Education in India: Modern Period*, Baroda: Acharya Book Depot.

Mukhopadhyay, M. and Madhu Parhar (eds.) (1999), *Indian Education: Development since Independence,* New Delhi: NIEPA and Vikas.

——— (eds.) (2007), *Education in India: Dynamics of Development*, Delhi: Shipra.

Murdoch, John (1904), *India's Greatest Educational Need: The Adequate Recognition of Ethics in Her Present Transition State,* London and Madras: n. p.

Naik, J.P. (1979), 'Equality, Quality and Quantity: The Elusive Triangle in Indian Education', *International Review of Education,* vol. 25, nos. 2-3, pp. 167-85.

National Curriculum Framework for School Education, NCERT 2005, NCERT Publication, New Delhi.

Nehru, J.L. (1946), *The Discovery of India*, Calcutta: Signet Press.

Neill, Stephen (1970), *The Story of the Christian Church in India and Pakistan*, Michigan: William B. Eerdmans Publishing Company.

Nurullah, Syed and J.P. Naik (1962), *A Student's History of Education in India*, Calcutta: Macmillan.

Oldenburg, Veena Talwar (1989), *The Making of Colonial Lucknow, 1856-1877*, New Delhi: Oxford University Press.

One Step Forward: The Report of the First Conference of Basic Education, Poona, October 1939, Sevagram, Wardha: Hindustani Talimi Sangh.

Oram, A. (1996), *Women Teachers and Feminist Politics, 1900-1939*, Manchester: Manchester University Press.

Pandey, Gyanendra (1983), 'The Bigoted Julaha', *Economic and Political Weekly*, vol. 18, no. 5, 29 January, pp. PE19-PE28.

Panikkar, K.M. (1953), *Asia and Western Dominance,* London: George Allen & Unwin.

Paranjpe, R. (ed.) (1938), *A Source Book of Modern Indian Education*, Bombay: Macmillan.

Parulekar, R.V. (ed.) (1945), *Survey of Indigenous Education in the Province of Bombay (1820-1830),* Bombay: Asia Publishing.

Pernau, Margrit (ed.) (2006), *The Delhi College: Traditional Elites, the Colonial State, and Education Before 1857*, New Delhi: Oxford University Press.

Porter, Andrew (1985), 'Commerce and Christianity: The Rise and Fall of a Nineteenth Century Missionary Slogan', *Historical Journal*, no. 28, pp. 597-621.

Prasad, Rajendra (1949), *Mahatma Gandhi and Bihar: Some Reminiscences*, Bombay: Hind Kitab Limited.

Ramakrishnan, R. (1994), *Press and Politics in an Indian State: Mysore 1859-1947*, New Delhi: Delta Publishing House.

Raman, Sita Anantha (1996), *Getting Girls to School: Social Reform in the Tamil Nadu Districts, 1870-1930,* Calcutta: Stree.

Ramusack, Barabara (1990), 'Cultural Missionaries, Maternal Imperialists, Feminist Allies: British Women Activists in India, 1865-1945,' *Women's Studies International Forum*, vol. XIII, no. 4, pp. 309-20.

Rao, M. Shama (1936), *Modern Mysore: From the Coronation of Chamaraja Wodeyar X in 1868 to the Present Time,* Bangalore: Higginbothams.

Rao, Parimala V. (2007), 'Women in the Nationalist Discourse: A Case Study of Tilak's Approach to Women's Education and Emancipation', in S. Bhattacharya (ed.), *Development of Modern Indian Thought and the Social Sciences*, New Delhi: Oxford University Press.

——— (2007), 'Women's Education and Nationalist Response in Western India: Part I Basic Education', *Indian Journal of Gender Studies*, vol. 14, no. 2, pp. 307-16.

——— (2010), *Foundations of Tilak's Nationalism: Discrimination, Education and Hindutva*, New Delhi: Orient Blackswan.

Ray, Bharati (ed.) (1995), *From the Seams of History: Essays on Indian Women*, New Delhi: Oxford University Press.

Ray, G.N. (2004), 'Transition from Information Society to Knowledge Society: An Indian Perspective', http://presscouncil.nic.in/speed11.html.

Ray, P.C. (1899), 'The Problem of Scientific Education in India', *Calcutta Review*, vol. CVIII, pp. 347-95.

——— (1932), *Life and Experiences of a Bengali Chemist*, vols. I-II, Calcutta: Chuckervertty, Chatterjee & Co.

Richey, J.A. (ed.) (1922), *Selections from the Educational Records*, Part 2, *1840-1859*, Calcutta: Superintendent Government Printing, India.

Rudolph, S.H. and L.I. Rudolph (1972), *Education and Politics in India: Studies in Organization, Society and Policy*, Cambridge: Harvard University Press.

Sahasrabudhey, Sunil (1983), 'Gandhi and the Challenge of Modern Science', *Gandhi Marg*, V, September, pp. 330-7.

Sangari, Kumkum, and Sudesh Vaid (eds.) (1990), *Recasting Women*, New Brunswick: Rutgers University Press.

Sangwan, Satpal (1988), 'Indian Response to European Science and Technology 1757-1857', *The British Journal for the History of Science*, vol. 21, no. 2, pp. 211-32.

——— (1990), 'Science Education in India under Colonial Constraints, 1792-1857', *Oxford Review of Education*, vol. 16, no. 1, pp. 81-95.

Sanyal, S.P. (1918), *Education in U.P. 1912-1917*, Benares: n.p.

Sarkar, Benoy Kumar (1946), *Education for Industrialization: An Analysis of Forty Years of Jadavpur College of Engineering and Technology, 1905-45*, Calcutta: Chuckervertty, Chatterjee & Co.

Sarkar, Sumit (1973), *The Swadeshi Movement in Bengal, 1903-1908*, New Delhi: People's Publishing House.

Satthianadhan, S. (1894), *History of Education in the Madras Presidency*, Madras: Srinivasachari and Co.

Sen, D. and. A.K. Chakraborty (eds.) (1986), *J.C. Bose Speaks*, Calcutta: Puthipatra.

Sen, J.M. (1933), *History of Elementary Education in India*, Calcutta: Book Company Ltd.

Sen, Keshub Chunder (1936), *Letters on Educational Measures to Lord Northbrook*, ed. G.C. Banerjee, n.p.

Sen, S.N. (1991), *Scientific and Technical Education in India: 1781-1900*, New Delhi: Indian National Science Academy.

Seshadri, P. (1935), *The Universities in India*, London: Oxford University Press.

Shariff, A. and NCAER (1999), *India Human Development Report: A Profile of Indian States in the 1990s*, New Delhi: Oxford University Press.

Sharma, Narinder Kumar (1976), *Linguistic and Educational Aspirations Under a Colonial System*, Delhi: Concept.

Sharma, Usha and B.M. Sharma (eds.) (1995), *Women's Education in British India*, New Delhi: Commonwealth Publishers.

Sharp, H. (1904), *Rural Schools in the Central Province*, Calcutta: Government Printing.

—— (ed.) (1920), *Selections from the Educational Records, Part 1, 1781-1839*. Calcutta: Government of India.

Shouric, Arun (1994), *Missionaries in India: Continuities, Changes, Dilemmas*, New Delhi: ASA Publications.

Shrivastava, M. and C. Chowdhary (2006), 'Marketing Education: Where are we Heading?', *Social Change*, vol. 36, no. 3, pp. 177-94.

Shukla, Suresh Chandra (1978), 'Education, Economy and Social Structure in British India', *National Journal of Education*, vol. I, nos. 1 and 2, pp. 112-26; 70-80.

Sinha, Mrinalini (2006), *Specters of Modern India: The Global Restructuring of an Empire*, London: Duke University Press.

Sircar, Mahendra Lal (1869), 'On the Desirability of a National Institution for the Cultivation of the Sciences by the Natives of India', *Calcutta Journal of Medicine*, no. 2, pp. 287-88.

——(1877), *The Indian Association for the Cultivation of Science*, Calcutta.

Sitaramayya, Pattabhi B. (1952), *Basic Education: The Need of the Day*, Sevagram, Wardha: Hindustani Talimi Sangh.

Srinivas, M.N. (1969), *Social Change in Modern India*, Berkeley and Los Angeles: University of California Press.

Thakurta, Tapati Guha (1992), *The Making of a New Indian Art*, Cambridge: Cambridge University Press.

Thomas, F.W. (1891), *History and Prospect of British Education in India*, Cambridge: Deighton Bell.

Thomson, Mark (1995), *Gandhi and His Ashrams,* Bombay: Popular Prakashan.

Tilak, J.B.G. (2007), 'Inclusive Growth and Education: On the Approach to the Eleventh Plan', *Economic and Political Weekly*, 22 September pp. 3872-7.

Trevelyan, C.E. (1838), *On the Education of the People of India*, London: Longman, Orme, Brown Green and Longmans.

Tyabji, Nasir (1995), *Colonialism and Chemical Technology and Industry in Southern India 1880-1937*, New Delhi: Oxford University Press.

Vermani, R.C. (1983), *British Colonialism in India*, Delhi: Authors Guild Publications.

Visvesvaraya, M. (1920), *Reconstructing India,* London: P.S. King and Sons, 1920.

——— (1934), *Planned Economy for India*, Bangalore: Bangalore Press.

Viswanath, Susan (2000), 'The Homogeneity of Fundamentalism: Christianity, British Colonialism and India in the Nineteenth Century', *Studies in History*, 16, pp. 221-40.

Viswanathan, Gauri (1988), 'Currying Favor: The Politics of British Educational and Cultural Policy in India, 1813-1854', *Social Text*, no. 19/20, (Autumn), pp. 85-104.

——— (1989), *Masks of Conquest: Literary Study and British Rule in India*, New York: Columbia University Press.

——— (1998), *Outside the Fold: Conversion, Modernity and Belief*, New Delhi: Oxford University Press.

Vyasulu, Vinod (1989), 'Nehru and the Visvesvaraya Legacy', *Economic and Political Weekly*, vol. 24, no. 30, 29 July, pp. 1700-4.

Wanchoo, H.N. (1934), *Studies in Indian Education*, Allahabad: Allahabad Law Journal.

Watt, C.A. (2005), *Serving the Nation: Cultures of Service, Association, and Citizenship*, New Delhi: Oxford University Press.

White, E. (1885), *Education Report on Public Instruction in the North-Western Provinces and Oudh* for the year ending 31 March 1885, Allahabad: n.p.

Wise, T.A. (1854), *Thoughts on Education in India: Its Object and Plan*, London: Smith, Elder & Co.

Wolpert, Stanley (2001), *Gandhi's Passion: The Life and Legacy of Mahatma Gandhi,* New York: Oxford University Press.

Wood, Ernest (1917), *Selected Articles on National Education,* Hyderabad, Sind: Sind Publishing House.

Wright, W.H. (1885), *The Muir Central College, Allahabad: Its Origin, Foundation and Completion*, Allahabad: Government Press.

Zachariah, K. (1936), *History of Hoogli College, 1836-1936*, Alipore: Supt. of Govt. Ptg., Bengal Government Press.

Zastoupil, Lynn and Martin Moir (eds.) (1999), *The Great Indian Education Debate: Documents Relating to the Orientalist-Anglicist Controversy, 1781-1843*, Richmond: Curzon.

Index